A HISTORY
OF
CORNWALL

Other works by F E Halliday published by House of Stratus:

Chaucer and His World
Dr Johnson and His World
Thomas Hardy
The Poetry of Shakespeare's Plays
Robert Browning
Shakespeare (The Life of)
Shakespeare in His Age
A Shakespeare Companion
Shakespeare and His Critics
Unfamiliar Shakespeare
Wordsworth and His World

A HISTORY
OF
CORNWALL

F E HALLIDAY

HOUSE OF
STRATUS

First published in 1959 by Gerald Duckworth & Co. Ltd

Copyright © 1959, 1975, 2001 Sebastian Halliday

All rights reserved. No part of this publication may be reproduced, stored in a retrieval system, or transmitted, in any form, or by any means (electronic, mechanical, photocopying, recording, or otherwise), without the prior permission of the publisher. Any person who does any unauthorised act in relation to this publication may be liable to criminal prosecution and civil claims for damages.

The right of F E Halliday to be identified as the author of this work has been asserted.

This edition published in 2001 by House of Stratus, an imprint of House of Stratus Ltd, Thirsk Industrial Park, York Road, Thirsk, North Yorkshire, YO7 3BX, UK.
Also at: House of Stratus Inc., 2 Neptune Road, Poughkeepsie, NY 12601, USA.

www.houseofstratus.com

Typeset by House of Stratus, printed and bound by Short Run Press Limited.

A catalogue record for this book is available from the British Library and the Library of Congress.

ISBN 0-7551-0817-5

This book is sold subject to the condition that it shall not be lent, re-sold, hired out, or otherwise circulated without the publisher's express prior consent in any form of binding, or cover, other than the original as herein published and without a similar condition being imposed on any subsequent purchaser, or bona fide possessor.

For
Sebastian and Mary

1 October 1958

List of Illustrations

Front Cover:
    St Michael's Mount at sunset, The National Trust/Peter Cade
Back Cover:
    Fowey town and harbour, The National Trust/Dan Flunder
    Endpapers, © Cornwall 1610 by John Speede, courtesy of
    www.oldmap.co.uk

Contents

Preface To The Second Edition

When my father decided to write his *History of Cornwall* some forty years ago there was no single book dealing with the history of the county from prehistoric to modern times. His history filled this gap admirably and, even at the time of the second edition, it was essentially alone in the field. Since then a number of other books have appeared which also trace the entire course of the history of the county in varying degrees of detail. The original justification for publication is thus no longer valid. However the book is very widely cited and is valued and sought after by all who are interested in Cornwall and its history. It is therefore appropriate to reissue it in its original form. It is a splendidly written and vigorous account of Cornish history and can stand comparison with any more recent volume.

In fact it remains remarkably up-to-date, both in its general interpretation and in detail. Recent advances in archaeology have somewhat changed the picture of Cornwall's prehistory, especially in relation to dating in the pre-Christian era; the interested reader should consult any recent specialist text. In other respects my father's account is of real value and is a fine piece of historical writing. The main text has therefore not been altered; however I have added a very brief epilogue outlining significant developments in the last part of the twentieth century and prospects for the new millennium.

Sebastian Halliday
St Ives, Cornwall.
July 2000.

Preface To The First Edition

When, some two years ago, I was asked to write a History of Cornwall, I hesitated with what I hope was a becoming humility; although there could be few subjects more fascinating, who was I, a Saxon, a foreigner, to approach such a formidable undertaking? And I thought of the sixteen thousand documents that Charles Henderson had collected for his projected History. Yet there was no History of Cornwall. Since the publication of Carew's *Survey* in 1602 more books had been written about Cornwall than about any other county, but the histories were either parochial – the parish is far more important to the Celt than to the Saxon – or dealt with special periods or subjects. There was no single book that covered the whole period in any detail from prehistoric to modern times, from the age of stone to the age of atomic power. I began to consider my qualifications for the task.

Perhaps, I persuaded myself, it was not necessary to be a Cornishman to write a History of Cornwall; at least a foreigner could write more objectively. Then, I had known Cornwall for more than thirty years, since my first visit to Tintagel as a young man, and for eleven years I had lived not far from the Land's End. Although by no means a professional historian, I had read some history at Cambridge, even taught some history, and archaeology had always been one of my favourite pursuits. Moreover, I had made a special study of certain aspects of late medieval, Elizabethan and Caroline Cornwall, done some original research, and published two books on the periods. Again, I was well acquainted with the county; I had walked over the greater part of Penwith, and had explored most of the places of historical and archaeological interest as well as those famed for their beauty, as far north as Morwenstow, as far east as Mount Edgcumbe and Cotehele. I had even been down a tin mine. Finally, I had long since fallen in love with Cornwall. There was no question of disloyalty. A man's love for his native county resembles his love for his mother, which is in no way weakened if he falls in love with another woman, and it is certain that a second love is an immense enrichment of his experience. I loved Cornwall for its beauty: for its coast and ever-present sea, not grey here, but flashing opal and sapphire; for its clean northern plateaus and deeply wooded southern estuaries; for its quiet granite hills, rich green fields and little grey hamlets and towns; even for its rapid changes of temper, for its squalls and storms; and for its sun, which shines higher, brighter and longer than elsewhere in Britain, rising and setting on the horizon and not in a belt of haze, even in winter striking vertical rock faces with equatorial splendour. And I loved it for its character: for its strength, although an outcast among counties; for its appearance of having known and suffered so much, yet without any trace of disillusionment, but having rather an air of expectancy; for its human virtues of patience and endurance; for its mystery, for what it concealed as well as for what it revealed, for its past as well as its present; in short, for its history. Yet not so much *its* history as *their* history: the lives of the thousands of men and women who had worked and died here, a few of them leaving an individual, all of them a communal, memorial – the Cornwall of their day. For I liked the Cornish people. Perhaps there is some affinity between Cornishmen and Yorkshiremen, for after all the La Tène Celts established themselves splendidly in the Yorkshire Wolds. I began to write my History.

It is a story worth the writing: the story of the builders of the great chambered tombs of West Penwith, of the entrance graves of the Fortunate Isles, of Bronze Age stone circles and Iron Age citadels; of the coming of the Saints; of Arthur and Mark, Tristan and Iseult, Tintagel and Castle Dore; of the Black Prince, Restormel and his Duchy; of the dissolution of the monasteries and the Tudor rebellions; of the Armada and war with Spain; of the Civil War and Sir Bevil Grenville; of the preaching of Wesley; of the making of the railway; and woven throughout this great pattern of the centuries the two threads of the sea and Cornish tin.

I hope I have succeeded in working all this material into a coherent narrative with an organic unity and structure, though the vastness of the theme has compelled me to draw largely on the work of others, specialists in their particular periods, notably

Dr H O'Neill Hencken, Canon L E Elliott-Binns, Dr A L Rowse, Dr Mary Coate, Dr John Rowe, Mr Hamilton Jenkin and the late Charles Henderson. Most of the books and periodicals to which I am indebted will be found in the Bibliography.

Perhaps the main difficulty has been the prehistory, for archaeology is in such a state of activity and flux, the latest hypotheses tumbling before the most recent discoveries, that little remains stable for long. For example, the work of Mr Charles Thomas over the last ten years is rapidly transforming the little Gwithian peninsula into one of the classic sites of British archaeology, the pattern of which is just beginning to emerge. Even the professional prehistorian, therefore, would hesitate to claim that his description of pre-Norman Cornwall was the true one, and I can only hope that mine is, broadly speaking, true, and if I have often made sweeping and overconfident statements it is – apart from ignorance and incompetence – only because continual qualification would be wearisome.

Mr A Guthrie has very kindly read the first three chapters of my manuscript, Mr R Morton Nance and Dr A C Todd the remainder, and I am most grateful to them for their criticism and advice, as I am to Mr Charles Woolf of Newquay for his generous co-operation in taking so many photographs specially for this book. I am also grateful to Mrs Harvey of the Morrab Library in Penzance, Mr J H I Cable, Director of Penzance Public Library, Mr H L Douch, Curator of the Museum of the Royal Institution of Cornwall, and Mr P L Hull, the County Archivist, for all the willing help that they have given me.

F E Halliday
St Ives, Cornwall.
November 1958.

Prelude

For the greater part of the thousand million years or so in which Britain has been a-building we must imagine our country as a scrap of land that was the sport of a sea running from east to west, sometimes submerging it, sometimes, as the waters changed their outline, leaving it attached to one or other of the continents that formed their northern and southern shores. It is this rhythm of submersion and emergence that has made the scenery of Britain, of England in particular, so varied, perhaps the most varied of any small country in the world. The oldest rocks are in the north and west, the newest in the south-east, so that when we make the three-hundred-mile journey from London to the Land's End we travel also in time, back towards our beginning, at an average rate of a million years for every mile.

For untold ages the land that was to form the little peninsula of Cornwall lay under this tropical sea. Then, some three hundred million years ago, after the convulsion that threw up the towering mountain ranges of north Wales and Scotland, the Devonian sandstone and slates began to be laid down under the ocean that covered western Europe. For forty million years sun and wind and rain wore away those Caledonian peaks, high as the Himalayas, the debris settling at the bottom of the sea to form the rock that now covers the greater part of the surface of Cornwall. It was the age in which life spread from sea to land: vegetation first, luxuriant and tropical, and then the fishes that had learned to breathe with lungs, first of the amphibians.

There followed fifty million years when limestone was deposited in the shallow waters that lapped the then east coast of Cornwall, roughly the line of the river Tamar, and to the north, beyond what is now the Bristol Channel, layers of millstone grit that supported the swamps and tree ferns that were to be compressed into coal measures. Towards the end of this humid Carboniferous period, about two hundred and forty million years ago, came another convulsion, when the rocks of Cornwall and Devon were violently folded into the Armorican mountains, almost as high as the Alps are today. The fiery matter that lay beneath the oldest sedimentary rocks thrust itself into the folds, where it solidified as granite, while gases and boiling liquids forced their way through fissures in the heat-transformed and hardened aureoles round the granite domes to form metallic veins: tin, copper, lead, silver and even gold. Although Cornwall as we know it had not yet been created, the raw material from which it was to be carved was there, the great buckled layers of sandstone, slates and shales supported by intrusive domes of granite far below.

For a hundred million years a burning sun splintered the rocks of these raw and angular mountains, while wind and rain pursued their polishing process and torrents carried away the debris to form new red rocks about their bases. The first mammals appeared, and Cornwall was once more covered by shallow waters and then again by sea, the period when chalk was laid down over eastern England, the age of giant reptiles, of Allosaurus and Tyrannosaurus, beasts for whom man would have made but a mouthful. Then at last the worn and rounded stumps of the Cornish highlands began to show again above the sea, and after the earth-throes that flung up the Alps and Himalayas, some thirty million years ago, the pattern was almost complete. The sea retreated, and slowly the lowlands emerged, forming a high coastal platform and linking the granite island of Bodmin Moor with those that lay farther west, though a tropical sea still flowed between the Land's End and the Isles of Scilly. These granite bosses were all that remained of the great Armorican range that had been thrust up two hundred million years before.

Soon after the Alpine upheaval the climate began to change. Tropical conditions gave place to those more temperate, and then, about a million years ago, when the first creature that could be called man made his appearance, the ice thrust out its fangs from the Poles. It gripped England as far south as Severn and Thames, and though Cornwall was never scored by glaciers it was reduced to an arctic region by freezing winds that blew off the great ice sheets. Four times the ice advanced before it began its last retreat; then the climate gradually improved, grass flourished where once tundra mosses grew, trees gained a foothold, and new animals crossed the chalk downs that still bridged England and France. The dwindling ice caps released huge volumes of water, and seas lapped higher until, some eight thousand years ago, shortly after the ice had withdrawn approximately to its present limits, the chalk barrier was breached; the waters flowed between Atlantic Ocean and a marshy North Sea, flooding up the river valleys of southern England, submerging the forests that fringed them, and forming great natural harbours like those at the mouth of the Tamar and Fal.

So, after millions of years of shaping, emerged the Cornwall that we know, the long delicately stepping leg and toe reaching out towards the Atlantic, olive-green over the seaworn sandstone lowlands, silver-grey, fawn and tawny in autumn on the lichened granite heights that once lay far below the peaks of the great Armorican mountains. A land of stones, immemorially old, of cliffs falling sheer to the sea, of hills lacerated by Atlantic rains and gales, or shrouded in sullen mists, yet under the sun a land whose colours are more luminous, whose contours are cleaner, whose masses bulk ampler than those of other counties, the deep blue of whose sea is shot with purple and green and guarded with the gold and silver of its sands and driven foam. A land of stones, an appropriate setting for the men of the age of stone with whom its human history begins.

Like Catullus' Sirmio it is an all-but-island. Sea-surrounded on three sides, its eastern boundary is the river Tamar, which, rising almost on the northern coast, flows due south until it reaches the tidal waters of its intricate estuary. Almost equally spaced from east to west rise the great granite bosses of Bodmin Moor, Hensbarrow Downs, Carnmenellis and the West Penwith Moors. Each is the centre of a region bounded by lowland routes that thread between them from sea to sea, the most important in early times being those that ran from the only two estuaries on the northern coast, from Camel to Fowey in the centre, from Hayle to Mount's Bay in the west. The reason for this early importance becomes at once apparent if we glance at a map showing the neighbouring lands. Cornwall lies exactly halfway between

Ireland and Brittany, and in days when ships were little more than cockleshells, traders, travellers and even leaf- and millstone-sailing saints preferred an overland route to the stormy passage between the Land's End and Scilly. The southern estuaries that lacked a corresponding outlet on the higher northern coast, those of the Tamar, Looe and Fal, were to gain in importance during the Middle Ages.

One other region remains to be mentioned, that to the south of the Carnmenellis granite and severing Helford estuary, the peninsula that forms the heel of Cornwall and the only part of the British mainland that lies within the latitude of the forties. Here is the high, wild, sea-polished plateau of Goonhilly Downs and the Lizard, a Celtic name that so felicitously matches that of the streaked and mottled serpentine of which it is made.

A History Of Cornwall

I

The Stone Age

During the warm interglacial periods of the Ice Age Britain was inhabited, though very thinly of course, by palaeolithic man, man of the Old Stone Age, who, by taking refuge in caves and crouching over the fire that he had learned to control, even managed to survive the last glaciation. This was Neanderthal man, an unattractive-looking creature, shaggy, shuffling and ape-like, using simple flint implements that are known as Mousterian. But, although sufficiently tough and hairy to withstand the cold, his shambling wits were no match for the late palaeolithic race that superseded him round about 100,000 BC. Cro-Magnon man was a splendid specimen of humanity both physically and mentally: six feet tall and with a long head that housed a brain as big as ours, it was he who in Aurignacian and Magdalenian times produced the great wall paintings in the caves of southern France and northern Spain. In the more rigorous climate of England, however, the struggle for existence seems to have been too exacting to allow him leisure for such spiritual explorations, though he carved bone with his flint chisels and added refinements to his armoury of weapons: harpoons for example, and a mechanical device for throwing a spear. For he was a hunter, armed with bow and flint-tipped arrows, pursuing the herds of reindeer, bison, horse, mammoth and woolly rhinoceros that roamed the steppe-like grasslands. But as the climate improved his way of life declined; the game that he had hunted for thousands of years moved ever farther north as trees invaded the grasslands, and lacking the tools to check the spreading forests he was unable completely to adapt himself to the new conditions.

Although Cornwall had little natural shelter, and flint was confined to pebbles on the shore, too small to make large tools, the region had at least one advantage to offer the men of the Old Stone Age: it was farther from the ice fields than the country to east and north. Both Neanderthal and Cro-Magnon man occupied Kent's cavern near Torquay and, in summer at least, may have pursued their game far into the west. Perhaps the hand axe found near the Lizard, of chert from the Devon-Dorset border, was lost on one of these hunting expeditions. In any event it is the only evidence there is to suggest that palaeolithic man ever ventured as far west as Cornwall.

About 7,000 BC, when the ice had withdrawn to the Poles, fresh immigrants bringing what is known as the mesolithic, or Middle Stone Age, culture arrived in England from the continent. Those who came from the east, paddling their dugout canoes over the shallow waters and swamps of what is now the North Sea, had heavy stone axes with which they were able to fell trees and establish themselves in clearings in the forests. Part of a paddle and two of the birch trees they felled have recently been found at one of their settlements near Scarborough, the oldest piece of navigational gear and the oldest felled trees yet discovered anywhere. But the mesolithic people who came from the south, possibly south-west France, lacked these woodland tools and had to settle on forest fringes, in sandy regions and along the open country of the coasts, some of them in Cornwall. There are traces of their occupation near the Land's End and at Gwithian, where hundreds of their small flint implements, 'microliths' made from the local pebbles, have been found, and no doubt they settled in Scilly along the flint-strewn shores that have since sunk far below the sea; for the sea level was rising as the climate improved. Here then, beside the coves and sand dunes of the Cornish coast, with their arrows, darts and harpoons, tipped and set with tiny flints, they hunted small game and birds and speared fish. It was a poor, unheroic sort of existence in comparison with the spacious life of the Aurignacians and Magdalenians, the hunters and artists who had once pursued big game across the English steppes. Then, to add to the discomfort of mesolithic man, the climate changed again, warm dry summers giving place to weather much wetter, to the summers puffing with wind and rain that we know only too well; oak supplanted pine, and the unchecked forest grew even denser. Some time before this England had been severed from the continent, so that it is with mesolithic man that our island history begins.

Rarely, I think, are we fully aware of the debt that we owe to our ancestors, to the thousands of years of accumulated knowledge and skill that we inherit, so that each generation is able to begin where its predecessor had to abandon its progress. We take our way of life for granted, our language, our books and music, the comfort of our homes, their warmth and light, the variety of our foods, the ease of transport; though we may still marvel at the most recent inventions, at the aeroplane, television and atomic power, we rarely give a thought to the fundamental things that made such refinements possible, that took so many thousands of years to evolve: to the fields of wheat, herds of cows, flocks of sheep, to the loom and the wheel of a simple cart. Yet, suppose it were possible for a community of modern Europeans to grow up in some isolated part of the world, quite ignorant of their rightful heritage, what would be their way of life? Would they know by instinct how to speak articulately, how to make a fire or wheel, that wild animals can be domesticated, the wool of the sheep spun and woven into cloth, that grasses and bushes can be cultivated and their yields of grain and fruit immeasurably increased? Of course not; theirs would be a miniature Stone Age society, less advanced than that of mesolithic man with his inherited skill of chipping flints.

We may, therefore, sympathetically imagine the way of life of late mesolithic man, potentially not unlike ourselves, as he clung precariously to the shores of Cornwall five thousand years ago. Summer, with its long, comparatively warm days, may well have been a delight. While some of the men speared fish off the coast, others, armed with flint-tipped darts and arrows, and helped perhaps by dogs which they had tamed, hunted deer, boar, hares and other game, snared birds and stole their eggs. The women too collected food, limpets and mussels from the rocks, berries and nuts from the brakes and copses. At home, perhaps no more than a windbreak, they tended the children, scraped the skins, sewing them into clothing with bone needles, for spinning and weaving were unknown arts, and prepared the food, for though there were no pots in which to boil and cook, meat could be roasted on spits and fish grilled on the embers. But winter was another matter, and in stormy weather near the Land's End, when fishing was impossible, no game abroad, and the autumn fruits exhausted, life must have been hard indeed. Primitive man lives perforce from day to day, or at least from week to week, for hunters and gatherers are fearfully dependent on fortune and, unlike farmers, cannot store or otherwise ensure a constant supply of food. Yet, in the third millennium BC mesolithic man, even in remote Cornwall, was on the verge of a great economic revolution.

The change of climate which, in England, reduced the Stone Age hunters of the open country to squatters along the coasts, made more than amends by stimulating the early civilisations of Egypt and Mesopotamia. On the fertile plains beside the Nile, Tigris and Euphrates peasants began to grow crops of wheat and pasture cattle. Villages sprang up where the crafts of pottery and weaving were developed, then towns where merchants bought and sold their wares, transporting them in carts and sending agents in ships to open up new markets and find new sources of raw materials. Finally cities, where mere building became princely and priestly architecture and the art of making bronze was evolved and practised. As the population increased the poorer and more adventurous peasants pressed north and west, along the shores of the Mediterranean, until they found new land in the south of France. Thence they pushed slowly north until they came to the Channel, not quite so broad as it is today, and saw the coast of England. Embarking in their primitive boats, laden with livestock, they crossed the straits and landed on the northern shore. And so, round about 2500 BC, neolithic man, man of the New Stone Age, arrived in England.

For he was still in the Stone Age, his ancestors having left the Middle East before the discovery of metal, and all he brought with him were his sheep, cattle, dogs and seed corn, the craft of pottery, though not apparently of weaving, and more serviceable forms of weapons and tools, in particular leaf-shaped arrowheads and polished stone axes and adzes. Yet it was a revolution as great as any in the history of man. No longer was he merely a hunter and gatherer, altogether dependent on nature, but a farmer who could make nature serve his own ends.

These new immigrants from the Mediterranean were a short, dark, long-headed and energetic people, who spread over the open chalk uplands of southern England where they made characteristic 'causewayed camps', and it is from one of these, on Windmill Hill near Avebury, that they take the name of the Windmill Hill people. They were a peaceable folk and their camps were not forts but pounds, a series of concentric banks and ditches pierced by causeways, into which a few small tribes probably drove their cattle to be identified, gelded or slaughtered at the end of the summer.

The most westerly causewayed camp so far discovered is at Hembury in Devon, but Windmill Hill people reached west Cornwall, for on the granite heights of Carn Brea, overlooking modern Camborne, are the remains of one of their settlements. Though much disturbed and confused by later occupations, the foundations of their little round stone huts can be seen, and excavation has revealed their characteristic tools and weapons, and fragments of pottery resembling Hembury ware. It is a wild region still, where we can easily imagine these early settlers at work: the younger men hunting in the surrounding lowlands, the older men tending the herds and tilling their little plots on the southern slopes of the hill with stone hoes, deer-horn picks and shoulder-blade shovels, the women outside their huts grinding corn between polished pieces of granite, scraping skins and making round-bottomed bowls and cooking pots which they sometimes decorated sparingly with grooves or rows of dots. There were no pieces of flint in Cornwall big enough to make axes, but the hard greenstones outside the granite aureoles served well enough, and they have been found all over the county and even beyond, notably in the Windmill Hill area. Apparently there were a number of factories – one was near St Ives, another near Penzance and a third near Callington – and their products were traded with the eastern centres, perhaps in exchange for flint. One wonders what happened to the mesolithic hunters. There cannot have been many; no doubt they lingered for a time along their fishing beaches, but eventually they must have been absorbed by the newcomers to whom they taught their own traditional crafts, so modifying the first neolithic culture.

And so farming, and with it a primitive civilisation, first came to Cornwall. Yet it is not of farming, nor of axes and pottery, that we think when we summon up remembrance of neolithic Cornwall, and if this were all that remained the long tenure of the land by these Mediterranean settlers would pass almost unnoticed today. But one other thing besides their crafts and tools they brought with them to England, the tradition, derived ultimately from their ancestors in the Middle East, of burying their dead collectively and magnificently under great mounds of earth and stone, the long barrows of the chalklands, sometimes more than two hundred feet long and fifty feet broad.

There are no barrows of this type in Cornwall, but some centuries after the arrival of neolithic man in Britain there was another and more immediate contact with the culture of the Mediterranean. We cannot be certain of the details, but it seems that sometime before 2000 BC explorers from the Aegean, short dark men of much the same stock as the Windmill Hill farmers, sailed west, possibly in search of copper and tin, the raw materials of bronze. In the south of France and Iberia, that is Spain and Portugal, they elaborated their traditional method of burying their dead under mounds of earth into building megalithic forms of mausoleum, tombs constructed of gigantic slabs of rock over which they heaped their barrows. From Iberia these adventurous colonists, impelled by prospects of profit, sailed in their bawbling vessels, possibly made of skin, up the rocky coasts of western Europe and across the Bay of Biscay to Brittany and Ireland, and then round the north of Scotland to the Orkneys and beyond, until their long and hazardous mission spent itself on the eastern shores of the North Sea. And wherever these daring seafarers landed, perhaps the most audacious explorers in history, they established their custom of communal burial under chambered barrows and the cult of the earth goddess of the eastern Mediterranean. It may have been about 1800 BC when these Iberians, as they are sometimes called, reached Cornwall, possibly in search of tin, and probably from south-east Ireland, where they had first settled and worked copper.

Although these megalith builders were pioneers in the use of metal, it is customary and convenient to think of them as still in the Stone Age, for one of the chief characteristics of the neolithic cultures was collective burial, and it is of the great stone monuments which they erected for their dead that we think when we call to mind neolithic Cornwall, for after nearly forty centuries these remain when so many more recent memorials have perished. They are the earliest architecture in our island, most of them on ridges overlooking the sea, though the chambered tomb at Pawton is near Wadebridge and Trethevy Quoit on the southern edge of Bodmin Moor.

1. Trethevy Quoit.

2. Trethevy Quoit.

There cannot have been many of these Irish immigrants who joined their distant cousins, the neolithic farmers, as many years before the beginning of the Christian era as we are after it, perhaps no more than a hundred, but such hardy adventurers, with a knowledge of metals and a well-developed religion, must have established themselves as a superior caste, and no doubt the chambered tombs were for the families of their priestly chiefs. We may imagine the building of Trethevy Quoit. First a deep rectangular trench was dug, then five great slabs of granite, some twelve feet high and five feet wide, were hauled into position on wooden rollers where they were raised with levers and rawhide ropes until their bases sank into the trench to form three walls of a chamber. This was then sealed by another stone set back from the entrance, so forming an open antechamber or forecourt, though a gap was left at one of the bottom corners of the sealing stone, big enough for a man to crawl through. Finally, an earthen ramp was built against the back of the chamber, and up this the gangs of straining men inched the massive capstone, or quoit, until it covered the tomb. Perhaps the hole at the front of the capstone was bored as an aid to this operation of heaving and levering. What strange ceremony was performed over the body we shall never know, but when it had been lifted through the hole into the inner chamber and laid on its side with knees drawn up to the chin, food and drink, weapons and tools were left for the journey to the shadowy world, and the ritual probably completed by a sacrifice in the antechamber and a mournful dance and chanting about the sepulchre. For generations the chamber was used as a family vault and then, when it was full, or when the last of the line had been buried, earth was heaped over the tomb to form a high circular mound.

The rain of centuries washed away the soil, and peasants of the Roman or Arthurian times scattered it over their fields until all that remained to their wondering eyes was the great stone sepulchre. Presumably they found the skeletons, for there is no record of any discovery in historical times. For the credulous countryfolk of the Middle Ages it was another relic of the time of Gogmagog and the other giants, whose pastime it was to throw great rocks about the hills and play quoits with the capstones; the tomb at Pendarves near Camborne, indeed, is known as The Giant's Quoit. More prosaically, though enchantingly, John Norden the Elizabethan described Trethevy Quoit as 'a little howse raysed of mightie stones, standing on a little hill within a feilde ... an arteficiall holl 8 inches diameter, made thorowgh the roofe very rounde, which served as it seemeth to putt out a staffe, wherof the howse it selfe was not capable'. Yet more knowingly, antiquaries of a later age called these Stone Age tombs 'Druids' Altars'. Any mysterious relic of the past could conveniently, and vaguely, be attributed to those Celtic priests.

It is in the remote west, however, that there is the greatest concentration of megalithic tombs on the Cornish mainland, along the northern heights of the Penwith moors. On the ridge overlooking the village is Zennor Quoit with its huge displaced capstone, eighteen feet long and half as wide, surrounded by the remains of its forty-foot barrow. On a neighbouring height is Mulfra Quoit, and three miles farther west the perfect mushroom of Chun Quoit, dwarfed by the vast expanse of the downs.

Between the two are Lanyon Quoit, a spectacular though mutilated relic, West Lanyon Quoit and the strange Men-an-Tol, the Stone with a Hole, possibly all that remains of a vanished tomb, the porthole through which the body was lifted into the chamber. Perhaps this passing of the body had some magical significance that lingered in the unconscious minds of later generations, for until quite recent times parents passed their children through the stone, 'nine times against the sun', as a cure for rickets, and they themselves would crawl through to ease their aches and cricks in the back. It is still locally known as the Crick Stone. There is a similar holed stone at Tolven, near Gweek on the Helford river.

Few of these chambered tombs, however, had portholes or even an antechamber, and the majority are simply rectangular boxes of stone. Very little has been found in them since records have been kept, for their contents were long ago plundered and scattered, but human bones lying 'in a promiscuous state' are reported from West Lanyon Quoit, opened in the eighteenth century, and a whetstone was found in the chamber of Zennor Quoit, indicating a knowledge of metals. The strange thing is that these people who built so splendidly for their dead failed to build enduring habitations for themselves, and we know little or nothing about their settlements. Perhaps they were semi-nomadic, but certainly they attached tremendous significance to their religion and ritual of burial.

A century or so after the arrival of these first megalith builders from Ireland another band of Iberian immigrants landed in Cornwall, this time probably from Brittany, bringing with them a somewhat different tradition of tomb-building. Their chambers were much smaller and lower, and approached by a passage with an entrance at the edge of the barrow. They are indeed little more than passages some fifteen feet long, four feet wide and three feet high, walled and roofed with big stone slabs, for the central chamber is normally indistinguishable from the passage, and for this reason are generally known as entrance graves. There are about a dozen, most of them still

covered with the remains of their low round barrows, the best
preserved being the group on the hills above Zennor: Gundry's
Cave on Trewey Hill, two at least near Treen, and another near
Pennance Farm.

But rich in megalithic tombs as are the wild Penwith
uplands, the last isolated outcrop of the ancient granite is far
richer. From the cliffs at the Land's End, or from the hills
behind, the tiny Isles of Scilly, the Fortunate Isles, can be seen
on the horizon, beyond the sea that is said to cover the lost
land of Lyonesse. It is in itself a prospect to give birth to legend,
even without the strange trophies to be found there. For the
islands are riddled with graves, like those on the mainland
built by the immigrants from Brittany, some of whom settled in
Scilly. When they arrived, perhaps about 1700 BC, the present
islands were probably forty or fifty feet higher than they are
today, forming hills round the edge of one large island. Since
then the land has gradually sunk, submerging the once
cultivated central lowland, and leaving the present kite-shaped
archipelago which, on the map, seems to soar towards the
Land's End, its tail streaming back into the south-west, until
at Bishop's Rock it is lost in the Atlantic. It must be this
subsidence that accounts for the legend of Lyonesse, so
nostalgically described by early chroniclers, the country of
Arthurian romance and of Sir Tristan, which was suddenly
engulfed by the sea. As, however, the submergence must have
been very slow and not cataclysmic, the story, much as we
should like to believe it, is less probably the memory of such a
protracted occurrence than a later invention to account for the
ancient walls that run into and under the sea.

Yet in spite of all that has been lost there are still at least fifty
chambered tombs on the Isles of Scilly, one-fifth of the total
number in England and Wales, an astonishing proportion and
concentration in so tiny an area. It seems, however, that, isolated
on their sinking island, the descendants of the original megalith
builders went on burying their dead in these tombs, and even
building new ones after the same pattern, well into the Bronze

Age when elsewhere collective inhumation had given way to cremation and single interment. Thus, one tomb on Gugh, with the enchanting name of Obadiah's Barrow, was originally used for inhumation, then refashioned in the Bronze Age and used for some time longer for cremations. Then, in the recently opened Knackyboy Cairn on St Martin's four hundredweight of Bronze Age pottery were found, representing more than seventy urns, each of which held the burned remains of one person. In addition there were pieces of bronze, eight glass beads and a star-shaped one of faïence, suggesting traffic with their old home in the Near East. The earliest tombs, like Innisidgen Cairn on St Mary's, were probably built soon after 1700 BC, but Knackyboy was built five hundred years later and apparently used for another five centuries, representing an average of one burial every six or seven years.

In spite of this great concentration of the dead there are few traces of the living on the islands beyond the remains of a few stone huts on St Martin's, those at Halangy Porth on St Mary's being Romano-British. No doubt most of the early settlements were on lower ground now engulfed by the sea, and most of the tombs on the hills that remain as islands, and this, together with the fact that the graves were used over a period of a thousand years may account for the numerical discrepancy between the homes of the dead and the living.

Perhaps, however, there is a genuine element of folk memory in the early stories related about islands lying off Cornwall and Brittany. According to classical writers of late pagan and early Christian times there was something mysterious about them: they were delectable lands inhabited by gods, or by heroes, or by women, and strange ceremonies were performed there. Or they were occupied by holy men who sailed there from the mainland, or by the dead, who were ferried across from ports along the coast. The Celts of Wales and Ireland also had stories about an island of the dead and a land beyond the sea inhabited only by women, stories that are recalled by the legend of the death of Arthur, who, when mortally wounded in his last great battle in the west, was carried away by queens to the island of Avalon. Can it be, therefore, that the Isles of Scilly really were islands of the dead? That the bodies of their most illustrious men were rowed across from Penwith to be buried there? Or, like the legend of Lyonesse, are the stories merely the fabrications of later people to account for this mysterious burial ground?

A History Of Cornwall

II

The Bronze Age

Although history falls naturally into a sequence of 'periods' that can be neatly labelled and dealt with one by one, it is easy to make the error of imagining them more sharply defined than they really are, to forget that the end of one epoch is much like the beginning of the next, and that there are very few abrupt transitions. For example, it may be said that the Victorians lived in the age of steam engine and gaslight, whereas we live in that of petrol engine and electricity, yet most of our trains are still driven by steam and many of our stations lighted by gas, or even by oil lamps. And in prehistory, when progress was so desperately slow, it is even more important to bear in mind these periods of transition, often centuries long, when the old culture continued alongside the new. Thus, there was no abrupt change from the late Stone Age to the Age of Bronze, and flint and metal implements existed together for hundreds of years.

The megalith builders probably brought a knowledge of metals with them from the Mediterranean, but shortly before they landed in Cornwall another metal-using people invaded southern and eastern Britain, from Dorset to Scotland. These were the Beaker Folk who came originally from central Spain, one branch of them by way of the Rhine valley, where they mixed with and absorbed some of the formidable Battleaxe people of Nordic stock. They are called Beaker Folk from the characteristic waisted drinking cups with which they so liberally littered the trail of their migrations, to the great content of present-day archaeologists. They were a powerful, warlike, round-headed people, restless and adventurous, more interested in their cattle, hunting and trade than in the duller pursuit of tilling fields. As a result they were semi-nomadic and have left little trace of their domestic life, though we know that they had the art of weaving, for woollen and linen cloth has been found in their graves. Like neolithic man they buried their dead in a crouching position, not in communal graves, however, but singly, under circular mounds of earth, the round barrows that stud and rivet the hills. Beside the body they placed weapons and food for the new adventure, often a bronze dagger and nearly always a beaker, symbols almost of their conquest of the country, for it may be that they had some form of alcoholic liquor that corrupted the islanders much as Stephano's sack corrupted Caliban. In any event the peaceable, slightly built neolithic farmers were no match physically for the stalwart warriors with great stone battleaxes and daggers of bronze. Those who stayed were subdued and probably lost everything to their conquerors, but some no doubt found refuge with their cousins beyond the Tamar, swelling the basic Cornish population of short, dark people, popularly, though quite erroneously, called 'Celts'.

Although the more advanced culture of the Beaker Folk spread eventually into the far south-west, they themselves do not seem to have occupied the area in any great numbers. The deep valley of the Tamar was already beginning to isolate Cornwall from the rest of England, and such traces of the Beaker Folk as there are appear to belong mainly to the more settled period after their irruption, to the Early Bronze Age proper. In one of the barrows on Trevelgue Head, near Newquay, was a cist containing a skeleton with knees thrust up to the chin. It crumbled when touched, but beside it lay the polished granite head of a battleaxe, and other battleaxe graves have been found near Padstow and Looe. Beakers are rare, but two have been found as far west as the Land's End, both of them in cists, and one, now in St Buryan church, accompanied by a flint knife. Most of the bronze daggers have come from graves, but one was discovered on an ancient tin-working site near Mevagissey. This, with the discovery of a mould for making the first, flat-bladed type of bronze axe, suggests that tin was worked in Cornwall in the Early Bronze Age, though it does not follow that the craft was brought by the Beaker Folk, who were not themselves skilled workers in bronze; almost certainly it came from Ireland, whose smiths supplied them, and where copper was abundant and had long been worked. Pure copper, however, is a soft material, and only when mixed with some alloy, such as tin to form bronze, can it be forged into really serviceable tools and weapons. Tin is a rare metal in Europe, and Cornwall with its vast virgin deposits was at the beginning of an industrial revolution.

The original deposits of tin are veins, or lodes, in the aureoles surrounding the granite hills. As the overlying rock was worn away some of these lodes were exposed, the loose material being gradually washed down the hillsides and valleys in fan-shaped 'streams' of heavy black stones and sandy particles, sometimes several feet thick, and covered with layers of earth. It follows that there are three ways of working tin: either 'streaming', or digging into a cliff face where a vein is exposed, or mining by sinking shafts into the lodes. Naturally the first tinners with their primitive tools would take the easiest course of streaming, and that they did so is confirmed by Richard Carew, who tells how in the sixteenth century picks of wood and horn were found in ancient stream works 'along with little tool-heads of brass which some term thunder-axes'. 'They make small show of any profitable use,' he adds, but these bronze axes would be useful for making 'tyes', wooden troughs in which the lighter waste was washed out of the heavy grains of ore which sank to the bottom. When the tin stones had also been pounded into grains on the neighbouring rocks the 'black tin' was ready for smelting in pits or rough granite furnaces fired with wood. Carew, not without irony, relates the belief of Elizabethan tinners that the tin streams were washed down by Noah's Flood, and even in the eighteenth century they were generally thought to be tokens of the truth of the Bible story.

The development of tin working naturally brought prosperity to Cornwall, but so did the expanding trade of Europe as a whole.

The west was growing up. No longer was it inhabited entirely by small self-sufficing communities, but both the individual and society were becoming dependent on specialists, on the skilled miners and knappers of flint, on the tin streamers and smiths who forged bronze implements. Division of labour implied an internal trade, which inevitably led to a traffic abroad, so that, however darkly, we may see the beginning of modern times in the Early Bronze Age.

Ireland was rich not only in copper but also in gold, and the easiest route for her trade with the continent lay by sea to the north Cornish coast, then overland to the southern harbours and across the Channel to France. For transport by sea was simpler, perhaps even safer, than through the almost trackless wastes and forests of Wales and the English midlands, though

3. Gold collar and nugget.

the short haul across the Cornish peninsula was preferable to the dangerous passage round the Land's End. We can imagine the arrival of the Irish boats, the run up the sand, the unloading of the precious bales under the direction of the merchants, and then the chaffering with excited natives as the crews bartered bronze axeheads for tin, for they would scarcely return to Ireland without a cargo. The merchants were now in the hands of the Cornish, who carried their wares up the tracks between the hills and down to the upper reaches of the southern rivers where their dugouts were moored. Then, after more bargaining and payment in bronze or gold, the goods were stowed, the merchants embarked, and the crews paddled down the river towards the open sea.

If the market were eastern England or France, or somewhere along the North Sea coast, the route across Cornwall would be from the Camel estuary, by way of modern Padstow, Wadebridge and Bodmin to Lostwithiel and the river Fowey; if the destination were Brittany the overland passage was only a few miles up the Hayle river to St Michael's Mount, the valley that severs the West Penwith massif from the rest of Cornwall. It is, as we should expect, along these two routes that the richest trophies of the Irish traffic have been found. From St Erth at the head of the Hayle estuary come two early bronze axeheads, slender and unflanged, three more from St Blazey near Fowey, elaborately engraved with geometrical patterns characteristic of Ireland at this period, and another from the northern end of the route at Harlyn Bay near Padstow. And it was here that a labourer found a number of pieces of metal, apparently brass horse-trappings, all but two of which he threw into the sea. They proved to be crescent-shaped necklets of pure gold, beaten fine by skilful Irish smiths and decorated with patterns similar to those on their axeheads. They must be among the first real luxuries ever to come to Cornwall, worn no doubt about their necks by long-since-vanished women, not only as foils to their beauty but also as symbols of the wealth and importance of their lords, who bartered tin or cattle in exchange for them. Two more of these golden lunulae have been found: one at St Juliot, Thomas Hardy's St Juliot not far from Padstow, the other in Gwithian parish, at the end of the defile between Hayle and the Mount. They are the only golden crescents that have been found in England, some indication of the importance to Cornwall of this western sea-borne traffic. Perhaps the beautiful little ribbed gold beaker, found with a skeleton and a bronze dagger in a large barrow above the Hurlers, is of about the same period.

The passage between Ireland and Cornwall was only part of the long trade route established by the megalith builders from the Mediterranean to Brittany and the north of Scotland, and it was probably along this route that came the blue faïence beads found in a barrow near the Land's End. They came either from Egypt or Crete, possibly as early as 1600 BC, and are among the first products of the great eastern civilisations to reach England.

Owing to this Atlantic seaboard traffic, Cornwall had more in common with the culture across the Channel than with that beyond the Tamar. The entrance graves of the two regions were similar, and so was their pottery. The typical Cornish pot of the Early Bronze Age is biconical, rather like a plant pot with a short inverted one above it, a shape that does not occur in England outside the south-west, though it is characteristic of Breton ware, and British influence was confined virtually to the decoration made by pressing cords into the plastic clay. Again, when the Bretons added handles to their pots, so did the Cornish, and both developed the custom of burning their dead exceptionally early in the Bronze Age. Intercourse must have been further encouraged by the working of tin, and it may be that bands of Bretons, attracted by the new venture, helped to swell the growing population of west Cornwall. Perhaps, with their advanced megalithic tradition, they inspired the erection of some of the great stone monuments there, the circles and menhirs and the only alignment in Cornwall, the Nine Maidens near St Columb Major.

Yet far the finest of these monuments were the work primarily of the Beaker Folk farther east in Wiltshire, where their tradition of building circles of wooden posts within an earthwork – woodhenges – was transformed into stone by their contact with the megalith builders. Stonehenge, on the vast expanse of Salisbury Plain looking so small and forlorn when seen from a distance, so grand from its approaches, is two concentric stone circles enclosing a double horseshoe sanctuary, the whole temple, for such it must have been, being surrounded by a ditch and outer bank. Then there is Avebury, which, according to Aubrey who saw it in the seventeenth century, 'doth as much surpass Stonehenge as a cathedral doth a parish church'. Certainly, in sheer extent it does: the surrounding ditch, a quarter of a mile in diameter and fifty feet deep, forms a circular platform or plinth on which the temple is set. This consists, or used to consist, of a great circle of stones along the inner edge of the ditch and two double circles within, each built about a central group of stones. What were the mysteries celebrated we do not know, though it seems probable that they were connected with the sun. Perhaps the sun itself, the bringer of light, was worshipped, a very different religion from the cult of the earth goddess that lingered in west Cornwall, a cult with which one always associates darkness and torches and the sounds of a night sea.

As the culture of the Beaker Folk did not completely submerge that of the far south-west there are few of these embanked circles, or henge monuments, in Cornwall, and all are significantly at the eastern end. There is one near Callington, another near Lanivet, and a third on the southern slope of Hawk's Tor in the middle of Bodmin Moor. This is the Stripple Stones, much ruined now, but the ditch remains, and on the outer bank Bronze Age people must have assembled to watch the ritual performed by their priests, much as their descendants of medieval times were to watch the miracle plays performed in their rounds. It is a strange thought this, that the ultimate origin of Shakespeare's theatre, the wooden O of the Globe, may have been the wood or stone circle of the Bronze Age.

There are nine more circles on, or in the neighbourhood of, Bodmin Moor, the most interesting being the group known as the Hurlers, so called because they were thought to have been men turned into stone 'for profaning the Lord's Day with hurling the ball'. Many of these eastern circles are associated with hamlets of stone huts, with the living, that is, rather than with the dead, for barrows about them are few. There are no circles in central Cornwall, but among those of the far west there is a significant reversal of emphasis, for here the remains of dwellings are few

4. The Hurlers.

and barrows are many, as are also stories of petrified people and legends of slaughter, a further indication perhaps that the west was more concerned with the cult of darkness, death and the earth than with that of light, life and the sun.

The biggest of these western circles is the Nine Maidens at Boscawen-Un, north of St Buryan, where neighbouring barrows have yielded burned bones and other relics of the Bronze Age. The name 'Nine Maidens' is curiously persistent, for there are five of them in Penwith, in addition to the alignment at St Columb Major and the Nine Stones near Altarnun. Legend has it, of course, that they are girls turned into stone for dancing on the Sabbath, but this is merely the attempt of medieval Christianity to moralise these outlandish memorials, *maiden* being a corruption of *maedn*, late Cornish for *maen*, a stone. Apparently 'nine' is also a corruption, for there was once a circle at Goon-Nawmen, the Down of the Nine Stones. This takes us back to Celtic times. But why 'nine', a number that bears no relation to the number of stones in the circles? Can it be that there is any connection with the curious story told by Pomponius Mela in the first century, that an island off Brittany was inhabited by nine virgins with strange powers of magic?

There is a variation of the name in the Merry Maidens near Lamorna, a circle close to which are two tall single stones, the Pipers, who were petrified for playing the tunes to which the maidens danced. The whole group was once surrounded by barrows and Bronze Age bones and ashes, now scattered, and another legend lingers about this prehistoric burial ground. It is the scene of the last great battle in the west, when the Saxons under Athelstan defeated King Howel and his Cornish forces; the Pipers represent the rival Kings, and about them are buried the bodies of the slain. It is possible, for standing stones may be of almost any date, though the origin of the legend may well be something much older, a folk memory perpetuating some Bronze Age engagement commemorated by the circle and barrows. Perhaps the Pipers are memorials to two of the heroes or chiefs.

The battles of the later years of the Early Bronze Age can rarely have been more than inter-tribal affrays, grim little skirmishes fought on the wild moors with dagger and axe, for there were no foreign invaders to repel during the four centuries that followed the arrival of the Beaker Folk. Soon after 1500 BC, however, heralding the Middle Bronze Age, small bands of warriors from Brittany invaded the chalklands of Wessex and established themselves as masters of southern England, dispossessing the Beaker chieftains as they had dispossessed the neolithic farmers, and as the Norman knights, twenty-five centuries later, were to dispossess the Saxon aristocracy.

They owed their ascendancy largely to superior weapons. The flat bronze dagger and axe were easily buckled and broken, but the new rulers had smiths who forged daggers strengthened with a slender central rib, and axeheads with flanges and a stop ridge that prevented the splitting of the haft when a heavy blow was struck. It was not long before the bronze dagger was attached to a shaft and became a spear, while by a parallel development the ribbed blade was lengthened until it was no longer a dagger to be clutched in the fist but a thrusting weapon, a rapier more than two feet long. It is a sobering thought that even in the Bronze Age man's progress is to be measured largely in terms of the efficiency of his weapons.

Yet not altogether so. Whatever internal broils there may have been, the five centuries of the Middle Bronze Age, roughly from 1400 to 900 BC, were free from foreign invasion, and a period of steady if unspectacular advance in the arts of peace, as the various strains in the population intermingled and were grafted together to form a people with a common culture. Agriculture, which had been neglected by the Beaker Folk, was to some extent revived, and though the bronze-smiths were too busy making swords to think of ploughshares – a woman with a hoe served well enough – barley was grown to supplement their food crops and flax for the manufacture of linen. Trade expanded, and to the gold from Ireland, now in the form of torques, twisted ribbons of metal made into necklets and girdles, was added the amber of the Baltic. The traffic in amber was particularly important; so important that a new trade route was opened up for it, from the hitherto isolated Baltic, south across the passes of the Alps to the Adriatic, and the gleaming fossilised resin with its magical power of attraction enchanted even the princes of Crete.

It seems probable that the development of new overland routes through Europe led to a slackening of the old Atlantic trade. It is only what we should expect. With the gradual clearing of the forests and the making of tolerable tracks for pack animals, transport by land and river would become quicker, easier and safer than by the western seas, which must have taken a fearful toll of the Bronze Age boats. The Irish trade would be affected in a similar way. Once the English midlands had been made passable it would pay to ship gold and bronze from Wicklow to north Wales or the Mersey, and then carry it overland, to south-east England and the continent. If this happened it would be disastrous for Cornwall, for though she still had her tin for export the demand would inevitably fall, and in any event her prosperity depended less on her tin than on her position athwart the

Atlantic trade route. That it really did happen, and that for the greater part of the Middle Bronze Age Cornwall was cut off from the growing prosperity of the rest of England is suggested by the paucity of finds belonging to this period.

We should not expect to find much in the graves, for even in eastern England it was no longer the custom to leave extravagant and precious objects with the dead. Bodies were now generally burned, and their ashes buried in urns under round barrows of earth or stones. 'Some apprehended a purifying virtue in Fire,' wrote Sir Thomas Browne, 'refining the grosser commixture, and firing out the Aethereal Particles so deeply immersed in it.' Perhaps, then, this fiery dissolution betokens some change of religious belief, a more spiritual view of man, whose soul was in need of no physical aid in the next world. Or perhaps cremation was merely a device to get rid of the dead and their ghosts, the maimed rites and paltry offerings the economy of a society more conscious of material values.

It is not, then, the poverty of the Cornish burials of this period that is surprising, the fact that little or nothing has been found with the huge biconical cinerary urns, but the poverty of other finds. A few bronze axeheads have been discovered, but only one rapier and one spearhead. There is no amber, and there is no gold, unless the hoard found at Amalveor in Towednack near St Ives is of this period. This consists of six plain bracelets and two torques, one a girdle and the other a necklet of three twisted ribbons of gold. But although the torque is a form characteristic of the Irish goldsmiths of the Middle Bronze Age, the bracelets, of which another has recently been found near Liskeard, appear to be later, so that the hoard as a whole almost certainly belongs to the Late Bronze Age.

It seems then that we should think of Cornwall in the Middle Bronze Age as cut off not only from eastern England, as it always had been, but also from the west, from the stimulating contact with the Mediterranean as well as from the lucrative traffic with Ireland. Of course an occasional foreign boat would run into harbour, but generally speaking the period must have been one of stagnation. Fortunately the climate was warmer and drier than it is now, and the inhabitants of the little villages probably passed their uneventful lives in comparative comfort. There cannot have been more than a few thousand of them altogether, a mainly pastoral people eking out the food supplied by their herds and scanty agriculture with that obtained from hunting and fishing. Tin streaming may have been almost abandoned for lack of copper with which to make bronze, though had they known it there were immense deposits of the precious ore not far below their feet. And so some twenty generations of Cornish Bronze Age men and women were born, laboured, died and were burned, leaving so many handfuls of ashes to add to the urns under the barrows.

It was probably about the middle of the ninth century BC that the long somnolence of the Middle Bronze Age in Cornwall was broken by the arrival of fresh immigrants from the continent. These were the Celts of France and western Germany, a people whom it is by no means easy to define. Like the inhabitants of England they were a mixture of various races, of tall fair long-headed Nordics, of stocky round-headed Beaker Folk, of short dark long-headed Iberians, the descendants of the megalith builders who had absorbed the even older strain of mesolithic man. Yet, despite this racial mixture, for the short swarthy Greeks at least the typical Celt was a tall, fair, muscular, blue-eyed barbarian who spoke a strange language, although it was one allied to their own, for both were branches of the parent Aryan tongue. Possibly the natives of Britain, being descended from similar stock, already spoke a language akin to the newcomers, but if any trace of the old Iberian tongue remained, from now on it must have been swamped by Celtic, the language of the ancient Britons, which was to be preserved as Welsh and Cornish. Perhaps, however, something of the Iberian syntax survived, and this may account for the peculiar word-order of the Cornishman even today when he speaks English, 'Are you going to do it?', for example, becoming, 'Going to do it, are 'ee?' It is interesting to note that many constructions in Cornish resemble those in non-Aryan Hamitic languages, and the Iberians were almost certainly a Hamitic people, coming ultimately from Egypt and north Africa.

These first Celtic immigrants, squeezed out of their continental homes by the expanding peoples of central Europe, were not numerous but as the pressure increased, immigration became invasion, and by the end of the eighth century Celtic refugees were pouring into England along the whole of the eastern and southern coasts, even as far west as the Land's End. They brought with them a more advanced culture and better tools, for their bronze-smiths were a highly skilled caste, merchants as well as founders, who travelled about buying old bronze which they melted down and forged into the improved shapes that they had invented. Among their weapons was a leaf-shaped spearhead and a double-edged slashing sword, more formidable than the rapier, while for protection there was a small circular wooden shield with a central boss of bronze, or even, for those who could afford it, entirely of bronze. Then there was the new socketed axe, much firmer than the old flanged type – two moulds for making them have been found near Camelford; for the smith himself there were punches and small anvils, for the carpenter chisels and saws, for the farmer sickles and – at last – ploughshares; they were, it is true, merely glorified hoes that scratched the soil, but at least they were hoes that were pulled by oxen instead of pushed by women.

For these Celtic immigrants of the Late Bronze Age practised mixed farming like their neolithic predecessors, and agriculture, comparatively neglected since the incursion of the pastoral Beaker Folk a thousand years before, now became the basic occupation in the economy of man. Agriculture is a stabilising and civilising influence, for it ties man to the soil he has tilled, and this in turn encourages building and the domestic arts. Spindle whorls and clay weights for stretching the warp threads in the upright looms bear witness to the improvements in spinning and weaving, and bronze cauldrons that could be hung over the fire suggest the savours of the new dishes that the housewives of the age were able to prepare.

Agriculture, improved tools and more nourishing food all spelled prosperity, and the rising standard of living of these settled communities led inevitably to an increase in population, as is witnessed by the number of funerary urns that have been unearthed. Two of their first-discovered burial grounds are in Dorset, and it is from these sites that the Celtic invaders of the Late Bronze Age have derived their name of the Deverel-Rimbury people. There is nothing very beautiful about the grey barrel-shaped and bucket-shaped urns, and their hugger-mugger method of interment is in startling contrast to the great stone memorials of the megalith builders and rich burials of the Early Bronze Age. Rarely was anything of value deposited with the dead, who were packed into urnfields, or buried in the side of an old tumulus, or at best commemorated by a small round barrow piled over their ashes. Whatever his religious beliefs may have been, it seems clear that the increasing prosperity of Bronze Age man made him think more of his life on earth and less of the shadowy existence in the next world.

At last, after its long period of isolation, Cornwall began to share in the prosperity that had eluded it in the Middle Bronze Age. The Deverel-Rimbury people settled along the south coast of the western half of the county, where the mild climate favoured their husbandry and the sunny southern slopes of the hills afforded plenty of pastures for their flocks and herds. The extreme west particularly attracted them, for this was the principal tin-working region, and here they seem to have settled in still greater numbers. They can be traced by their characteristic urns, usually found under barrows, often in small stone cists, the human ashes sometimes accompanied by most strange grave-fellows: the skull of a goat and bird bones at St Just, the bones of three birds, a rabbit and toad in another cist at Gunwalloe.

Many of the Late Bronze Age implements that have been found in the last few centuries have since been lost, but a double-edged sword remains and a small bronze saw, discovered with a number of axeheads in 1813. Apparently a similar hoard was turned up near St Michael's Mount in the early sixteenth century, for Leland writes in his *Itinerary*, 'there was found of late yeres syns Spere Heddes, Axis for warre, and Swerdes of Coper wrappid up in lynid scant perishid nere the Mount in S. *Hilaries*

Paroch in Tynne works'. These hoards, several of which have been found in the western half of the county, are particularly informative, for they appear to be the stock-in-trade of itinerant bronze-founders, lost perhaps in some accident or after being hidden in a moment of peril. Not only are there axeheads, spearheads and swords, many of them broken, probably old weapons past repair which the smith had bought as scrap metal, but there are also 'jets' of bronze left over from casting, some small bars of gold, and even a piece of tin from a hoard in the rich ore-bearing district of St Just.

Cornwall, then, appears to have benefited from its contact with the advanced culture that the Celts brought with them from the continent. But more than this: there are indications of a revival of the ancient Atlantic seaboard traffic. This is what we should expect when central Europe was in a state of ferment, the overland routes endangered, and when the first sailing ships were replacing primitive paddle boats. A long pin with an amber head has been found near Fowey, and many of the socketed axeheads are of foreign type: French, Welsh and Irish. And that trade began to flow again between Cornwall and Ireland is confirmed by the rich finds of gold ornaments. The Towednack treasure, already mentioned, is probably of this period, and the hoard of six large gold bracelets from Morvah, between St Ives and the Land's End, certainly is, for three of the bracelets have the characteristic Irish trumpet-shaped ends of the Late Bronze Age. Pieces of similar ornaments have been found near the Lizard and the Land's End.

All the most important finds of the Late Bronze Age have come from the extreme west of Cornwall, evidently the most prosperous part of the county as well as the most highly populated. The itinerant bronze-smiths, after working their way along the south coast, naturally stayed longer in this, the main tin-streaming region, where incidentally they mixed an abnormally large proportion of tin with their copper when smelting bronze. Then, this developing industrial area inevitably attracted Irish merchants, who now sent their wares for the continent up the Hayle valley to St Michael's Mount rather than by the longer route between the upper reaches of the Camel and Fowey rivers.

Towards the end of the Bronze Age the pattern of present-day Cornwall was beginning, however dimly, to emerge, and if only we could take an aerial view of the county in the middle of the fifth century BC, when Socrates was a young man in Athens and Pericles building the Parthenon, the scene would be not altogether unrecognisable. There would, of course, be no towns, but the main tracks and their crossings would indicate the places where they were to develop in later ages. The extreme north-east of the county, without natural harbours and without tin, is almost deserted, but following the track from the Tamar, past the Hurlers and Trethevy Quoit, we should see tiny settlements on the southern slopes of Bodmin Moor, though many of them lie farther north along the little De Lank river which flows into the Camel. The round houses have low granite walls and vary in size from about six to thirty feet across, and in the centre of the conical roof, supported by posts and thatched with branches and turf, is a hole for the escape of smoke from the fire on the hearth below. Beds and settles of heather, and perhaps stone shelves are ranged round the walls. Surrounding the huts are little fields enclosed by earthen banks and dry stone walls, and not far from Rough Tor is the large rectangular cattle pound now known as King Arthur's Hall. It may be that these villagers are descendants of the pre-Celtic people who were driven into the high hills by the invaders and built the stone stronghold on the top of Rough Tor.

At the western end of the moor the track falls steeply into the gap between the granite hills, and where it is crossed by the route from the Camel to the Fowey estuary is a small settlement, the site of modern Bodmin. From here the track follows roughly the line of the present main road towards Hayle, avoiding the wooded and swampy valleys to the south. Carn Brea, once a neolithic settlement, is still occupied, but the greatest activity is along the valley of the marshy Hayle river up which boats are plying with goods, gold and bronze from Ireland and Wales, which are unloaded halfway across the isthmus to finish their journey to the port at St Michael's Mount on the backs of horses and men. More packhorses are converging on the Mount from the West Penwith moors, for this is the great tin-streaming region. A winding track girdles the granite, defining the line where the hills sink into the coastal plateau: under the steep northern escarpment from Hayle to the Land's End, then back towards Mount's Bay, past standing stones and stone circles, where the slopes are gentler, though the intersecting valleys deeper. Like the threads of a spider's web, or the spokes of a wheel, other well-worn paths fan out from the Bay across the moors to the gaps in the northern hills, where they join the coastal track, and here are many of the principal tin streams and the hamlets of the workers: Sperris Croft, Wicca Round, Trewey-Foage, Kerrow, where a longstone was erected over the urns of a Late Bronze Age burial.

It is the region of the neolithic quoits, now some fifteen centuries old, and already largely denuded of earth and even stranger perhaps to the Bronze Age tin workers than they are to us today. No doubt religious ceremonies are still performed within the stone circles, but they probably bear little resemblance, apparent resemblance at least, to those for which they were built a thousand years ago. Perhaps they are also used for secular purposes, as open-air council chambers and tribal meeting places where chief or priest presides. We cannot say. Nor can we say what legends still lingered about the Isles of the Dead, just visible on the western horizon beyond the Land's End.

A History Of Cornwall

III

The Iron Age

It was at about this time, in the fifth century BC, that the progressive deterioration of the climate drove the harassed farmers of northern France and the Netherlands to look for new land for their growing numbers and expanding agriculture. The shores of England appeared to offer them scope and refuge, and so further bands of Celtic immigrants crossed the Channel to join the descendants of those who had made the same venture hundreds of years before. As their ways of life were not unlike and there was no lack of land waiting to be developed, the newcomers settled comparatively peacefully in the south and east in the characteristic Celtic pattern of scattered hamlets and farms.

In one vitally important matter, however, they differed from their predecessors: their weapons and farming implements were made of iron. Iron had long been known in the eastern Mediterranean: the Greeks were using it more than five centuries before this time, and from them the knowledge passed to the warlike Celts of central Europe, who developed the so-called Hallstatt civilisation, which covered roughly the first half of the first millennium BC. It was from their Hallstatt kinsmen that the Celtic farmers of France learned the use and manufacture of the new metal, and as it became cheaper and more plentiful, within the reach of those who could afford but few of the rare and costly implements of bronze, there was a corresponding rise in the standard of living. But bronze was by no means altogether displaced. Iron was essentially utilitarian, far more efficient for weapons and tools, for sword-blades and daggers, for sickles and ploughshares, but bronze was more beautiful, more comely for ornament, for sword-hilts and scabbards, for brooches and bracelets, and even for some domestic functional objects, cauldrons for example, it was superior to iron.

This imported Hallstatt culture of eastern and southern England seems scarcely to have affected Cornwall, which for some time longer remained in the Bronze Age. Early in the third century, however, there was a fresh Celtic irruption, this time very different from the peaceful infiltration of the Hallstatt farmers. The restless and vigorous central European Celts were bursting their confines. Some of them had already crossed the Alps, descended on Italy and sacked Rome, and now, having plundered Delphi, they were pressing eastwards into Macedonia, whence they were to force a passage into Asia Minor. Trade followed in the wake of plunder, and this contact of the barbarians with the Mediterranean transformed their old Hallstatt culture into that which takes its name from La Tène, a fortified post on the shores of Lake Neuchâtel. In exchange for the northern products of amber and tin they imported the luxuries of the south, particularly wine, and with it bronze and earthenware bowls and cups, enriched with classical designs. It was probably these stylised Greek plant forms, particularly the palmette or honeysuckle, that inspired the Celtic craftsmen, in whose hands they developed into the graceful curvilinear designs that are the great glory of Celtic art.

War, conquest and wealth led to a new form of social organisation, or at least to the consolidation of an already existing pattern. The Hallstatt farmers of France and England were only amateur warriors, resorting to arms in defence of their fields and folds, but the La Tène warriors were professionals. Organised war demands some sort of military hierarchy: a chief and an aristocracy wealthy and powerful enough to control the peasants on whose support they must depend. How wealthy and powerful were these warrior chiefs may be judged from their burials. One of them, in the Marne district of France, lies at full length between two iron tires and bronze axle trees, all that remains of the wheels of his war chariot; at his left side are iron spearheads and a long iron sword, and at his right a bronze-bladed knife. On his breast are four bronze buttons and a bronze fibula to fasten his cloak, and at his feet lie his pointed helmet, bridle bits and trappings for two horses, a Greek flagon and a drinking cup of the fourth century BC.

These were the warriors who, in the third century, thrust into England bent on conquest. But the southern farmers were not easily subdued. Hastily they threw up fortifications on the hilltops, earthen ramparts strengthened with palisades, and though some of the raiders remained in the south, others followed the line of least resistance up the less populated eastern half of England to Lincolnshire and Yorkshire, where they developed an advanced form of their culture.

At about the same time as this eastern invasion other bands of La Tène warriors from western France crossed the Channel in search of a richer prize. This was the tin of Cornwall. Towards the end of the fourth century BC the Greek geographer Pytheas had sailed round Spain and up the coast of France to Britain, part of which he explored. His account of his voyage has been lost, but extracts are quoted or paraphrased by later writers, notably by Diodorus Siculus, a Sicilian Greek historian. According to Diodorus, the inhabitants of that part of Britain called Belerion, or the Land's End, 'are very fond of strangers, and, from their intercourse with foreign merchants, are civilised in their manner of life. They prepare the tin, working very carefully the earth in which it is produced. The ground is rocky, but it contains earthy veins, the produce of which is ground down, smelted and purified. They beat the metal into masses shaped like astragali, and carry it to a certain island lying off Britain called Ictis. During the ebb of the tide the intervening space is left dry, and they carry over into this island the tin in abundance in their wagons. Now there is a peculiar phenomenon connected with the neighbouring islands, I mean those that lie between Europe and Britain, for at the flood tide the intervening passage is overflowed, and they seem like islands, but a large space is left dry at the ebb, and they seem like peninsulas. Here then the merchants buy the tin from the natives and carry it over to Gaul, and after travelling overland for about thirty days, they finally bring their loads on horses to the mouth of the Rhône'.

After trying to reconstruct events from the relics that prehistoric man has left behind him of his painful upward struggle, from his shelters and hovels, monuments and graves, weapons and tools, ornaments and pottery, it is exciting to come at last upon the first contemporary description of Cornwall, and one would give much to have the remainder of the account. If this extract really is a plain unvarnished paraphrase of the Pytheas story, it is a remarkable picture of the civilisation of West Penwith at the end of the Bronze Age. Who the foreign merchants were we do not know for certain, but there is no reason to suppose that they were Phoenicians, a speculation first advanced by Camden in the sixteenth century. Probably they came from Brittany, whither the tin was shipped, and perhaps it was from them that the Cornish learned how to make wagons and to convert their trackways into passable roads. It seems the most likely explanation, for Diodorus tells us that the tin was carried to Marseilles by way of Narbonne, which must mean that it was taken up the valley of the Garonne, and it would be prudent, essential maybe, to put in first at some haven in south Brittany before continuing the voyage down the coast. And we know that in the time of Caesar the Veneti used to sail for Britain from the harbours of this region.

If this was the ancient tin route to the Mediterranean, there can be little doubt that the island of Ictis was St Michael's Mount, for its description as an island at full tide and a peninsula at the ebb exactly depicts it today. It is true that the old Cornish name for the Mount was *Carrek Los y'n Cos*, the Grey Rock in the Wood, and that once there may have been a forest between it and the shore, but if so it was probably long before the time of Pytheas.

We may then picture the Cornish tinners 'beating the metal into masses shaped like astragali', that is into ingots resembling Grecian dice, loading them on their primitive wagons, and at low tide driving them across the causeway to the little sheltered harbour on the landward side of St Michael's Mount. There the Breton merchants bartered their southern wares for them, stowed them in their leather-sailed ships and transported them to the mouth of the Loire, where, after a pause for revictualling, they were taken up the Garonne as far as Toulouse, and then overland through the Gap of Narbonne between the Cevennes and Pyrenees to Marseilles. It must have been a perilous journey when the marauding Celts from the alpine region were thrusting west and north, and no doubt many of the precious cargoes were intercepted and seized. But valuable as was the plunder from waylaying an occasional convoy, it would be far more profitable to capture its source of supply. And so, in the third century BC, plundering warrior bands of La Tène Celts descended on Cornwall.

The tinners and farmers of west Cornwall were not a warlike people. No doubt they squabbled and fought among themselves, but for centuries they had lived comparatively peaceful lives, untroubled by foreign aggression, and if, as is probable, the skeletons found in the cemetery at Harlyn Bay are theirs, they do not seem to have been physically equal to coping with such an emergency. They lie near the sea, more than a hundred of them, in parallel lines of black slate cists, and probably as many more are still under the dunes that have covered so much along the exposed western-facing stretches of this coast. Most of them lie on their right side, with knees drawn up to their chins. Very little was buried with them: a few slate knives, two bronze brooches that may have come along the tin route from the south of France, some iron bracelets, two mice in the grave of a child. They were a small people, the women just over five feet, the men only three inches taller, and most of them long-headed. It looks as though the predominant strain was that of short, dark neolithic man, though a number of rounder heads suggests a mingling with the earlier Celtic immigrants, and an occasional broad head a contact with the Beaker Folk.

It is a singularly moving sight, this cemetery by the sea, and the small crouching figures, so old, yet so seemingly young, like children yet to be born, appear pathetically unequal to the task of repelling a powerful opponent. Of course they may have been nimble and tough, but they were ill equipped to defend themselves against the invaders. Armed only lightly with weapons of bronze, they were no match for the La Tène warriors with their iron-tipped spears and long iron swords, sharp and double-edged. Probably they withdrew into the hills where, like the Hallstatt farmers farther east, they tried to secure themselves within hastily constructed fortifications, but if so they were soon dislodged and subdued, and their conquerors converted their makeshift hilltop refuges into permanent strongholds from which they could overawe and reduce them to subjection.

Chun Castle, on the north coast not far from the Land's End, is one of these citadels. It stands seven hundred feet high on top of a hill overlooking a rich tin-streaming region and the village of Morvah, the site of the treasure of gold bracelets, buried perhaps to prevent their being seized by the invaders. Close by, on the gently falling western slope, is Chun Quoit, and one wonders what the newcomers made of it, a monument as remote from their age as Roman London is from ours. The castle, almost a hundred yards in diameter, was surrounded by a ditch, crossed by a causeway leading through the so-called Iron Gateway of the outer wall, a massive structure of dry masonry some six feet thick and faced with granite blocks. The entrance passage then turned left along the line of the wide inner ditch, so that any intruder exposed his unprotected right flank to the defenders until he reached the gateway through the inner wall, which may have been fifteen feet high or more. Within the spacious central enclosure, and ranged round the inner wall, were the rooms, or houses, of the chief and his garrison. Given a sufficient store of food, the defenders of such a castle could laugh a siege to scorn, for a well ensured a plentiful supply of water.

Chun Castle is now only a ruin, its ditches choked and its outer walls fallen, though still formidable even in decay, and in its prime the tall concentric walls crowning the hill must have been among the most impressive sights in Britain, certainly a citadel to impress the subject folk below. No doubt the conquerors, in return for their 'protection', exacted tribute of food and fuel from the natives, and especially of tin, for inside the fortress was a furnace where the chief's smiths smelted the ore, and both tin and iron slag have been found beside it. Presumably the metal was sent down to St Michael's Mount, where it was exchanged for a product even more precious, the wine of the south, imported in amphorae of red Mediterranean ware. It must have been a good, if intellectually limited, life, for even when the hill was shrouded in mist and guards had to be doubled, it was snug enough round the fires of the little houses huddled against the great circling walls. And in summer it must have been idyllic: the patterned fields below, the opal and sapphire of the sea, the Isles of Scilly beyond the Land's End, and the Lizard away to the south-east. No remains of chariots have been found, but on a shimmering summer afternoon, when looking idly at the great gateway with its massive granite uprights, it is not difficult to imagine a flash of horses, wheels, a streaming cloak and a glittering helmet.

Three miles to the south of Chun is Caer Brane, a similar though more dilapidated citadel of mainly earthen ramparts, and five miles to the east stands Castle-an-Dinas, dominating the route that runs down to St Michael's Mount. It was described by William Borlase two hundred years ago, when considerably less ruinous than it is today. Then it consisted 'of two stone walls built one within the other in a circular form surrounding the area of the hill. The ruins are now fallen on each sides the Walls, and shew the work to have been of great height and thickness; there was also a third and outmost Wall built more than halfways round, but was left unfinish'd. Within the Walls are many little inclosures of a circular form about seven yards diameter with little Walls round them of two, and three feet high; they appear to me to have been so many huts, erected for the shelter of the garrison; the diameter of the whole Fort from East to West, is 400 feet, and the principal Graff or Ditch is 60 feet wide: towards the South the sides of this mountain are mark'd by two large green paths about ten feet wide, which were visibly cleans'd by art of their natural roughness for the more convenient approach to this garrison: near the middle of the Area is a Well almost choak'd with it's own ruins, and at a little distance a narrow pit, it's sides wall'd round, probably dug for water also, but now fill'd with rubbish'.

Dr Borlase, confusing *Dinas*, a fort, with *Danes*, attributed these castles to the Vikings, and he did not know that many of the little ruined villages on the flanks of the hills were of the same period as the citadels. Some, like Sperris Croft and Wicca Round, had first been occupied in the Bronze Age, but others were built early in the Iron Age. The round granite-walled huts of Bodrifty on the western slope of Mulfra Hill were built in the early fourth century BC by settlers who reared sheep and grew corn in their tiny lyncheted fields, only about an eighth of an acre in extent; they still ground their grain on saddle querns, made pottery by hand, for the potter's wheel was as yet unknown in Cornwall, and probably worked iron. They were primarily farmers, however, and agriculture made another great advance in the Iron Age.

Relations between village and citadel would gradually become easier until, in course of time, the conquerors came to be accepted as natives, their stronghold as a tribal centre and general place of refuge, a primitive acropolis. And as the second century BC drew to its close there was need of refuges and strongholds. The Cimbri and other Teutonic barbarians were overrunning northern France, and now that ships were becoming comparatively large and seaworthy there was no telling when or where a crew of reckless and heavily armed pirates might run up an open beach in search of booty. The sea was no longer a defensive moat but a menace, and Cornwall with its immensely long coastline was particularly vulnerable. The Veneti of Brittany had a similar and even more urgent problem which they met by building cliff castles along their coast, and as it was they who shipped most of the tin from Cornwall they probably taught the Cornish the art of fortifying their headlands. They were singularly well equipped to do so, for they had recently become acquainted with the latest offensive weapon, the sling, a device for hurling stones, which in hands as skilful as those of the Balearic islanders in Hannibal's army was as deadly as the medieval longbow. In defence, therefore, the essential thing was to keep the slingers at a distance, and one way of doing this was to increase the number of ramparts in front of the principal fortification.

All the way round the coast, therefore, the Cornish built new and strengthened old cliff castles: from Rame Head in the south-east to Black Head in St Austell, from Dodman Point to Maen Castle at the Land's End, and then along the north coast from Cape Cornwall to Kelsey Head, from Pentire Point to Tintagel. One of the finest of these is that on Trevelgue Head, a promontory just north of Newquay. A series of ramparts across the neck protects it from the mainland, one of the ditches being a natural chasm that would have to be bridged, and other earthworks defend the weakest points on the cliffs overlooking the sea. Within such a stronghold the defenders would be safe against anything but invasion and a permanent occupation of their countryside.

The defensive device of multiple ramparts was naturally applied to hilltop fortresses as well, and soon there was scarcely a hill in Cornwall that was not crowned with an earthwork. Carn Brea, the great granite outcrop near Camborne which seems to have been continuously occupied since neolithic times, was ringed with a series of stone walls like a medieval walled town. The defences of Castle Dore were remodelled, and it may be that 'the third and outmost wall' of Castle-an-Dinas, noted by Borlase, was added at this period, and numerous sling stones within Chun Castle and Tregear Rounds, near Port Isaac, suggest that here too there was a strengthening of defences. Warbstow Burrows in the north-east is one of the finest of the late Iron Age forts, but finest of all is the other Castle-an-Dinas in St Columb Major parish. 'It seemeth (in time past),' wrote Carew dryly, 'to have been a matter of moment, the rather for that a great causeway (now covered with grass) doth lead into it.' It was indeed a matter of moment. The fortress controlled the main route along the county, the tin-working area round about Roche, and the track that connected it with the little haven of St Columb Porth beneath Trevelgue Head, from which the tin was probably shipped.

Cornwall, however, had little iron, and it may have been in search of its ore that traders and colonists from the south-west worked their way up the Bristol Channel towards the Forest of Dean and south Wales, taking with them their knowledge of the new offensive and defensive tactics of war. This would account for the numerous Iron Age fortresses in the north-east of Cornwall, a region that had hitherto been of little importance and very thinly populated. Some of the venturers, reinforced later by further immigrants from Brittany, settled at Glastonbury, halfway between the tin of Cornwall and the iron of Gloucestershire, where they developed their peculiar and advanced La Tène civilisation in lake villages built on piles and protected by water instead of by ramparts. By the end of the first century BC the whole of this south-western region, from the Cotswolds to the Land's End, was loosely bound together by the Celtic culture that the La Tène warriors and seafaring Veneti had brought to Cornwall.

Paradoxically, however, in Cornwall most of the memorials of the Iron Age are in the materials characteristic of the preceding periods, in the stone of their fortresses and villages, and bronze of their ornaments. Pottery is scarce, for the invaders established the practice of burying their dead without burning, so that there are no funerary urns, and the unburned bones have mostly perished in the damp sour soil of their cemeteries. For the same reason there is a scarcity of iron remains. The nobler bronze is virtually imperishable, but iron rusts and quickly crumbles in the mists and rains of Cornwall, and most of the tools that survived the damp have been thrown away as so much valueless scrap metal.

However, articles of bronze are much more varied than those of the previous age, testifying to the rapid advance in culture. Brooches, in the form of elaborate safety pins, were now used to fasten clothing, and circular necklets were worn with a hinge on one side and a clasp on the other. One of these has been found near Hayle, studded with small pieces of glass and engraved with a typical Celtic design. Pottery goblets were no longer the only drinking vessels, for a large wooden tankard bound with hoops of bronze and with a bronze handle has been unearthed in a tin stream near Mevagissey. It is possible that some of the beautiful bronze horse-bits and buckles similar to those found in Somerset were made in Cornwall, for a stone mould from Camelford might have been used for casting them. Then, from the neighbourhood of Warbstow Burrows not far away, comes a handsome bowl of hammered bronze, apparently turned on a lathe. It is late work, possibly of the first centuryad, and remarkable for the stylised head of a ram in relief on one side, the great curves of the horns being the detail that had most interested the Celtic artist. But the best example of the art of the period comes from the cemetery of Trelan Bahow near the Lizard. The unburned bones have all crumbled away, but one of the graves, apparently that of a lady of rank, contained bronze brooches, bracelets, rings, blue glass beads, and a bronze mirror. Though not as beautiful as those found at Desborough and at Birdlip in the Cotswolds, this Cornish mirror is a very fine one, and the engraved ornament of its back – scrolls and circles within circles – reflects the sophistication, as its burnished front once reflected the faces, of the women who adorned themselves with such care, and used tweezers and other delicate instruments as aids to their beauty.

These luxuries and refinements, as well as improved agricultural, industrial and domestic implements, all point to a rapid cultural development and rise in the standard of living. Industry implies trade, and trade in turn inevitably leads to a medium of exchange, to some form of money. The lake dwellers of Glastonbury, rich in iron from the Forest of Dean, had long, sword-shaped currency-bars of iron, and it may be that their kinsmen in Cornwall used a similar clumsy form of money, but if so it has perished along with their iron sickles and weapons. But, to quote Borlase, 'In the month of June 1749, in the middle of the ridge of Karn-brê hill, were found such a number of Coins of pure Gold, as being sold for weight, brought the finder about 16 pounds, sterling'. Apparently the whole of the able-bodied population of Camborne turned out that midsummer to dig on the top of Carn Brea, for 'Near the same quantity was found by another person near the same spot, a few days after; all which were soon sold and dispers'd: some were much worn and smooth'd, not by age, or lying in the earth, but by use, they having no allay to harden, and secure them from wearing'.

Most of these coins probably came from Gaul, where they were first minted in the second century BC, their model being the standard gold coin of Philip of Macedon, father of Alexander the Great, which on one side had the head of Apollo crowned with a laurel wreath, on the other a man driving a chariot and two horses. These Celtic coins were in circulation in south-east England by the beginning of the following century, and it seems probable that at about the same time the Gauls used them to pay for their imports of Cornish tin. Probably they remained in circulation in Cornwall long after the Roman conquest, for Roman coins are very scarce west of the Tamar until the middle of the third century.

They are strange, barbaric objects. Perhaps the reader has played the Christmas game in which a number of people sit with pencil and paper in a semicircle, each copying from his neighbour the picture that is drawn by one at the end of the line. If so, he will know that the copy that emerges at the other end rarely bears much resemblance to the original. In the same way the Gaulish coins, copied from copies, show a progressive degeneration. The Celtic artist naturally seized upon the curves. Apollo's face disappears and the obverse is filled with flames, butterflies and crescents, representing his hair, laurel wreath and ear, while on the reverse the horses' bodies are also reduced to crescents, their legs becoming dumb-bells, and the chariot wheel a series of circles. It is an admirable example of the difference between the Greek and Celtic genius, the one expressing itself in forms precise, balanced and concrete, the other spontaneous, unpredictable and abstract.

By the beginning of the Christian era a hundred generations of men had modified the natural landscape of Cornwall. To the memorials of the dead, the great stone tombs and monuments of neolithic man, to the stone circles and grass-grown barrows of the Age of Bronze, the men of the Iron Age had added their trophies of the living, their citadels, forts, cliff castles and villages. Most of these had been built on high ground, those of the first two ages for religious reasons, those of the last from more practical motives of defence, but as the climate worsened and mists and coarse vegetation crept down the flanks of the moors, villages were pushed farther down the slopes, and the little fields spread their filigree of silvery walls from the bases of the hills towards the cliffs and sea. Pack animals had trodden the principal tracks into primitive roads, and it may well be that the origin of the present tortuous route from Hayle to the Land's End was a prehistoric way linking hamlets that are now represented by medieval villages and farmsteads.

The western half of Cornwall was the industrial area, far more important and more highly populated than the agricultural east. In the valleys the tinners had piled up mounds of earth in their search for the ore of the tin streams, and here were most of the little havens, protected by forts, from which the metal was shipped by Irish merchants and Veneti traders, notably St Michael's Mount and Hayle, though the numerous fortifications along the Helford

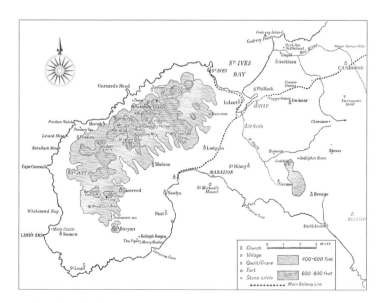

5. *The Penwith Hundred.*

river suggest that here, despite the dangerous approach athwart the Manacles, was a rival port.

All this material progress meant that the people of the Late Iron Age, a predominantly Celtic people now, speaking the musical Celtic tongue, were better clothed, better housed, better fed, and probably, therefore, taller and stronger than their Bronze Age predecessors. And they were better organised in larger tribal groups, probably with a well-developed social hierarchy, from the chief down to the assistant at the plough or forge. For the people as a whole, no doubt, this organisation spelt security, but for the warrior aristocracy it meant something more than defence, and ships, chariots, iron swords and slings gave scope for ambitions very different from those inspired by improved looms and ploughs and querns. The beginning of the Iron Age in Britain was the beginning of the age of iron.

Presumably the Cornish had their priests like other Celtic peoples. Neolithic man's cult of the Earth Goddess appears to have been succeeded in the Bronze Age by worship of the Sun God, and this in turn by the religion practised by the Celtic priests, the Druids, though no doubt Druidism was modified by elements that lingered from the preceding cults. According to Caesar the Druids of Gaul in the first century BC were a priestly and scholarly aristocracy, entry to which could be gained only by a long novitiate. They taught astrology, geography and natural science, and believed so firmly in the immortality of the soul that it was said they would even lend money on condition that it should be repaid in the next world. Mistletoe and oak were held in the highest veneration, and when the one was found growing on the other, a priest clad in a white robe would cut the golden bough with a golden sickle, and two white bulls were sacrificed below. But their religion demanded grimmer sacrifices than bulls. 'The whole nation of the Gauls,' wrote Caesar, 'is much given to superstition, for which reason those who are afflicted by a dangerous disease, and those who are involved in wars and dangers, either make human sacrifices, or vow that they will do so, and use the Druids as their agents at these ceremonies; for they think that the divine power cannot be conciliated unless a human life is paid for by a human life. They have public sacrifices ordained in this same fashion. Some tribes make great images, whose limbs, woven of wickerwork, they cram with live human victims, and then place fire below and slay them by the flames. They consider that thieves and highwaymen and other criminals are the sacrifices most pleasing to the gods; but when the supply of such victims has failed, they have been known to lay hands on wholly innocent persons.' Again, according to Caesar, the origin of Druidism was in Britain, and Gaulish novices were sent there to learn its mysteries.

All this led the eighteenth-century antiquary, William Stukeley, to find the hand of the Druids everywhere in the antiquities of Britain: Stonehenge was their temple, and cromlechs were their altars. His contemporary, William Borlase, was rather more cautious, and though he devoted twenty-three chapters of his *Antiquities of Cornwall* to the Druids he rejected the theory that the Cornish quoits were altars, and very sensibly suggested that they were sepulchral monuments or altar tombs, though for 'one of the Chief Priests or Druids, who presided in that district, or of some Prince, a favourite of that order'. Their gigantic size he considered might be owing to our forefathers' exceeding in proportion the present race of mankind. He found that the summit of Carn Brea had all the paraphernalia requisite for Druid worship: circles, standing stones, remains of cromlechs, a grove of oaks, a cave, a religious enclosure and rock basins for collecting holy water. He attached great importance to these rock basins, and at Carn Leskys, near St Just in Penwith, he found one associated with little vermicular grooves which he supposed were 'divinatory chanels' into which the blood of the unhappy victim flowed.

It must be remembered that eighteenth-century antiquaries laboured under the insuperable difficulty of having to reconcile their findings with the fact, established by Archbishop Ussher, that the world had been created in the year 4004 BC. But in one thing at least Stukeley and Borlase may have been right, or partially right. Although the stone circles were built long before the time of the Druids, there is evidence to suggest that two more circles were added to Stonehenge in the Iron Age, presumably by the Druids who used it as a temple. And if Stonehenge was used by the Celtic priests it is possible that other ancient stone circles were used as well, including those of Cornwall, from the Hurlers on Bodmin Moor to the Nine Maidens of Boscawen-Un near the Land's End.

But although the Druids have left no certain, visible monuments of their religion, they appear to have left enduring memorials in the minds of men. The belief that passing children through the hole of Men-an-Tol will cure them of rickets could be a superstition of the Druids, derived perhaps from an even earlier age, and their art of divination may be preserved in the old custom of placing two crossed pins on top of the stone and foretelling fortunes by their movements. And again, the fire festivals so dear to the Cornish are probably the sacrificial fires of the Druids in modified form. It used to be the custom to draw the figure of a man on Christmas 'stocks', or Yule logs, before setting them alight, and at the great Celtic festival of Midsummer, when fires were lighted on the hilltops, as they still are, children were swung through the flames, sometimes so perilously close as to singe their clothes.

So long as Cornwall remained on the old Atlantic trade route from the Mediterranean her main cultural contacts had been by sea and from the west, rather than by land from the east, and at certain favoured periods, therefore, she was in the van of British civilisation. Such a period was the Iron Age, when the La Tène culture had been imposed on her from western France, and had spread east and north to the Cotswolds and beyond. But by the middle of the first century BC these palmy years were over. In 56 BC Julius Caesar destroyed the floating castles, the high flat-bottomed boats, of the Veneti in a great sea battle off the coast of Brittany, and soon the whole of France was added to the Roman Empire. Henceforth the culture of the Mediterranean came to Britain across the eastern narrows of the Channel, and for fifteen hundred years the region that lay beyond the wastes of Dartmoor and the severing Tamar was little more than a backwater, cut off from the mainstream of civilisation.

A History Of Cornwall

IV

The Romans
55 BC – AD 410

In north-east Gaul an even tougher people than the Veneti opposed Caesar's schemes of conquest. These were the Belgae, whose original Celtic stock had been invigorated by intermarriage with barbaric German tribes from beyond the Rhine. Some of them had crossed the Channel to establish themselves by force in eastern Kent, from which base they reinforced their kinsmen's resistance to the Romans, and it was this that decided Caesar to invade Britain. It would be easier to crush the Belgae of Gaul if those of Britain were broken first.

In the late August of 55 BC Caesar sailed from Boulogne with a force of about ten thousand men, and landed near Deal. The moon was full, and a high tide driven by a north-easterly gale wrecked many of his anchored transports and damaged the galleys drawn up on the beach, while the British resistance was fierce. It is worth noting the battle tactics of the Belgic charioteers, which probably resembled those of the western Celts. 'First,' wrote Caesar, 'they gallop round the enemy and hurl darts at him, which often puts his lines in disorder, and then they fill in the gaps among their cavalry, leaping down and fighting on foot.' These chariot fighters were as skilful as they were formidable: 'They can drive and turn their teams on the steepest slopes, sometimes running forward along the pole to stand on the yoke, and then springing back nimbly into their chariot.' Caesar sent a rosy report to the Senate describing his expedition as a success. But it was a failure. He had gained nothing but a few hostages, contact with the Britons and a knowledge of a dozen miles of their coast.

His second expedition in the following year was more successful. The Kentish tribes were defeated and, after a heroic resistance, the Belgic chief north of the Thames, Cassivellaunus, had to sue for peace, and Caesar returned to Gaul with a number of slaves and a promise of tribute. Given the opportunity he might have conquered Britain, but revolt in Gaul followed by civil war in Italy occupied him for the next few years, and by 44 BC he was dead. It was exactly a hundred years before the Roman cohorts returned to Britain.

In the course of this century the Belgae of eastern Britain pushed ever farther west, as far as Dorset, where they were checked for a time by the Celtic inhabitants, probably kinsmen of the Cornish invaders, Veneti driven out of Brittany by Caesar, for they fortified their stronghold of Maiden Castle in the western manner with line upon line of huge ramparts. But it was only a matter of time before the Belgae overran them, attacked the Glastonbury lake dwellers, and stopped only when they reached the wild country of central Devon.

The great Belgic chief, or king as he may now be called, of this period was Cunobelin, Shakespeare's Cymbeline, whose reign covered the first forty years of the first century AD. Although his capital was in the far east, at Colchester, his kingdom embraced most of southern England, and for the first time in its history a large part of Britain was united under a single ruler. *Rex Brittonum* he was called by the Romans, who were allowed to establish trading stations within his territory, notably on the site of London – a Celtic name – while Roman merchants, maybe Italians as well as Gauls, settled in other important centres. In the time of Caesar, Cicero had dismissed Britain as merely a potential source of unskilled labour, slaves ignorant of literature and music, but by the middle of Cymbeline's reign the country was exporting not only slaves but gold, silver, iron, hunting dogs, and even corn and cattle, while in return she received luxuries such as amber, ivory, glass, pottery, necklaces and bracelets. The free and flowing Celtic design was modified by contact with the restrained and ordered art of Rome, and Cymbeline's coins, the silver and copper ones at least, were struck after the Roman pattern, sometimes with his head, imitated from that of Augustus, on one of their faces. This peaceful Roman penetration was to make the conquest of Britain comparatively easy.

These critical events in eastern Britain, from Colchester almost to Exeter, had little direct effect on Cornwall, the repercussions of Belgic conquest and Roman commerce growing fainter and fainter as they travelled westward, until they had almost spent themselves by the time they reached the Land's End. Coins of Cymbeline are very scarce west of Wiltshire, and none has been found in Cornwall, though a number bearing the name CATT have been discovered in the south-west, one near Carn Brae. They resemble the gold Macedonian stater already described, and are presumably the coinage of some petty western king who imitated Cymbeline in minting his own money.

Yet if the impact of Belgae and Romans was not directly felt in Cornwall, there were indirect, and sometimes unfortunate, consequences. It is ominous that among the British exports of this period there is no record of tin, Caesar indeed being the last writer of classical times to mention the Cornish metal. The explanation is probably quite simple. After the defeat of the Veneti Brittany was merged in the Empire, and the old Atlantic trade route between western Britain and the Mediterranean was severed. Moreover, the Romans had just discovered another supply of tin in Spain. The foreign demand for Cornish tin, therefore, virtually ceased. Cornwall was reduced to a limited home market for its principal industrial product, and the first two centuries of the Christian era were probably a period of some impoverishment.

There must have been a considerable migration of people. Although most of the eastern Celts probably remained in their native homes and hamlets under the dominion of their Belgic conquerors, we can imagine a number of them fleeing with their scanty possessions, driving their cattle across the Tamar, and settling in the sparsely populated east and centre of Cornwall. Then, there must have been many in Brittany who, preferring their old barbaric freedom to the yoke of Rome, crossed the Channel to join their kinsmen in western Cornwall. Owing to the decline of the tin trade this part of the county already had as many people as its restricted arable and pasture could support, and there are signs of migration from the region, for buildings characteristic of the Land's End area now appear along the west coast of Scotland, not only fortresses similar to Chun Castle, but also underground galleries like the Cornish fougous, and even courtyard houses resembling those in West Penwith.

6. *Chysauster village.*

Some thirty of these villages of courtyard houses have been discovered on the hills of the Land's End region, built apparently about the first century AD and occupied throughout the Roman period. The most famous is Chysauster on the flank of the hill topped by Castle-an-Dinas. It consists of at least eight houses, characteristically oval, four on either side of a sickle-shaped street. The outer door of each house opens on to a central court, round which are other doors leading into round or oval rooms, a large one at the far end, built in the thickness of the walls. The smaller rooms may have had corbelled roofs of stone, like that of the chamber at Bosporthennis, but the bigger ones were probably thatched, and some of them paved. There was also an elaborate system of drains, some of which ran through the houses, and one at least emptied itself into a large basin in the courtyard, where the water may have been used by tinners as well as housewives. Behind each house was a little terraced garden, and beyond these again small fields defined by earthen banks. Porthmeor village is similar, its houses built on terraces on the gently sloping shoulder of a hill near Gurnard's Head – these villagers had an eye for a view – and, like Chysauster, Porthmeor has a fougou.

It is not easy to say exactly when, or even why, these subterranean galleries were built, though it is significant that they are always associated with forts or courtyard villages, with which, therefore, they appear to be contemporary. The romantic and credulous Norden defined a fougou as 'a wonderfull deepe hole or cave, which the Welsh call an *Ogo*, the Cornish a *Googoo*', and he described Pendeen Vau as 'a holl or deepe vaute in the grounde, whereinto the sea floweth at high water, verie farr under the earth; manie have attempted, but none effected, the search of the depth of it'. A century and a half later Norden got the retort impatient from the Age of Reason. 'The sea,' wrote Borlase, 'is in truth more than a quarter of a mile from any part of it. The common people also thereabouts tell many idle stories of like kind, not worth the reader's notice, neglecting the structure, which is really commodious, and well executed.' Borlase knew, for the fougou was in the grounds of the house where he was born.

And well executed these underground chambers certainly are, their lintelled doorways in particular having claims to be considered as architecture, that at Boleigh being carved, apparently, with the figure of a god. Essentially, a fougou is a slightly curved trench, some fifty feet long, wide enough for a man to stand in with his arms outstretched, walled with dry masonry, roofed with massive stone slabs and covered with earth. The entrance is low and narrow, and generally there is some sort of obstruction over which anybody unacquainted with the place would stumble, for of course it is quite dark inside. This suggests that it was a refuge, a hiding place that might escape detection if there were a sudden raid, and it would have been a brave, or foolhardy, buccaneer who first crawled through the tunnel and stuck his neck through the tiny doorway into the gallery. The slight curve too may have had a defensive purpose, though perhaps after all these underground chambers were primarily storehouses, and that at Carn Euny, below the citadel of Caer Brane, seems to have been used as a habitation, perhaps in very cold weather. The gallery is exceptionally spacious and there is a unique refinement, a side passage leading into a round and lofty room with corbelled roof. Fougous are commonest in the Land's End area, though there are one or two on Bodmin Moor, and the best preserved of all is at Halligye, near Trelowarren, not far from the Lizard.

Although excavation throws no light on the tribal organisation of the period, it helps us to imagine the kind of life led by these Iron Age Cornishmen of about the time of the Roman conquest. Their houses look spacious today because of their courtyards, but they may have had to share these with their cattle, and the little rooms were probably slum-like with overcrowded families. The women spun, wove and made pottery copied from Roman models and turned on a wheel, and labour-saving rotary querns indicate another advance in civilisation, and suggest a new domestic noise, a more continuous crunching than the daily rubbing on a saddle quern. There may have been some tin streaming and smelting, but the men were primarily farmers, keeping cattle, sheep, goats, and pigs, and wresting the land from the grip of swamp and bracken, clearing surface stones and boulders and building them into cyclopean walls round the enclosures which they tilled. Perhaps the people who lived within round or oval earthworks on the less forbidding lower ground east of the Hayle river were the streamers with whom the Romans mainly dealt when they began to buy Cornish tin, while their more conservative countrymen kept to the hills.

When Cymbeline died, about 40 AD, his kingdom soon began to fall to pieces, offering a perfect opportunity for Roman intervention. There was no lack of advisers eager to urge the Emperor to seize it, and in the year 43 Claudius despatched a powerful army to add Britain to his dominions. The Belgic territory was rapidly overrun, but the Brigantes north of the Humber checked the Roman advance, and the massacre of the Druids in Anglesey was followed by a serious revolt of the Iceni of Norfolk under their golden-haired queen Boudicca. Wales was the next problem, but this was effectively occupied by the year 70, and ten years later the great governor Agricola was able to begin his drive into the north. But he failed to subdue the wild Caledonian Picts, and in 123 the Emperor Hadrian sealed off Scotland from England by building a defensive wall from Solway to the mouth of Tyne. Antoninus Pius advanced the frontier as far as the line of the Forth and Clyde, where he built a second wall, but it proved too costly to hold, and by the beginning of the third century the northern limit of the Empire was defined by the original wall of Hadrian. There was no attempt to add Ireland to the Empire.

Roman Britain, therefore, was confined to England and Wales, though there was a vast difference between the south and east and the remainder of the country. Unlike the Belgae, the Brigantes and the Celts of Wales had never come into contact with Roman civilisation, and clung fiercely to their old tribal customs, so that their remote and mountainous regions were never settled, but remained areas of military occupation patrolled by three legions with headquarters at York, Chester and Caerleon. The legionaries built roads to connect their fortresses with London, and another great highway, the Fosse Way as the Saxons were to call it, ran from Exeter to Lincoln, where it joined Ermine Street, the road to York and the Wall. Along these magnificent paved roads marched the relieving cohorts, passing through peaceful, smiling country as far as Lincoln, Chester, Gloucester and Dorchester, after which they entered the savage territory of still prehistoric Celtic Britain.

The Pax Romana was a very real thing, and from the end of the first century generations of Romanised Britons lived in the south-east of the province undisturbed even by rumours of war. Towns sprang up equipped with all the amenities of Roman civilisation, baths, theatres, temples and other public buildings; ports too, from which the products of the country were despatched. Metals were a particularly valuable prize, and soon after their invasion the Romans were working the lead of the Mendips and Shropshire, the iron of the Weald and Forest of Dean, and even a gold mine in Wales. Not, however, the tin of Cornwall.

The countryside was less Romanised than the towns, and much of the land was cultivated in the old Celtic manner of small hedged fields, the peasants continuing to live in their primitive houses and hamlets. The wealthier farmers, however, built villas after the Roman fashion, adorned with frescoed walls and tessellated floors, and cultivated their fields in long strips with heavy ploughs driven by slaves or serfs.

It must be remembered that a 'Roman' was any citizen of the Empire, and comparatively few of those in Britain would come from Italy or the Mediterranean. Soldiers and civil servants were recruited largely from Gaul and the north, whence also came many of the foreign merchants, while British town dwellers and wealthy farmers soon became as Roman as any other people on the outskirts of the Empire. Most of the foreign civilians lived in towns, and it was they who taught the natives the Latin tongue, introduced them to the literature and art of Rome, and to the gods of the Roman pantheon, soon happily confused with local deities. Roman rule was harsh only when its authority was challenged, as by the Druids, and tribal customs were tolerated, even encouraged, provided the chiefs and aristocracy spoke and dressed like Romans and were loyal to the Empire which had brought them peace, prosperity, literacy and an immeasurably higher civilisation. For the well-to-do at least, life in southern Britain of the second century may well have been more idyllic than that of any other period in our history.

Very little of this Roman civilisation filtered into Cornwall, which was in a peculiar position. Unlike Scotland it was a part of the Empire, unlike Wales and northern England there were no fortifications along its border, no patrolling legionaries. No doubt, owing to their ancient contact with the Mediterranean the Cornish were more civilised and peaceful than the Welsh and Brigantes, and the Romans, having no urgent need to develop such a westerly trade in tin, lost interest in their new province when they reached the wilds of Dartmoor. Exeter, or Isca Dumnoniorum, the capital of the Dumnonii as they called the Celtic tribes of Devon and Cornwall, was their most westerly town, and though three villas have been discovered in Devon they are all significantly near the Dorset border.

However, as we should expect, a few Roman pioneers pushed into Cornwall in the hope of making a fortune out of tin. Some two miles west of Bodmin, on a low hill overlooking the river Camel, they built a small rectangular enclosure at Tregear, 'the Fortified Homestead', still known as the Campfield. Within, and in the neighbouring streamworks have been found pieces of early Samian pottery, a bronze brooch, rings and other small objects. Perhaps one of these early settlers was Lesbius, the potter who made the basin bearing the inscription LESBIUS F, 'Lesbius made this'. If so, he is the first inhabitant of Cornwall whose name we know. They also left a few coins covering the century from 60 to 160, from the reign of Vespasian to that of Antoninus Pius. Maybe the first adventurers made their fortunes, but by the end of the second century the tin streams appear to have been worked out and the site abandoned.

It is just possible that other early pioneers pushed even farther west, as far as the richer tin area near the Land's End. In 1727 the antiquary Thomas Tonkin wrote to Borlase telling him how 'in the year 1700 some Tinners opening a Barrow of Stones, call'd Golvadnek Barrow [Calvadnack near Carn Brea], came at last to some large ones dispos'd in the nature of a vault, in which they found an Urn full of ashes, and a fine chequer'd brick pavement, which, together with the Urn they ignorantly broke to pieces; they found also in the same place several Roman Brass Coins of the second size, and a small instrument of Brass set in Ivory, which I suppose the Roman ladies made use of about their hair'.

According to Tonkin the coins were of the second century. Again, Borlase himself records how in 1723 some workers at Kerris, near Newlyn, discovered a similar vault, 'the floor pav'd with stone', containing 'a plain fair Urn, of the finest red clay', and some coins which were not preserved, 'because of Brass'. Eighteenth-century antiquaries were much given to romance, and the accounts are not very convincing, particularly as Borlase goes on to record a discovery of coins of Julius Caesar, which, however, he did not himself credit.

Nevertheless, apart from the evidence of Tregear, it seems probable that Cornwall attracted a few Roman adventurers in the course of the first two centuries of their occupation of Britain: fragments of early Samian pottery have been found as far west as Carn Euny, and coins of the period, mainly of the same century as those at Tregear, 60 to 160, have been picked up along the coast, most of them on the southern side and towards the west. It looks as though the Romans, or at least a few hardy prospectors, in their first enthusiasm at the conquest tried to exploit the Cornish tin deposits, pushing their trade by sea along the south coast, and perhaps also down the Bristol Channel from Gloucester. Presumably there was also an early military reconnaissance, probably by sea, and a few landings to test the temper of the people, but there seems to have been no attempt to effect any sort of official occupation.

Perhaps it was the appearance of Roman troops, or rapacious traders, that led the natives of Porthmeor to fortify their village – the head of an ensign has been found at St Just a few miles away – and Romans too who gave them the idea of making a paved road and paved courts within their fortification. Certainly its paved area gives the ruined village a more Roman appearance than any other visible remains in Cornwall. Moreover, a few second-century coins, pieces of glass, and native pottery copied from Roman models are further evidence of some commerce with eastern England. But the contact was very slight, and the Dumnonii beyond the Tamar were left to pursue their old tribal life undisturbed by Roman soldiers and officials.

About the middle of the third century, however, there was a change. The Empire, torn at its centre by civil war and ravaged on its fringes by barbarian invaders, was in decline, an empire on the defensive. The Saxons were already raiding the south-east coast of England, and when the commander of the Roman fleet in the Channel proclaimed himself ruler of an independent Britain the Scots broke through the denuded defences of the Wall. The pretender's successor was defeated, the province once again brought within the Empire, and after Diocletian's reorganisation of the imperial structure at the end of the century Britain enjoyed a short Indian summer of prosperity. But it was a prosperity mainly of the countryside. Roman civilisation was based on city life, and in Britain the towns proved too expensive a luxury to be supported by the produce of the land, so that as early as the third century the essentially Roman element, the town, began to decline, while the old Celtic way of life based on agriculture reasserted itself. In short, after 250 not only was the Empire as a whole in desperate need of money to strengthen its frontiers, but the British economy, already strained by the parasitic towns and by the expense of keeping an army of forty thousand men along the Welsh and Scottish marches, now had to finance the defence of the south-east coast against the Saxons. Moreover Spain, the chief source of tin within the Empire, had been ravaged by barbarians. No wonder the Roman authorities turned at last to the organised exploitation of Cornish tin.

There was no occupation of the county, for there were no cohorts that could be spared. The tin was worked by the natives, bought by Roman officials, and carried by sea, there being no main road west of Exeter and the old Celtic track along the peninsula would be quite inadequate for the long-distance transport of such a heavy commodity. The Romans paid cash, and thousands of their copper and silver coins, mainly of the century from 250 to 350, have been discovered. These are most concentrated in the far west, though they are numerous as far east as Truro, and at Carhays a hoard of two thousand five hundred was found in a tin jug. Such jugs and other vessels of tin and pewter now became common in eastern Britain, and at Bosence, near St Michael's Mount, a tin saucer and jug were unearthed while Borlase was writing his *Antiquities of Cornwall*.

Bosence is a small rectangular enclosure, possibly a fortified station occupied by Roman officials and a small detachment of soldiers. It is what we should expect in the neighbourhood of a port, and similar camps on the Helford river suggest that the Romans used this huge natural harbour as a base for the export of tin. Perhaps, too, the much bigger camp on the delectable site of Golden, overlooking the then navigable Fal just south of Grampound, was also a Roman station. The famous geographer Ptolemy mentions a Roman town called Voliba somewhere in Cornwall, and though 'town' is altogether too grand a word for anything in Roman Cornwall, early forms of the name – Leland calls it Wolvedon – approximate to Ptolemy's Voliba. Altogether there are twenty or thirty rectangular earthworks that may have been Roman.

There is little to suggest that Roman civilians migrated to Cornwall and made their homes there. It is true that at Rock, across the Camel from Padstow, a number of Roman ornaments and other relics have been found – glass, pottery, brooches and so on – but as there are no signs of Roman building it seems probable that the site was once a village of fisherfolk who traded with Roman merchants entering the Camel estuary. Perhaps the large wedge-shaped ingot of tin found at Carnanton, not far from Padstow, was destined for these traders. It is said to have the stamp of a helmeted head and buckler resembling that on some fourth-century coins, and the inscription, DDNN, an abbreviation of *dominorum nostrorum* '(the property) of our lords the Emperors', which is the usual formula on metal bars and ingots of this period. Cornish tin, then, was probably government property, and its working in the hands of government officials.

Even the only villa so far discovered in Cornwall, at Magor between Camborne and the coast, seems to have been merely an amateurish imitation of a Roman model, but it is especially interesting as it was apparently built in the late second century, before the development of the tin trade, a period particularly poor in Roman remains. We can reconstruct what happened with some degree of probability. Soon after the middle of the second century a young Cornishman left his native village to seek his fortune in the prosperous, Romanised east of England. After a successful career in the army or civil service he returned to his old home where, with the help of native craftsmen, he built himself the kind of house to which he had become accustomed. There were, to the great admiration of his neighbours, six or seven rooms with plaster-painted walls, two of them with fireplaces, and a long corridor with a handsome, though plain, tessellated pavement. The house looked very grand and was no doubt comfortable, but it lacked a Roman thoroughness: the Celtic masons fumbled when it came to making a right angle, and the sanitary arrangements were something less than imperial. There was some rebuilding and additions were made, but soon after the death of the original owner the villa was abandoned, probably because the foundations were inadequate and one of the walls collapsed. For thirty or forty years the empty house decayed, but it was just habitable, and on the revival of the tin trade was reoccupied for a time, probably by tinners who worked the neighbouring streams. It is an exceptional, indeed unique, example of the penetration of Roman civilisation into Cornwall, but that such a house could be built at all shows that the Cornish of the early third century were by no means barbarians.

We might expect the Romans to have taught the natives how to build paved roads from some of their tin streams and smelting houses to the ports from which the metal was shipped, yet the only one that has been discovered is the short stretch made by the villagers of Porthmeor within their fortification, though Chun Castle and Bosullow courtyard-house village are said to have been connected by a paved way, which must have formed part of the ridgeway running from the tin region of St Just to the Hayle valley and its ports.

However, two milestones, one at St Hilary of about the year 305, the other at Breage some fifty years earlier, suggest that there was a road, though not necessarily paved, leading to Porthleven from the direction of St Michael's Mount. Such a road, running close to Bosence in the rich tin-streaming region of Penwith, is likely enough, but it is not easy to account for two other milestones of the same period at Tintagel. One was found serving as a lich-stone at the entrance to the churchyard, the other as a gatepost at Trethevey, two miles to the east, but why the Romans should build a road along this majestic but barren strip of coast is an archaeological puzzle – unless they worked the fine light slate of Delabole and shipped it from Bossiney.

We might expect to find a road along the line of the prehistoric track between the Camel and Fowey rivers – Tregear would have been halfway – but this route had probably fallen into disuse. The Romans were concerned merely with getting the tin down to a port on the coast, and only a few short stretches of road would be necessary, or even packhorses on an old track would often serve, for transport was almost entirely by sea, and perhaps the recently discovered milestone east of Redruth was on such a track between the rich tin region of Carn Brea and the river Fal. They reached the Isles of Scilly, where the discovery of a few late silver coins adds colour to the tradition that the islands were the 'insula Sylina' to which Emperor Maximus banished the heretical Spanish bishop Instantius in 384.

There are very few visible remains of Christianity of the Roman period in Britain, and none in Cornwall. Yet as early as the second century there were a few Christians in eastern England, and by the beginning of the fourth century it had produced its first martyr, St Alban, who probably perished under the persecutions of Diocletian. Britain may also be said to have produced the first Christian Emperor, for it was at York that Constantine the Great was proclaimed Augustus in 306, after which, assuming the championship of Christianity and fighting under its standard, he defeated his rivals and established the faith as the official religion of the Empire. A British Church was organised and flourished, and British bishops, though poorer than their continental brethren, attended many of the Councils of the fourth century.

If the vigour of a Church may be judged by its heresies, that in Britain was vigorous enough by the end of the century, when it produced the celebrated heresiarch Pelagius. However, it was not in England but in Rome that he preached what seems to have been his very reasonable heresy against the doctrine of original sin. Overborne in argument by St Augustine and excommunicated, he disappears from history, but his Commentary on St Paul's Epistles has survived – the oldest book known to have been written by a Briton.

Despite the vigour of the stripling British Church in Romanised England, it is unlikely that by the time of Pelagius it had converted more than a fraction of the heathen population outside the towns, and even more unlikely that it had converted the countryfolk of Cornwall. There was a kind of vacuum between Exeter and central Cornwall where the influence of the Romans was very slight, for they had little incentive to push into the wild area of Dartmoor and beyond, and the tin industry and its sea-borne trade were virtually confined to the area west of the Camel and Fowey rivers. Of course there might be a few Christians among the sailors who put in at their ports and the officials who camped near the coast, but their influence would be slight, and in any event the traffic in tin faltered and probably ceased altogether soon after 367 when the combined Picts, Scots and Saxons broke through the defences and ravaged the greater part of the civilised province. Perhaps there was some conversion of the Cornish from the west, by sea from southern Gaul, by way of the old Atlantic trade route – the Bretons were still mainly heathen – but there is little evidence for this, and it seems improbable that there were many Christians in Cornwall when, in 410, the Romans withdrew from Britain, leaving their former province to the mercy of the barbarian invaders.

But as Roman rule flickered and was suddenly extinguished, its smouldering religion leaped into flame. The old pagan deities offered cold comfort to the Britons no longer protected by the legions and faced with a desperate future, but Christianity was consolatory and promised a better life after the disasters of this world. Thus when the bishops Germanus and Lupus crossed from Gaul in 429 to confute the Pelagian heretics of now independent Britain they were besieged by thousands of converts demanding baptism. Moreover Germanus was a man of war as well as a bishop, and when the Britons were opposed by the united powers of Picts and Saxons he took command of their army on condition that those who were still heathen should be baptised before the battle. Then, as the enemy advanced, the British raised the cry of 'Hallelujah', and the startled pagans, thinking themselves surrounded and outnumbered, dropped their arms and fled. Baptism on such a scale was no doubt exceptional, but the activities of Germanus are an indication of what was happening, and many of these neophytes as well as Christians of longer standing would be among the refugees who fled westward before the plundering Saxons, some of them as far as Cornwall, where they helped to prepare the way for the coming of the Saints.

Cornwall must have seemed an uncouth country to their eastern eyes. They would see scarcely a sign of the Roman province to which they had been accustomed: no towns, no temples or churches, no public buildings, and only in the far west would they see one or two modest villas and a few miles of road to remind them of what they had lost. The people still lived in rude stone houses like those of the fisherfolk of Gwithian, or huddled together in villages under the old hilltop citadels – Chun, Trencrom, Carn Brae, Castle-an-Dinas, Tregear Rounds, Kestle – where tribal chiefs still dwelt. By Roman standards they were barbarians, yet they were something more than this, and there must have been those who listened enthralled to descriptions of the vanished splendours of the Roman province, and to the Roman tongue that some of the refugees could speak. No doubt their eastern British dialect sounded strange to the Cornish Britons, and there would be a number of words that were new to them, borrowings from the Latin which the newcomers had incorporated in their native Celtic, *medicus* and *coquina*, for example, becoming *medhek* and *kegyn*, physician and kitchen.

The towns and churches and villas were burning in eastern England, though the Saxons, even if they had wished to do so, could not easily destroy the Roman roads to which they gave their own fantastic names; but paradoxically in remote and unromanised Cornwall two other legacies of Rome survived, at least for a time, alongside the Celtic and far older pre-Celtic traditions, Christianity and the Latin language.

A History Of Cornwall

V

The Dark Ages
410 – 1066

The two centuries that followed the withdrawal of the Romans, when their civilisation was destroyed and the first faint pattern of England traced over its ruins, are a period of almost unrelieved darkness, for the illiterate heathen Saxons left no contemporary record of their conquest. But we can imagine what happened: bands of tall fair-haired warriors thrusting rapidly into the country along the Roman roads, pillaging and burning, slaughtering and enslaving the Romanised Britons who failed to escape to the mountains of Wales or the remote Devonian peninsula. Then in their wake came the women and children, and Saxon settlements spread farther and farther west into the country that they had devastated. At last a British leader arose, Ambrosius Aurelianus, who about the year 500 defeated the Saxons at Badon Hill, probably in Wiltshire, and checked their westward expansion. There followed half a century during which the Saxons consolidated their conquest and a number of petty kingdoms emerged, the chief of which was Wessex, the realm of the West Saxons. Under their king, Ceawlin, they resumed their westward advance, overran Dorset, and in 577 defeated and killed three British kings who opposed them at Dyrham, a few miles north of Bath. Although the Saxons did not follow up their success by pushing still farther west, and another century was to elapse before they did so, their victory at Dyrham marked an epoch, for it severed the Britons of Wales from those 'of the Devon' peninsula, and from this time the fortunes of the two Celtic regions diverge, the regions that had never been Romanised, but now, ironically, the sole depositaries of all that remained of Roman civilisation.

For one effect of the Saxon conquest had been to make the Romano-British fugitives fanatically Christian. Not only did they consider themselves Roman citizens still, defenders of Roman civilisation against the barbarians, but also defenders of the Roman faith against the heathen. Such a one was Ambrosius Aurelianus, who, according to the lachrymose Welsh monk, Gildas, was the only faithful, strong and truthful Roman left alive, except of course Gildas himself, who, born on the very day of the Battle of Badon, inherited his virtues. We can picture how the Romanised Britons who found refuge in the south-west converted their heathen kinsmen, and how the imperial religion passed along the peninsula until it reached the already partially Christianised Celts of west Cornwall, who now became inheritors of the Christian Empire of which they had scarcely been aware. And it is here that we find the earliest relics of Cornish Christianity, rude tombstones or memorial stones, some of them bearing the emblem under which the Emperor Constantine had fought, the Chi-Rho monogram formed by the intersecting X and P of the Greek ΧΡΙΣΤΟΣ, 'Christ'.

There are a dozen or more of these stones erected in the fifth and sixth centuries, that is round about 500, the period of Aurelianus, King Mark, Tristan and King Arthur. They are pathetic memorials, for they seem to commemorate more than the British dead – the passing of Roman civilisation itself. For though the inscriptions are in Roman capitals, the letters falter and the spelling fumbles, *fili* often becoming *filli*, and *hic iacet* degenerating into ic iacit. The Latin tongue, the last relic of Rome save Christianity itself, was foundering. At St Erth one of these pillar stones records how *Cunaide hic in tumulo iacit. Vixit annos xxxiii*: 'Cunaide lies here in the grave. She lived thirty-three years.' On the bleak Penwith moors near Men-an-Tol is the tall Men Scryfys, or 'Written Stone', commemorating Rialobran, the 'Royal

Raven', probably a tribal chief and possibly the giant Holiburn of Cornish folklore, who was said to live on neighbouring Hannibal's – or Holiburn's – Carn. Still farther west in the church of St Just is a small stone with the XP monogram on one side and on the other, *Selus ic iacit*, a memorial maybe to Selevyn, the brother of St Just.

Much the most interesting of these early monuments, however, is between Fowey and Castle Dore on the old trade route running north towards Bodmin. Castle Dore was originally a small fortified village of the second century BC, the defences of which were strengthened a hundred years later to meet the threat of the sling. Then, after being abandoned during the Roman period, the fort was reoccupied by a Cornish king whose subjects built his wooden palace within its ramparts, the great aisled hall, chamber, chapel, kitchen, stable and barn. The inscription on the neighbouring stone reads, *hic iacit Cunomori filius*, 'here lies the son of Cunomorus'. It is difficult to decipher the name of the son, but the father may well be the British King 'Marcus, dictus Quonomorius' with whom St Paul, probably the saint who gave his name to the church near Penzance, is said to have stayed in the sixth century, no doubt on his way from Wales to Léon on the north-west coast of Brittany. The other name of Quonomorius was Mark, so perhaps the Cunomorus of the stone is the semi-historical King Mark of Cornwall, whose citadel was Castle Dore, and whose kingdom may have been defined by the great earthwork known as the Giant's Hedge, running from the river near the castle to Looe, some eight miles to the east. It seems possible that an older name for the castle survives in Carhurles, the name of an adjoining building, which suggests that it was once the castle of someone called Gourles. As the husband of King Arthur's mother, Igraine, was Gorlois, it may well be that Mark succeeded him as Duke or King of Cornwall. Even more exciting is the probability that the scarcely legible name on the stone is Drustans, and that it once marked the grave of Tristan, who, according to early versions of the story, was buried by Mark in a tomb close to his beloved Iseult. However, the Tristan of the story is Mark's nephew, not his son, and the evidence of the Castle Dore stone must not be pressed too far, though it is quite possible that the original relationship was changed to give a less shocking version.

Whether the story of Tristan and Iseult be historical or merely a fable, it is one of the great love stories of the world, and in its early, if not original, form the scene was set in the country round about the Fowey and Truro estuaries, where the sea runs into the hills and the woods slope down to the sea. King Mark's castle was then called Lancien, a name perpetuated in the old manor of Lantyan, within which stood the church of St Samson at Golant, where Mark and his queen worshipped. Iseult presented her best dress to the church, where it was preserved and exhibited on feast days. The Forest of Morrois in which the fugitive Tristan and Iseult found refuge is the great wood of Moreis, as it is called in Domesday, now Moresk, near Truro. After crossing the Truro river at La Mal Pas, the present Malpas, Iseult reached La Blanche Lande, where the Cornish Chirgwin perpetuates the name of White Land given to those lovely quartz-strewn downs. Here too is Carlyon, perhaps the Caerleon where some say that Tristan was born, in the kingdom of Loonois, or Lyonesse.

But the version with which we are most familiar today is that of Sir Thomas Malory, written almost a thousand years after the events he described, by which time the original Celtic story had become a medieval romance whose knights were those of the Wars of the Roses. Yet much of the early magic is recaptured in the apparently unpremeditated prose of the *Morte d'Arthur*, and we can scarcely fail to feel some excitement when we read, 'It was a king that hight Meliodas, and he was lord and king of the country of Liones, and this Meliodas was a likely knight as any was that time living. And by fortune he wedded King Mark's sister of Cornwall …'

The scene, however, is not the Fowey estuary and Castle Dore, but the savage northern coast and great riven headland of Tintagel, undermined by sapping waters that rumble and boom in its caverns. It was here that young Tristan defeated the Irish knight who had came to fetch the tribute demanded of King Mark by the King of Ireland, and from 'a chapel that stood upon the sea rocks' that he 'leapt out and fell upon the crags in the sea' when his jealous uncle tried to seize him. Again it was to Tintagel Castle – not, alas, the one whose ruins we see today, for that is medieval – that he returned to be once more with his Iseult, and in a neighbouring forest that he went distracted for her love, harping and weeping together. Unfortunately Malory did not know the original tragic ending of the black sail of Brittany, and all we have is a casual report of his death in another story, a cowardly stab in the back from his uncle Mark: 'Also that traitor king slew the noble knight Sir Tristram, as he sat harping afore his lady La Beale Isoud, with a trenchant glaive, for whose death was much bewailing of every knight that ever were in Arthur's days.'

The romance of Tristan became inextricably interwoven with the legendary history of King Arthur, and in Malory he actually becomes one of the knights of the Round Table. But the first mention of Arthur is in the *Historia Britonum*, a compilation of about the year 685 which has come to be known by the name of Nennius, its ninth-century editor. Nennius has little to say: 'The Saxons increased in numbers in Britain' until they were checked, not however by Ambrosius Aurelianus, Gildas's hero, but by one Arthur or Arthurus, who 'used to fight against them in company with the kings of the Britons'. Arthur, however, was not himself a king, but *Dux Bellorum*, a title that seems to have descended from the old Roman *Dux Britanniarum*. He defeated the Saxons in twelve battles, the sites of which cannot be identified with any certainty, though the tenth was at Chester and the last at Mons Badonis, the Badon Hill victory of about 500. On that one day, we are told, 'nine hundred and sixty men fell before the assault of Arthur, and no one felled them save he alone'. The legend of Arthur was fairly launched.

In the fertile brain of the twelfth-century Geoffrey of Monmouth, or Geoffrey Arturus as he liked to call himself, this simple story of Arthur blossomed into luxuriant fantasy. Arthur, we learn, was born at Tintagel, the son of Igerna and Uther Pendragon, King of Britain, who by the devices of Merlin was made to resemble Gorlois, Duke of Cornwall, Igerna's husband.

After defeating the Saxons, Picts and Scots, restoring the churches of York, and adding Ireland, Iceland, Gothland and the Orkneys to his domains, Arthur turns his talents to Europe and subdues Norway, Dacia, Aquitaine and Gaul. This leads to a successful war against the Romans, on the way to which he kills a Spanish giant on the top of Mont St Michel. But as he is crossing the Alps on his march towards Rome, news arrives that his nephew Modred, to whom he has entrusted Britain, has seized the crown, married his queen Guanhumara, and made an unholy alliance with the heathen Saxons and his other enemies. Arthur returns to Britain, and in a great battle at Richborough defeats Modred, whereupon Guanhumara flees from York to Caerleon, where she finds refuge in a nunnery. After another defeat at Winchester, Modred retreats into Cornwall, where in the last great battle in the west, on the river Cambula, he is killed. 'But the famous Arthur himself was wounded to the death, and being carried thence to the Isle of Avalon to be cured of his wounds, he resigned the crown of Britain to his kinsman Constantine, the son of Cador, Duke of Cornwall, in the five hundred and forty-second year of our Lord.'

So, according to Geoffrey of Monmouth, Arthur was born and died in Cornwall. Of course the extravagant old chronicler worked from still extant traditions as well as from his own embroidering fancy, and shortly before he wrote there is record of the belief that not only was Arthur a Cornishman, but also that he was still alive and one day would return to champion the British people. In the year 1113 certain canons of Laon came to England with the miracle-working relics of Our Lady of Laon, to raise money for their new cathedral. From Exeter they made their way towards Cornwall, where they were told that they were now in the land of the famous King Arthur, and when they reached Bodmin a cripple who sought a cure assured them that Arthur was still alive. This, leading to a dispute and almost to bloodshed, so offended Our Lady of Laon that she was quite put out of the giving vein, and the cripple departed unhealed.

Cornwall, particularly the north-east part of the county, is haunted by memories of Arthur. Camelford, of course, is Camelot, and Slaughter Bridge, a mile higher up the river Camel, the scene of his last battle. Then there is Arthur's Hall on Bodmin Moor, and Dozmary Pool into which Bedivere threw the sword Excalibur. Tintagel is King Arthur's Castle, and underneath is Merlin's Cave, while not far away is Warbstow Burrows and Arthur's Grave. Kelly Rounds is another of Arthur's castles, and Damelioc (St Dennis) the stronghold where Uther rid himself of the superfluous Gorlois. Not far away is Arthur's Hunting Seat at Castle-an-Dinas, once, it is said, surrounded by a forest full of game, and as proof that the tradition is true there is a stone bearing the hoof marks of Arthur's horse. The far west has its own Arthurian cult. There is a Merlin's Rock off Mousehole, and at Sennen is Table-Men, the stone on which Arthur dined with Cornish kings after being summoned from Tintagel to repel a Danish invasion. Even two of the Isles of Scilly are known as Great and Little Arthur.

This catalogue is by no means exhaustive, and of course other western counties, as well as Wales and even Scotland, have similar Arthurian associations. For example, Glastonbury is said to be Avalon, Apple Tree Isle, where, according to Giraldus Cambrensis, in 1191 the tomb of Arthur was discovered in the abbey. His skeleton was of heroic proportions, in his skull were ten wounds and at his feet lay Guinevere and a tress of her yellow hair.

Much of the old Welsh legendary literature has survived, but that of Cornwall has perished, the ancient stories and ballads that would have thrown more light on the dim and shadowy figure of the authentic Arthur. For there is no reason to doubt that in the early sixth century there was a British leader of that name, who may well have been born and died in Cornwall, though that he fought the Saxons there is most unlikely, for in his day their frontier still lay a hundred miles beyond the Tamar, where we may imagine him defending the hilltop fortresses of Dorset, counter-attacking and putting the heathen to flight. We may be sure, however, that this British warrior bore little resemblance to the Victorian gentleman celebrated by Tennyson in his *Idylls of the King*, or even to the fifteenth-century hero of the *Morte d'Arthur*; nor was Camelot 'a city of shadowy palaces', but a simple Iron Age citadel of earthen ramparts and wooden huts like Castle Dore.

Arthur, we are told, was succeeded by his kinsman Constantine, and we catch a glimpse of him and this period of comparative security in Damnonia, that is Devon and Cornwall, in the chronicle of his learned and hysterical contemporary, Gildas. Britain has kings, but they are tyrants, he groans; they have an abundance of wives and yet are given to fornication and adultery; they make war, but their wars are against their own countrymen; they exalt the proud and the enemies of God, and treat the holy altar before which they swear by the name of God as if it were merely a heap of stones. Of this horrid abomination, Constantine, the tyrannical whelp of the unclean lioness of Damnonia, is not innocent, for in the very year in which Gildas wrote, he swore a dreadful oath not to practise deceit against his countrymen, and then in the habit of a holy abbot seized the two sons of Modred from their mother and murdered them before the altar. The priests are little better than the kings: false, impudent, deceitful, arrogant, covetous, ambitious, ravenous wolves, belly beasts, lustful, indecently entertaining strange women, and worst of all, like Simon Magus, trafficking in church preferment.

No doubt Gildas was a disappointed man, and his lamentations need not be taken too seriously – according to another story, for example, Constantine abdicated his throne and preached the gospel to the Picts and Scots – but they do reflect the real barbarousness of the age of Arthur, and the shortcomings of a Church that had already become sufficiently wealthy to be accused of corruption. Probably this was the period when some of the quarrelsome chiefs or kings of Damnonia, flushed with their success against the Saxons and needing some outlet for their energies, invaded and colonised Brittany. Arthur, it will be remembered, is said to have conquered Gaul. In any event, by the beginning of the seventh century northern Brittany was known as Damnonia, though it may have been a hundred years and more before the central region got the name of Cornouaille. The traditional explanation of this invasion, of this inversion of the old order of events, that panic-stricken Damnonians were already fleeing from the eastern heathen, is possible, even though the Saxons had not then reached Devonshire; but it is also possible that they were fleeing from another invader, this time Christians from the north – the Irish.

Even as early as the fourth century the Gaelic Celts of Ireland were adding to the Romans' troubles by raiding the western coasts of Britain, and it was on one of these raids, about the year 405, that they carried off the sixteen-year-old son of a Romano-British priest as a slave. This was young St Patrick, who, after escaping from his captors, had a vision bidding him convert the Irish, most of whom were still heathens dominated by the Druids. In 431, therefore, he sailed to Ireland, where, until his death thirty years later, he laboured in his mission of organising a Christian Church. So successful was he that before long Ireland had its own missionaries, eager to support the British Church threatened by the heathen Saxons, and in the sixth and seventh centuries these Irish saints arrived in Wales and Cornwall, whence they could easily cross over into Brittany, so linking all four countries together in their work.

Unfortunately, most of the Lives of the Saints, preserved in the monasteries, were destroyed at the Reformation, though Leland was just in time to see a few of them and to make a note in his *Itinerary*. One of these was a *Life of St Ia*, which no doubt he found in the church of St Ives. She was a nobleman's daughter – most of the saints were noblemen's children: it was more edifying so – who with St Elwine and many others came to Cornwall and landed at Pendinas, 'the peninsula and rock wher now the town of St Ies stondith', and there an accommodating 'Great Lord in Cornewaul', one Dinan, built a church for her. According to another account St Ia was too late to join the party of saints when they sailed from Ireland, so she followed St Fingar, the Cornish Gwinear, and the others on a leaf. Landing at Hayle, they crossed the dunes to the village of Conetconia, where, however, Theodoric, King of Cornwall, most inhospitably slew all those he could lay hands on. 'The castle of Theodore,' Leland adds, was 'almost at the Est Part of the mouth of Hayle Ryver, now, as sum think, drounid with Sand.' No doubt it was, and no doubt it still is drowned under the towans that engulfed the little chapel of another of the martyrs, Gwithian. Gwinear was another victim, and his church, a medieval one, stands on the scene of the massacre on Connor Downs, not far from that of his sister Piala at Phillack, where there is a stone with a XP monogram of the period. Meriadoc, the Breton prince and patron saint of Camborne, was more fortunate, for according to the medieval miracle play *Meriasek*, he escaped the clutches of Theodore, or Teudar, who was eventually defeated by the Christian Duke of Cornwall whose palaces were at Tintagel and Castle-an-Dinas.

There were other Irish saints who worked near the Land's End: Buriena, Levan, Sennen, and the jovial Just, who coveted and pocketed a piece of plate belonging to his great friend Keverne, who, however, did not allow the light-fingered saint to get home with his booty. No doubt such escapades were exceptional, and we can imagine these missionaries of the age of Arthur attaching themselves to the retinue of some tribal chief – preferably one more sympathetic than Teudar – whom they converted and persuaded to build a church. Then the holy man, or woman, would come to the site to pray and fast for forty days, eating only a little bread and a few eggs, and drinking only milk and water – Sundays excepted. The building was thereby consecrated, the pious founder popularly received the title of saint without the formality of canonisation, and he set about interpreting in approximately Christian terms the age-long pagan superstitions that lingered about the place. Especially revered were wells and springs, like that beside which St Madderne built an oratory. Into the divining fountain girls dropped pins that would tell them when their wedding day would be, and the healing properties of its waters acquired such fame that it became one of the most frequented places of pilgrimage in Cornwall. Votive rags were hung on the thorns that grew around the shrine, as no doubt they were hung about similar holy places in neolithic times – and as they still are at Madron to this day. Stones, too, were objects of veneration, and had therapeutic qualities equal to the springs. For example, children who drank the water of St Piran's Well and were passed through a cleft of rock by the sea were cured of a variety of diseases, and the rite was a sovereign remedy for rickets. It is the superstition, going back perhaps to neolithic times, which we have met before at Men-an-Tol.

St Piran is the most famous of all Irish saints who came to Cornwall – he arrived on a mill-stone. A gang of heathen Irishmen had tied him to the stone, rolling it over the edge of the cliff into a stormy sea, which thereupon was stilled, and the saint floated calmly over the water to the sandy beach of Perranzabuloe. There are those who doubt not only the adequacy of his transport, but also whether he ever set foot in Cornwall at all. Yet is not Piran the patron saint of Cornish tinners, said indeed to be the discoverer of tin? Then, Exeter Cathedral was once the fortunate possessor of one of his arms, while according to an inventory of 1281 at St Piran's church itself was a reliquary containing his head and a hearse in which his body was placed (for processions), as well as such trifles as a tooth of St Brendanus and another of St Martin. And they were still there in 1433, when Sir John Arundell left 40s to enclose the head of the saint in the best and most honourable way they could. But more convincing than any record of relics are the ruins of the forlorn little oratory half-buried in the waste of shifting towans of Penhale Sands. There is nothing to prove that it was built by Piran, but it is sixth- to eighth-century work in the manner of the Celtic chapels of Ireland, and the earliest church, unless the remains of St Elidius on Scilly are older, not only in Cornwall but in the whole south-west of England.

There is plenty of evidence, then, of the coming of Irish missionaries to Cornwall after the Roman withdrawal. Probably, however, the gospel was preceded by the sword. The legend of Tristan is full of references to Ireland, and at the beginning of the story, when he comes to Tintagel, Cornwall is subject to the Irish king to whom it must pay a triennial tribute of youths and maidens. Tristan defeats the Irish collector of this iniquitous tax, an episode that leads to his visit to Ireland and the tragedy of his love for Iseult, the king's daughter. Then again, according to a ninth-century Irish source, 'the power of the Gael was once great over Britain', and long after the time of Patrick that power was felt in the south-west, even as far east as Glastonbury, and in Cornwall they had a fortress called after an Irish king. Perhaps, after all, Teudar was trying to repel something more hostile than an invasion of missionaries, and we can understand why King Mark entrenched himself near the south coast at Castle Dore, and threw up the defensive rampart of the Giant's Hedge.

Further evidence of Irish influence, whether peaceful or warlike, is afforded by the early memorial stones, a few of which bear ogham inscriptions, a tedious form of writing of Irish invention, in which letters are represented by combinations of long and short strokes in the manner of the Morse code. Two of these stones are at Lewannick, a few miles from Launceston, each with an inscription in Roman capitals which is repeated in abbreviated form in ogham lettering: [Hi]c iacit Ulcagni, 'Here lies [the body] of Ulcagnus', becoming simply Ulcagni,' of Ulcagnus'. All but one of these ogham stones are in the north-east of the county, not far from Tintagel, which suggests that there is a basis of fact underlying the romance of Tristan and Mark. However, as not all the names of the people commemorated are Irish, it may be that invasion came partly from Wales, where Irish settlers had established themselves by the late fourth century.

For Welsh saints came to Cornwall as well as Irish and Breton, sometimes apparently in battalions, like King Brychan with his three wives, concubines, twenty-four sons and twenty-five daughters, all of them saints. More reputable was Samson whose journey across Cornwall in the time of Mark and Arthur is recorded in a Life written not long after his death. After landing at Padstow he stayed with the abbot of the recently founded monastery of Docco in the district of Tricurius, that is at St Kew (another Welshman) in the Hundred of Trigg. Then with a cart and horses he and his monks set off along the old trade route towards the south coast, but he had not gone far before he saw a number of people dancing round a heathen image on the top of a hill. He paused, therefore, to convert and baptise them, and to slay a dragon, before pursuing his way to Golant, near Castle Dore, where the church still bears his name. Then from the Fowey estuary he sailed to Brittany to found the Monastery of Dol. Evidently Cornwall was by no means altogether Christian at the beginning of the sixth century.

The *Life* of St Petroc, 'captain of Cornish saints', confirms this. The son of a Welsh king, he sailed to Ireland with sixty of his nobles, where he spent some years in a monastery before crossing to Cornwall and landing at the river Camel. There he astonished the heathen natives by striking water out of a rock, and there he met Samson and a certain Bishop Wethnoc, who hospitably made over his monastery at Padstow to his guest and his followers. Petroc remained there for thirty years, practising an austere religious life, before making a pilgrimage to Rome, Jerusalem and India, where he lived for seven years nourished only by a single fish placed before him by the divine will at appropriate hours. On his return to Cornwall he reformed a horrible man-eating monster, one of Teudar's pets, and converted Constantine, a rich chieftain, presumably Arthur's successor and Gildas's abomination.

Of course much of this *Life* of Petroc is merely medieval elaboration, but there are elements in it that suggest an early origin. It is the Celtic, not the medieval Church that is described; there are no diocesan bishops, no metropolitans, and no mention of the Pope. Wethnoc is a Celtic bishop living in a monastery, and Petroc, like Samson, merely the ascetic leader of a company of monks, a typical Celtic saint, for monasticism was the most characteristic feature of the Celtic Church.

There were a great many of these Celtic monasteries in Cornwall: according to Charles Henderson ninety-eight of the two hundred and fifty-four parishes were originally monastic foundations, and the total number of monasteries was considerably more. But when we try to picture them we must not think of the splendid churches, cloisters and chapter houses of medieval times, but of a number of simple huts or cells built about a little church, like St Piran's, according to no regular plan. The remains of one of these early communities can be seen on the headland at Tintagel, a series of tiny rooms with earthen floors and walls of turf except for the lower courses of stone. Life was very hard: beds were of hide or straw, food was simple and meagre, while long hours of labour in the fields alternated with periods of study and the celebration of services in the chapel. Then, like the medieval friar, the Celtic monk travelled about the neighbouring countryside teaching and preaching to the barely civilised peasants. He must have looked a strange sight in his bulky cloak of skins or undyed wool, his long back hair falling over his shoulders, the front of his head jaggedly shaved from ear to ear to represent the crown of thorns.

Although we can see little that is sharply defined through the mists that obscure these two centuries from 400 to 600, we can at least catch glimpses of looming figures and confused events that give us some idea of the Cornwall of the period, when the Saxon was no immediate danger and his frontier had not yet reached Damnonia. We see a number of petty kings and chieftains squabbling and fighting among themselves, Arthur perhaps and Rialobran, Constantine, Mark in Castle Dore and Teudar in Trencrom or Gwithian. We see the Irish taking advantage of the strife and raiding the northern shores, and Irish, Welsh and Breton missionaries founding monasteries and ministering to the people, some of them no doubt charlatans and almost as pagan as their congregations, others bringing with them a culture that came ultimately from southern Gaul and Italy. And if we are to believe Gildas, the original austerity of the Celtic Church was already becoming corrupted by the middle of the sixth century. We see the people increasing in numbers, and moving down the hills from their old Iron Age villages in search of better agricultural land, and we see new hamlets, or *trevs*, springing up along the lowland tracks and in the neighbourhood of monasteries, many of them with the prefix *lan*, signifying a monastic enclosure, Lanvean for example, or Lanherne.

The remains of one of these early settlements has recently been discovered at Gwithian, a few hundred yards from the chapel of the saint among the towans near the mouth of the Hayle river. There are traces of fifth-century huts, but these were replaced, probably in the sixth century, by new ones on the same site. The inhabitants worked the local iron which made the neighbouring stream run red, kept cows, sheep and pigs, horses and dogs, and apparently amused themselves with gamecocks. As we should expect, they were great eaters of fish, treading their bones into the floor, and it was probably the women and children who collected mussels, limpets and oysters, of which they were inordinately fond. It was the kind of life that must have been lived, and was to continue, for centuries, and the only remarkable change was in their pottery. After the Roman withdrawal these Gwithian people made pots after the Roman pattern to which they had been accustomed, but round about 550 a new style of 'grass-marked ware' appears – so called because the bottoms of the vessels retain the impression of the grass on which they were put to dry before firing – possibly introduced by the Irish saints who landed here, for it resembles the domestic pottery of northern Ireland. It may be, then, that there were two distinct Irish invasions: the first round about 500, when the north-east coast was invaded from Wales, the second later in the century, when saints and settlers landed in west Cornwall from Ireland itself.

The far west, however, for perhaps two thousand years the most flourishing and advanced part of the country, was losing its supremacy, for the tin trade had sadly declined. Indeed, the last we hear of Cornish tin until well after the Norman conquest is at the end of this period, when in about 600 an Alexandrian seaman sailed with corn to Britain, relieved a famine, and returned with a cargo of tin. Pre-eminence had shifted to the centre, to the region of Arthur and Mark and of the prehistoric trade route between the Camel and Fowey rivers, now trodden by missionaries on their travels between Ireland, Wales and Brittany. It is the region where Christian monuments are thickest, and at the northern end of the route was the famous monastery of St Petroc which gave its name to Padstow, the ecclesiastical capital of Cornwall until the Saxon conquest.

By the year 600 the Saxons had destroyed the last vestiges of Roman civilisation in eastern England, and in the west it had been almost forgotten. True, Latin of a sort was the language of the clergy and their services, but they no longer thought of their Church as a legacy of Rome: it was theirs, it was Celtic. Then, just at this critical moment, in 597, St Augustine landed in Kent and began the conversion of the Saxons to Roman Christianity.

The Saxons, or English as we may now call them, responded remarkably quickly to the proselytising of Augustine and his followers. Within forty years King Edwin of Northumbria had accepted the faith, and in Wessex Birinus had baptised King Cynegils, who gave him Dorchester in Oxfordshire as his ecclesiastical see, with a diocese that stretched from Surrey to the Severn. In the north, Celtic missionaries speeded the joyful work, but the result of this particular form of division of labour was a divided Church, roughly Roman in the south and Celtic in the north. The main differences seem trivial today – the date of Easter, the correct form of tonsure – but to seventh-century zealots they were not, for they involved the far more serious question of independence or subjection to Rome. At the Synod of Whitby in 664 the dispute was decided in favour of Rome, and England was once again brought within the mainstream of western civilisation as an ecclesiastical Roman province.

All except the south-west. The Celtic Church of Damnonia had not been a party to the decisions of Whitby, which were abhorrent to its fierce spirit of independence. Even when it was a part of the Empire, Damnonia had never been subject to Rome in anything but name, and the liberal Celtic genius that expressed itself in the flowing lines of its art was fundamentally opposed to the Latin passion for order and formal organisation. The Celtic chief was head of a clan rather than ruler of a defined territory, and in the same way a Celtic bishop, where one existed, was an abbot responsible for Church affairs in a vaguely limited area round his monastery. So while Theodore of Tarsus,

Archbishop of Canterbury, divided and subdivided England into dioceses and parishes, the Cornish Church remained obstinately and formlessly monastic and, if we may judge by the memorial stones of the seventh century, came even more under the influence of the Irish, whose missionaries had withdrawn from England after their repulse at Whitby. No wonder that when Aldhelm, the English Bishop of Sherborne, urged Geraint, the first recorded Damnonian king since Constantine, to make his clergy adopt the Roman Easter and tonsure his overtures were indignantly rejected.

That was in the year 705 when the westward Saxon advance had been renewed and eastern Damnonia overrun. Taunton was occupied and fortified as a royal burgh, and by 710 Exeter was in English hands. It should be remarked that this offensive of the early eighth century was very different from the earlier Saxon advances that Arthur and Aurelianus are said to have stemmed; then it was a Romano-British defence of the remains of Roman civilisation threatened by heathen Saxons, now it was a defence of one of the last Celtic strongholds and of a Celtic Church against what may be called a Romano-Saxon invasion. Yet the fact that the Saxons were now Christians made no difference to the Damnonians; perhaps it only increased their bitterness. The English were foreigners, near-barbarians, who wanted to impose their way of life on them, and though they no longer wished to destroy Christianity were determined to alter its form.

However, checked perhaps by Geraint, who was apparently killed in battle at Langport, the Saxons were not yet ready to tackle the savage highlands of Dartmoor, and it was another century before they moved far beyond the Exe. For yet another century, therefore, the Cornish pursued their own peculiar Celtic way of life, uninfluenced by Saxon layman or by Roman priest. It is important to remember this eight hundred years of isolation, almost half the history of Cornwall in Christian times. The Romans during their four-century occupation of Britain seem rarely to have set foot there, and after their withdrawal it was exactly another four hundred years before the Saxons crossed the Tamar.

When at last invasion came it came swiftly. In 814 Egbert collected the forces of Wessex, invaded Damnonia and 'laid waste the land from east to west', compelling its kings to do him homage. Eleven years later the Cornish rebelled, only to be defeated again at Gafulford, probably Camelford, where Slaughter Bridge may commemorate Egbert's bloody victory rather than Arthur's last battle against Modred. Egbert followed up his conquest of Cornwall by routing the army of the rival English kingdom of Mercia, and so becoming the first king of all England. But he was also the last king of all England for some time. Already the Danes, or Vikings, were raiding the English coast much as the Saxons had done in the last days of the Roman occupation. When, therefore, a great Danish fleet appeared off Cornwall in 838 the Celtic Christians seized their chance, joined hands with the heathen Norsemen and prepared to expel the Saxons. But Egbert was too quick for them. Marching rapidly westward he crossed the Tamar and at Hingston Down near Plymouth routed the forces of the unholy alliance. The Danes fled to their ships, and the Cornishmen renewed their oaths of allegiance, which they were never to break again. Hingston Down was their last battle against the Saxons. It was also the last battle fought by Egbert. He died in the following year, and the Danes descended on England. Cornwall was to escape lightly from this new scourge, but Ireland, undisturbed by Roman and Saxon, was less fortunate: within a few years it had a Viking overlord and its golden age was over. Yet other Norsemen settled on the French shore of the English Channel, giving their name to the province that they seized – Normandy.

Although Egbert had devastated Cornwall and incorporated it in Wessex, it was still, and for a hundred years to come, allowed its native rulers. The successors of Egbert up till the time of Alfred, towards the end of the century, were too busy coping with the Danes to pay much attention to this remote and unrewarding region, and English influence did not spread far beyond the eastern part of the county. Egbert himself seized the fertile lowlands of the north-east as a possession of the Crown, and English place names soon mingled strangely with the Cornish.

Stratton, of course, is pure Saxon, as are Week St Mary and Poundstock, but sometimes an English suffix was added to the original Celtic, so forming a queer though often musical hybrid such as Morwenstow, or more uncouthly, Kilkhampton. The land was divided into estates, or manors, according to the Saxon custom – they were exceptionally big, perhaps because they were the old tribal territories – and with three of them Egbert endowed the See of Sherborne. One was Lawhitton on the Devonshire border, and another Caellwic, probably the neighbourhood of Kelly Rounds, King Arthur's reputed castle. These were both on the route to Padstow and the third manor of Pawton. This covered an enormous area on the west bank of the Camel, but did not include Padstow itself. The land belonged to the monastery of St Petroc, so that by this alienation Egbert was both strengthening the English See of Sherborne and reducing the authority of the Cornish ecclesiastical capital. No doubt it was his way of persuading the Celtic Church to accept the usages of Rome.

Cornwall was too poor and too remote to attract the attention of the Danes, but by the time of Alfred's accession the situation in England was critical. By 878 the Danes had reached the borders of Devon, and Alfred was trapped in the marshes of Somerset. The Cornish clergy, particularly those along the coast, had good reason to be nervous, and some of them buried their treasure under the debris of an old tin-stream at Trewhiddle near St Austell. One wonders what happened, for they never returned to claim it. And it was worth the reclaiming. Almost all the objects are silver: coins of Mercian and Wessex kings, rings, a brooch, a small box, a number of silver straps decorated with black enamel, a silver chalice and a knotted scourge of plaited silver wire. The scourge is unique, and the chalice, plain but beautifully proportioned, is the earliest piece of English church plate known. English, for the treasure is not a Celtic one, and it shows that some Saxon influence had reached at least the middle of Cornwall by the latter part of the ninth century.

Thanks to the genius and exertions of Alfred, when he died in 900, the Danes had been forced to come to terms, and England was on the way to becoming a civilised and literate country. His successors made it a united one, and Alfred's grandson Athelstan found time to bring even Cornwall under English rule, exactly a century after it had been conquered by Egbert. His methods were conciliatory and statesmanlike. In 931 he created a diocese of Cornwall, appointing Conan, a Cornishman who had presumably accepted the ways of Rome, its first bishop with his see at the monastery of St Germans. It was an astute move, for the ecclesiastical capital of the county was now on the eastern border instead of in the centre at Padstow, where the old Celtic monastic tradition was strongest. However, even here Athelstan was conciliatory, compensating the monastery of St Petroc with a grant of the manor of Nywanton. He even made a small grant to the monastery of St Buryan, near the Land's End, probably because it had accepted Roman usages, and to encourage the others. Apparently the others were encouraged, for many of the monasteries converted themselves into collegiate churches served by a body of canons instead of monks. Although the old Celtic monastic tradition must have lingered, religious strife was at an end by the time of Athelstan's death in 939, and the bishops of Cornwall who succeeded Conan at St Germans were all Englishmen enforcing the rules of Rome. That the policy was a successful one is suggested by the fact that the three Cornish manors with which Egbert had endowed Sherborne were transferred to St Germans.

Politically, too, strife was at an end. However much the Cornish may have resented it, they had to accept the inevitable occupation of their country by the Saxons, and the system of government that they imposed. Their chiefs or petty kings were reduced to a humbler status, possibly as lords of extensive manors, and replaced by English officials who, with their alien speech, pushed farther and farther west. It is a strange experience to read the inscription on the tenth-century stone in the churchyard of Lanteglos-by-Camelford: *Aelselth 7 Genereth wohte thysne sybstel for Aelwyneys soul 7 for heysel* (Aelselth and Genereth made this monument for the soul of Aelwine and for themselves).

We can trace this English infiltration more in detail in the pages of the so-called Bodmin Gospels, the only Cornish monastic book that has survived from the Dark Ages. Written in the late ninth or early tenth century, probably in France, and crudely illuminated, it is not merely a Latin version of the Gospels, but a book for liturgical use, indicating the portions of the Scriptures to be read at Mass. It soon came into the possession of St Petroc's monastery at Padstow, or Petrocys Stow as the Saxons called it, and this in itself shows that the monks had accepted the Roman form of Service introduced by the English. Far more interesting than the book itself, however, are the entries on the flyleaves and margins – presumably because it was their most valuable book – entries that record the ceremonies of manumission, or freeing of slaves, before St Petroc's altar. There are forty-seven of these entries, covering the century from 940 to 1040, and altogether a hundred and twenty-two slaves thus secured their freedom. Of these the names are overwhelmingly Celtic: apparently ninety-eight Cornishmen to twelve Saxons and twelve nondescripts with Latin or biblical names such as Prudens and Noah. The Cornishmen were probably descendants of slaves of the period of Cornish kings, and not wretches enslaved by the Saxons, for the Saxons were not much given to slavery, and of the thirty-three liberators twenty-four have Saxon names and only five Celtic. Perhaps some of the Saxon slaves were descendants of prisoners captured during the wars with Wessex.

These Cornish names in the Bodmin manumissions are, with the place names in some of the Saxon charters, the earliest examples of Cornish, but, to our infinite loss, none of the entries themselves is written in Cornish, thirty-eight being in Latin and the remaining nine in English, the usual formula being either, 'Hoc est nomen illius hominis quem liberavit ...' or 'Thes ys thaes manes nama dhe X gefreade ...' (This is the name of the man whom So-and-so freed). It was because the ceremony was for the good of the liberator's soul – who knows how many years docked from purgatorial pains? – that it was so solemnly celebrated and recorded before witnesses, as when Cenmenoc, 'pro anima sua', liberated Benedic on the altar of St Petroc in the presence of Osian the priest and Morhaitho the deacon. Evidently Osian was an Irishman, and the young deacon Morhaitho was to become something of a professional witness, for he appears in twelve of the manumissions, in the later ones as a priest. Nearly all the witnesses are monks of St Petroc, most of them Cornish – two being called Mark and Modred – but a third of them are English, and their number significantly increases as the years go by.

In some of the longer entries we catch poignant glimpses of the lives of the people in this remote angle of England a thousand years ago, and wonder what was the whole story that lay behind the episode. Why, for example, did Aelsig buy Ongynedhel and her son Gydhiccael from Thurcild 'with half a pound' at the church door at Bodmin, paying Maccos the hundredsman four pennies for toll – silver pennies of Edward the Elder and Athelstan were circulating in Fowey at this time – and then set them free? This is a late entry, and it is just possible that the president of the hundred court was the Macos of Domesday Book, who held the manor of Forsnewth in St Cleer at the time of the Conquest. Then there is Putrael, who seems to have lapsed into the position of a penal slave to Aefric for some crime or other. The unfortunate man approached Aefric's brother, Boia, and offered him sixty pennies if he would intercede for him. Boia agreed, and eventually Putrael secured his freedom by paying Aefric eight oxen at the church door at Bodmin, in addition of course to the sixty pennies that Boia demanded. Boia seems to have been the dean who witnessed the liberation of Codgiuo for the soul of Maccos the hundredsman, and 'the priest of Bodmin' who held the substantial manor of Pendavy in Egloshayle in the time of Edward the Confessor.

Clearly, the English penetration of Cornwall was proceeding apace during the golden age of the Saxon monarchy. The last quarter of the tenth century, however, was disastrous. The great line of Saxon kings came to an end with Edgar, and when Ethelred succeeded in 978 the history of England became little more than a record of rapine and murder. The Danes took advantage of the anarchy, fastening ravenously upon the country until by 1016 it had been absorbed into a great northern empire under a Danish king – Canute.

Fortunately for Cornwall, most of the fighting was in the east, but in 981 a Danish fleet descended on the north coast and sacked 'Petroces stow'. Presumably the monastery was looted, for shortly afterwards it was transferred to Bodmin, comparatively safe from these rapid coastal raids. It was just as well, for a few years later another fleet sailed plundering along the whole length of the north coast, then, rounding the Land's End, turned east and up the Tamar, harrying the country as far as Lydford and Tavistock. Perhaps it was on this raid that Olaf Tryggveson put in to the Isles of Scilly, where he found a hermit who prophesied that he would soon become King of Norway. Olaf was so impressed and gratified that he allowed himself to be baptised, promised Ethelred, in return for a handsome consideration, that he would never again attack England, and sailed away to deliver Norway from its lecherous usurper. Few men can ever have served England better than the unknown hermit of Scilly.

It was shortly after the move of St Petroc's monastery to Bodmin that an illuminating episode occurred. The wife of the great Saxon ealdorman Ethelweard, lord of the manor of Liskeard, wished to free a bondwoman in her service, though without the trouble of going the twelve uneasy miles to Bodmin, even for the good of her soul, for which the liberation was to be made. The Abbot therefore sent four of his clerks to Liskeard with the precious bell of St Petroc, on which the ceremony was performed before numerous witnesses of the great lady's household. Soon afterwards Ethelweard himself went to Bodmin and freed the woman 'for his own soul on the altar of St Petroc' in the presence of a number of clergy, including the Abbot and Burhwold, the Bishop of Cornwall himself. 'And,' added Ethelweard fluently – Ethelweard was a chronicler as well as a descendant of King Alfred's brother – 'whosoever shall infringe this freedom shall be accursed of the Lord God of Heaven and His Angels.'

It is to this period of Saxon conquest and settlement that the first stone crosses of Cornwall belong. Still one of the most familiar and characteristic sights of Cornwall, they would be far more prominent in the tenth-century landscape, empty almost of building save for field walls, hovels and hamlets. Deriving ultimately from the prehistoric standing-stones, many of them were set up, like the earlier Christian memorials, to commemorate the dead, but some marked cross-tracks, some praying-stations and other sacred sites, perhaps even sites of open-air churches before granite ones were built. And yet one cannot help feeling that they were primarily protests, silent and even unconscious, against the Saxon intruders, symbols of Celtic nationalism. Perhaps it is not altogether fanciful to imagine this host of four hundred or more shafted crosses gathering near the Land's End where they are thickest, advancing through Wendron to meet the oncoming alien near Bodmin, where, being checked, only a few – though among them the noblest – broke into the eastern hundreds. Most of these crosses are wheel-headed, some bearing the figure of the crucified Christ as at Sancreed, others covered with interlacing ornament as at Cardinham and St Neot, others again with incised design as at Lanivet, where the figure of a man with a tail is cut in the shaft. The first to be mentioned in history was the one that stood as a landmark above St Piran's oratory, perhaps even then among the piling towans almost as forlornly as today, when in a charter of 960 King Edgar referred to the 'Cristes-mace' by the church of Perran-in-the-Sand. And sometimes a Saxon set up a cross of his own, like the otherwise unknown Aelnat of Tintagel, who 'ficit hanc crucem pro anima sua'.

The twenty years or so of Danish rule can have had little effect on Cornwall, though the constant threat of Viking raids must have drawn Celt and Saxon closer together in a common defence of the country. In any event the government of Wessex was primarily in the hands of the great English earl, Godwin, and when in 1042 Edward the Confessor succeeded to the throne the old English line of King Alfred was restored. During the first half of the eleventh century, therefore, the Saxon settlement of Cornwall continued with little interruption.

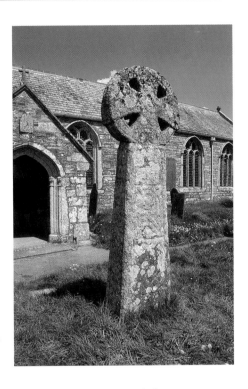

7. Cardinham cross.

The Saxons took over the local government of the country, substituting their feudal system for the Celtic form of clan ownership of land. Under its shire-reeve or sheriff the county was neatly divided into six hundreds, later increased to nine, and the subdivision into manors, each under the jurisdiction of its lord, was pushed farther and farther west. Naturally the old tribal centres and strongholds of the Cornish chiefs often became the new manorial capitals, the Saxons frequently adding their word *tun* to the original Celtic name, Binner, Cally, Winnian becoming Binnerton, Callington, Winnianton, while Henlis became Helston, the capital of one of the largest and most valuable manors. It was in these tiny 'towns', perhaps no more than a few cottages clustered at a crossway, or about a manor house or church, that the Saxons chiefly settled, establishing their own system of cultivation in open fields split up into a patchwork of strips or allotments. The Celts, however, mistrusted these towns, preferring to live in isolated farmsteads and *trevs*, where, until caught up in the feudal system, they pastured their stock and cultivated their tiny fields and gardens.

There is one of these late Dark Age settlements on the north coast at Mawgan Porth, occupied probably from about 850 to 1050, from the time of Alfred to the Norman conquest, throughout the period of the Bodmin manumissions therefore, and one cannot help wondering if any of the villagers were among those who were freed before the altar of St Petroc. There were at least three houses of the courtyard type, though very different from those at Chysauster and Porthmeor, roughly rectangular rooms being built on each side of a rectangular courtyard, straight lines instead of Celtic curves, no doubt in imitation of the Saxons. The walls were almost seven feet high, and probably roofed with branches and turf, supported by timber uprights. The principal room, the 'long house', was thirty-three feet long by fifteen wide, though one end was used as a cattle shed, which was separated by a low wooden partition from the living quarters. In the middle was a cooking-pit, and along the walls were short box beds of slate – snug enough in winter, though doubtless overfull of smoke and smell. The other rooms, occupied perhaps by the families of married sons and daughters, were smaller, though without the added warmth of a byre. Outside was a terraced garden, and not far away a cemetery, where the bodies, many of them children, were buried in slate coffins with their feet to the east.

Like the Gwithian folk, they kept oxen, sheep and goats, horses, dogs, cats and gamecocks, and ate quantities of shellfish, a peaceful community of fishermen and pastoralists rather than tillers of the soil. Again like the Gwithian folk of this period, where there are remains of a similar long house, they made an ingenious kind of cooking pot with clay bars across enlarged lips on either side, by which it could be suspended over the fire. The origin of this bar-lip pottery appears to have been Frisia, where the Saxons came from: possibly therefore, when the old traffic with the east was severed in the eighth century by the Arabs who overran the Mediterranean shores, the Cornish turned to Frisian merchants for their trade, and found with them another outlet for their tin.

In the first half of the eleventh century sand began to blow up from these western-facing beaches on the north coast, and then, shortly before the Norman conquest, the dunes advanced so rapidly that the villagers of Gwithian and Mawgan Porth packed up their belongings and moved to higher ground, the former to Godrevy, the latter probably to Lanvean, two miles up the valley.

The Saxons also organised the Church after their own model. The Bodmin Gospels show that even as early as the tenth century the Celtic form of service had been abandoned in favour of the Roman, at least in the eastern half of the county. The old Celtic form of monasticism inevitably crumbled. Some of the estates that had supported the monasteries were transferred to other foundations, as the manor of Pawton – the Mawgan Porth settlement was probably in Pawton – had been transferred from St Petroc's to Sherborne, and sometimes the monasteries themselves were transferred: St Michael's Mount, for example, had long had a community of Celtic monks, but it became a Benedictine house under Edward the Confessor, who gave it as a daughter-church to the Norman monastery of Mont St Michel. Others again, like St Buryan, were reconstituted as collegiate churches. The parish system was reorganised, boundaries firmly defined, and though most of the new parishes were centred on a Celtic monastery, church or oratory, only about one in three achieved this distinction. Finally, when Bishop Burhwold died, about 1040, Cornwall was deprived of its own bishop. St Germans lost its cathedral status, and the diocese was combined with that of Devon under the Bishop of Crediton. Ten years later the see was moved to Exeter, where it was to remain for more than eight hundred years, until the foundation of the diocese of Truro in 1876.

By the year 1050, more than two centuries after Egbert's conquest, the Saxon settlement of Cornwall must have been fairly complete, though English influence was far stronger in the east, rapidly declining beyond the line of the Camel and Fowey rivers, until in the far west, in the Land's End and Lizard peninsulas, it was quite swamped by the old Celtic way of life. After leaving the little monastery of Launceston, dominated by the fortified hill of Dunheved, the westbound traveller might see, if he crossed the almost trackless moor, clusters of old huts long since abandoned for the lowland *trevs*. Bodmin, centre of the cult of Petroc, was much the biggest town in the county, and may have had a hundred houses or more as well as its monastic buildings. Both Launceston and Bodmin might have their open fields after the Saxon model, and there, perhaps, English was already beginning to compete with Cornish as the language of the people. But west of Bodmin signs of English occupation would become rarer, and the traveller might journey all the way to the Lizard or the Land's End without seeing anything bigger than a Celtic hamlet or a Celtic field, without hearing a word of Saxon speech, and if previously he had crossed a stream by an English ford it was now by a Cornish *res*. Mounds turned up by the digging tinners, wayside and churchyard crosses, and deserted hilltop citadels of Celtic kings became more frequent, and when the traveller crossed the river Hayle and climbed the granite massif of West Penwith he was in the pre-Celtic country of the megalith builders, of petrified dancers and barrows stripped to the stone.

In the late autumn of 1066 rumours flowed along this central ridgeway of a battle far away in eastern England, where English Harold had fallen before the conquering sword of William of Normandy.

VI

The Early Middle Ages
1066–1337

For very few beyond the upper and educated classes of Cornwall, the Saxon overlords, officials and clerks, would William's victory at Hastings have any meaning. Even in the eastern half of the county it would be rare to find a peasant who had ever heard of Harold or his father Godwin, and for most of the Celts of the Penwith and Lizard peninsulas Arthur was probably still their

8. *Land's End.*

king. Yet even as far as the Land's End, though not yet awhile as far as Scilly, the hand of the Norman was to make itself felt.

South-eastern England submitted, and on Christmas Day, 1066, William was crowned at Westminster. But resistance was not yet at an end. The family of Godwin held great estates in Devon and Cornwall, and it was to Exeter that they naturally retreated when London and the east were lost. Early in 1068 William marched on the city with an army which, for the first time, had Englishmen in its ranks, and when the citizens refused to admit him he dragged a hostage before the walls and put out his eyes to teach them what resistance to the Norman entailed. After a siege of eighteen days Exeter surrendered, but William was merciful, and the citizens escaped with no worse penalty than building a castle at their own cost. Devon submitted with Exeter and, after a show of strength beyond the Tamar, so did Cornwall. William's initial clemency was politic, for when in the following year the men of Devon and Cornwall marched on Exeter to expel the Norman garrison, the citizens helped in its defence. The rising was put down by William's lieutenants, while he dealt mercilessly with the far more serious rebellion in the north.

By 1072 England was completely subjugated, and William turned to the consolidation of his conquest. This was achieved mainly by a systematic extension of the feudal system. Although the Saxons had a rudimentary form of feudalism, there had been thousands of freeholders in England subject to no lord, but now every holder of land was to be the tenant of his feudal superior and every man was to have his lord. The ownership of all the land was vested in the king, and from him the tenants-in-chief held their estates in return for military service, and again the tenants-in-chief let some of their manors to sub-tenants in return for feudal dues, while part of the manor itself was let to peasants in return for labour on the lord's demesne, or home farm. Of course it was in practice far more complex than this – a man might be both a tenant-in-chief and a sub-tenant, for example – but such an ideal presentation of the system makes its working easily comprehensible. Wealth and power depended on the holding of land, and the basic unit of the system was the manor. No wonder

William ordered the making of a detailed survey of his kingdom, manor by manor, showing its lord, its size, how it was farmed, how many tenants and labourers there were, how much stock, and how much he could wring out of it in taxes.

The *Domesday Survey* of 1086, therefore, is an invaluable source of information about the land and its inhabitants twenty years after the Norman conquest. It sounds dull, but a little imagination will quicken the bleak catalogue. Here, for example, is a picture of Climsland, near the Devonshire border, towards the end of the Conqueror's reign:

> The King has a manor called Climeston, which Earl Harold held in the time of King Edward. Therein are 5 hides, and they rendered geld for $2^{1}/_{2}$ hides. Twenty-four teams can plough these. Of these the King has in demesne 1 hide and 3 ploughs, and the villeins have 4 hides and 17 ploughs. There the King has 30 villeins and 24 bordars and 9 serfs and 7 beasts and 200 sheep save 13, and of woodland three leagues in length and 1 league in breadth, and 3 acres of meadow, and of pasture 4 leagues in length and as much in breadth.

As a hide was 768 acres this was a large estate, one of the many Saxon *tons* or large *vills* once belonging to the House of Godwin and now taken over by William as a royal manor. It was probably farmed after the English pattern, in strips in three great open fields, by the peasants who lived in the village surrounding the church. Each villein would hold some thirty acres of this arable land in return for helping to farm the king's demesne, and the bordar was a similar tenant on an even humbler scale. As the wealth of a lord depended on his having sufficient labour to work his home farm, neither villeins nor bordars were allowed to leave the manor without his consent, though otherwise they were comparatively free and had the benefit of their lord's protection. The serf, in spite of the manumissions, much more common among the Celts than among the English – there were twenty-three serfs on the royal manor of Helston – held no land, and though he had some rights he might be virtually a slave. Climsland was in good agricultural country with a high proportion of arable, for one plough and its team of oxen was reckoned as being capable of cultivating about a hundred and twenty acres.

At the other extreme is the little manor of Trevillein near St Veep, in the King Mark country, a typical Celtic *trev*, and the original home of the Trevelyan family, where two serfs looked after the stock on a hundred acres of grassland. Or again there is the manor of Whitesand in Sennen:

> The Count has a manor called Witestan, which Alwald held in the time of King Edward, and now Ralf holds it of the Count. There is 1 ferling of land, and it rendered geld for half a ferling. Therein is half a plough and 1 serf and 8 beasts and 8 swine and 40 sheep and 40 goats and 12 acres of woodland.

A ferling and half a ploughland mean much the same thing, about sixty acres, but as there is no mention of a plough presumably there was no arable, and the serf and his family, crowded into their miserable hovel at the Land's End, would just be able to manage the little flocks and herds. No doubt the pigs rooted in the wood, but some of the goats would have to be milked, and some of the 'beasts' too if they were cows.

Apart from the highlands and woodlands – and there was far more woodland than there is today – it seems as though only about half of the land that might have been cultivated had been reclaimed from the original waste even at the end of the eleventh century. The population was correspondingly small, and most of it concentrated in the Saxonised east, more suitable for arable than the poorer and wetter western uplands, though there was a relatively thickly populated belt along the old trade route between Hayle and Mount's Bay. According to Domesday there were about 1,700 villeins, 2,400 bordars and 1,100 serfs, to whom must be added the 7 tenants-in-chief, 97 sub-tenants, clergy and a few half-freemen, some 5,700 adult males in all, making a total population of perhaps 20,000, about the same as that of present-day Penzance.

The lord of the manor of Whitesand, it will have been observed, was 'The Count'. This was Robert, Count of Mortain and half-brother of William, who invested him with more than two-thirds of the county, so that, though he never assumed the title, he was in fact the first Earl of Cornwall. Not content with his estates – he was the greatest landowner in England after the king, with eight hundred manors in twenty counties – he seized even more: some of the manors of St Petroc, a hide here and a hide there from other church lands, and the old Sunday market on the Bishop of Exeter's manor of St Germans, a valuable institution to its lord, was 'reduced to nothing by reason of the market which the Count of Mortain has established hard by at a certain castle of his, on the same day'. These descendants of the Vikings had lost none of their ancestors' flair for business, and no wonder they built themselves castles to which they could modestly retire. This one, 'hard by St Germans', was Trematon, superbly sited on the north bank of the Lynher, Carew's beloved river, where it flows into the Tamar estuary. It was held by Reginald de Valletort, one of the thirty-three estates that he held of Robert, forming the honour of Trematon, which remained in the hands of his descendants for almost two centuries. Even more important than Trematon was the grim stronghold that Robert built for himself at Launceston, the military key to the county.

A number of manors under one great lord was called an honour, and after Trematon the biggest honour in Cornwall was that of Cardinham, held by Richard Fitz Turold, Robert's steward. The third great sub-tenant of Robert was Turstin with twenty-two manors, the chief of which was Bodardel, now the name of a farm on the outskirts of Lostwithiel. As sheriff, Turstin was the most important man in Cornwall after Robert, among other duties being responsible for collecting taxes and making an annual account to the Exchequer, for calling together the military forces, and presiding, with the bishop, over the shire court. When the male line of Turstin failed in the twelfth century his heiress married the heir of Cardinham, so uniting in the possession of the Cardinham family two of the greatest honours in Cornwall.

As the Saxons had dispossessed the Celtic chiefs, so the Normans had dispossessed the Saxons, and only fifteen small English sub-tenants remained. Yet the Normans were not numerous, probably no more than eighty lords of manors, and many of those with estates outside Cornwall would rarely be resident, but their power was out of all proportion to their numbers: they were the rulers of Cornwall, under a Norman king and a Norman earl. There were in addition a number of Bretons, a contingent of whom had fought with William at Hastings. One of these was Alvred, Robert's butler, ancestor of the family of Montague, and another Blohin, founder of the family of Bloyou, who held two manors in St Teath. There must have been a strange confusion of tongues between Tamar and the Land's End: Cornish spoken by the great majority of the population, mainly villeins, bordars and serfs; English by the dispossessed upper classes and some of the eastern peasants; French by the Norman overlords and their officials, and Latin by the clergy, or at least by the few with some pretension to learning.

As Domesday was essentially a survey on which to base taxation, the only mention of Church affairs is a catalogue of ecclesiastical landholders, though here again the record is enlivened with touches of human nature. The Abbot of Tavistock was the one head of an external religious house holding land in Cornwall, and after the description of his six manors he added the pathetic note – we can imagine him dictating his protest – 'From the Abbey of Tavestoch have been taken away 4 manors which Abbot Suetric had bought in the time of King Edward with the money of the church. Now the Count of Mortain holds these manors unjustly. Now the Abbot claims them to the use of the church.' The biggest of these holders of church lands was naturally the Bishop of Exeter, who had a hundred hides and four hundred tenants. Although the bishops had been among the first to recognise William as their sovereign, the Norman king had no more intention of leaving the Church in English hands than he had of leaving the country as a whole, and most of the old bishops were soon replaced by Normans. However, the Saxon Bishop of Exeter, Leofric, was allowed to stay, possibly because he was an old man. He died in 1072 and was succeeded by Osbern, a Norman whose father had been William's guardian, and who had come to England before the Conquest.

To the businesslike and bustling Normans the English clergy must have seemed exasperatingly easygoing and inefficient. Many of them were married, and in their way of life and even in appearance scarcely distinguishable from their parishioners. And the monasteries by no means came up to Norman ideals. There was therefore a general reformation, in which some of the Cornish monasteries were suppressed and others organised after a stricter fashion. The Norman abbot of Mont St Michel sent a prior and twelve monks to the new Benedictine monastery of St Michael's Mount, where the church was consecrated in 1135, and at about the same time a Benedictine priory was founded at Tywardreath overlooking St Austell Bay, a daughter house of SS Sergius and Bacchus of Angers. It is strange that the Cornish, after their early devotion to monasticism, should have taken so little interest in their medieval monasteries, all eight of which were small and dependent on some foreign house or one outside the county: the Priory of St Nicholas on Tresco in Scilly, for example, was merely a cell of Tavistock Abbey.

The new semi-monastic order of Augustinian Canons reached Cornwall at the beginning of the twelfth century, and under the reforming Bishop Warelwast a number of old houses were reorganised according to their rules. One of these was Bodmin Priory, built on a site chosen by a holy hermit in the days of the Saints, a pleasant site beside a stream in a sheltered valley. The undisciplined secular canons were reconstituted as Augustinians, and having built themselves a new church they presented their old one to the town, to which it still belongs. Of course they took with them the shrine of St Petroc, which brought in a considerable income from pilgrims' offerings, though shortly afterwards one of their number stole the body of the saint and carried it off to Brittany. Fortunately it was recovered, and the head and some of the bones were placed in an ivory casket, relics that brought such prosperity that from a village of a few score houses at the time of Domesday it grew to be the biggest and wealthiest town in medieval Cornwall. Today scarcely a trace is to be seen of the splendid Norman church and the monastic buildings that surrounded it.

Launceston Priory went through a similar transformation. The original town was built round the old monastery of St Stephen from which it took its name of Lan Stefanton, but when Robert of Mortain filched the lordship from the secular canons and moved the market to the site of his castle at Dunheved on the south side of the little river Kensey the inhabitants had to follow, and Dunheved acquired the name of the old town of Launceston. It was beside the river, at Newport, between St Stephen and the castle, that the Augustinians established by Bishop Warelwast built their new priory.

The old Celtic monastery and Saxon cathedral of St Germans was also converted into an Augustinian house and, as at Launceston, a new church built, the nave being for the use of parishioners. Fortunately most of this remains, and the austere west front relieved by its splendid portal of seven receding orders is the finest piece of Norman architecture in Cornwall. When, in the fourteenth century, the Abbey of St Germain at Auxerre presented St Germans with relics of the saint it became a favourite place of pilgrimage where indulgences were profitably purveyed to the faithful. But the relics of St Germanus could never compete in popular favour with the head of St Piran, the bones of St Petroc at Bodmin, and the milk of the Blessed Virgin at St Michael's Mount, the most popular shrine of all.

How far the Norman conquest, and particularly the activities of its Earl, disrupted the economic life of Cornwall it is impossible to say, but it seems clear that the meagre resources of the county were exploited and drained by the new owners, many of whom lived in other parts of the country and were interested only in what they could exact. There are whole sections in Domesday in which every entry finishes with a variation on the same refrain: 'The Count has a manor which is called Tucowit [Tucoyes in Constantine] … This is worth 5s, and when the Count received it, it was worth 60s.' Tolgollow in Gwennap 'is worth 4s, and when the Count received it, it was worth 20s'. Trescow and Gear both declined from 25s to 5s, and Skewis in Cury 'has been entirely wasted, and when the Count received it, it was worth 15s'. It is true that the value of some of the manors rose in the same period, the twenty years between the Conquest and Domesday, but these by no means offset the general decline, and how poor the county was may be judged by the fact that the average value of a ploughland in Cornwall was 5s 6d, the lowest in the country – it was over 30s in Kent – and even in the middle of the twelfth century a tax of 2s a hide brought in only £23, when the average for England as a whole was £150.

It can have made little difference to the county when, after rebelling against William Rufus at Pevensey, Robert of Mortain died in 1090, for his son William saw even less of his Cornish estates than his father. He too proved a rebel. When Henry I refused him the Earldom of Kent in addition to that of Cornwall he supported Duke Robert of Normandy in his claim to the English throne, but at Tinchebrai in 1106 the rebellion was broken and William captured. Henry was not a vindictive man, but he inflicted the severest penalty that Norman law allowed against a treacherous vassal, and condemned him to lifelong imprisonment. Incidentally almost, he ordered his eyes to be put out. However, William was freed shortly afterwards, some say because of a miracle, and he became a monk at Bermondsey where he died about 1140. Henry I retained the Earldom of Cornwall for himself.

It was in the year after Tinchebrai that William Warelwast was consecrated Bishop of Exeter. A diplomatist of repute who had done the state some service at the time of Rufus's dispute with Anselm, he now did far greater service to posterity by beginning the building of Exeter Cathedral. Although his nave and apse have been replaced, the great towers still stand like twin Norman keeps above the transepts, unique in the architecture of England.

The firm reign of Henry I was followed by the anarchy of Stephen, last of the Norman kings. As Henry's only legitimate son had been drowned when the *White Ship* foundered, he had tried to secure the succession for his daughter Matilda, wife of Geoffrey Plantagenet, Count of Anjou, and though many of the barons swore to support her, the Great Council, thinking a woman no match for those iron times, conferred the crown on her cousin, Stephen of Blois, son of the Conqueror's daughter. In 1135 Stephen rounded the Land's End and landed in Whitesand Bay, no doubt to the astonishment of the descendants of the serf who had run the little farm there in the days of the Conqueror. But Stephen, generous and easygoing, proved unequal to his task, and there followed long years of civil war between himself and the supporters of Matilda, a conflict that was kept alive by the feudal magnates for their own ends. It was a fearful period. 'They forced the folk to build them castles,' wrote the last compiler of the English Chronicle, 'and when the castles were finished they filled them with devils and evil men. They took those whom they suspected to have any goods, both men and women, by night and day, and put them in prison for their gold and silver, and tortured them with pains unspeakable. Some they hung up by their feet and smoked them with foul smoke; some by their thumbs or by the head, and they hung burning things on their feet. About the heads of some they put a knotted string which they twisted till it went into the brain. Others they put in a chest that was short and narrow and not deep, and they put sharp stones in it and crushed the man therein.' In the west country people were reduced to eating raw herbs and roots and the flesh of dogs and horses, while the harvest rotted in the fields because the peasants had run away or died of famine.

No doubt things were not as bad as this in Cornwall, far from the central scene of rapine. Yet the castles sprang up. Some of them, however, were there before the time of Stephen, though none the less sinister for that. Trematon and Launceston, 'Castle Terrible' as it was called, are mentioned in Domesday, and Tregony was built soon afterwards by the Norman family of Pomeray. At about the same time the Cardinhams and Turstins built their strongholds, one of which was Restormel, magnificently seated above Lostwithiel and an ancient ford across the river Fowey. Then came the 'adulterine' castles of Stephen's reign. One was at Kilkhampton, built probably by Matilda's half-brother, the bastard Robert of Gloucester, and another at Truro, high above the town. But most famous of all is the fabled castle of Arthur and Mark, Tintagel, buttressed by the promontory rock and girdled by the ocean itself. It was begun about 1140 by Reginald, Earl of Cornwall, another of Henry I's illegitimate sons, and another half-brother of Matilda's.

Reginald was also the newly acquired son-in-law of William Fitz Richard, the formidable Lord of Cardinham, whom Stephen had appointed his lieutenant of the county. But Fitz Richard's ambitions proved too strong for his loyalty and, treacherously declaring for Matilda, who after all might now almost be considered one of the family, he persuaded Reginald to assume the title of Earl of Cornwall. Between them they held many of the Cornish castles, including Launceston, from which bases they caused such destruction that the Bishop of Exeter put them under the ban of the Church. Stephen acted with unusual energy. Advancing into Cornwall at the head of an army, he seized the rebel castles and conferred the Earldom on the ruthless Alan of Brittany, whom he left to deal with Reginald. However, though Reginald was expelled, he had his reward. When Matilda's son, Henry II, came to the throne on Stephen's death in 1154, he confirmed him in his title of Earl of Cornwall and accepted him as one of his most trusted advisers. The long anarchy was at an end, and Henry destroyed more than a thousand of the adulterine castles, including those of Cornwall. A few stones remain, but of most of them even the memory has perished.

Another man who profited from the civil war in Cornwall was Richard de Lucy. In 1140 he was at Bodmin with Count Alan of Brittany, and it was probably after his services to Stephen at this critical period that he received a grant of some of the confiscated estates of the Cornish rebels. His fief was largely in the Tristan country, for his head manor was Lantyan, once the residence of King Mark, and another Kenwyn by the Truro river and the forest of Moresk. Part of Kenwyn was admirably placed for development as a town, with consequent profit to its lord, for although almost in the centre of the county it was at the head of the great tidal estuary of the Fal and on the main route from Grampound and the east. But as the Cornish did not take kindly to town life, to encourage them de Lucy seems to have converted part of the villeins' holdings into free-burgage tenements, where those who settled would become freemen. Thus Triueru, or Truro, became a borough with a court of its own and the right of managing its own affairs independently of the original manor of Kenwyn.

Shortly before his death Stephen appointed de Lucy his Chief Justiciar, an office in which Henry II very wisely confirmed him, for he proved to be the most able and reliable of his advisers – 'Richard the Loyal' he called him. If de Lucy gave a written charter to Truro it has perished, but in any event it was essential to get one from the Earl, without whose approval no borough could possibly prosper. Reginald agreed, and it may have been in 1173 that he granted a charter to his 'free burgesses of Triueru', confirming de Lucy's privileges and adding three more much prized ones: freedom from the jurisdiction of his hundred and county courts, freedom from tolls in all markets and fairs in the county, and the right to distrain upon their fellow burgesses for debt – they already had the right of *Infangenethef*, of hanging their own thieves. Henry II himself confirmed Reginald's charter, and so one of the first boroughs in Cornwall came into existence. Others were soon to follow.

The granting of town charters and creation of small borough courts nibbled at the authority of the hundred and county courts, and at the same time their power was limited from above by the institution of travelling justices who brought the authority of the king directly into the shires. The process had been begun by Henry I, but was greatly extended by Henry II in 1166, when six circuits, soon reduced to four, were created, round each of which three judges travelled administering the justice of the king. Cornwall was grouped in the south-western circuit with Dorset,

Wiltshire, Somerset and Devon, the assizes normally being held at Launceston, beyond which, on the miserable Cornish roads, the justices could scarcely be expected to travel. Their arrival was welcomed neither by the feudal magnates nor by the common people, who, terrified that their misdemeanours would be discovered, took to the woods and moors when the watchman on Launceston church tower announced their appearance on Polston Bridge over the Tamar.

Henry II further undermined the power and independence of his barons by offering them the tempting bait of paying a money rent for their estates instead of supplying him with a quota of troops, an arrangement that had the double advantage of allowing him to hire a mercenary army and at the same time discouraging the warlike proclivities of his vassals. And again he strengthened his position when, by the Assize of Arms, all freemen – later extended to all males – were made liable for military service, though the efficiency of this militia was impaired by its being on a shire basis, so that no man could be made to serve outside his own county, a limitation that was to affect the fortunes of the Civil War in the seventeenth century.

Despite this strengthening of the central government, there was still the danger of feudal fragmentation under a weak or absentee king, and when Richard I went crusading there was another outbreak of trouble. Richard, with good reason distrusting his younger brother John, excluded him from the regency when he was abroad, though he allowed him the revenues of Cornwall and the other south-western counties. Soon after his departure John began intriguing against the regents with the aim of seizing England for himself. He was joined in his design by some of the barons, including Henry de Pomeray, who, in 1194, occupied St Michael's Mount by disguising his men as pilgrims. However, when he heard that Richard had returned he was so terrified that he died of fright, or so the story went, 'whereon,' as Carew put it, 'the old cell and new fort were surrendered'. John too surrendered, crawling to Richard's feet and asking for pardon, which his brother magnanimously granted.

Henry II had reserved the Earldom of Cornwall for John, but as he was only eight years old when Reginald died in 1175 he made the late Earl's illegitimate son, Henry Fitz Count, Constable of Launceston and gave him the county in farm. John never received the Earldom, and when he became king in 1199 confirmed Henry in his position, though this did not prevent his joining the baronial party that forced John to sign Magna Carta. The leader of the barons in their struggle against the king was Robert Fitz Walter, who had inherited some of the vast estates of Richard de Lucy, including part of his Cornish fief and the manor of Truro.

It is at this period that the authentic history of the tin industry may be said to begin. Although there is no reason to doubt that tin streaming was practised by the Cornish during the four centuries between the Roman withdrawal and the Saxon conquest of the county, then under the Saxons and finally under the Normans, there is no record of their so doing, even in Domesday, and the last mention of British tin is in the Life of St John the Almsgiver, who died in 616. Then almost six hundred years later, in 1198, appears a letter that throws light on the condition of the industry in the twelfth century. When Richard I left England again in 1194, this time never to return, the task of governing the country devolved upon the Justiciar, Hubert Walter, as also the task of raising money for the king's French war. Although Hubert was not over-literate – he was incidentally Archbishop of Canterbury – he was an astute man of business and sent William de Wrotham into the west country to see how far the taxes on the tin of Devon and Cornwall might be stepped up to help finance Richard's expensive hobby. De Wrotham was appointed Warden of the Stannaries, that is of the tin works, and made his report. Not many years before, he discovered, the annual output of tin was little more than seventy tons, most of it coming from west Devon, and the tax of approximately 5s a ton in Devon and 10s in Cornwall produced only £17.

The main weakness was the amateurish organisation of the industry. The tinners were not a distinct class of worker, but farmers as well, villeins subject to labour on their lords' demesnes and to the jurisdiction of the manor and hundred courts. Their one privilege was the customary one of 'bounding', that is of searching for tin on any piece of land, and working it within the bounds of turf they set up to mark their claim, subject of course to a payment to the lord, which took the form of 'toll tin', originally one-fifteenth of the product. De Wrotham's immediate concern was the raising of revenue, so calling together representatives of the tinners, with their help he standardised the weights of the slabs subject to tax, clapped another mark on each half-ton, and organised a department of officials to supervise its collection. In 1198 he was able to send Hubert a sum that was far greater than the total revenue of Cornwall from all other sources.

King John was not slow to see the attractions of the industry, and in 1201 issued the first charter to the Stannaries. It was brief, but to the point. The tinners were confirmed in their privileges 'of digging tin, and turfs for smelting it, at all times, freely and peaceably and without hindrance from any man, everywhere in moors and in the fees of bishops, abbots and counts, and of buying faggots to smelt the tin without waste of forest, and of diverting streams for their works, as by ancient usage they have been wont to do'. Moreover, the only magistrate with jurisdiction over the tinners was to be their warden, and he alone might summon them from work for either civil or criminal matters. By 1214 production had risen to six hundred tons. No wonder, for, to the great indignation of the manorial lords, all their villeins were turning tinners, and one of the clauses of Magna Carta was that no lord should lose the services of his men whether they dug tin or not. But Henry III confirmed his father's charter to the tinners, who soon became a state within a state. They had their own courts, their own laws and their own taxation; they acknowledged no lord, were subject to no manorial dues or constraints, and obeyed the king only when his orders were transmitted through their warden.

For the remainder of the thirteenth century the Stannaries were under the Earls of Cornwall, Richard and his son Edmund. Richard was the second son of King John, only a year younger than his brother Henry III, who succeeded to the throne in 1216 as a boy of nine. Henry's was a long, turbulent, but very important reign, for his attempt at personal rule led to another struggle with the nobility, from which emerged the beginnings of parliamentary government. In 1225, when he was only sixteen, Richard was granted the county of Cornwall and its tin works, and two years later the Earldom. In his youth he showed little gratitude to his brother, supporting the baronial party in their opposition to the king and his foreign favourites, but after the death of his first wife in 1240 – he was in Cornwall at the time – he married the queen's sister and became one of Henry's firmest, though not altogether uncritical, adherents. With his great riches he bought sufficient votes to secure his election as King of the Romans in 1257 and was crowned with the silver crown of Germany at Aachen, the ancient capital of the Holy Roman Empire, but after two years spent in trying to win support in Germany he returned to England, a king without a kingdom, as mediator between Henry and the baronial opposition. According to a contemporary satire, the earliest in the English language, Richard, 'The king of Germany', was not unwilling to consider a bribe:

The Kyn Of Alemaigne bi mi leautè
Thritti thousent pound askede he
For to make the pees in the countrè

But negotiations broke down, and at the Battle of Lewes in 1264 the royal brothers were captured by Simon de Montfort. However, in the following year de Montfort was defeated and killed at Evesham by Prince Edward, and the remaining days of Henry and Richard were comparatively peaceful and uneventful.

The Cornish people had seen very little of their first Earls, not that they would have regretted that, for they can scarcely have ached with desire to see their grasping Norman overlords, but in the course of his long and restless life – long by medieval standards – Richard paid a number of visits to the county. His headquarters were at Launceston, where he added to the old Norman castle of Robert de Mortain, but he also had his eye on Tintagel, which his father, Lackmoney as well as Lackland, had granted to Gervase de Hornicote. Richard therefore offered his heir a number of manors in exchange, and such an offer from a king's brother being little short of a command, or even a threat, in 1236 he secured possession of the castle, adding the curtain wall and great ward on the mainland, which was linked to the island by a bridge. We can understand why the medieval legends of Arthur and Tristan crystallised about this grim and dream-like castle in its fabulous setting of precipice and sea.

Some of the most important events in Richard's career were associated with Cornwall. He was there when his first wife died in giving birth to his eldest son Henry, he spent Christmas at Launceston shortly before his coronation as King of the Romans, and there he collected the troops that he led to defeat at Lewes. He lost not only the battle but also his estates, though he recovered them after de Montfort's death, and resumed his hobby of collecting Cornish castles. Perhaps he had an eye for the picturesque, though his object was more probably the prosaic one of consolidating his position in the county. The de Cardinham heiress, Ysolda, was persuaded to part with her castle of Restormel to her 'most serene prince and lord', together with her demesne lying on the east side of the highway from Bodmin to Lostwithiel, its freemen and villeins, park and wood, three mills, the town of Lostwithiel, the waters of Fowey and the fishing therein. It was a covetable acquisition. Of the big castles there remained only Trematon, now two centuries old and still in the hands of its original Norman owners, and in 1270 Richard rounded off his collection by buying it from Roger de Valletort. His position in Cornwall was now impregnable. Yet he had not much longer to live. He had married for a third time, apparently very much for love, when he was sixty, but the great joy of his life was his eldest son Henry. In 1271 he was murdered by two of Simon de Montfort's sons while listening to a service in the church at Viterbo, and the news broke Richard's heart. He died early in the following year, unwanted in

Germany, unloved in England, and was buried in Hailes Abbey, the great Cistercian house that he had founded in the Cotswolds. His brother Henry survived him only a few months.

One of Henry's last acts had been to invest Edmund, Richard's son by his second wife, the beautiful Sanchia of Provence, with the Earldom of Cornwall, so that the new king and new earl, who succeeded to their estates at about the same time, were first cousins. But Edmund took little part in the great events of the reign of Edward I beyond helping to finance his exploits, on one occasion placing the entire revenue of Cornwall at his disposal. He was more interested in religion than in politics and campaigning – though once during Edward's absence abroad he crushed a Welsh rebellion – and was particularly interested in his father's foundation at Hailes. He presented the abbey with the celebrated crystal vase containing the Holy Blood of the Lord, and when the church was burned down in the following year – no doubt because it was not grand enough to house the precious relic – he rebuilt it on a lavish scale around a splendid shrine. He also endowed it with some of his Cornish possessions, with land at Helston, for example, and presented it with the advowson of Paul church – Rewley Abbey got that of St Wendron. Where his sympathies lay in the sharp dispute between the king and clergy we do not know. In 1296 the Pope issued the bull of *Clericis Laicos*, forbidding the Church to grant money to a temporal prince without papal permission, whereupon Convocation refused a subsidy to the king. Edward promptly replied by outlawing the clergy, many of whom suffered real hardship, some of the Cornish clergy being imprisoned in Launceston gaol, and William Bodrugan, Archdeacon of Cornwall, was fined for publishing the bull.

Edmund's favourite residence in Cornwall was Restormel – he had good taste, though he must have been torn between Restormel, Trematon and Tintagel – and he modernised the castle by replacing the wooden structures inside the keep with buildings of stone. It is the most perfect of all Cornish castles, a circle of stone, sheer unbuttressed walls surrounded by a moat, the medieval version of prehistoric Chun. A mile below, at the limit of the navigable Fowey, lay the little town and port of Lostwithiel, its name so old that its meaning has long been forgotten. It received its first charter in the twelfth century, at about the same time as Truro, and now Edmund of Cornwall, looking down from the battlements of Restormel, decided to make it the capital of his county. So there he built the splendid 'Duchy Palace'. There was the great Shire Hall for the sessions of the county court, where the freeholders met to elect two county members for Edward I's Model Parliament of 1295 and the Hall of Exchequer of the Earldom – almost all that remains of the palace – and the Coinage Hall, for Lostwithiel was one of the stannary towns, where the tinners had to bring their blocks of metal to be weighed, assayed and stamped. Adjoining it was the stannary gaol, for the reception of those convicted before any of the stannary courts. It had a sinister reputation, like the Devonshire gaol at Lydford where, it was said, prisoners were hanged first and tried afterwards, and if found not guilty a priest would pray for their souls. Edmund's palace then – not be it noted his residence – was to Cornwall what the Palace of Westminster was to London and the country as a whole, the seat of government.

Although Edmund lavished money on his little town of Lostwithiel and the great abbey of Hailes, for some reason or other he took little or no interest in Cornish religious houses, and there were at least four within a few miles of Restormel. There was the little Cluniac cell of Carroc on the other side of the river, and though this was too insignificant to be of much interest, we might have expected him to help the Benedictines at Tywardreath, very much in need of help at this time, a handful of poverty-stricken monks in a decaying priory. Then there were the Augustinians at Bodmin with their relics of St Petroc – not comparable perhaps to the Holy Blood of Hailes – who were also in trouble, not financial as at Tywardreath, but ecclesiastical, things coming to such a pass in 1284 that Bishop Quivil excommunicated their forward prior. And also in Bodmin was the new and flourishing Franciscan friary that Earl Richard had helped to found. Yet Edmund seems to have contented himself with patronising local hermits, spiritual descendants of the early Saints, one of whom, Brother Philip, lived in the hermitage in the park, where he sang masses for the souls of departed earls. There was also Brother Robert on an island in the river. Perhaps he looked after a coastal beacon, a nicely complementary occupation of those who sought a cloistered virtue, saving lives as well as souls. The hermitage at Restormel was destroyed at the Reformation; one on the top of Carn Brea, probably serving another beacon, was pulled down last century, but the remaining one at Roche was surely the most spectacular of all, a granite tower built into a granite pinnacle, the hermit's cell below, his chapel above.

Edmund died in 1299 and was buried, or at least his bones were buried, at Hailes. He was the last Earl of Cornwall to reside in the county. Among his possessions recorded in the valuation of his estate were 'the little castle of Restormel and the town of Lostwithiel, with a deer park and a toll arising from the road between them near Penkekes-crosse, worth 6d yearly. Also the fishery in the river Fawe, from the port of Polruan to the bridge of Resprynn, so long as two oxen yoked together could go up the river'. These and all the other vast possessions of the Earldom reverted to the Crown, though they did not long remain with Edward I. He died in 1307, leaving a languid and extravagant young man as his heir.

One of Edward II's first acts was to recall his great favourite Piers Gaveston, an upstart Gascon adventurer who had been banished by Edward I, and to invest him with the Earldom of Cornwall, an honour that had formerly always been reserved for princes. But Gaveston did not last long. His arrogance infuriated the nobility, who forced Edward to banish him again, and when he returned in 1312 they publicly executed him as a traitor. Edward had his revenge. With the aid of his new favourites the Despensers, father and son, he built up a king's party which defeated the baronial opposition at Boroughbridge in 1322. His most implacable opponent, his cousin Lancaster, was killed, others were imprisoned, but Roger Mortimer escaped to France. Sir Otto de Bodrugan, one of the rebellious knights of Cornwall and owner of a castle near Dodman Point, was fined a thousand marks and an annual tribute of a tun of wine. More fortunate was Thomas Lercedekne of the eight-towered castle of Ruan Lanihorne, for he was on the winning side, at least for the moment.

The Despensers were more generally abhorred than Gaveston had been, and it was popularly supposed that they were responsible for the breach between Edward and his queen, Isabella of France, and for his seizing all the possessions with which he had endowed her, including the revenues of Cornwall. However, she was allowed to go to France with her young son Edward, who was to do homage for his father's French territory. There she fell in love with Roger Mortimer, and together they formed a plan to overthrow the Despensers. Walter Stapledon, Bishop of Exeter, who had accompanied the queen, scandalised by her intimacy with Mortimer, escaped from Paris in disguise to warn the king, but the fleet that Edward assembled – there were four ships and eighty-four men from Looe, two ships and forty-six men from Fowey – could not prevent the landing of Isabella and her lover in September 1326. London declared for the queen, and when Edward fled into the west country the mob broke loose and attacked those whom they considered her principal enemies. One of these was Bishop Stapledon. His house was sacked, and he himself seized on the steps of St Paul's as he was seeking refuge. The rioters dragged him into Cheapside and cut off his head, which they sent to the queen as a token of their loyalty; his naked body they left in the street, and it was not until the following March that it was buried in Exeter Cathedral near the high altar. Meanwhile Edward, having been captured and compelled to abdicate in favour of his young son, had been murdered at Berkeley Castle by the orders of Mortimer. It is perhaps the most sordid period in our history, and the episode was not yet quite over.

Edward III was only fifteen when he ascended the throne, and for the next three years the government was in the hands of Isabella and Mortimer. But by the time he was eighteen he was strong enough to strike. Declaring himself of age, he placed his mother in honourable confinement and ordered the execution of

Mortimer. Although he had been crowned in 1327, his reign really began when he thus assumed power in 1330, the year in which his first son – he was to have far too many sons – was born.

Soon after his accession Edward had created his younger brother, John of Eltham, Earl of Cornwall. He was only a child at the time and could take little interest in his Cornish estates and castles, untenanted by any Earl since the death of the great builder Edmund thirty years before, and now crumbling away. A host of officials under a steward, a most desirable office, administered the Earldom, but at this time nobody seems to have paid much attention to its buildings. Tintagel's great hall was roofless and ruinous, and even Restormel was decaying, though John de Kendall was appointed its keeper for life with a salary of 3d a day and an annual robe. Earl John died in September 1336, and in the following March Edward III raised the Earldom to a Duchy and created the seven-year-old Prince Edward, later to be known as the Black Prince, the first Duke of Cornwall, the first duke indeed that England had ever known.* In the same spring he ordered a fleet to attack the shipping in the ports of Normandy. The Hundred Years War had begun.

This change in the status of Cornwall in 1337, coinciding with the beginning of the great French war, is a convenient date at which to pause and review the changes that had taken place in the thirteenth and early fourteenth century. It is indeed almost essential to make such a survey at this point, for the civilisation of the Middle Ages had just reached perfection and was about to suffer a shock that would lead to its gradual disintegration. Since the time of John towns had begun to compete in importance with the manors, industry and trade with agriculture, and population was increasing, as was the power of the central government and the smaller country gentry at the expense of the old feudal baronage. Moreover, England had become a nation, the upper

* It is important to note that the county and the Duchy are not the same thing. The Duchy is merely a number of estates in Cornwall – and elsewhere – which belong to the Duke, the eldest son of the Sovereign.

classes were beginning to speak English instead of French, and the Hundred Years War, the first large-scale continental struggle in which England had ever been engaged, was as much an expression of this nationalism as it was an attempt to safeguard and extend the foreign market.

But like the Welsh, subdued by Edward I, and the Bretons, still struggling for independence against the French and English, the Cornish had their own nationalism. Perhaps those in the eastern half, where there must have been much intermarriage with the English, were already taking pride in being members of a greater nation, but for the unmixed western Celts the English were foreigners, their language a foreign language, and though they had to obey English laws they pursued their old way of life as much as possible, living in hamlets and avoiding towns. Even as late as 1327 there were more foreign than native burgesses in Tregony, Grampound and Fowey, all near the centre of the county.

Cornish towns were not a natural Celtic growth, a spontaneous development of villages into larger centres of population, but speculations of English feudal magnates and ecclesiastical landholders who foresaw the profit that would arise from urban rents from tolls of markets and fairs, and some thirty boroughs were founded in this period. It was of course essential to have suitable sites, and the southern half of the county was particularly rich in these, where the arms of sunken estuaries ran up far into the land making the hamlets by their lowest fords or bridges potential ports as well as market towns for country produce. Truro, founded by Richard de Lucy in the middle of the twelfth century, is an excellent example. Penryn, on a lower arm of the Fal estuary, is another. This was a shrewd move by Bishop Brewer in 1236 – the bishops of Exeter were expert manipulators of real estate, and not slow to see the worldly advantages of trade between their diocesan ports and Gascony, when that province became part of the dominions of English kings. Penryn had another advantage: it was much nearer the sea than Truro, and naturally attracted much of its foreign trade. Tregony, far up the river Fal in the shadow of

Pomeray castle, was less fortunate. In the early Middle Ages it was a busy little port with a quay at the end of its street, but the gradual silting up of the river ruined its seaborne traffic and reduced it to a small market town, 'a verie poore towne graced somtymes with *Pomery* castle', wrote Norden in 1600. Lostwithiel on the Fowey was in a similar situation to Truro, an inland port and market town. So too was Helston on the little tidal river Cober, though the formation of Looe Bar cut it off from the sea as early as the thirteenth century. However, the town was strategically placed at the entrance to the Lizard peninsula and continued to prosper, partly because the burgesses took over the ancient tin port of Gweek, where they set up their gallows to warn over-enterprising foreigners that not only had they the right to hang thieves caught within their borough, but also those caught beyond its limits.

The first step in the creation of a borough was the granting of a charter by the lord of the manor on which it stood. This was normally subject to confirmation by the king, but in Cornwall very few towns received royal confirmation before the fourteenth century as the Earl's authority sufficed. The privileges were substantial, and though they varied in detail were essentially much the same: making the burgesses virtually freemen instead of villeins, giving them limited rights of self-government with their own court, and exemption from a number of feudal dues. Thus Robert de Cardinham's charter to Lostwithiel at the end of the twelfth century allowed each burgess to hold his burgage, that is his house, garden, and strips in the open fields, for the very reasonable rent of 6d a year. He could leave it by will or sell it if he wished, provided his heir or the new tenant paid a fine of 12d. The townsmen were subject to no court but their own, though this was exceptional, for most charters granted exemption from the hundred court only and not from that of the shire. They were allowed to give their children in marriage without their lord's permission, and to elect a reeve as their representative. On the other hand, the reeve was responsible not to them but to the lord, who also retained for himself and his bailiffs the office of judges in the borough court, so that although the burgesses were comparatively free they were in the last resort still subject to their feudal lord.

John of Eltham's charter to the burgesses of Grampound at the end of this period, in 1332, though not the first, was a particularly generous one. The town was in the old manor of Tybesta, one of the biggest of the Earl's demesne estates, a single street, as it is today, running down to a bridge over the Fal. From this bridge it derived its importance and its name Grand Pont, or in Cornish Ponsmur, for it lay on the main southern highway from Callington to Truro and Helston, and before Tregony had a bridge this was the lowest one across the river. Earl John confirmed the townsmen in their privileges of _Infangenethef_, of hanging thieves in their borough, of exemption from various dues throughout the county, such as payment for the upkeep of bridges and the use of stalls in markets, and of farming the manor mills along the river, but in addition granted them the right to form a merchant gild and to hold a weekly market and two fairs a year. The good burgesses of Grampound were in clover.

The manorial mill – grindstones worked by a water-wheel – was a valuable source of revenue to its lord, for all his tenants were bound to bring their corn to be ground there, and to pay a toll for the privilege. If they were found surreptitiously using an old-fashioned quern in their own home they were fined, as was Richard Pope – an English name, be it noted – who in 1297 had to pay 3d at Tybesta for evasion. The Tybesta mills were already being farmed by the burgesses of Grampound for an annual rent of 53s 4d and they were evidently as careful as the lord's bailiff to see that nobody evaded paying his due.

Tybesta also had a tucking mill, and though this was not the property of the lord his permission would have to be obtained, and a payment made, as it involved the use of his water. Tucking is the west-country word for fulling, the final process in the manufacture of woollen cloth, when it is dipped in water and pounded with stones or hammers. A fulling mill, it will be remembered, played an important part in one of Don Quixote's most memorable adventures, when one dark night he and

Sancho heard the eerie sound of roaring waters accompanied by regular blows and a clanking of iron and chains. The trade in raw and manufactured wool had become one of England's greatest sources of wealth, and though Cornwall contributed little in the way of export – its sheep had 'little bodies and coarse fleeces, so as their wool bare no better name than Cornish hair', wrote Carew of these early times – the people made cloth for their own use, and tucking mills, though many of them were post-medieval, can be traced all over the county: Tuckingmill on the Red river near Camborne, for example. The manufacture was, of course, a domestic one, and we can imagine the women of Grampound in their cottages, spinning from their distaffs, weaving on their primitive wooden looms, and taking the cloth down to the fulling mill by the river to be finished.

The right to have a merchant gild was a much valued privilege, for it immensely increased the prestige of the burgesses thus to be able to form an association of craftsmen and traders with the monopoly of trade in the borough, and power to enforce rules against foreigners – any non-townsman was a foreigner – perhaps even to wring further concessions from their lord. Inevitably the gildsmen assumed control of borough affairs, so that when Earl Richard allowed those of Launceston to build themselves a Gild Hall it was tantamount to building a Town Hall, and the terms have become almost synonymous. The gild was also a charitable association, and when one of its members died the others arranged for him to be decently buried and prayed for, and if necessary made provision for his widow and children. Bodmin, Helston, Liskeard and Lostwithiel all gained permission to have merchant gilds in the thirteenth century.

These merchant gilds eventually split up into craft gilds, associations of masters engaged in the same trade, but their development in Cornwall was, like everything else, slower than elsewhere. For one thing, the Cornish were individualists and little given to combining, and then towns were so tiny at the beginning of the fourteenth century – even in 1377 Helston, Penryn and Looe had under three hundred inhabitants – that few of them can have had more than two or three of the same trade. Bodmin was bigger, and perhaps it was there that craftsmen first organised themselves in separate gilds.

Markets were profitable institutions for their owners, who collected rents for the stalls set up in the streets, or sometimes in the churchyard, tolls for the right of trading, and a purchase tax on goods sold. It was difficult to do anything in the Middle Ages without somebody else getting something out of it, and we can understand why Reginald de Valletort set up a market at Trematon to compete with the bishop's at St Germans – the bishop held his on Sunday (as did Reginald) when the maximum number of people could attend – and why Robert of Mortain stole that of the Launceston canons – it was worth 20s – by moving the site to his castle. The burgesses also gained, for a market brought trade and traders to their town, and, if they managed to farm it from their lord, they pocketed any surplus above the rent. Naturally they were jealous of their rights and eager to gain a market before a neighbouring rival, for it was unusual to have two markets close together. Thus, when Lelant secured one in 1296 the fisherfolk of the growing port of St Ives had to buy and sell at the licensed centre of trade three miles away. Incidentally they had to go to Lelant to be baptised, married and buried, as its own little church was merely an unconsecrated chapel of ease.

The right to hold a fair was even more profitable and more to be prized, for a market was a purely local function, an occasion for business and gossip, whereas fairs, which generally lasted a week, or at least three long summer days, attracted people from far and wide and, though a considerable amount of business was done, were something in the nature of a holiday, and visitors in holiday vein were prodigal spenders. But although fairs were an excuse for merrymaking and junketing, for dancing and wrestling, ogling and drinking, sideshows and peepshows, to the great profit of minstrels, balladmongers, charlatans and pickpockets, the Autolycuses of the period, they were also a necessity in medieval times. At markets merely local produce was exchanged, and only at fairs was it possible to buy the wares of distant counties and foreign countries, essential goods as well as luxuries such as spices, perfumes, wines and silks. Moreover fairs were a mart for the exchange of ideas, an annual expansion of the spirit beyond the horizons of the parish within which most medieval men and women were confined for the rest of the year. There were no fairs in Cornwall comparable to those at Stourbridge and St Ives in Huntingdonshire, which had an international reputation, and though most of the market towns had their fairs, the Cornish, still suspicious of towns and large congregations of people, held their principal ones at out-of-the-way places, where the villages of Summercourt and Goldsithney have since arisen.

If then we could travel back and make a rapid survey of Cornwall in the middle of March 1337, when the young Black Prince became its Duke and daffodils and primroses sweetened the indefinite edges of the roads, we should find about thirty of these chartered boroughs, most of them on the southern side of the county. They were all very small, none of them save Bodmin with more than a hundred little houses, though most of them had a biggish church, while a castle or monastic buildings added greatly to the size of some, as did the Duchy Palace to Lostwithiel. Along the central ridgeway were Launceston, the only walled town in the county, and Bodmin, much the biggest and wealthiest, with its priory church, in the lady chapel of which was the shrine of St Petroc, and on its southern side the cloisters, monks' dormitory, refectory, chapter house, prior's lodging, pond and culver house, a much-prized monopoly of manorial lords, who generally built these dovecotes in their tenants' fields so that they could feed on their corn. There was also at Bodmin a century-old Franciscan friary. Fifteen miles farther west was the little borough of Michell, a mere street along the main road, for which in 1239 Walter de Ralegh secured a royal charter for a weekly market and a yearly fair. It was at the height of its prosperity at this time, but was soon to decline as its site had few natural advantages.

The southern highway, from Tavistock across the Tamar, was marked by Callington, Liskeard, Lostwithiel, Grampound (with Tregony three miles lower down the Fal), Truro,

Helston and Marazion, the natural centre for pilgrims visiting St Michael's Mount.

On the north coast was Padstow, with Tintagel and Bossiney not far away, but their day was almost over, and owing to their decline Camelford failed to develop into anything more than a street of houses at the river crossing, its parish church two miles away at Lanteglos.

The southern estuaries were now coming into their own, and here on the Tamar was Saltash, granted a charter in 1190, and high up the tidal Lynher, beyond Trematon, the old cathedral town of St Germans. On the Fal were Penryn and St Mawes, though the latter never came to much. But the future lay with the ports at the entrance to the estuaries: with Plymouth just across the Tamar in Devonshire, with East and West Looe on either side of their river, with Fowey, mainly a colony of foreigners whose splendid church had just been consecrated by Bishop Grandisson in 1336, and already at the mouth of the Fal, below Penryn, a number of villages went under the collective name of Falmouth.

Some of these towns were already returning members to Parliament. It may be that some of them were represented in the momentous Parliament called by Simon de Montfort in 1265, the year of his triumph and fall, momentous because for the first time burgesses were summoned to supplement the knights from the shires. It is true that the towns represented were only those favourable to de Montfort's cause, but it was the beginning of borough representation and of the House of Commons. Edward I followed the example set by the rebel de Montfort, and there must have been Cornish burgesses in his first Parliament of 1275, though the Model Parliament of 1295 is the first for which we have a record of the members' names. Cornwall, like the other counties, was represented by two knights of the shire and two burgesses from each of five boroughs: Launceston, Bodmin, Truro, Liskeard and Tregony. Helston was added later and Lostwithiel displaced Tregony, these six towns continuing to return members fairly regularly to the medieval Parliaments. It was not a very desirable privilege, particularly in Cornwall, some three hundred miles of medieval road from Westminster, and the same members were rarely elected twice. Then the county and boroughs had to support their representatives, paying 4s a day for a knight and 2s for a burgess while they were on duty, which included time spent in travelling. This was reckoned as taking four days each way, though in foul weather it must have taken the Helston burgesses far longer than that. However, Cornishmen were more conscientious than most, and attended more than half the Parliaments to which they were summoned.

Many of the biggest and most important towns of modern Cornwall, though none of them big by English standards, were no more than villages in the middle of the fourteenth century. Camborne, Redruth and St Austell had to wait for the Industrial Revolution, while Newquay, St Ives and Penzance were still little fishing ports, as were Mousehole, Newlyn, Porthleven, Mevagissey and Polperro, which have never grown into anything much more.

Cornish ports and ships first appear in official records at the beginning of the thirteenth century in the reign of John. The king himself owned the nucleus of a royal navy, fifty galleys or long ships for war which were stationed at various ports, though none of them in Cornwall. In addition Dover, Winchelsea, Rye and the other towns on the south-east coast which formed the Cinque Ports, in return for certain privileges, were bound to supply a number of ships and men – in the reign of Henry III fifty-seven ships and one thousand two hundred men – who served for fifteen days at the expense of the towns, beyond that time being maintained by the king. This feudal array, however, good work though it did, was not an unqualified success, for it was as much given to piracy as to the king's service, finding it just as profitable to plunder English ships as those of France: in 1297, for example, on an expedition to Flanders the Cinque Ports fleet scuttled twenty Yarmouth ships under the eyes of the king himself. Then during the anarchic reign of Edward II the Cinque Ports were in a state of open war with the ships of the Fowey river. Apparently the Cornishmen had rescued one of their fellows who was accused of murder from a Cinque Ports ship, killing some of his captors in the affray, and the Portsmen were now hunting down any vessels coming from the Fowey. The king issued a writ ordering the men of Kent and Sussex not to molest those of Fowey, Lostwithiel and Polruan, nor to prevent their trading in the Cinque Ports, but it had no effect and soon the eastern ports were at war with those of the west. According to Leland the west-countrymen then took the initiative, and 'the Shippes of Fawey sayling by Rhie and Winchelsey wold vale no bonet being requirid, wherapon Rhy and Winchelsey Men and they faught, wher Fawey Men had victorie, and therapon bare their Armes mixt with the Armes of Rhy and Winchelsey: and then rose the Name of the Gallaunts of Fowey'. Leland heard the story at Fowey more than two centuries after the event, by which time no doubt it was highly embellished, but it illustrates the danger of the feudal array and the insolence of a privileged and semi-private navy. Little more is heard of the Cinque Ports fleet after this time, and kings came to rely on the national militia, the ancient obligation of coastal towns and counties to provide ships and men in time of need.

This was why King John sent orders in 1205 to the bailiffs of the Cornish and other west-country ports to secure expert shipwrights and sailors to build and man vessels for his service. But in the thirteenth century the Cinque Ports fleet generally sufficed and little use was made of the power to impress ships and men. In 1301, however, Cornwall was ordered to supply ships for the Scottish war, one from Fowey and one from Looe. But the Fowey ship failed to turn up, and in the levy of the following year the two Looes were grouped with Saltash, Fowey with Lostwithiel, Polruan, and even Bodmin, and security taken from the owners that the ships, one from each group, really would appear. This time Looe seems to have defaulted, for in 1303 Edward I, with regal courtesy, asked the burgesses of Launceston, Liskeard and Polperro to help those of Looe and Saltash to furnish a ship as they alone could not afford to do so. But by 1306 the royal patience was exhausted, and Edward ordered the steward of Cornwall to commit reluctant seamen to the gaol in Launceston Castle.

Yet the king's service had its compensations. Before the days of marine insurance legitimate trading was a risky business: if a ship escaped wreck in a storm, or, as Chaucer put it, 'casuelly the shippes botme rente', there was always the danger of piracy, and there was no saying what a cargo would fetch when it was discharged. But the king promised – not quite the same thing as a guarantee perhaps – a definite rate for the fitting and hire of ships that he commandeered, and the pay was generous: sixpence a day for officers and threepence for the men. However, less orthodox forms of maritime enterprise were probably more profitable, particularly for the Cornish, thrust far out into the Atlantic. In 1226 a merchant vessel of Bruges was plundered at Falmouth by the crews of four English ships, and in 1312 a ship lying at Fowey was seized and sold abroad by the men of the estuary, and the owner held prisoner at Lostwithiel.

The Cornish already had a reputation for plundering wrecks, though of course the practice was common enough all along the English seaboard. In Cornwall the right to wreckage, originally vested in the Crown, passed to the Duchy and eventually to the lords of manors along the coast, wreckage including whales and porpoises – William de Aumarle was fined in 1346 for making off with a porpoise – but the Cornish coastal dwellers cared for none of these legal niceties. So, when William le Poer, coroner of Scilly, went to Tresco in 1305 to take charge of the salved cargo of a wreck, he was seized by a mob led by the prior of St Nicholas and held captive until he bought his freedom. A few years later an Irish vessel, wrecked at Porthleven, was broken 'into little pieces' by the natives, including a number of clergy, and picked so clean that not a trace remained either of cargo or ship.

Apart from fishing and their less legitimate activities the Cornish seamen were mainly engaged in the export of their one major product, tin, though they preferred to hug the coast – running the gauntlet of the Cinque Ports – as far as London, whence the metal was carried mainly in French and Italian ships, to venturing across the stormy Channel approaches and the Bay of Biscay. By the fourteenth century new overland trade routes had been opened, and Cornish tin passed not only through France to Marseilles, but also through Bruges to Venice, Constantinople and the Near East, where it was used for plating the insides of copper vessels. The medieval passion for hanging and ringing bells in their church towers was a great stimulus to the industry, as was also the invention of an even noisier and decidedly more cacophonous instrument, the cannon. Thanks then to bronze bells and brazen cannons, symbols of peace and war, the production of tin in Cornwall reached a record figure in 1337, the year of the creation of the Duchy – perhaps almost an allegory.

Meanwhile, in 1305, Edward I had confirmed John's charter of 1201, and the tinners had secured their strange privileges and independence: their rights of bounding, of trial before their own courts, and of exemption from ordinary taxation. The mining areas were divided into four provinces or stannaries, tracts of unenclosed land on and around the primeval granite bosses, where the tinners could set up their bounds and their stream works. Bodmin Moor, the source of the Fowey river, was known as Foweymore; between Bodmin and St Austell, and centring on Hensbarrow Beacon, was Blackmore, now the weird china clay region for which the name of Whitemoor would be more appropriate; Tywarnhayle embraced St Agnes on the north coast and the area of Carn Brea, and the combined stannaries of Kerrier and Penwith included the Godolphin Hills and the western granite peninsula from Hayle to the Land's End. Within these wild and vaguely delimited tracts of moor the tinners worked and lived, subject only to the law of their stannary courts for all matters save those of life, limb and land. These courts were normally held in each district every three weeks under the presidency of the steward appointed by the warden, though what exactly was the procedure we do not know as there are no records before the sixteenth century. It is clear, however, that the tinners were very jealous of their rights, and if brought up before another court could insist that half the jury should also be tinners.

We must, then, imagine these medieval tinners at work on the desolate slopes of the moors, with their iron-tipped shovels and picks turning over the earth and sinking small shafts in search of the alluvial tin swept down from the parent lode. When found, they diverted a stream of water into the working to scour away the lighter rubbish, leaving the heavy particles of ore at the bottom, thus accelerating the process of nature by washing silt into the rivers, so that towns and villages that had once been little ports reached by the tides, such as St Erth and St Blazey, were cut off from the sea. Large nodules had to be crushed before the baser matter could be separated from the ore, and this was often done by pounding them with heavy rounded stones in cavities on the granite boulders. These depressions may still be seen on the rocks in tin-streaming districts, circular mortars about nine inches across, worn quite smooth by the pounding and grinding of the ancient tinners. The romantic Borlase attributed them to the Druids, bowls that drained the blood of their dreadful sacrifices. Small stones and gravel were generally crushed in a crazing mill, a sort of rotary quern consisting of two grindstones.

After grinding into sand and washing, the 'black tin', as the ore was called, was ready to be converted into metal, or 'white tin', by smelting. The earliest form of furnace was simply a small pit in which a fire was kindled, the ore thrown on the top, and the metal gathered from the ashes. 'Jews' houses' were a refinement in which the fire was contained in a sort of inverted cone of hard clay some three feet high, and fanned to a greater heat with a pair of bellows. These primitive furnaces were made and worked by the streamers themselves, but by the fourteenth century a class of regular 'blowers' had apparently developed. These men had their blowing houses, huts built of rock and turf and covered with thatch, in which they worked their more elaborate furnaces, or 'castles', made of large blocks of stone clamped together with iron. Charcoal was used as a fuel, and the great bellows worked by a waterwheel created an intense heat. The blast drove the smelted tin through a small hole at the bottom of the furnace, where it ran into a stone trough, whence it was ladled into a heated iron cauldron and tested for purity. If it proved sufficiently fine it was poured into smaller moulds of moorstone and allowed to cool, when it was ready for sale, or rather for transport to the coinage town of the stannary.

The term 'coinage' has nothing to do with the minting of coins, but comes from the French coin, a corner, the quality of the tin being judged by a small piece cut from a corner of the block by the assay master. There was a coinage town for each of the four stannaries, Liskeard and Lostwithiel for the two eastern ones, Truro and Helston for the others, and twice a year all the tin that had been smelted had to be carried to one of these centres to be tested and taxed. The blocks, stamped with their owners' names, were stored in the blowing houses until a few days before the royal officers arrived, when files of packhorses carried them down from the moors to the towns. On the first day of the coinage tinners, merchants, pewterers and other tradesmen assembled in the coinage hall, and at noon the weighing and testing began, each block that was passed as satisfactory receiving an official stamp as a guarantee of quality.

It was a lengthy business, and the tinners might be kept waiting a week or more to their loss and the corresponding profit of the townsmen, for whom these assemblies meant a spell of bustling trade. Then, not only had the tinners to pay for their stannary privileges at the rate of 4s for every hundredweight of metal before they were allowed to sell it, but soon the medieval abuses crept in and all the petty officers of the coinage demanded their fees and gratuities: porters, weighers, cutters, all expected a fee in addition to gift money, drink money, dinner money, and even the use of the beams and scales had to be paid for. Moreover, as there were only two coinages a year, the tinners, unless they were hired men, might be hard pressed for money before they could legally sell their produce again, and be driven perforce to borrow. As the moneylenders were usually the Cornish and London merchants who bought their tin, they were at a disadvantage and the rate of interest was correspondingly high, often as much as fifty per cent, with perhaps a promise to deliver so much tin at a certain price at the next coinage.

No better way of encouraging illicit trade could have been devised than these taxes, exactions, delays and frustrations, and even by the end of the twelfth century the Cornish had added tin smuggling to their other unconventional activities. Wandering tinkers haunted the stream works and blowing houses, buying ore by the bowl and uncoined metal by the pound – it must be remembered that pure tin is almost as heavy as lead – and selling it in the southern ports to specialists in the art of conversion into small blocks of 'pocket tin', which were readily bought by seamen and travelling pewterers, or smuggled by night aboard ships that put into Fowey and Mevagissey ostensibly to buy Cornish slate and stone.

The expansion of the tin industry and establishment of towns were two of the main factors leading to a rise in population. At the time of the Conquest there were fewer than twenty thousand people in Cornwall, but by the time of the creation of the Duchy in 1337 there were probably about three times as many, exerting a corresponding pressure on the land and its produce. But agricultural methods and implements changed little in the Middle Ages, and were woefully inadequate by modern standards. Ploughs drawn by teams of two, four or even more oxen could turn only a few inches of soil, and there was insufficient manure to feed the land as cattle had to be slaughtered at Michaelmas owing to lack of winter fodder. It was a vicious circle – shortage of crops meant shortage of manure which in turn meant shortage of crops – a circle that could be broken only by the discovery of better methods of arable farming. And Cornwall was even more backward than most counties: much of the land was moor and waste, there were few regions of really rich soil, and both the English strip farming in open fields round the towns and the far more prevalent Celtic farming in tiny enclosed fields were uneconomical. It followed that if no more produce could be raised from a given piece of land the area of cultivation had to be extended, and in the course of the thirteenth century hundreds of new farms came into existence. A start was made as early as 1204, when the Cornishmen paid the needy King John the huge sum of two thousand two hundred marks and twenty palfreys to rid themselves of the detested Forest Law, which preserved a great part of the country as a royal hunting ground. New tracts of land were thus freed for reclamation, and slowly the frontiers of cultivation were pushed up the slopes of the hills that had been abandoned by Bronze Age farmers nearly two thousand years before, some of their huts, no doubt, being reoccupied by medieval peasants. We can still see some of these medieval intakes and settlements, and find them recorded in the legal documents of the age. In 1284 the Prior of Launceston made over to William of Trewortha and eleven others, in consideration of a rent of four silver shillings, the tract of moor that lies between Lynher and the leaping Withey Brook, the priory reserving for its other tenants at Caradon the right to pasture their cattle there in the summer – a significant clause describing what was apparently the customary medieval practice. The moor is still called Twelve Men's Moor after these twelve tenants of the reign of Edward I, and there on the bank of the Withey Brook, nine hundred feet high and surrounded by hut circles of the Bronze Age, is Trewortha farm, all that remains of the medieval hamlet save a few shadowy foundations. Almost as high was the little village of Temple, two miles south of the Stripple Stones on the desolate track across Bodmin Moor. The settlement was made by the Knights Templar in the twelfth century, presumably as a refuge for travellers, but after their suppression in 1312 it passed to the rival order of Hospitallers. Their little church was outside the bishop's jurisdiction, and one could be married there without the formality of banns, a circumstance that led to Carew's sour remark that 'many a bad marriage bargain is there yearly slubbered up'. Church and even churchyard have gone, but there are still a few houses and inhabitants, and Merrifield farm close by is one of those built by the thirteenth-century colonisers of the waste.

Far more important than the military orders of the Templars and Hospitallers were the friars, who arrived in England at the beginning of the thirteenth century and soon founded two houses in Cornwall. As, unlike monks, they were not confined to their monastery, but travelled abroad preaching and ministering to the poor, they naturally established themselves in the most populous centres, the Franciscans or Greyfriars at Bodmin, the Dominicans or Blackfriars at Truro. The friars were by no means altogether to the liking of the other clergy: the monks resented the diversion of charitable bequests from their own foundations, and the secular clergy their interference in parish affairs, particularly their popular preaching, collection of alms and hearing of confession. Wealth corrupted their original ideals and things were very much worse at the end of the fourteenth century when Chaucer described the merry friar who was far better acquainted with rich merchants and their wives, with innkeepers and barmaids, than with lepers, beggars and other outcasts of society:

And he had power of confessioun,
As seyde him-self, more than a curat,
For of his ordre he was licentiat.
Ful swetely herde he confessioun,
And plesaunt was his absolucioun;
He was an esy man to yeve penaunce
Ther as he wiste to han a good pitaunce.

Chaucer's friar was at least licensed to hear confessions, or claimed to be, but not all friars were equally scrupulous, and Bishop Brantingham warned the Archdeacon of Cornwall to keep his eyes open for these unlicensed friar-confessors.

The Augustinian canons of Bodmin can scarcely have welcomed the arrival and fraternal competition of the Franciscans, who soon became so popular among the townsmen and neighbouring gentry, and attracted such endowments that they were able to add a third great church to the town and another block of monastic buildings. At Truro the Dominicans, apparently under the patronage of the Reskymer family, settled on the west side of the town in the valley of the little river Kenwyn, and in September 1259 Bishop Bronescombe of Exeter consecrated their church. On the previous day he had consecrated the chapel of St Mary, which was to become the parish church and nucleus of the Victorian cathedral.

It was Bronescombe who, a few years later, founded the most famous of all Cornish collegiate houses, Glasney, a kind of minor cathedral within the diocese, with a provost, eleven canons in priests' orders, seven vicars and six choristers. The church was at the bottom of the bishop's park at Penryn, and the canons set about erecting the buildings on a monastic plan, with cloister, dormitories, chapter houses and refectory. Bronescombe endowed the college with a number of livings, most of them in the neighbourhood of Penryn, others, such as Sithney and Zennor, farther west, in the hopes of making his new foundation a stronghold of ecclesiastical discipline in the remotest region of his diocese. The canons, however, were not for long a model to the laity, and in 1330 Bishop Grandisson had to order them to fence their garden and stop poaching in his park.

The growing prosperity and population of the county in the thirteenth century inevitably led to a great building of churches, a movement that was encouraged by a succession of devoted bishops of Exeter, most of whom were themselves great builders: William Brewer who added the chapter house to Warelwast's Norman cathedral, Walter Bronescombe who began the rebuilding and in 1280 was buried close to his new Lady Chapel, and Peter Quivil who continued his work and transformed the Norman towers into transepts. But the Cornish would be little interested in the splendours of their cathedral far beyond the Tamar, few of them would ever see it, though no doubt they took a pride in the building or rebuilding of their own parish churches.

There must have been some two hundred Norman churches in the county at the beginning of the century, from the old cathedral of St Germans on the Devonshire border to the collegiate church of St Buryan near the Land's End, but few extensive traces of the original work remain, so much have they been altered, enlarged and restored in later times. Tintagel is early Norman at its bleakest, squat and grey with fortress-like slits of windows, but the monumental nobility of later Norman can be seen in the north arcade and south doorway at Morwenstow. The font is also Norman, though of a very primitive oval shape, and there are more than a hundred Norman fonts in Cornwall, a surprisingly large number. Perhaps the finest is that at Bodmin, a great foliated bowl supported by a central shaft and four slender columns with capitals of winged angels' heads. There is a similar one, almost as good, at Roche.

Towards the end of the twelfth century, or at the beginning of the thirteenth in Cornwall, the new Gothic principle of construction was introduced. Norman walls and piers had to be massive enough to carry the dead weight of the superstructure, but Gothic was engineering in stone, a framework of shafts, arches, ribs and buttresses held in equilibrium by thrust and counter-thrust. Walls were scarcely necessary save to enclose the space between the buttresses, and as the style developed most of this was taken up by stained-glass windows with elaborate tracery. We can see this transition from Norman to Gothic at Morwenstow, where the round arches of the late Norman bays are continued eastward in the pointed Early English style of the thirteenth century. Yet, although there was so much building during this century of faith, there is little of it left in Cornwall, mainly because the men of the fifteenth century preferred their own light and airy Perpendicular style and had no scruples about demolishing the work of their ancestors.

However, St Anthony-in-Roseland, although much restored a hundred years ago, gives a fair idea of what a Cornish church looked like at the end of the thirteenth century: a simple nave, chancel and transepts, with a tower over the crossing. No later builder thought it worthwhile adding to the church of this remote parish at the tip of the Gerrans peninsula, so that there are no Decorated or Perpendicular aisles and porches, and no west tower, so characteristic of Cornish churches. Then, as we should expect, Lostwithiel, the town so much favoured by Earl Edmund and the capital of the county in the thirteenth century, has more early Gothic than most places. The church tower is Early English, and the octagonal lantern and spire – a rare feature in Cornwall – were added in the Decorated style of the early fourteenth century. The great east window and grotesquely carved octagonal font are of the same period, and among the best examples of Decorated work remaining.

Although not in Cornwall, one other foundation of the period remains to be mentioned: Stapledon Hall, one of the earliest halls of residence in Oxford and the origin of Exeter College, founded in 1314 by Walter Stapledon, the Bishop of Exeter who was to perish at the hands of the London mob a few years later. The original foundation was for twelve scholars, eight of whom were to come from Devonshire and four from Cornwall, so that the college has always had a strong west-country connection. John of Trevisa, born probably at Crocadon in St Mellion, was there in the middle of the fourteenth century when Chaucer was a boy, and translated the Latin *Polychronicon* of Ralph Higden, which version contains the earliest description of England in English. He has much to say about the English tongue: 'for men of the est with men of the west, as yt were under the same part of heyvene, acordeth more in sounynge of speche than men of the north with men of the south'. Again, and more significantly, 'John Cornwaile, a maister of grammar, chaunged the lore in gramer scole and construction of Frensche into Englische; and Richard Pencriche learned that manere techynge of hym, and othere men of Pencriche'. Unfortunately he says nothing about his native Cornish, but as he came from Tamarside and passed most of his life in Gloucestershire he probably knew little about the language.

A History Of Cornwall

VII

The Late Middle Ages
1337–1485

In 1337 when Edward III, still only twenty-five though ten years a king, made his seven-year-old son Duke of Cornwall and advanced his own claim to the crown of France, all seemed set fair for a reign of unprecedented glory and prosperity. And the next ten years seemed only the prelude to a yet more brilliant future. It is true that the Scottish border was in a continual state of turmoil, and that in 1339 the Cornishmen from Saltash to Mousehole were mustered to repel the French, who were raiding the coast as far west as Plymouth, even Bodmin being called upon to supply four ships and its leading burgesses imprisoned at Lostwithiel, until the government discovered that Bodmin was not a port. However, the western ports promised seventy ships of a hundred tons or more, and no doubt some of them were in the royal fleet that won the great naval victory of Sluys in 1340 and gained for England the command of the Channel. Then in 1346 Edward, accompanied by the young Duke of Cornwall, now Prince of Wales, collected a huge fleet, to which Cornwall contributed its quota and a contingent of infantry, landed in Normandy and marched on Paris, then north towards the Straits of Dover. Trapped by overwhelming French forces on the Somme, the English gave battle at Crécy and, thanks to their archers, overthrew the old-fashioned chivalry of France, finishing their campaign by capturing Calais, which for two centuries remained a possession of the English Crown.

It was a dazzling triumph, brilliant as it was barbarous and ultimately futile, and Edward and his court celebrated in feasting and in dancing. But there was a spectre at the revelry. By the summer of 1348 the Black Death from the east had reached Normandy and, in spite of the prayers of the Bishop of Bath and Wells, in August it fastened on the village of Melcombe Regis in Dorset. Thence it swept in every direction with terrifying speed, and Devon and Cornwall were soon infected. Small black pustules appeared on the body, there was a spitting of blood, and in a few hours the victim was dead. All classes were affected, though the mortality was greatest among the poor and the devoted clergy, the young and the strong, those whom the country could least afford to lose. Naturally the towns, whose houses huddled over stinking kennels, were particularly vulnerable, and Bodmin, where the conduit water ran through the graveyard and the filth was washed down through the houses into the streets, suffered badly. Only two of the canons of the priory were spared. And if we look at the rolls of incumbents in churches, even as far west as Constantine and Phillack, we shall nearly always find that there was an induction, sometimes more than one, during that dreadful year of 1348–9. The worst was over in England by the end of 1349, but Wales and Scotland were devastated in the following year. How many died we do not know with any certainty, but estimates suggest that almost half the people of the country perished, perhaps two million in all. Cornwall, with few towns of any size, seagirt and remote from the worst areas of infection, probably escaped more lightly than most counties, but even here the population may have fallen in that single year from sixty thousand to forty thousand.

The economic and social effects of the Black Death were revolutionary. The lord of the manor now found himself faced with a shortage of labour, and the labourer was not slow to exploit his new value. The villeins demanded their freedom, and if it were refused fled to other manors or the towns – Ralph Vyvyan's bondmen found refuge in Scilly – where their new employers, also short of men, would be unlikely to betray them. Free labourers demanded higher wages, and this with a dearth of food and other commodities led to a rise in prices. The government, obstinately convinced that business should be as usual, replied with repressive measures, and landowners by enclosing part of their estates and turning them into sheep farms for which little labour was required. In short, the medieval organisation of the manor was breaking down, a new middle class of yeomen farmers and merchants was emerging, while the labouring classes, dissatisfied with their lot and disillusioned by a corrupt Church, were beginning to ask,

> When Adam delved and Eve span,
> Who was then a gentleman?

The Black Death had struck savagely at the Cornish tinners, and its effect on the industry was disastrous. After the record coinage of six hundred and fifty tons in 1337 production had fallen to two hundred and fifty tons by 1355, and so serious was the situation that the Black Prince issued a proclamation that all tinners and owners should expend as much labour and capital on the tin works as before. But the order had little effect, and it was not until sufficient time had passed to allow the recruitment of new men that there was much improvement. Then in the last decade of the century there was a spurt, production reaching eight hundred tons in 1400.

However, the French war brought prosperity to the Cornish ports. Their ships were now beginning to trade direct with the continent instead of leaving the traffic to foreigners, and a new class of merchants and contractors, like the Bonifaces and Michelstows of Fowey, made money out of supplying merchantmen and vessels of war. Then in 1354 the Black Prince himself came down to see his Duchy. His visit was heralded by an order to John de Kendall to repair the castles, particularly Restormel, of which he had long ago been appointed keeper, and on August 20th the Prince arrived, a young man of twenty-four in the pride of life and fame, accompanied by many of the knights who had fought with him at

Crécy. All Cornwall flocked to Restormel to see their Duke, to pay him homage and to present petitions; the burgesses of Helston asked for a charter, and the Dominicans of Truro received a present of ten oak trees from the park, with which they finished the building of their friary.

The Prince stayed at Restormel only a fortnight. A year later he was in Gascony at the head of an English army, and again a year later, in September 1356, he routed the French at Poitiers and brought back their captive king, whom he led in triumph through the streets of London. In 1363 he was again at Restormel, this time raising money and troops before setting out for Bordeaux, where he maintained the most brilliant court in Europe. Four years later he led a successful expedition into Spain to restore Peter the Cruel to the throne of Castile, but when he recrossed the Pyrenees with the remnant of his army it was as a dying man, for on the hot Spanish plains he had contracted a lingering and mortal disease. His father, Edward III, was now sinking into premature dotage, a besotted old man completely under the influence of his mistress, who was herself controlled by the Prince's younger brother, John of Gaunt. When therefore, after a period of truce, the French war was resumed, there was no repetition of Crécy and Poitiers, but only the Black Prince's massacre of the people of Limoges, and John of Gaunt's trail of slaughter from Calais to Bordeaux. This bestial ferocity only infuriated the French and stiffened their determination, and when they defeated the English fleet off La Rochelle the south coast lay open to their depradations. Cornwall escaped lightly, though in 1375 the *Trinity* of Fowey was one of thirty-nine merchantmen captured or destroyed by the French.

And so the reign of Edward III, which had begun with such brilliance, ended in disaster and disgrace. The old king – yet he was only sixty-five – died in 1377, by which time all his French conquests had been lost save five coastal towns, including Calais. The Black Prince, 'that flower of English knighthood', according to Froissart, 'the Lord Edward of England, Prince of Wales and Aquitaine', and, he might have added, Duke of Cornwall, had died a year before, leaving an only son, Richard of Bordeaux, aged ten.

When the Black Prince died the Duchy and its revenues reverted to the Crown, for by Edward III's charter the title and estates were limited to the eldest son of the reigning monarch, and Richard was the son of the Prince of Wales. There is an important distinction between the titles, for whereas the sovereign's eldest son is created Prince of Wales by special investiture he is born Duke of Cornwall. The title therefore remained dormant during the reign of the childless Richard II, being revived in 1399 when his cousin Henry IV seized the crown and invested his eldest son, the future Henry V, with the dukedom. Owing to lack of male heirs there have often been long periods of dormancy, and the title was held for only seventy-five of the years between the death of the Black Prince and the accession of James I in 1603. As a result many of the estates were granted away during this period of civil war and childless queens, and after the Black Prince's day the Cornish castles were untenanted and neglected. Restormel, which once echoed to the talk and laughter of the knights of Crécy and Poitiers, soon fell into silent ruin. So too did Tintagel, Tristan's Tintagel, which declined into a prison where Richard II confined John of Northampton, Lord Mayor of London, and Thomas Beauchamp, Earl of Warwick. Launceston was ever a prison, and when Leland saw Trematon in 1538 the ruins of that also served as a prison. Trematon, however, was splendidly placed to repel any raiders up the Tamar, and served as a fort for another century or so, the constable, Henry Kirksted, being supplied in 1386 with twelve pounds of gunpowder – 'pulveris gunnorum' – for his newfangled defensive weapons.

There was need of gunpowder at Trematon at this miserable period of the war with France, now joined by Spain, when their ships were sailing unmolested along the southern coast, burning the fishing villages and ports – Fowey was burned in 1378 – and slaughtering their inhabitants. And there was justification for the complaint of the Cornish in Parliament, that as their able-bodied men had been impressed for the navy they were unable to resist the marauders, and for their appeal that the government should send down troops to protect them. The government replied by ordering all landowners to remain on their estates by the sea, and gave the sheriff, Otto Bodrugan, power to enforce the order. Yet it was not for lack of ships that things had come to this pass – Fowey could supply John of Gaunt with four when he sailed after castles in Spain – but for lack of organisation and competent leadership.

This mismanagement of affairs under John of Gaunt, coupled with an iniquitous poll tax that was levied to pay for it, precipitated the latent discontent of the peasants, already stirred up by the speeches and rhymes of John Ball, while at the same time Wycliffe and his 'poor priests', the Lollards, were preaching to eager open-air congregations against the wealth and corruption of the Church. Although there was no rising in Cornwall comparable to the Peasants' Revolt of 1381 in other parts of England, there were a number of minor outrages, directed chiefly against the clergy. The condition of the collegiate church at Crantock had long been unsatisfactory. Despite a reorganisation by Bishop Stapledon, Grandisson discovered that the canons had let their houses to laymen, some of which were being used as taverns and some, apparently, as brothels. The tenants were evicted and excommunicated, and Grandisson completely reorganised the college. That was in 1352, but thirty years later the dean was a pauper and not one of the canons was resident. Glasney College was in an even more unsavoury state. A visitation revealed that much of its property was unaccountably missing – ornaments, vestments, five hundred marks – that the buildings were dilapidated and services irreverently conducted; no wonder, when the canons were toying with their doxies in their houses. We can understand therefore, when the preaching of the Lollards, the message of John Ball and news of the Peasants' Revolt filtered into Cornwall, why the officiating priest and clergy were assaulted in Crantock church, and John Calesteke, priest, was dragged through the streets of Penryn and bound to a cross. A much more grisly affair occurred in St Hilary parish, where one John Browder seized and bound another priest, Walter Sancre, and cut off his head, which was carried to London on a spear.

The man largely responsible for the savage repression of the Peasants' Revolt was Robert Tresilian, a Cornishman born near

St Buryan and educated at Exeter College, Oxford. Appointed Lord Chief Justice for the occasion, he conducted his bloody assizes, sparing none, it was said, who came before him for trial, and under his direction hanging, quartering and disembowelling proceeded apace. At St Albans he hanged fifteen serfs whose crime had been no more than that of rising for their liberty, and ordered a far more barbarous death for the captured John Ball himself. It was Tresilan who sentenced John of Northampton to imprisonment at Tintagel, though very reluctantly, as he feared reprisals from the king's opponents among the barons. His fears were justified, for when John of Gaunt's son, Henry of Derby, and the other Lords Appellant gained control of the government in 1388 he was denounced as a traitor and hanged at Tyburn. Some of his estates were confiscated, but others passed to Sir John Colshull who married his widow; one of the manors was Tremodret in Duloe, where the chancel aisle of the church houses the tombs and effigies of the family.

A truce, followed by peace with France, brought the first phase of the Hundred Years War to an end, and with it, to the profit of Cornwall, a renewal of the pilgrim traffic, particularly to the popular shrine of St James at Compostela. Pilgrims from Ireland and Wales landed at Padstow – there was a big Irish population at Padstow – and either took the short cut by way of Bodmin to Fowey, where the *George* and the *Mary* (140 tons) awaited them, or before embarking made their way to St Michael's Mount along a route defined with chapels dedicated to St James. In May 1396, when Chaucer was describing a pilgrimage to Canterbury – May was the month of pilgrimages and Chaucer's favourite month – William Rose carried forty pilgrims to Santiago de Compostela in his ship, the *Seinte Marie* of Truro. We can only hope they got there and back safely – with their cockles in their hats – for though England and France were officially at peace, private war was still rampant in the Channel. The French complained that English seamen were constantly ravaging their coast and accused the Cornishmen of open piracy, while the English replied with similar complaints and accusations against the French.

Parliament ordered the Cornish ports and even some of the inland towns to build and equip ships at their own cost, and made a grant to the prior of St Michael's Mount for the maintenance of a garrison, as a fortress able to protect the neighbouring country. But the Mount was too far away to protect Looe from the raid of five French and Spanish galleons in August 1405, when nineteen fishing boats were sunk, their crews drowned, and the town sacked and burned.

Apart from these maritime diversions, however, Cornwall was fortunate in having little history at the turn of the fourteenth century, for medieval history is largely a record of foreign war and civil war. It meant little to the people of Cornwall that Richard II was deposed and murdered in 1399, and that his cousin, Harry of Derby and of Lancaster, succeeded him as Henry IV, the first of the Lancastrian kings. It is true that his son, the twelve-year-old Prince Henry, became Duke of Cornwall, but he was never to set foot in his duchy, and rarely was the county more isolated than in the fifteenth century, when no more earls or dukes with their gay and glittering companies rode over Tamar bridges on their way to Lostwithiel and Restormel. None of the great nobles who held land in Cornwall was resident there, though Sir Hugh Courtenay, son and heir of the Earl of Devon, lived at Boconnoc in the middle of the fifteenth century; and though the handful of burgesses elected to Parliament would bring back highly coloured news from Westminster, there was little other contact with the capital save through the travelling justices, who very rarely got beyond Launceston. Even the bishops of Exeter were rarely seen in the western part of their diocese, and even Peter Quivil, who had once been vicar of Mullion, hardly ever returned to Cornwall.

Soon after his accession in 1413 Henry V, having ordered his bishops to pray for peace, renewed the Hundred Years War by reviving the claim of Edward III to the crown of France, although by lineal succession he was not even the legitimate king of England. To enforce his claim he began the building of a royal navy, and in 1415 collected a huge fleet of one thousand four hundred ships for the campaign, so like that of Crécy, which led to the dazzling victory of Agincourt. Cornish ships were in the fleet, 'a city on the inconstant billows dancing', which sailed from Southampton to Harfleur, and a contingent of Cornishmen fought at Agincourt under a banner bearing a device of two wrestlers. Sir John Cornwall and Sir John Trelawny lived to feast their neighbours on the anniversary of that Saint Crispin's day, but the body of Sir John Colshull was brought home to rest in Duloe church.

Three years later another Cornish Sir John, Sir John Arundell of Lanherne, contracted to supply the king's uncle, the Duke of Exeter, with 364 men-at-arms and 770 archers for service in France, and then in 1420 came the Treaty of Troyes, whereby Henry was to marry the daughter of the crazy French king and succeed him on the throne. But it was not to be. Henry V died in 1422, and under his son Henry VI, at times almost as crazy as his French grandfather, the great empire across the Channel was gradually lost. After the English had burned Joan of Arc as a witch the end was certain, and by 1453 the Hundred Years War was over. England was left with the solitary possession of Calais.

Cornwall had been mainly concerned with the profitable business of transporting troops and supplies, and some idea of the strength of its merchant marine may be gained from the lists of vessels that were impressed during five of the last years of the war. Fowey supplied nineteen transports, the largest of which was of three hundred tons, a biggish ship in those days; Saltash supplied six; Landulph five; Looe five; Truro, Penryn and Falmouth sent two each, and Mevagissey one. Particularly interesting are the four supplied by Penzance and two by Marazion. In 1427 William Morton of St Michael's Mount had complained that there was no harbour for large vessels between the Lizard and the Land's End, and asked for help in completing his stone pier that would shelter two hundred ships of any tonnage in Mount's Bay. Fortunately Parliament granted Morton the right to collect dues from ships using the harbour, including one shilling yearly from 'strange' fishing boats coming for hake.

The man in the field and the workshop, the peasant, yeoman and craftsman who supported the monstrous incubus of war, must have rejoiced when they heard that the long struggle with France was ended. But there was to be no peace in England yet awhile, for the hundred years' foreign war was immediately followed by a thirty years' civil war, the Wars of the Roses between the Henrys of Lancaster and the Edwards and Richards of York. It was a ferocious struggle, and though Cornwall was far from the main scenes of battle and carnage most of the leading gentry were involved, and near-anarchy spread to the far west.

It was of course a great time for the lawless seamen of Fowey, who, like the county as a whole, identified themselves with the cause of Lancaster, and particularly with Warwick the Kingmaker, whose badge of a ragged staff they incorporated in the splendid church tower which they were building out of the proceeds of their questionable practices. Norman, Breton, Spanish and even Plymouth ships were attacked and despoiled, until in 1457 a Breton fleet settled old scores by burning part of the town, which, in the absence of Thomas Treffry, was gallantly defended by his wife. 'Wherapon,' wrote Leland, 'Thomas Treury buildid a right fair and strong embatelid Towr in his House: and embateling al the Waulles of the House in a maner made it a Castelle: and onto this Day it is the Glorie of the Town Building in Faweye.' Treffry had come into money by marrying the daughter of the wealthy John Michelstow, and he too inserted the Warwick device in his fine new house of Place. Fowey was irrepressible and its gallants were soon 'skumming' the seas again, having strengthened their base with towers on either side of the river, between which a great chain was slung.

This was the period when the feud between the Courtenays, Earls of Devon, and the Bonvilles reached its climax over a dispute about the stewardship of the Duchy of Cornwall, in 1455 the Earl even attacking Exeter cathedral with his retainers. These retainers, little private armies in the pay of the nobility and gentry, were a legacy of the French war and the curse of the time, and it was to be one of Henry VII's first acts to abolish them. At a level lower was the feud between Thomas Clemens and John Glyn of Morval over the deputy-stewardship of the

Duchy. The story is one of almost unbelievable ferocity and lawlessness, culminating early one Saturday in August when Clemens's men lay in wait for Glyn and 'at four o'clock in the morning horribly slew and murdered him, clove his head in four parts and gave him ten dead wounds in his body, and when he was dead cut off one of his legs, and one of his arms and his head from his body to make him sure'. It is a measure of the anarchy of the time that although numerous warrants were issued for the arrest of Clemens he was still at large in 1476 when he is last heard of.

After the Battle of Tewkesbury in 1471 and the murder of Henry VI, the Prince of Wales (and Duke of Cornwall) and all Lancastrian heirs to the throne – except the boy Henry Tudor, safe from the Yorkist knife in Brittany – Edward IV was firmly established on the throne, and there was a period of comparative order. However, Cornwall was the scene of the last forlorn Lancastrian revolt against Edward. In September 1473 the Earl of Oxford, after an unsuccessful attempt to land in Essex, slipped down the Channel and seized St Michael's Mount by the old stratagem of disguising his men as pilgrims. There he was besieged, not very convincingly, by the sheriff, Sir Henry Bodrugan, and then by his successor Richard Fortescue, who cunningly enticed his men away by promises of pardon and reward. After a four months' siege, when only a few of his followers were left, Oxford surrendered on promise of his life. He was imprisoned, but ten years later was to escape and fight for Henry Tudor at Bosworth.

When the Mount was safely in his hands again King Edward took the opportunity of chastening his loyal but lawless subjects of Fowey, who not only refused to obey his officers but were disrespectfully given to lopping off their ears. In 1474 he sent down commissioners who, under pretence of discussing naval affairs, lured the leading burgesses of Fowey, Polruan and Bodinnick to Lostwithiel, where they imprisoned them and executed one of their number. Their goods were confiscated, the chains defending their haven handed over to their rivals of Dartmouth, 'and their wonted jollity transformed into a sudden misery'. The great days of Fowey were over, and it was soon to be eclipsed by Plymouth and Falmouth, but its spirit was unbroken, and four cases of flagrant piracy during the troubled years of 1483–5 suggest that the local industry continued to flourish.

Edward's strongest supporter in Cornwall was Sir Henry Bodrugan, whose home was high on the cliffs of Chapel Point near Mevagissey. A freebooter of the school of Fowey, like the Gallants he laboured in his piratical vocation, on one occasion chasing a Breton ship into St Ives, whence he brought back its cargo to Bodrugan. At the beginning of the civil war his political allegiance was conveniently ambiguous, and it was only after Oxford's surrender on the Mount and a final frolic with the earl's Lancastrian filibusters that he decided that Edward IV was the man, and finally plumped for the Yorkists. He was an equally ardent supporter of Richard III, who succeeded his brother Edward in 1483, having got rid of his two nephews and an elder brother who stood inconveniently between him and the crown. But most of the Cornish gentry remained loyal to the house of Lancaster and, headed by Edward Courtenay of Boconnoc, declared for Henry Tudor, a determined young man of twenty-six still waiting in Brittany for his chance to claim the throne. It came in October of that year, but a few days before the forces of the west country were to rise and be joined by Henry, a great storm flooded the rivers, preventing the junction of the rebel forces and driving Henry back to the Breton coast. Richard advanced rapidly on Exeter, and the bishop, Peter Courtenay, withdrew to Bodmin where he and his cousin Edward, Sir Thomas Arundell, Richard Edgcumbe, John Treffry and others proclaimed Henry before taking ship for Brittany. This was the celebrated occasion on which Richard Edgcumbe was chased through his own woods at Cotehele by the conscientious Bodrugan, and only escaped by throwing his cap and a large stone into the Tamar, so making his pursuers think that he had drowned himself. Thus says Carew, and he should have known, for Richard was his great- great-grandfather. Moreover, as proof of the story, the chapel that he built in gratitude for his deliverance still stands on the cliff above the river gorge. As a reward for his loyal services Richard III gave Bodrugan the manors of Trelawne and Tywardreath, and other Yorkist supporters in the west received suitable compensation at the expense of the Lancastrians, Sir James Tyrrel, who had been largely responsible for the murder of the princes in the Tower, receiving the confiscated estates of the Arundells.

Meanwhile the Lancastrian exiles in Brittany swore homage to Henry, who in turn promised to marry Elizabeth of York and so unite the rival royal houses. On August 7th, 1485, he landed at Milford Haven, where John Treffry was one of those on the shore to meet him and be knighted on the spot. A fortnight later Richard III was killed at Bosworth and the victor crowned on the battlefield as Henry VII. The Wars of the Roses were over, and the golden age of the Tudors had begun.

The Cornish people could do with an age of gold – though they were in fact to find a considerable proportion of alloy – for there had been no spectacular progress in the county since the Black Death almost a hundred and fifty years before, years of almost constant war and grinding taxation. The population of course had grown in spite of wars and frequent returns of the plague: at the time of the poll tax of 1377 it seems to have been about forty-five thousand, and a hundred years later was probably much the same as it had been before the calamitous mortality of 1348–9, that is, about sixty thousand. After that year the farms that had been established high up in the hills in the thirteenth and early fourteenth century had been abandoned, and the hungry bracken again engulfed the fields that had been so painfully won from the waste. Even if the mouths to feed were once more as many as they had been in 1348 there was no need to push the margin of cultivation to the former heights. Some of the lowland wastes, waterlogged and scrubby land, must have been reclaimed for arable, some improvements made in the art of farming, and in lower-lying and more sheltered districts there may even have been an extension of the larger-scale English open-field system. Moreover, cultivation by serfs is notoriously wasteful, and the comparatively free peasantry that emerged in the fifteenth century, a peasantry working for itself or for money wages, would produce far heavier crops than when doing compulsory week work and boon work for its lords.

Most of the peasants were now customary tenants or copyholders, that is, holding at the will of their lord according to the custom of the manor. In Cornwall holdings were generally for three lives, husband, wife and child, the tenant paying a capital sum when he took possession as well as an annual rent, and on the expiration of the third life the family would either be evicted or the lease renewed on payment of a fine. This was very different from the original feudal organisation of the manor, when the serf was bound to the soil, yet although the manor was breaking down as an economic unit it was still the basis of rural society.

We can see how the manor controlled the lives of its members towards the end of the Middle Ages from the court rolls of the manor of Michell, the little borough set up on the Bodmin road in the early thirteenth century and now held by the Arundells of Lanherne. The records cover the hundred years from 1443 to 1546 and at the end of the fifteenth century there were seven free tenants and twenty copyholders. The lord held courts leet twice a year and courts baron rather more frequently, at all of which his steward presided. At Michaelmas the sworn body of tenants elected their representative for the year, the reeve and two officers to taste the ale and weigh the bread, for the price and quality of these were controlled by law. Those who had broken it were fined, and it was generally assumed that all brewers had done so, for all were written down and if found innocent were acquitted with the note *non brasiavit* – 'he did not brew'. When a tenancy lapsed it was the reeve's duty to see that the new tenant did fealty to the lord and paid his fine. The yearly fair was another valuable source of income to the lord, the profit rising steadily from 16d in 1443 to 32s 6d in 1541. And even the manorial pound brought in its contribution, any stray beast being put there and charged 'herbage' until claimed, or if unclaimed becoming the property of the lord.

At the beginning of the period the leet is concerned mainly with manorial nuisances and minor breaches of the peace. Thus in 1444 John Cary was presented for leaving his field and garden fallow – and presumably unweeded – to the hurt of his neighbours. Two years later Andrew Ranlyn was accused of obstructing a road so that other tenants could not drive their carts along it. In the same year John Trewhila claimed £10 damages from Robert Jobe, chaplain, for beating him twice and making him ride to fetch wine for Mass – though there was plenty in the church – as a result of which his horse, worth £2, had died. Then, some years later we find the reeve presenting John Iryshe for assaulting John Breton, two excitable though non-Cornish Celts representative of the many foreign burgesses of this period. With the coming of the Tudors there was a general tightening up of discipline, and concern with the law of the land as well as with the customs of the manor. Thus, after making a by-law dealing with stray pigs – Henry Hogge had been beating Remfry Coyswarn's pigs – a leet of 1497 ordained that anybody harbouring a suspicious woman for three days and nights should be fined 40d. And six years later Isabella Martyn was presented for keeping a common brothel, not only a local nuisance but also contrary to law. No wonder the Arundells were able to begin the building of a fine new house at Lanherne.

As the manor was the basis of rural society, so was the gild the basis of society in the borough, for not only did the gildsmen regulate their own crafts, but they were also the principal burgesses who controlled the affairs of the town as a whole. Launceston was the first town to have a mayor instead of a provost or portreeve, but by the end of the fifteenth century Lostwithiel, Liskeard, Bodmin, Helston and Truro all had mayors. The distinction was important, for though the portreeve might be elected by the burgesses he was responsible to the lord of the manor, but a mayor was responsible to the burgesses themselves. The population of the towns naturally grew more quickly than that of the county as a whole, though they were still very small: Bodmin, much the biggest, may have had as many as three thousand souls, and the others between five hundred and a thousand. Bodmin also had some forty gilds, mainly religious associations, though little is known about them, and the most illuminating document relating to gilds is that of the Cobblers of Helston. There were seven of these master cobblers and 'householders of the borough of Helston' on whose behalf their priest, James Michell, drew up rules in 1517. The master was to teach his apprentice all his cunning in his craft, and each was to deal fairly with the other. No member was to buy false stuff out of covetousness, to the deceiving of his customers and the displeasure of God. The poor or unfortunate brother was to be provided for, and at the gild's own altar in the church prayers were to be said for all the lives and souls that God willed they should pray for. We can take these rules as characteristic of any craft gild in the fifteenth century, Cornish or English, and they show how closely religion was associated with the ordinary business of life in the Middle Ages.

The port towns were doing well, thanks largely to the wars, official and less official. Fowey was still prosperous in spite of its chastening experience at the hands of Edward IV, and was able to supply Henry VII with a fleet of six ships ranging from a hundred and twenty to two hundred tons, which only two or three other towns on the south coast could have done. It also had much the biggest share of Cornish foreign trade. This was chiefly with Brittany, from which came cargoes of salt, linen, woollen cloth and canvas, the Cornish exporting tin, hides, herrings and pilchards: raw materials and food in return for manufactured goods. The most valuable import, however, was wine from the south of France and Spain. Even Padstow's main trade was with Brittany, though the ancient intercourse with Ireland remained important, a market for tin and source of coarse woollens and – significantly – timber.

Although tin was Cornwall's chief export, the fifteenth century was a period of depression for the industry. No doubt Henry V's renewal of the French war stimulated the home demand for the manufacture of the cannon whose fatal mouths gaped on girded Harfleur, but the export trade must have suffered. After the record of eight hundred tons in 1400, tin production had fallen to four hundred by 1455 and was little more than five hundred at the end of the century.

The Cornish gentry were beginning to dabble in tin as well as in trade, for though their main occupation was the cultivation of their estates, the absence of great nobles with their attendant dynastic strife encouraged these peaceful – or comparatively peaceful – pursuits. Many of these estates were quite small, their manor houses no more than farmhouses, but their owners had the right to coat armour and were immeasurably proud of their families and jealous of their claim that in Cornwall were the best gentlemen. The Pomerays, Chamonds and St Aubyns were of Norman descent, but the Carmynows claimed King Arthur as their ancestor, and Coswarths and Polwheles maintained that they were in Cornwall before the Conquest, as the Trevelyans undoubtedly were. Other ancient families were the Reskymers, soon to die out, the ill-fated Tregians, the Bassets, Roscarrocks, Trevanions of Carhays, Arundells of Lanherne, Arundells of Trerice, and Grenvilles of Stowe. William Edgcumbe had founded the fortunes of his family in the fourteenth century by marrying the heiress Hilaria de Cotehele; a century later Alexander Carew inherited the manor of Antony from his mother, a daughter of Sir Hugh Courtenay of Boconnoc, and by the fifteenth century the arms of the Godolphins, soon to make a fortune out of tin, were carved on the splendid rood screen at St Buryan. Some families holding land in Cornwall, such as the Champernownes, were resident mainly in Devonshire.

Few of these medieval families had houses of any consequence, and even of these little remains today. The hall of Trecarrel is now, alas, a barn, and how humble were the houses of some of the minor gentry may be judged from the recently discovered remains of the home of the Godrevy family in Gwithian. Originally it was nothing more than a single room about thirty feet long and twelve wide, divided by a wooden screen, on one side of which was the hall, on the other the cowshed, like the Dark Age 'long room' at Mawgan Porth and 'sooty byre and hall' of Chaucer's poor widow. Then round about 1400 the house was modernised: a stone wall replaced the wooden screen, the cows were expelled and their shed made into another room with a solar above – the medieval equivalent of a drawing-room – approached by a ladder from the hall. And this three-roomed hovel, for it was little more, was the manor house of Crane Godrevy until it was abandoned when the sand began to pile up again early in the sixteenth century. Then, 'in this park was the house of Sir Henry Bodrugan', wrote Leland in the reign of Henry VIII; 'the ancient dwelling of the Grenvilles' at Stowe was replaced by another great house in the late seventeenth century, and even of this nothing remains but the terraced foundations and stables; the mullions of medieval Antony have long been the humble stones of neighbouring field walls and stiles. Lanherne and Trerice were rebuilt in Tudor times, and so was Cotehele, though some of the old walls survive, as do the chapel and great hall with its timber roof built by Richard Edgcumbe, Bodrugan's rival, at the end of the fifteenth century. Even the main glory of Place at Fowey, the great bay windows, was an early Tudor addition.

Yet if medieval manor houses of any architectural pretension were few, there was a great building of churches after the county had recovered from the ravages of the Black Death. The rebuilding of Bodmin church was begun in 1469, and at the far end of the county we may take St Ives. By the end of the fourteenth century it was a flourishing little fishing town, but still without a church in which its children could be baptised, its young couples married and its dead buried, and the parishioners still had to resort for their sacraments to the distant mother church at Lelant, a little port then sadly in decline owing to the silting up of its harbour. In 1409 they petitioned Bishop Stafford, pointing out that they had built a chapel, made a cemetery and were quite prepared to support a parish priest. They also petitioned the Pope, or rather one of the Popes – this one was an ex-pirate – for there were three characters in search of the office at the time. At last in desperation they set about rebuilding their chapel on a grand scale in the late Decorated style, with two aisles and a great granite west tower a hundred and twenty feet high. It was a typical Cornish church of the period, though bigger than most, with wagon-roofs and no clerestory, the nave and aisles crouching low against the wind, in marked contrast to the vertical lines of the tower. It was almost eighteen years a-building, and in October 1428 Bishop Lacy came down to consecrate it for the performance of all sacraments save burial. Not until 1542 did St Ives – and Towednack – secure the right to a cemetery of its own.

The church at Launcells at the other end of the county is typically English rather than Cornish, light and airy with slender shafts and big Perpendicular windows. Fixed pews were rare until the late Middle Ages, and the special pride of Launcells is its fifteenth-century bench ends carved with symbols of the Passion: a table with flagon and loaves for the Last Supper, or two feet disappearing into a cloud symbolising the Ascension.

Near the middle of the county on the wooded southern slopes of Bodmin Moor is St Neot church, half Cornish, half English in design and feeling, with granite battlements on its porch and aisles, and pinnacles on its buttresses. Almost entirely of the fifteenth century, it is the only church in Cornwall – indeed apart

9(a). St Neot. St Neot church.

9(b). The Death of Adam. St Neot church.

from Fairford in Gloucestershire the only parish church in England – which retains the greater part of its stained glass, the storied windows that were the visual counterpart of the principal episodes in the Bible and the lives of the saints. It was an art that came to an end with the Renaissance when medieval conventions were ignored, moreover an art so vulnerable that it was almost entirely destroyed by the fanatical Protestants of the Reformation and the Puritans of the Commonwealth. But here in the windows of St Neot we may still see the story of the Creation, and the story of Noah, from his building of the Ark – a beautiful fifteenth-century ship, modelled perhaps after the *Christopher* (captain, John Treffry) or *Gabriel* of Fowey – to his so regrettable drunkenness. Then there is the moral story of the felicitous and comfortable life of St Neot, whose very fish were miraculously caught, grilled and served to him in bed, a fine foil to the misfortunes of St George, who was himself grilled before his final gruesome tortures and martyrdom. And again, there is the first episode of the Legend of the Rood: Seth placing three seeds from the fatal Tree of Knowledge in the mouth of his father Adam as he lies dying in his four-poster.

This episode was taken from the Cornish miracle plays. The Cornish tongue was still spoken by the great majority of people, a musical language resembling the Welsh but even more like that of the Bretons, so many of whom were resident in the coastal towns. There had been a time when Cornish kings were patrons of poets and encouraged the writing of ballads and romances such as the original story of Tristan and Iseult, and even as late as the fourteenth century an unknown poet had written the long *Pascon agan Arluth*, the *Passion of Our Lord*. By the fifteenth century, however, the upper and educated classes spoke and read English, and as the great mass of Cornish speakers were unable to read there was no more incentive to write in the native language than there was to perpetuate its literature with the printing press, the newfangled device that came in with the Tudors.

There was, however, one immensely important form of literature that was an exception. Plays are written primarily to be seen and heard, not to be read, and when performed can be understood and appreciated by an illiterate audience as easily as by a literate one. Moreover they can be used as a vehicle of instruction and exhortation. In the Middle Ages, therefore, the Cornish clergy wrote plays about the lives of their innumerable saints for the edification of their parishioners, who were no doubt to perform them. Only one of these has survived, the fifteenth-century *Bewnans Meriasek*, or *Life of Meriasek*, the patron saint of Camborne, incidentally the only extant saint's play in the literature of our country. It begins delightfully with a picture of a genial pre-Reformation Cornish priest, much given to drink, teaching small boys their alphabet and Latin:

> *Master.* Come sit down nicely,
> Meriasek, among the children,
> And look at your books,
> Or recite a short piece;
> There will be some delay in teaching you,
> But the fees are not much.

> *First Scholar.* 'God speed': A, B, C;
> At the end of the verse that one is D;
> I don't know any more in the book.
> I have only been in the school
> Since late last night.
> After breakfast I will learn more
> As well as I can, my master.

> *Second Scholar.* E, S, T, that is 'est';
> What's next I don't quite know.
> Master, don't beat me,
> For I shall be none the better:
> If only I could have breakfast
> I should improve.

More ambitious are the three long plays of *The Origin of the World*, *The Passion of Our Lord* and *The Resurrection*, collectively known as the *Ordinalia*, a Cornish cycle comparable to the English cycles of

York, Wakefield, Coventry and Chester. They were written in the fourteenth century, almost certainly by one or more members of Glasney College, for Penryn and its neighbourhood are frequently mentioned, as when Solomon gives his masons the parish of Budock and the Seal Rock 'with its territory', a joke that would be relished by the local audience, for the rock is a barren and dangerous crag in the middle of the harbour entrance. Throughout the three plays runs the beautiful Legend of the Rood, one episode from which is depicted in the glass of St Neot church. The three seeds that Seth places in Adam's mouth grow into the tree that becomes the king post of Solomon's Temple and the cross on which Jesus suffers his martyrdom. More than a hundred years after the writing of the *Ordinalia* another version of *The Creation* was made, the *Gwryans an Bys*, remarkable for its lengthy and illuminating stage directions in English.

The Cornish miracle plays compare very favourably with the English ones, and are particularly interesting because of the uniqueness of much of their material. There are moments of real dramatic intensity, as when Adam, old and weary of life, sends Seth to Paradise to ask the watchful angel when he is to be released, and if God will pardon him at the end. Then there is the episode of the Three Marys looking for the risen Christ, or again the lyrical lovemaking of David and Bathsheba – one thinks of the scandalous goings-on at Glasney at this time:

Damsel, er dha jentylys,
dysqua dhym a'th kerensa ...

Lady, in thy gentleness,
I beseech thee, love me;
Never have I seen a woman
Pleases me above thee;
Thou shalt have my palaces,
All my halls and chambers;
Be my love and live with me,
And I thy lover ever.

But although the object of the plays was to instruct and their themes were essentially serious, they were very sensibly garnished with plenty of comedy and horseplay to make the matter savoury. In *Meriasek* our old friend Teudar, maker of martyrs, becomes a figure of fun as the Mohammedan Emperor of Cornwall. After being worsted in argument by the saint, the Moslem heavily defeated by the Christian, he calls for his executioners – stock comic characters and clearly the great favourites of the audience – who fail to hear him and are soundly beaten for their indolence. The prompter's notes give us some idea of the dumbshows and noise of the entertainments: 'here the dragon aredy in the place … her a gon in the dragon ys mouthe aredy and fyr … sum of the soudrys [soldiers] y-swolwyd'. And nobody could complain that the opening of *The Creation* was without incident: 'Let them fight with swordes, and in the end Lucyfer voydeth & goeth downe to hell, apariled fowle with fyre about him burning, and every degree of devylls of lether & spirytis on cordis runing into the playne'. It is crude, childish stuff, but then the unsophisticated men and women of the Middle Ages were in many ways little more than children, ignorant, credulous and emotionally unstable, at one moment thrilled into religious ecstasy, the next revelling in farce, bawdiness and brutality.

They must have looked forward eagerly to the performance of these plays on festival days and flocked to the open-air theatres, the 'rounds' of western Cornwall, like those remaining at St Just and Perranzabuloe, circular banks of earth on which they stood about the playing place or *plen-an-gwary*. There on the east side they would see the main stage with the hut of Heaven and throne of God approached by steps, and on the north the mouth of Hell belching fire from its working jaws. In the middle would be one of the main localities in the play, Meriasek's chapel perhaps, and round the sides the tents where the principal characters remained until called upon to perform. Under a blue sky it would be the gayest of scenes – white canvas, coloured flags and costumes – a place in which to chatter and drink until the trumpets sounded from Heaven, the celestial doors opened, and God appeared enveloped in a linen cloud to create the world.

The long cycle of the *Ordinalia*, extending over three days, would be performed during some major religious festival and general holiday such as Whitsuntide, and in a great *plen-an-gwary* like Perran Round, which is some fifty yards across, but *Meriasek* was played on the saint's day in a smaller local round, as were all the other long-lost plays written by parsons about the saints of their particular parishes. These saints' feasts were also celebrated

10. Perran Round.

with hurling matches between neighbouring parishes, a game not unlike lacrosse in which a silver ball was hurled from hand to hand, the goals in the unenclosed parts of the western hundreds, as between St Ives and Newlyn, often being separated by miles of the wildest moorland. Or again there was wrestling, for which the Cornishmen were famous: they fought at Agincourt, it will be remembered, under their banner of two wrestlers, and Henry VIII, himself a great wrestler, ordered a number of them to attend a sporting festival at Calais.

The life of the medieval peasant was one of labour within the limits of his parish, and very few of those in Cornwall would ever cross the Tamar into England, but because his life was so confined he was much more aware of the passage of the months and sensitive to the rhythm of the year than we are today, and every so often found emotional release as well as physical refreshment in unrestrained celebration of the seasons in the pagan rites of his prehistoric ancestors, which the Church had so wisely transformed into Christian festivals.

May Day and the coming of summer was, as it still is, celebrated at Padstow by the parade of a hobby horse with snapping jaws, a fearsome beast the mere sight of which is said to have repelled a French raid during the Hundred Years War. The main Helston revels were a week later on one of the festivals of St Michael its patron saint, Furry Day or feast holiday, and took the form of dancing through the streets, first by the gentry and then more boisterously by the burgesses, their servants and the peasants. At midsummer came the pagan festival of bonfires, their lighting on the hilltops and the leaping over them beside the ancient quoits and citadels. In the autumn, harvest suppers were preceded by the ceremony of crying the neck, when the last sheaf of gathered corn was the neck by which the corn spirit was caught to the cry of 'A neck, a neck, a neck; we have'n, we have'n, we have'n'. Christmas brought feasting, wassailing, guise dancing and the mummers' play of St George, pre-Christian in origin, symbolising the defeat of winter and miraculous revival of nature, the approach of spring. Thus with the year seasons returned, their rhythm woven harmoniously into the broader rhythm of human life, as one generation succeeded another and the level of the soil rose slowly round the walls of the waiting churches.

A History Of Cornwall

VIII

The Tudors
1485 – 1603

When, in 1485, Henry VII seized the crown, almost literally, from Richard III at Bosworth, the fortunes of his western followers were assured. The Courtenays were restored, Edward Courtenay of Boconnoc becoming the new Earl of Devon; Sir Thomas Arundell got back the estates that had gone to Sir James Tyrrel, and the Treffry brothers, John (knighted at Milford Haven) and William, received far more than they had lost. Richard Edgcumbe was knighted after Bosworth, and it was now his turn to chase the man who had hunted him through the woods at Cotehele. The story goes that Bodrugan escaped by jumping over the cliff near his home, still known as Bodrugan's Leap, and found refuge abroad. Anyway, escape he did, leaving his broad manors to be occupied by his old rival. Sir Richard served the new king well. After successful missions to Scotland and Ireland – sailing from Mount's Bay in June 1488 and returning by way of St Ives six weeks later – he was sent to Brittany, where he concluded a highly advantageous treaty before dying there in September 1489. He was buried in the church at Morlaix, and succeeded at Cotehele by his son Peter.

By this time Cornwall had a Duke again, the three-year-old Prince Arthur, who, thanks partly to the diplomatic skill of another Cornishman, Sir Richard Nanfan, was betrothed to the little Katharine of Aragon. Yet all was not well in the Duchy.

The tinners were depressed and discontented – a number of them raided Peter Edgcumbe's tin works at Tremodret – and then came the exactions levied to pay for a war against the Scots. For the people of Cornwall nothing could have been more remote than forays on the Scottish border, and nothing better calculated to infuriate the impoverished tinners, most of them in debt and entangled by usurers, than being taxed, and taxed heavily, to repel them. When, therefore, in 1497, the collectors began their exactions in the west they met with a sullen resistance, particularly at St Keverne near the Lizard, where the blacksmith Michael Joseph assumed the leadership of the people; and passive resistance was fanned into active revolt when Thomas Flamank, an eloquent Bodmin lawyer, voiced the popular discontent, and bands of men began to talk of marching to London to rid the king of his evil advisers.

Thus began, so many centuries after their conquest, the first Cornish incursion into England (Columbus was in America, Cabot in Newfoundland and Vasco da Gama on his way to India). In the long days of early summer the ill-armed Cornishmen marched through Devon and Somerset, picking up recruits on the way, until they reached Wells, where they were joined by Lord Audley, who now took over the command. By the beginning of June they were south of London in high hopes of being joined by the men of Kent. They were disappointed, however, and the fainter-hearted rebels began to slink away. And well they might, for Henry had an army of ten thousand men under Lord Daubeney ready to set out for Scotland, and this was the force that confronted the Cornishmen when they reached Blackheath on June 16th. Many of them counselled surrender, but their leaders had not marched to London to throw themselves on the king's mercy, and prepared for battle. That night there were more desertions. The next day, a Saturday, the rebels, armed only with bows, bills and other country weapons, were surrounded. The royal forces advanced, and the ill-organised Cornishmen, though they fought bravely enough, were soon routed. About two hundred of them were killed, Audley and Flamank were captured on the field, and Joseph was taken as he fled for sanctuary at Greenwich.

After the battle King Henry rode in triumph through the City, followed by the blacksmith, 'clad in a jacket of white and green of the King's colours, and held as good countenance and spake as boldly to the people as he had been at his liberty'. On the following Monday he and the other leaders were examined in the Tower, and a week later condemned to death. On Tuesday, June 27th, Flamank and Joseph were dragged on hurdles from the Tower to Tyburn, where they were hanged, disembowelled and hacked into quarters according to the custom of the age. As a peer, Lord Audley was treated less barbarously. The next morning he was 'drawn from the said gaol of Newgate unto the Tower Hill with a coat-armour upon him all to-torn, and there his head stricken off'.

The calamitous outcome of their insurrection only increased the resentment of the Cornish people and prepared them to seize any pretext for further revolt. It was not long in coming. Had they realised it, the indirect cause of their troubles was Perkin Warbeck, whose claim to be the younger of the two princes murdered in the Tower, and therefore rightful King of England, was supported by the Scots whose king had given him his cousin in marriage. When Warbeck heard that the Cornishmen were marching on London, he left Scotland with his wife and a few supporters, after an adventurous passage by way of Ireland arriving at Whitesand Bay near the Land's End on September 7th. He was rapturously received and, having left his wife with the monks of St Michael's Mount, advanced to Bodmin where he was joined by some of the lesser gentry and proclaimed Richard IV. With a force of about six thousand men he crossed the Tamar at Launceston just three months after Joseph and Flamank, and on September 17th appeared before the walls of Exeter. The city had been reinforced by the greater gentry under the Earl of Devon, yet the Cornishmen, without any guns or siege engines, broke down the eastern gate and fought their way into the narrow streets. Here, however, they were met by the Earl and his men, who, after desperate fighting, succeeded in driving them back outside the walls. The next day the rebels made another assault but were repulsed by the defenders' guns, and the dispirited rabble, depleted by desertion, struggled on towards Taunton.

By this time the king's forces under Daubeney were approaching Taunton, and there the courage of the wretched Warbeck failed him. After a show of preparing for battle he slipped away by night with a few of his men and, failing to reach the coast, took refuge at Beaulieu Abbey near Southampton. The Cornishmen were as infuriated as they were bewildered by the flight of their leader, whom they would gladly have torn to pieces had they caught him, and it was unfortunate for the Provost of Glasney that he should have fallen into their hands at this critical moment. He was one of the most conscientious collectors of the king's taxes, and there in the market place at Taunton they 'slew him piteously, in such wise that he was dismembered and cut in many and sundry pieces'.

When Henry arrived the remaining rebels surrendered, 'holding up their hands in asking mercy'. But the cautious king was not to be hurried. With his prisoners, among whom by now was Warbeck, he moved to Exeter where he stayed a month 'to order the parts of Cornwall'. This he did thoroughly after his fashion. Commissioners were sent into the west and in each parish somebody, often the parson, was made responsible for raising the fine levied as the price of rebellion, and altogether Henry managed to squeeze more than £600 out of the county, an enormous sum from such an impoverished region. For Henry the collection of money was much sweeter than the squandering of blood and most of the rebels were pardoned, only a few of their leaders being executed. Warbeck was spared, and his wife escorted with all courtesy from St Michael's Mount to Exeter, where Henry made the impostor confess that so far from being Richard, son of Edward IV, he was Perkin, son of a poor boatman of Tournai. For a time he was kept at Court, an object of wonder and derision, and hanged two years later when involved in another conspiracy.

So, because of the intrigues of a plausible young Fleming, Cornwall lay crushed and impoverished under the Tudor heel. We catch a glimpse of the far west at this period in a letter written by the Venetian ambassador to Castile when he with Philip I and his queen were held up at Falmouth by bad weather early in 1506: 'We are in a very wild place which no human being ever visits', he wrote, 'in the midst of a most barbarous race, so different in language and custom from the Londoners and the rest of England that they are as unintelligible to these last as to the Venetians.'

The barbarous and unintelligible race now had another Duke. In 1501 Prince Arthur had married Princess Katharine of Aragon, but six months later suddenly sickened and died, leaving his younger brother Henry heir to the throne. According to the original charter the Duchy of Cornwall should have reverted to the Crown, as the dukedom was limited to the eldest son of the king. A little characteristic Tudor pressure, however, persuaded the lawyers that Edward III had really meant 'the eldest surviving son', and Prince Henry succeeded his brother. Arthur was buried hugger-mugger in Worcester Cathedral and quickly forgotten, a special dispensation was obtained from the Pope, and Henry, aged eleven, was betrothed to his brother's young widow. A few years later, in 1509, the old king died and the momentous reign of Henry VIII began.

It began with a war against France, or rather with two wars. Cornishmen under Sir John Arundell and Sir Peter Edgcumbe were in the army that won the Battle of the Spurs, and the athletic Sir William Trevanion of Carhays, the king's companion, commanded one of the royal ships. There were repeated threats of invasion, taxation was heavy, and while the Cornish miners in France were semi-mutinous their companions at home rioted against fresh exactions. However, peace was made in 1525, and after the fall of Wolsey four years later Henry prepared for his struggle with the Pope, who had refused to grant him a divorce from Katharine. The Reformation Parliament called in 1529 was prepared, eager even, to support him, and in 1534 passed an Act of Supremacy making the king supreme head of the Church of England. The Pope replied by excommunicating Henry, and Henry again by the suppression of the smaller monasteries, three hundred and seventy-six of those with incomes under £200 being condemned by Act of Parliament in 1536. The dissolution was delayed by the protests in the north, culminating in the Pilgrimage of Grace, but was resumed after the crushing of the rebellion early in 1537. The king's main instrument in this expropriation was Thomas Cromwell, and during the next three years the richer monasteries met their fate as one by one they were bullied into surrendering their property.

There is no evidence to show that Cornish monasteries were any more corrupt than those elsewhere. Institutions that had grown up in response to an age that had passed, they were now stranded anachronisms that had long since lost their original ideals, and, obsolete as the feudal system, parasites clinging to, feeding on and encumbering the age of renaissance and nationalism, the time had come to shake them off. The little Benedictine priory of Tywardreath was one of the first to go – by the Act of 1536, its income being only £123 – and perhaps its condition was the worst of all. What that condition was is suggested by the injunctions of Bishop Veysey a few years before to the bibulous old Prior Collins and the other six monks of the house. They were to say matins shortly after midnight as their rules demanded; no brother was to go out alone, and all windows and doors by which women might enter were to be closed. Apparently the Benedictines of Tywardreath suffered from the same frailty as the canons of Glasney. But this was not all. The prior was still the nominal lord of the borough of Fowey, an encumbrance that his tenant Thomas Treffry was determined to get rid of. Treffry moved in the exalted circle of Cromwell himself and one day returned from London with a letter for Collins from that implacable Hammer of the Monks. There was no mincing of words. The king had heard that the town of Fowey was sore decayed owing to the lack of order and justice for which the prior was responsible, 'wherefore his Hignes thinketh that ye be veray unworthy to have rule of any towne that cannot well rule yourself'. Collins went, and shortly afterwards the priory was dissolved, the stones of its medieval walls being carried off for the secular erections of the new age.

The other Benedictine house of St Michael's Mount was more fortunate. In an age of nationalism and rivalry with the growing powers of France and Spain it was strategically too important to be demolished. The Crown kept possession until the end of the century, leasing it to the Millitons of Pengersick in consideration of their repairing the buildings and pier and maintaining five soldiers to defend it. 'Both fort and port of vaunt', wrote Carew, and because of its military and economic importance the original building remains much as it was in the Middle Ages, the only one in the county to do so.

The turn of the friaries came after the Pilgrimage of Grace. On September 20th, 1538, the Franciscans at Bodmin surrendered. The warden, two brothers and six lay-brothers seem to have been very poor – as they should have been – and had little to set against their debt of £16. Nor were the Dominicans of Truro, who surrendered two days later, in much better case; they too were in debt and their assets few. Both the houses came into the hands of the burgesses, and though the friary church at Bodmin survived until a century ago, when it was replaced by the present Assize Court, the buildings at Truro were used as a quarry and quickly disappeared, leaving only a name by the river – St Dominick Street.

Cromwell's main agent in the suppression of the western monasteries was Dr John Tregonwell, a Cornish lawyer who had done the king some service in ridding him of two of his superfluous wives, Katharine of Aragon and Anne Boleyn. In 1536 he was busy with the smaller monasteries, and it was not until after the Pilgrimage of Grace that he was able to devote his talents to the larger ones. Meanwhile Bishop Veysey at Exeter was preaching the new order: the king was to be acknowledged as Supreme Head of the Church; all Popish idolatry was to be abolished; relics and images were to be taken away; the Bible was to be set up in churches; the Paternoster, Creed and Commandments were to be taught and read in English or Cornish; births, marriages and deaths were to be registered; there were to be no more pilgrimages, and no more superstitious observations of holy days. Fortunately, and very sensibly, the king made some concessions to the Cornish, and parish feasts in honour of their Celtic saints managed to survive the iconoclasm of the Reformation.

There were three Cornish monasteries, all of Augustinian canons, which had survived the Act of 1536. None was big by

English standards, though each had an income of more than £200: Launceston Priory with £354, Bodmin with £270 and St Germans with £227. In February 1539 Tregonwell arrived at Launceston, where he found 'all things in good order', and on the 24th the prior and eight canons resigned their house to the king. At Bodmin, which surrendered three days later, there was the same number, a decrepit crew that included the 'blind and aged' Thomas Rawlyns, and Richard Luer, 'blind and of the age of 100 years'. The great days of Bodmin were over, where for a quarter of a century Thomas Vyvyan had presided autocratically, and not unprofitably, over the fortunes of the priory, in his later years combining his comparatively local office with the more extensive one of suffragan bishop, and passing his little leisure in the idyllic retreat of his manor house at Rialton, the sea on one side and his garden on the other. He died in 1533, shortly before Cromwell was appointed Vicar General and the harsh wind of the Reformation began to blow, and was buried in the priory church in a sumptuous tomb of black Catacleuse stone and grey marble, half medieval, half of the Renaissance, as befitted a princely cleric who linked the ages. Tregonwell was no sluggard, and, three days after the surrender of Bodmin, received that of St Germans from Prior Swymmer with his six canons and one novice.

The heads of the suppressed religious houses were generously compensated for their eviction. Shere of Launceston was given a pension of £100 and Swymmer of St Germans and Wandsworth of Bodmin each received one of £66 13s 4d. Perhaps they did not altogether deserve their rewards. The delay in dissolving the larger monasteries had given them time to parcel out property among their friends and relations, a patent here and an advantageous lease there. The Shere family had feathered their nests before the surrender, and Wandsworth added douceurs to the distribution of monastic possessions. He sent Cromwell a present of eight congers and promised a fee of £6 a year for life, 'trusting you will continue my good lord as you have ever done; and remember me and my brethren to the King's Commissioners at their coming into Cornwall for our poor living'. Nor did he forget his steward,

Nicholas Prideaux, who had secured his election after the death of Prior Vyvyan, so that when the king 'took his pleasure' he had plenty of grateful pensioners to support him as well as his poor living of £66 a year – some £2,000 of our money. The rank-and-file brethren were less liberally treated; most of them receiving pensions of some £6 a year with the choice of either becoming parish priests or earning their livings in some other way. Few chose to 'remain in religion', all the monks of Tywardreath, for example, opting for the licit indulgences of secular life. There appears to have been no great enthusiasm for a dedicated religious vocation.

In 1539 there was talk of creating a diocese of Cornwall with its see at one of the three big priories, whose confiscated possessions would endow it, but nothing came of the plan and the county had to wait another three centuries for a bishop of its own. The trouble was that Henry stood in urgent need of money and had to throw the monastic property on the market, to the great profit of speculators, merchants and the gentry. Much of the monastic revenue had come from tithes, compulsory payments from this parish and that, valuable securities which, in an age when land was virtually the only form of investment, were snapped up by laymen who thus came to have a considerable control over the Church. Nicholas Prideaux had already been rewarded with a very long and cheap lease of the tithes of a number of parishes, including Padstow, where his heirs were to build the splendid house overlooking the Camel estuary.

There followed the lease and sale of monastic buildings and demesnes. As early as the autumn of 1536 John Grenville had secured a lease of the Tywardreath estates, though they were soon to fall into the hands of the Protector Somerset. Carew has an amusing account of how John Champernowne got hold of St Germans: 'Now when the golden shower of the dissolved abbey lands rained wellnear into every gaper's mouth, some two or three gentlemen, the King's servants and Master Champernowne's acquaintance, waited at a door where the King was to pass forth, with purpose to beg such a matter at his hands. This while, out comes the King; they kneel down; so doth Master Champernowne;

they prefer their petition; the King grants it; they render humble thanks; and so doth Mr Champernowne. Afterwards he requireth his share; they deny it; he appeals to the King; the King avoweth his equal meaning in the largesse; whereon the overtaken companions were fain to allot him this priory for his partage.' Of course it was not really as easy as that, but the story gives us a glimpse of what was happening. Actually Henry leased St Germans to Champernowne in 1540 at a rent of £16 15s 11d. Some years later it was bought by John Eliot, a Plymouth merchant whose descendants still live in the priory whence Swymmer was evicted: Port Eliot as it was rechristened, a house remodelled in late Georgian times and standing in grounds laid out in the eighteenth century.

When the king's agent had stripped the lead from the roof of Bodmin Priory church, sold four of its great bells to the parish of Lanivet and its stones to the local builders, he found a tenant for the priory itself in Thomas Sternhold, versifier of the Psalms. Apparently he found the house, with its dovecotes, orchards and fishponds, so much to his liking that he bought it in 1545 for £100. Twenty years later his daughters, having married outside the county, sold it for £360 – a tidy profit even allowing for rising prices – to John Rashleigh, a prosperous merchant whose old house still stands in Fowey. But the Rashleighs preferred to live on the coast near their business. They built another house at Menabilly and split up the priory into a number of tenements: in 1567, for example, Robert James, a cooper, took a lease of 'a house called a Kitchen'. Two centuries later the dilapidated buildings were cleared away to make room for the present priory house.

Launceston Priory was soon stripped and demolished. After all, there were plenty of other churches in and about the town. St Mary Magdalene, indeed, had only just been finished, thanks to the generosity of Sir Henry Trecarrel, who seems to have been inspired by the lavish ornament of the new Tudor churches at Probus and Truro. The site of the priory was leased and then sold, and all that remains are fragmentary foundations by the river and a Norman doorway, now the entrance to the White Hart Hotel in the market place.

So perished the monasteries of Cornwall, and in their stead or out of their plunder the Tudor gentry and merchants, who thereby gentled their condition, built their new houses or enlarged their old ones: Port Eliot, Place at Fowey, Menabilly, 'Master Chamond's house and place of Launcells', Trerice, Mount Edgcumbe, Godolphin and Lanherne. The Reformation was a social as well as an ecclesiastical revolution: by the redistribution of tithes and monastic estates the clergy were brought low and the gentry and pushing middle classes exalted.

The dissolution of the monasteries coincided with another redistribution of property within the county. The son of Edward Courtenay of Boconnoc, Earl of Devon, had, like Henry VII, married a daughter of Edward IV, so that his heir, created Marquis of Exeter in 1525, was a first cousin of Henry VIII with a possible claim to the throne. It was dangerous to be a cousin to the king, particularly a Yorkist cousin, at a time when Henry was trying to beget a legitimate male heir, and wife succeeded wife almost annually. In 1538 the Marquis was arrested on a trumped-up charge of treason and executed. All his estates fell into the king's hands, including some fifteen manors in Cornwall, very conveniently as it happened, for Jane Seymour had just presented him with a son, the future Edward VI, and Cornwall had a Duke again. Henry took the opportunity to consolidate the Duchy estates, adding to them the forfeited Courtenay inheritance and another fifteen manors of which the monasteries of Tywardreath and Launceston had been relieved. Until this time most of the Duchy estates had been in the east, but many of the new ones were in the centre of the county and even farther west, the Isles of Scilly themselves becoming Duchy property. In the second half of the century when there was no Duke the direct power of the Crown was greatly increased, and it is significant that this was the period when Parliamentary representation rose to the astonishing number of forty-four members.

Henry, professing to sniff the odour of incipient rebellion in the so-called 'Exeter Conspiracy', still further strengthened his grip on the west country. In 1539 he set up a Council of the West, similar to the Council of the North after the Pilgrimage of Grace, with Sir John Russell as its Lord President. It was not necessary, and it did not last long, for the people of Cornwall had no intention of making a Perkin Warbeck out of the Marquis of Exeter, though they were perhaps a trifle uneasy about the changes that were taking place in their churches.

Fortunately we have a first-hand account of Cornwall at this critical period when the old order was going down before the new. Between 1534 and 1542 the young scholar John Leland, the King's Librarian, made a tour of England in search of records and other relics of antiquity, and having finished his travels proposed to write a survey of the country. He did not live to do so, but his notes remain. Let us follow him through Cornwall after his crossing of the Tamar by New Bridge some time in 1538.

He passed the priory, 'by a fair wood side' beside the little river Kensey, climbed the steep hill up to Launceston and, entering the gate in its wall, was much impressed by the castle, even in its half-ruinous condition one of the strongest that he had ever seen. West of the town the country was enclosed, with some woods and good corn land, but it soon gave way to marsh and moor with scarcely a tree, though there was more enclosure near Boscastle, 'a very filthy Toun and il kept'. Two miles farther down the wild coast he came to Bossiney, which, judging from the ruins of numerous houses, had been 'a bygge thing for a Fischar Town'. Sheep were grazing in the donjon of Tintagel Castle, but the drawbridge still linked the outer wards to the 'high terrible cragge environid with the Se'. Leland was a man of the new age, and yet, 'it hath beene a large thinge', he mused as he remembered its history. After visiting Port Isaac and Portquin he turned inland to call on Master Carnsew at Bokelly, 'a praty House, fair Ground, and praty Wood about it', an oasis in this treeless country. Thence by good corn ground, though still unwooded, to Wadebridge, where he crossed the seventeen arches of the great bridge built at about the time of Bosworth, the piers sunk on a foundation of woolsacks, or so he was told. Padstow was only a few miles down the estuary, 'a good quick

Fischar Town, but onclenly kept', perhaps because it was so full of Irishmen. It did a brisk trade with Brittany, many small Breton ships bringing their country's produce and returning with Cornish fish.

Retracing his steps to Wadebridge, he rode into the long street of Bodmin, filled like a fairground every Saturday when the market was held. It must have been a lovely little town, still dominated by the old monastic buildings at its sheltered eastern end: the great parish church, rebuilt less than a century before, the doomed priory close by, flanked by the house of the Greyfriars. 'The Shrine and Tumbe of S. Petrok' still stood at the east end of the priory church, and Prior Vyvyan lay 'before the High Altare in a High Tumbe of a very Darkesche gray Marble'.

From Bodmin he rode along the miry highway, wondering that there was no castle to be seen on Castle-an-Dinas, through Michell, 'a poore thorougfare' and no wood, to St Allen and Gwarneck, a manor of the Arundells of Trerice, where there was good arable and pasture. Apparently he met Sir John Arundell, knighted with Peter Edgcumbe after the Battle of the Spurs, whose son was to make Trerice into the loveliest of Elizabethan houses and become the father-in-law of Richard Carew.

And so to the tin-working region of the far west. Not very long ago, he was told, good tall ships used to sail up the Hayle river as far as St Erth, but now the haven was choked with sand brought down from the tin works. Sand, though this time blown from beaches, was also the curse of St Ives, for in the course of the last twenty years most of the houses, and even the little pier, had been 'sore oppressid or overcoverid with Sandes that the stormy Windes and Rages castith up there'. It is still a problem four centuries later. On the headland near the Chapel of St Nicholas, was 'a Pharos for Lighte for Shippes sailing by Night in those Quarters'. From St Ives he rode along the north coast to St Just and the Land's End, then back by St Buryan, whose dean and prebendaries 'almost be never ther', to Mousehole, 'a praty Fyschar Town'. He noted piers at Newlyn, Penzance and St Michael's Mount, where were also 'howses with shoppes for fyschermen', and perhaps it was from one of these little ports that he sailed for the Isles of Scilly, if sail he did, for there is an uncommon flavour of hearsay in his account of St Mary's, where the ground is so fertile that 'if a Man do but cast corn wher Hogges have rotid it wyl cum up'. We can forgive him for faltering at this passage beyond the Land's End, particularly when he heard that 'few Men be glad to inhabite these Islettes for al their Plenty' (a false note, surely) because of the French and Spanish pirates who carry off their cattle.

From Penwith he returned along the south coast, first calling on Sir William Godolphin, whose tin works were the greatest in all Cornwall. At Cromwell's request Sir William had just sent some of his expert blowers to London, apologising for their lack of English and need of an interpreter. No doubt they came from the blowing house that his younger son, Thomas, had recently made in a neighbouring valley. Helston he found to be a good market town with a mayor and privileges, and coinage twice a year. He called at Merthen on the Helford river, where 'Mr Reskymer hath a Ruinus Maner Place and a fair Park well woddid', and so to Arwennack, the Killigrew house on the brim of Falmouth haven. As the Killigrews owned most of the land round Falmouth they were understandably interested in the development of the little port – at the expense of its rivals farther up the estuary, Penryn and Truro. Their chance had come shortly before Leland's visit, when France and Spain were still at war. In 1537 a Spanish fleet put in to the haven, where it was attacked by French men-of-war. The French had the worst of it and were chased up the river almost as far as Truro, despite the protests of Sir John Arundell, who wrote to the king suggesting that blockhouses should be built at the mouth of the haven, 'else we shall have more of this business'. They did, for a few months later there was a hot encounter with the French in Mount's Bay, and it was hastily decided to build a fort on either side of the entrance to the Fal, at Pendennis Point and St Mawes. This was most satisfactory to John Killigrew, who owned Pendennis, and naturally became its first governor. No doubt he showed Leland round the proposed site on the peninsula, 'a Mile in Cumpace' and 'almost environid with the Se'. Penryn was already defended by stakes and a chain across the creek, at the end of which Glasney College was 'strongly wallid and incastellatid, have 3 strong Towers and Gunnes' – enough to repel the local doxies if not a foreign invasion.

Rivers fascinated Leland, and somehow he managed to make his way round the difficult country of the Fal, north to Truro, where the old castle was now clean down and the site used for 'a shoting and playing Place', then south to St Mawes, where the new castle, designed after the latest clover-leaf plan, was being built. And when, after passing through St Austell, notable for nothing but its church, and Tywardreath, whose priory was not yet down, he came to Fowey, 'walled defensably to the se cost', he found the man who was engaged in the building, and angling (successfully) for the captaincy, of the 'fortlet' at St Mawes. This was Thomas Treffry, with whom he stayed at Place, 'the Glorie of the Town', and for whom he wrote Latin inscriptions in praise of King Henry and the Duke of Cornwall, which were to be cut in the stone of the bastions at St Mawes.

Leland now made the circuit of the Fowey, which, like the Fal, he noted with satisfaction, was well wooded. He could find no trace of a castle at Castle Dore. The keep of Restormel was still standing, much as it does today, but the base court was 'sore defacid', the late thirteenth-century chapel unroofed, and there were tin works in the park. And Leland ventured a prophecy. Though barges with merchandise could still come within half a mile of Lostwithiel, the bridge was almost blocked with waste; 'the Sande that cummith from Tynne Workes is a great Cause of this: and yn tyme to cum shaul be a sore Decay to the hole Haven of Fawey'. At Polruan was a strong tower matching the blockhouse designed and partly paid for by Treffry at Fowey, but the chain that had once been slung across the river was now only a memory.

It is clear that Leland felt happier in the more English countryside of south-eastern Cornwall than in the wild north and west, and he became almost lyrical – and well he might – as he rode through the delectable lands of Celtic King Mark and Tudor Boconnoc towards Liskeard, 'by very pleasaunt inclosid Ground prately wooddid, plentiful of Corn and Grasse'. And Liskeard itself he saw in the same rosy light, standing on rocky hills, the best market town in Cornwall, saving Bodmin. The site of the castle overlooking the town was 'magnificent' – a rare burst of enthusiasm – though nothing but fragments of the walls remained. It was an easy ride to St Germans, a poor fisher town whose glory was the priory, on which John Champernowne already had an eye. And so along the northern bank of the Lynher, on the opposite shore of which lived the Carews, past the ruins of Trematon Castle to the ferry at Saltash. There, perhaps with a sigh of relief at leaving this outlandish western region, Leland crossed the Tamar and rode towards Plymouth.

Three years later England, in alliance with the Emperor, was again at war with France. In 1544 Henry laid siege to Boulogne, which, thanks largely to the younger Sir William Godolphin and a contingent of Cornish miners, was taken in September, a few days before the Emperor made peace, leaving England to carry on the war alone. The position was dangerous, invasion was expected at any moment, trenches were dug along the southern coast of Cornwall, and a fleet collected at Southampton. In the summer the French tried to force their way into the Solent, but after some inconclusive engagements an outbreak of plague drove them back to their own shores. It was at this time, on July 19th, 1545, that one of the biggest of Henry's ships, the *Mary Rose*, heeled over in a sudden squall and sank. Most of the five hundred men on board were drowned, among them her young captain, Roger Grenville of Stowe, who left behind him a little boy of three, Richard.

Peace was made in 1546, though this did not stop the profitable disorder in the Channel, the privateering and piracy of adventurers like William Hawkins and John Eliot of Plymouth, and John Killigrew of Arwennack. Six months later the blood-intoxicated Henry died and was succeeded by his son Edward VI, a sickly boy of nine.

The young king's uncle, the Duke of Somerset, became Protector. A liberal-minded Protestant and optimistic doctrinaire, he was

quite incapable of appreciating the complexities that faced him
and the delicacy with which he would have to tread in pursuit
of his aims. His inheritance was a formidable one. The treasury
was empty; prices were soaring owing to Henry's debasement
of the currency; trade was in confusion, and the acquisition of
monastic lands by the gentry had intensified the enclosure
movement and consequent unemployment and distress of the
peasants. In Cornwall, however, the discontent was mainly due
to the newfangled religion that the distant London government
was foisting on them. For the Cornish, particularly the purer
Cornish-speaking Celts of the west, were now as fanatically
attached to the Roman Church as they had been bitterly
opposed to it a few centuries before. Superstitious and therefore
conservative, they feared change and the unknown – with some
justice perhaps in Tudor times.

The Church had not yet been relieved of all its superfluous
wealth; the monasteries had gone, but chantries, religious gilds
and collegiate churches remained, and the needy government
sent out its commissioners to value the potential plunder. Much
the biggest of the Cornish collegiate foundations was Glasney,
with a provost, twelve prebendaries, ten priests, four choristers, a
bell-ringer and an income of £220 a year. It was not difficult to
find witnesses who were ready to swear that the buildings had
been neglected, and that the provost and his priests were more
given to drinking and the chase than to religion. In spite of
the attempt of the local gentry to retain the place as a fortress, the
church was stripped of its lead, bells and plate, the buildings were
sold, and soon there was little trace of where the three-centuries-
old college had stood. Crantock and the other collegiate houses
were dissolved and their lands seized by the Crown, though most
of their churches were spared, and St Buryan remained a deanery
for another three centuries.

But the Cornish people were less disturbed by what happened
to monasteries and colleges than by the changes in their parish
churches. In 1548 orders were issued that festivals were no longer
to be celebrated with such Popish paraphernalia as candles, ashes
and palms, there was to be no more making of holy bread

197

and holy water, and all images were to be removed. Busy in the overseeing of all this was William Body, who had leased the archdeaconry of Cornwall from an illegitimate son of Wolsey; an overbusy Body, for while he was happily destroying the images in Helston church a mob of a thousand men assembled, led by Martin Geoffrey, a priest of St Keverne – ominous name – and William and John Kilter of Constantine. The miserable Body took refuge in a house, but was dragged into the street and stabbed to death. The western justices could do nothing, but help soon came from the eastern gentry and the incipient revolt was crushed. Geoffrey was hacked into quarters in London, as were William Kilter and Pascoe Trevian, the actual killers, or so it was said, at Launceston. Several others suffered the same fate, and one nameless quarter was set up in Tavistock to remind the men of Devon of the dangers of rebellion.

There was need to remind them. In January 1549, Parliament passed an Act of Uniformity enforcing the use of a Book of Common Prayer, a simplified form of service in English instead of the old Latin Mass to which the people had been accustomed for centuries. The Prayer Book was first used on Whitsunday. The next day the outraged villagers of Sampford Courtenay in Devon made their priest put on his vestments and say Mass. The movement spread, and within a few days the Cornish parishioners were also demanding their Masses. Bodmin, as it had been in the time of Flamank and Warbeck, was the natural centre of resistance, and there the insurgents gathered under the leadership of the mayor, Henry Bray, and two staunch Catholic landowners, Humphry Arundell of Helland and John Winslade of Tregarrick. Many of the gentry with their families sought protection in the old castles. Some shut themselves in St Michael's Mount where the rebels (Carew calls them 'rakehells') besieged them, and a bewildering smoke-screen made of burning trusses of hay, combined with a shortage of food and the women's distress, forced them to surrender, fortunately without casualties. Sir Richard Grenville, former Marshal of Calais, the greatest man in Cornwall and father of Roger Grenville of the *Mary Rose*, found refuge in ruinous Trematon. Deserted by many of his followers, the unwieldy old man was enticed outside to parley. There he was seized, the castle surprised, the ladies stripped of their finery, and the men, including Sir Richard, bundled into Launceston gaol. Then the insurgents crossed the Tamar into Devonshire.

Meanwhile Somerset had sent Sir Peter Carew and his brother, Sir Gawen, to treat with the Devonshire rebels assembled at Crediton until Lord Russell could muster a sufficient force to cope with the rising. But the Carews were representatives of the very thing against which the people had risen, gentry who had profited from the spoliation of the Catholic Church with everything to gain by forcing through the Protestant Reformation, and their interference merely inflamed the rebels further. They chased the gentry out of the neighbourhood, imprisoning those whom they caught, and entrenched themselves behind the little river Clyst, four miles east of Exeter. At the end of June the Cornishmen arrived, and the combined forces closed on Exeter in the hope that the city would join them. But although they had many sympathisers within the walls, perhaps a majority, the mayor and corporation, very prudently remembering the fate of the 1497 rebellions, refused to open their gates, and a five weeks' siege began.

It was now that the rebels finally formulated the demands they sent to the government. The old Latin service was to be restored with all the ritual to which they had been accustomed, for, they added, somewhat illogically one would have thought, 'we will not receive the new service because it is but like a Christmas game'. The Cornishmen were on surer ground when they complained that they could not understand the new Prayer Book, 'and so we Cornishmen, whereof certain of us understand no English, utterly refuse this new English': And yet how many of those wretched peasants and tinners understood the old Latin? Finally, there were two significant demands directed against the gentry. Their servants were to be limited according to their income, and they were to restore half the monastic lands that had fallen to their lot. Probably very few of the gentry cared a straw whether the church service was in English or Latin and communion in one kind or two, but they were stirred to the bottom of their purses by the suggestion that they should restore the plundered property of the Church, and against those closed Protestant ranks the Catholic peasantry of the west had not a chance.

Yet it was a near thing in July. At the beginning of the month Russell had arrived at Honiton, only fifteen miles east of Exeter, though he dared not attack until the promised reinforcements of Italian and German troops arrived – the final humiliation of any government, to use foreign mercenaries against its own countrymen. And Exeter could not hold out much longer. The siege had lasted nearly a month, and the citizens, reduced to making bread out of the bran they normally fed to pigs, were on the verge of surrender. However, the rebels could not afford to wait until Russell was reinforced, and advanced to Fenny Bridges, within two miles of Honiton, to attack him. But Russell was too clever for them, surprising their main body in the marshy meadows, where they were saved only by the arrival of another band of Cornishmen. 'The fight for the time was very sharp and cruel,' wrote John Hooker, the Exeter historian, 'for the Cornishmen were very lusty and fresh and fully bent to fight out the matter.' They were thrown back, however, though Russell dared not pursue them far with hostile country behind him.

A few days later his mercenaries arrived under Lord Grey, and he was able to take the offensive. On August 3rd he left Honiton, striking across country along the ridge that runs south-west to Woodbury. The next day his troops forced the passage of the river at Clyst St Mary, where, after an alarm, he gave the order to kill all the prisoners they had taken. The final engagement came on the 5th. The rebels were outmanoeuvred and surrounded, 'and great was the slaughter and cruel was the fight, and such was the valour and stoutness of these men that the Lord Grey reported himself that he never in all the wars that he had been did know the like'.

The rebels fled, though not in utter disorder. The Devonshire men went north up the valley of the Exe, where they were overtaken and cut to pieces by Sir Gawen Carew, who left the corpses of their leaders 'hanging and tottering – as you know the wind will wave a man –' on gibbets from Dunster to Bath. For ten days Russell remained in rejoicing Exeter, where, encouraged by the liberated gentry, he dealt out justice to the rebel leaders in his hands. One of them was the vicar of St Thomas's, just outside the walls on the west bank of the Exe. He was hanged on a gallows from the top of his church tower, 'having,' wrote the good Protestant, Hooker, 'a holy-water bucket, a sprinkle, a sacring bell, a pair of beads and such other like popish trash hanged about him'.

Then came the news that the Cornishmen under Arundell had re-formed and taken up a position at Sampford Courtenay, the little village some fifteen miles north-west of Exeter, where the revolt had begun. Russell advanced with his troops, now reinforced with a strong contingent of Welshmen, and after a desperate fight stormed the village on the evening of August 17th. The rebels were finally broken, though most of them escaped in the dusk, including Arundell, who fled to Launceston. There he was captured and taken to London with Winslade, who had been caught at Bodmin. That winter, with two of their Devonshire comrades, they were hanged and dismembered at Tyburn. Sir Gawen Carew got all Arundell's estates, and Sir Peter all Winslade's, save Tregarrick and other Cornish manors that he had made over to his wife. She married again, and her husband, John Trevanion, made sure that her son William never came into his father's estates. He sold them to the Bullers and Mohuns and Trelawnys, and William Winslade, an impoverished Catholic exile, 'led a walking life with his harp to gentlemen's houses, wherethrough, and by his other active qualities, he was entitled Sir Tristram; neither wanted he (as some say) a belle Isoud, the more aptly to resemble his pattern'. Russell got the Earldom of Bedford and another vast grant of lands, including Boconnoc. It paid to be Protestant in the reign of Edward VI.

Russell had left the agreeable task of finally settling scores with the Cornish to Sir Anthony Kingston. A number of priests were hanged, including Richard Bennet, vicar of St Veep, who had previously been accused, strangely enough by John Winslade, of secretly harbouring a harlot in his house for ten years or more, and then murdering and burying her under the seats in his church. Perhaps Bennet received, obliquely, his reward. But even Richard Carew, no sympathiser with the rakehells, had to admit that Kingston 'left his name more memorable than commendable amongst the townsmen [of Bodmin], for causing their mayor to erect a gallows before his own door, upon which (after feasting Sir Anthony) himself was hanged. In like sort (say they) he trussed up a miller's man thereby, for that he presented himself in the other's stead, saying he could never do his master better service'. Nor had the townsmen of the far west any better reason to remember Sir Anthony with affection when John Payne, portreeve of St Ives, was strung up by his orders, an event commemorated on a plaque on the wall of the Catholic church four centuries later. Kingston himself had little longer to live. In Mary's reign he was involved in a plot to put Elizabeth on the throne, and died on his way to trial, probably by his own hand.

There were more important and more immediate casualties than Kingston. Sir Richard Grenville died shortly after his ordeal in Trematon Castle and Launceston gaol. Then there were the devout Catholic Arundells of Lanherne. When the rebellion began Sir John Arundell had refused to join Russell and even caused two Masses to be said. As a result he was detained in London, while his brother Sir Thomas of Wardour Castle, brother-in-law of Queen Catharine Howard, was active in the Catholic intrigue that led to the Protector's fall. Somerset was replaced by the Earl of Warwick, a quite unscrupulous man who cared nothing for religion and finally plumped for Protestantism purely as a matter of policy. In January 1550 the Arundell brothers were sent to the Tower, where Sir Thomas played the dangerous game of plotting to restore the man he had recently helped to overthrow. In October 1551 Somerset was seized, and executed the following January, Sir Thomas following him to the block a month later. Sir John was released in June and lived another five years, long enough to enjoy the Catholic reaction under Mary.

But the most distressing casualty of all was the Cornish language. No one had ever thought it worthwhile to make a

Cornish version of the Scriptures, and the new church services in English gradually accustomed the natives to a tongue that was at least more comprehensible than Latin. There were no books printed in Cornish, though in 1547 Andrew Borde published his *First Booke of the Introduction of Knowledge, the whych dothe teache a man to speake parte of all maner of languages* – including Cornish. For a taste:

> Gwrae, drewgh quart gwin de vi!
> *Wife, bring me a quart of wine!*

And even more essential than being able to ask one's wife for a drink on a visit to Cornwall, since for Borde the noblest prospect that a Cornishman ever sees is the highroad that leads him to England, was the question,

> Pes myll der eus a lemma de Londres?
> *How many miles is it from here to London?*

But guidebook Cornish was scarcely enough to perpetuate the language, and it had nothing to do with literature. Most of this – miracle plays and lives of the saints preserved in the churches – perished with the stained glass at the hands of reformers like Body. Without books and a literature a language must succumb to one that has both, and by the end of the century when Carew wrote his *Survey* very few people spoke Cornish in his, the eastern, end of the county, 'for the English speech doth still encroach upon it, and hath driven the same into the uttermost skirts of the shire'. It lingered on in remote places for some two centuries longer as the speech of the illiterate, but all that remains today is the musical intonation with which the people of the far west still speak the alien English.

Cornwall is the county of lost causes. Three times within fifty years its people had rebelled, and three times the Tudors had crushed them. Now, with an obsolescent language, symbol at once of their distinction and of their conservative Catholicism, they began to identify themselves with the gentry and middle classes, English-speaking and Protestant. Cornish nationalism was merged, though never submerged, in a greater English nationalism, which in Elizabeth's reign meant enmity with Spain and abhorrence of its religion and Inquisition. For Cornwall was no longer the backwater that it had been in the Middle Ages: in the sea-war with Spain it was once again the English frontier, as it had been in the days of the old Atlantic sea route; moreover it was the springboard in the race for the New World, a contest in which her seamen were inevitably to play a leading part, indeed some of them were already fishing off Newfoundland.

Under Northumberland the reformers went still more merrily to work. A second and more uncompromisingly Protestant Prayer Book was introduced, and non-attendance at church punished with imprisonment. The clergy were allowed to marry, more images were removed and more lights extinguished in the churches, while the stone altars of the Mass were carried out and wooden tables for communion carried in. Commissions were appointed to assess and seize the now superfluous apparatus of candlesticks, crosses, censers and so on, one chalice for communion and one bell to summon communicants being all that the needy government considered necessary for a normal church.

In Cornwall the commissioners were Sir Richard Edgcumbe, Thomas Treffry, Sir Hugh Trevanion, John Killigrew and Sir William Godolphin, names that run like a refrain throughout the Elizabethan age, all of them good Protestants whose estates bordered the richer southern coast from east to west. Amongst them they hunted out more than six thousand ounces of church plate, which Treffry locked up in St Mawes castle. At the same time the almost nonagenarian absentee Bishop of Exeter, Veysey, representative of a vanished age, was persuaded to make way for the zealous and puritanical Coverdale, translator of the Bible. Then, in order to strengthen support for his programme, Northumberland gave parliamentary representation to six more Cornish boroughs, Saltash, Looe, Camelford, Grampound, Michell and even tiny Bossiney returning two members each to the Parliament of 1552, most of them apparently government nominees.

Yet all went awry. Northumberland was defeated at the very centre, for in 1553 the young king died. He tried to persuade the country to accept his son's wife, Lady Jane Grey, as queen. She was proclaimed in Cornwall, and in Devon by Sir Peter Carew. But few people wanted Northumberland's nominee, and fewer still wanted Northumberland. He surrendered and was duly executed, and the Catholic Mary, daughter of Henry VIII and Katharine of Aragon, became queen.

Protestant reformation became Catholic reaction, and all was to be as it had been before Edward's unfortunate reign. The Prayer Book was abolished, the Latin Mass restored; the wooden communion tables were carried out, the stone altars carried in; the confiscated apparatus of candlesticks, crosses and so on were needed again, and Treffry had to disgorge the plate that he had locked in his castle of St Mawes, from the captaincy of which he was dismissed for his Protestant pains. Coverdale too was dismissed from Exeter, and somehow the senile Veysey was brought back from his retirement in Warwickshire to be reinstated as bishop. He did not stay long, and by the beginning of 1554 was back again in his beloved Sutton Coldfield, where he died before the year was out. He was replaced by James Turberville of Bere Regis in Dorset, one of the family that inspired the most famous of Hardy's novels. Coverdale was a married man, had been, to the scandal of good Catholics, a married bishop of Exeter, but now there were to be no more married clergy. Those who had married in Edward's reign were offered the choice between their wives and their benefices. Most of them chose their benefices. But then the Cornish clergy had not been so eager for matrimony as their brethren in the eastern counties, and only about a score of them were deprived of their livings.

There followed the burnings, but Cornwall produced only one martyr. This was Agnes Prest of Northcott in the parish of Boyton, on the banks of the Tamar. A simple, uneducated woman 'of a very little and short stature, somewhat thick, about fifty-four years of age', she sighed for the sermons that she had heard in good

King Edward's reign, and particularly detested the sacrifice of the Mass and restoration of images in churches. Her undoing began when she found a sculptor in the cathedral repairing the noses of statues that had been broken by the reformers, and offered her opinion. The artist was impolite, the lady violent. She was taken to prison, where everything was done to persuade her of her error, but she was not to be moved, and when argument had been exhausted, a last, and apparently unsuccessful, attempt was made to save her soul by burning her body outside the city walls.

One thing Mary could not restore: the monastic estates and tithes that the laity had acquired and were still eagerly trafficking in. The elastic-conscienced gentry were quite prepared to forget the last six unfortunate years and the doctrinal revolution since Henry's death, but emphatically were not prepared to surrender the lands they had gotten. However, Mary could at least restore the fortunes of her Catholic friends, and the lands of some of those who had incurred her father's displeasure. Chief among these was her young cousin Edward Courtenay, son of the Marquis of Exeter, who had been a prisoner ever since his father's attainder and execution fifteen years before. Mary lost no time in reinvesting him with the Earldom of Devon and restoring his western estates, including the manors that Henry had seized for the Duchy of Cornwall. As eligible as he was handsome, he was an obvious and popular candidate for the hand of Mary. But Mary had other ideas, cousins even more royal, and she accepted Philip of Spain's offer.

The news of her betrothal was greeted with dismay and raised anti-Spanish – rather than anti-Catholic – feeling to seditious pitch. Was England to become a mere dependency of Spain? A widespread rebellion was concerted under Sir Thomas Wyatt in the east and the Carews in the west: its object to marry Elizabeth to Courtenay and set her on the throne instead of Mary. In January 1554 the Carews were ready to receive the Earl in Devonshire, but Lord Chancellor Gardiner had frightened him into revealing the plot. Sir Peter Carew escaped to France, but Sir Gawen was taken, and Courtenay returned to the Tower, from which he had only just been released.

A year later he was allowed to go abroad, where he met Sir Peter and other west-country rebels and exiles, among whom were the brothers Edmund and Nicholas Tremayne, and Peter, John and Thomas Killigrew. The Killigrew brothers, sailing under French letters of marque, were hunting Spanish ships, one of which they sank off the Land's End, taking her cargo, worth £10,000, to Scilly, a favourite base for such exploits. Their father, Captain of Pendennis Castle, hid the culprits, but he and the younger John found themselves in the Fleet prison, and at about the same time Peter was clapped in the Tower. From privateering the Killigrews took easily and even more picturesquely to piracy, 'and for pyratts and rovers they have byn commonly knowen'. It was to prove a profitable and not unpatriotic pastime.

Courtenay abroad was inevitably involved in other conspiracies, in one of which the egregious Sir Anthony Kingston perished. But in the autumn of 1556 the Earl contracted a fever and died, relieving Mary of at least one of her anxieties. She had plenty of others. They killed her. She died two years later, hated by the people for whose love she had longed, and who now set all the church bells ringing in honour of her sister Elizabeth, the new queen.

Catholic reaction gave place once again to Protestant reformation, and all was to be as it had been, or pretty well as it had been, before Mary's unfortunate reign. Mass was abolished and the Prayer Book restored; altars were taken out and tables taken in, and images and superfluous apparatus of the Mass removed. The Catholic bishops, who refused to acknowledge Elizabeth as supreme head of the Church, were also removed, among them Turberville, who was replaced by William Alley. The parish priests were more amenable, and few of those in Cornwall surrendered their livings. Elizabeth had made it as easy as possible to accept the new order, for her policy was ever one of compromise, though here she offended her left-wing supporters, the Puritans, who thought that her Church settlement did not go far enough in their direction.

For the first ten years of her reign Elizabeth managed to live on comparatively friendly terms with Philip of Spain, but a crisis came in 1568 when the Protestant Netherlanders revolted against their Spanish overlords and were executed in their thousands by the Duke of Alva. Elizabeth watched uneasily, for she could not afford to see a strong Spanish base established within a few miles of the Kentish coast. There could be no question of open intervention, but it was no business of hers if English privateers were to sail under another flag in search of Spanish ships and plunder. Piracy of course was another matter, and a show could be made of checking that. Sir Peter Carew – of all men – was sent into Cornwall to make inquiries, but the difficulty was not only to catch pirates, but to get them convicted when caught. Everybody seemed to be in the business, even the parish priests as receivers of goods, though on the whole the gentry preferred the more respectable vocation of privateering. The zealous Sir Reynold Mohun, now lord of Boconnoc, laid information against the Killigrews and Sir William Godolphin, but little came of the matter, for the whole business was altogether too complex to unravel. William Hawkins and Richard Grenville were not above suspicion, and once at least Martin Frobisher found himself in Launceston gaol.

It was at the beginning of December 1568 that William Hawkins heard that his brother had been killed by the Spaniards. In the autumn of the previous year John Hawkins had sailed with six ships on his third slaving expedition, taking with him his young cousin Francis Drake. They had kidnapped negroes on the Guinea coast and shipped them off to the Spanish Main, where a little pressure persuaded the Spaniards to buy them, contrary to the orders of Philip II. Then, driven west by storms, they put in at the Mexican port of San Juan d'Ulloa to refit. While they were there a fleet of thirteen Spanish sail arrived, who, after professing friendship, attacked them. Only two of the English ships had escaped.

When the news of the disaster reached Plymouth it happened that a number of Spanish ships carrying pay for Alva's troops had been driven by storms and privateers into Fowey and Saltash. The treasure was a loan from Genoese bankers, and when Hawkins wrote to Cecil, Elizabeth's chief minister, the queen informed the Spanish ambassador that she had decided to accept the loan herself. Sir Arthur Champernowne of Dartington was ordered to superintend the operation of acceptance with all amicability, and he called in John Treffry to help. Sixty-eight chests of treasure were landed at Saltash and locked safely in Plymouth town hall, while Treffry had the satisfaction of seeing the Spaniards help to carry another thirty-two cases into his own house. Alva at once seized all English shipping in the Netherlands, to which Elizabeth replied by seizing all Spanish ships in English ports, many of them being in Cornwall. The queen had much the better of the bargain.

The report that William Hawkins had heard of his brother's death had been false. While these diplomatic exchanges were going on Drake arrived at Plymouth with the *Judith,* and a few days later John Hawkins put in to Mount's Bay with his crippled *Minion,* after a fearful passage from San Juan d'Ulloa. They had lost four of their ships, leaving a hundred men to the mercy of the Spaniards, who accused them, not of being smugglers engaged in an infamous traffic, which they were, but of being heretics, which was nothing to the point, and those who were not killed were reserved for a worse fate at the hands of the Inquisition. Anti-Catholic as well as anti-Spanish feeling rose sharply in England, and after the events of 1568 there could no longer be any pretence of friendly relations with Spain.

There followed a long period, some fifteen years, of cold war, during which Elizabeth innocently contrived to do as much damage as possible to Spain without involving herself in open hostilities which she could not afford. Privateering and piracy increased, with the Killigrews, still captains of Pendennis, at the centre of operations. The government must have been well aware of Sir John's activities, and it was very much in keeping with Elizabeth's diplomacy that he was appointed chairman of a commission to inquire into piracy in the west. There was of course no report, for the very good reason that Sir John failed to call together the other commissioners. No wonder, for when at last they made their report Peter Killigrew figured as one of the leading culprits. He had been provisioning pirates, including the notorious Captain Hicks of Saltash, at Helford, a favourite rendezvous. Soon it was the turn of yet another member of the family. A Spanish ship, driven into Falmouth, was boarded at midnight by a number of Killigrew's men, who threw most of the crew overboard, carried off the cargo to Arwennack and the ship itself to Ireland. Sir John, as chairman of the commission for piracy, could find no evidence to show by whom the deed was done, but the researches of the Privy Council soon revealed that his wife, Lady Killigrew, was the leading spirit in the enterprise.

Another lady at the other end of the county was involved in a similar though less nefarious transaction. In Mary's reign Sir Richard Edgcumbe had built the great house of Mount Edgcumbe overlooking Plymouth and the Sound, one of the noblest prospects in Britain. Richard Carew of Antony, only a few miles away, was born while it was a-building and knew the house well in Peter Edgcumbe's time, for Peter was his uncle, and he described it affectionately as 'builded square, with a round turret at each end, and the hall rising in the midst above the rest, which yieldeth a stately sound as you enter the same'. It was revolutionary in design, the first house in England to be built on this plan. Then, 'a little below the house, in the summer evenings seine-boats come and draw with their nets for fish, whither the gentry of the house walking down, take the pleasure of the sight, and sometimes buy the profit of the draughts'. But the scene was not always as idyllic as this, and in 1575 there was a less innocent diversion. There were rocks as well as pilchards below the house, and when some Spanish ships were driven on them, Peter being away from home, his wife seized the spoil and positively refused to surrender it. Peter supported her on his return, but when hauled up before the Privy Council had to agree to restore the goods. It was a politic gesture on the part of the government, anxious to make a show of defending the rights of innocent Spaniards.

But all these coastal and Channel activities paled into insignificance in the glare of Drake's achievements, and as a profit-sharer Elizabeth did not find it easy to convince the Spaniards that she did her best to obstruct his piratical ventures. Sailing with picked crews composed mainly of Devon and

Cornish men Drake made two reconnoitring trips to the West Indies before leaving Plymouth in the spring of 1572 and returning three months later laden with gold and silver seized on the Isthmus of Panama. When he returned to Plymouth in 1580 from his next great voyage, again ballasted with booty, it was after a three years' absence in which he had 'extended the point of that liquid line, wherewith (as an emulator of the sun's glory) he encompassed the world'. Had he known it, when he sailed past Lima early in 1579, John Oxenham, first of all Englishmen to sail the Pacific, was about to be burned there at an *auto-da-fé* after having been captured in possession of two Spanish treasure ships.

This part of the English Protestant offensive was obvious enough, gross as a mountain, open, palpable, however much Elizabeth might protest her innocence and make a show of bringing her unruly subjects to book. But the Catholic Spanish counter-offensive was subtler altogether, an insidious sapping operation that threatened the security and even the life of Elizabeth. In this Philip was greatly helped by William Allen's foundation of the English College at Douai for the training of Catholic mission priests to work in England, and by the Pope's Bull of 1570, declaring Elizabeth heretic and illegitimate, excommunicated and deposed. It was disastrous for the English Catholics, who were now faced with the cruellest of dilemmas, for they could no longer be loyal both to the Queen and to the Pope; henceforth every Catholic was suspect, a potential traitor, and the period of religious toleration was inevitably at an end.

The centre of Catholicism in Cornwall was Lanherne, the home of the 'Great Arundells' in the steep wooded valley that runs from St Columb Major to the sea at Mawgan Porth. Sir John, whom Northumberland had imprisoned with his even more influential and unfortunate brother, died in 1557, and was succeeded at Lanherne by his son, another John, knighted by Elizabeth during the happy decade of toleration. He married Lord Stourton's widow, his sister being the wife of another Catholic, wealthy Thomas Tregian of Golden, the Tudor house overlooking the valley of the upper Fal between Tregony and Grampound. When their son Francis married the daughter of his uncle's wife, Lady Stourton, the Tregians of Golden could scarcely have been more closely linked to the Arundells of Lanherne.

Francis made little attempt to conceal his Catholic practices, and when he succeeded to Golden in 1575 harboured one of the first seminary priests to come to England from Douai. This was Cuthbert Mayne, like Tregian a young man of about thirty, who passed as his steward and travelled openly between Golden and Lanherne, where he frequently stayed for a week or more to conduct the forbidden Catholic services. The Protestant gentry had a shrewd idea of what was going on in these two proud Catholic households, but it was only when Richard Grenville became Sheriff of Cornwall that any action was taken. Then, one day in June 1577, Grenville arrived at Golden with a dozen fellow magistrates and told Tregian that they had come to look for one Bourne, a fugitive from justice, who was said to be in the house. Tregian protested, but Grenville insisted, broke into the room where Mayne was hiding, and found him wearing an Agnus Dei, a wax medallion of a lamb blessed by the Pope. But more serious than this was a papal Bull of absolution. With grim satisfaction Grenville ordered Mayne and Tregian to be thrown into Launceston gaol, and took the opportunity of rounding up a number of other suspected offenders.

Richard Carew – he was only twenty-two – was one of the grand jury of Cornish gentry who returned a true bill against Mayne and his associates when they were brought up at the Michaelmas assizes. Mayne was found guilty of high treason for being in possession of a papal Bull, and half a dozen of his humbler confederates and companions were sentenced to imprisonment and forfeiture of their possessions. About twenty more were condemned as recusants, for not attending church, among them Sir John Arundell and Nicholas Roscarrock. Arundell and Tregian had been moved to London, but Tregian was returned to Launceston for the next assizes, when he too was sentenced to imprisonment and loss of his estates. The sheriff broke into Golden by night, evicted Tregian's wife and family, while Tregian himself was thrown into an underground dungeon at Launceston. Grenville was knighted for his services.

Meanwhile, Mayne had been executed. On November 30th he was dragged on a hurdle from Launceston gaol to the market place, where a gallows had been set up. The ceremony was performed with unspeakable brutality, and when his naked body had been hewn into quarters they were distributed to places where the sight of them would be most salutary: to Bodmin, Wadebridge, Tregony near Golden, and Barnstaple, Mayne's native town. His head was impaled on the gate of Launceston Castle, eventually being carried away to Lanherne where it was preserved as a precious relic. Mayne was the first of some two hundred seminary priests and Jesuits who suffered martyrdom for their faith in the last half of Elizabeth's reign, some of them being Cornish, like John Hamley of St Mabyn and John Cornelius of Bodmin.

As tension mounted and war with Spain became inevitable, the Catholics were subjected to even greater pressure, the Parliament of 1581 passing a ferocious Act making it treason to join the Roman Church or persuade others to do so; the celebration of Mass was punishable by a heavy fine and imprisonment, and failure to attend church by a fine of £20 a month. As £20 in Elizabeth's time was equal to about £600 today, only the very wealthiest families could afford the luxury of recusancy, in Cornwall only the Arundells of Lanherne. The rest had either to conform or go to prison. At last Sir John himself was caught harbouring Catholic priests in his London house. After being imprisoned in the Tower and then less rigorously confined, he died at Isleworth in 1590, his body being returned to St Columb for burial. Tregian, obstinately refusing to attend the Anglican service, passed most of his life in the Fleet prison, but was eventually allowed to go abroad, dying at Lisbon in 1608. His eldest son, another Francis and another recusant, followed him in the Fleet, where he occupied himself in compiling the most valuable of all anthologies of early English keyboard music, the so-called Fitzwilliam Virginal Book. Nicholas Roscarrock too was much in prison and once at least racked. Richard Carew remembered him 'for his industrious delight in matters of history and antiquity' – he wrote an account of the British Saints.

Many other families, the Penkivells of St Minver for example, suffered under the persecution, and by the time the war with Spain began the Cornish Catholics, most of them as loyal as their Protestant neighbours, were crushed and scattered, impoverished, imprisoned, or in exile.

While the Catholics were being rounded up and rendered harmless, efforts were made to strengthen the county's defences against invasion. One difficulty was the constant drain of men from the west country to suppress the dangerous risings fomented by Spain in Ireland. In 1574 a hundred Cornishmen were shipped from Padstow – full of Irishmen according to Leland – to take part in the ferocious and bestial struggle; two hundred more in 1578 and each of the following years, until the magistrates protested that there would be no men left in 'this little shire' to defend the coast. But still the drain went on until the rebellion was crushed in the early eighties, a campaign in which young Walter Raleigh distinguished himself by his courage and ruthlessness. Yet, despite this steady withdrawal of men, Cornwall could muster a force of four thousand, though their training and equipment – a few days in the year with bows and pikes – seem to have been sadly inadequate. However, there were garrisons of a hundred men for Pendennis, St Mawes and the Mount; Plymouth was defended by the fortifications on St Nicholas Island, and Scilly by the fort on St Mary's under the competent charge of Sir Francis Godolphin. Finally, the defensive system was strengthened when Raleigh was appointed Lord Lieutenant in 1585. The queen had already knighted her new favourite and made him Lord Warden of the Stannaries, so that he was now able to bring the tinners, with their right of separate muster, within the county organisation.

In the early eighties the international situation deteriorated rapidly. In 1580 the Jesuits added their underground activities to those of the seminary priests. In 1583 the Throckmorton plot to assassinate the queen was uncovered and the Spanish ambassador ordered out of the country. In 1584 William of Orange, leader of the revolt in the Netherlands, was murdered;

the Spaniards overran the southern provinces, and sixty miles of
coast opposite England offered a base from which to launch
invasion. At last Elizabeth sent a force to help the Netherlanders,
a campaign made memorable by the heroic death of Sir Philip
Sidney, 'the miracle of our age', as his friend Richard Carew
called him. The Spaniards seized all English shipping in their
waters, whereupon Drake sailed into Vigo, demanded the release
of the English crews, took some prizes, and went on to sack San
Domingo and Cartagena before returning to Plymouth with his
spoil. Without any formal declaration, the twenty years' war with
Spain had begun.

The years leading up to the Spanish war were momentous ones
for the tin industry, for war might cut off foreign supplies and
it was vital to increase the home production of metals of every
kind. By this time, however, the tin streams were almost
exhausted, and the only way to reach big quantities of ore was
by digging into the lodes. The age of mining had arrived. But
mining required far more capital than an association of simple
tinners could muster, and another and far more complex
technique as well. Although there had been a form of
elementary capitalism in the Middle Ages, capitalistic mining
really began at the time of the dissolution of the monasteries,
when the gentry were eager to exploit the mineral resources of
their newly acquired lands. The lead had been taken by Sir
William Godolphin, the hills on whose estates near Helston
were fabulously rich in tin, and whose works were the biggest
in Cornwall when Leland was there. Sir William died in 1575,
but his work was continued by his nephew and heir, Sir Francis
Godolphin, who devoted the greater part of his long life to the
industry, employed skilled German mining engineers, and had
'300 persons or thereabouts' working for him.

Peter Edgcumbe at the other end of the county was less
fortunate than Sir Francis, and the story of his misadventures was
a favourite one with his nephew, Richard Carew. Peter and his
friend William Carnsew of Bokelly employed a German mining
engineer called Burchard Cranach, 'addicting themselves but too

much to adventure their certain means upon the uncertain hopes of increasing them by finding rich mines, which Burchard promised to direct them where to find, as indeed he did. So when he had directed them where they should dig, at length after they had bestowed much labour and charge and were come to the sight of such plenty as they hoped the next day to make themselves rich, that night there fell into their work so great a quantity of loose earth and rubbish as they had no less to do to rid it than they had at first to open it. Upon which when they had again bestowed more charge to come to it the second time, they were again served as at the first, and forced to give it over for dear at the last'. That was the trouble in the early days: the workings collapsed owing to lack of skill and experience in shoring them up, and the mines began to take their toll of life. Or it may well have been that Burchard was an incompetent charlatan, for finding medicine more lucrative than mining he turned physician, cured Sir William Mohun of Boconnoc of a very dangerous sickness, and went to London where he was naturalised and set up business as Dr Burcot. That was in 1561, and in the following year he cured Lord Hunsdon, Shakespeare's future patron, 'of a very dangerous sickness'.

The story is worth telling at length, for not only is it a very good one, but it also gives us a rare glimpse of life in Elizabethan Cornwall. It was related by Carew to a few of his cronies one night at Antony House over the wine, and recorded by his son in his Memoirs.

'In the meantime the Doctor practised physic and did great cures, which made him much talked of and the more esteemed by my uncle, who, when going to London about some business, having occasion to talk to Lord Hunsdon, he found him sick of such a disease as posed all the London physicians. Thereupon my uncle commended Burcot's skill, and said he thought if any man could cure his Lordship, Burcot was like to be the man. Whereupon my Lord of Hunsdon entreated my uncle, upon his return into Cornwall where Burcot then was, to do him the kindness to send him up, as he did, and desired my grandfather to ride up with him, to defend him from any abuse might happen to be offered unto him because he was a stranger. And the old Mr Carnsew sent also with him an old and faithful servant of his house, called Roach, in colour to attend the Doctor, but indeed gave him a secret charge to have a diligent eye upon him, that from London he might not steal home into Germany before he had performed his promise concerning the mines.

'So when they came to London together he was by my grandfather brought to Lord Hunsdon, whom in short time he cured, and was by him brought and commended for an excellent physician to Queen Elizabeth, with whom when he had talked he told her, "My liege, thou shalt have the pox." At which speech she was so exceedingly offended that she said presently, "Have away the knave out of my sight." And within a while she fell extremely sick, so that none of her own physicians durst minister unto her, which danger of her life filled the Londoners' hearts and mouths with sorrow and lamentation.

'When she fell into so great danger by this sickness, some about her wished that Burcot might be sent for, which she consented unto, and two of the Court with a spare horse were commanded to bring him to the Queen. When old Roach saw them he imagined for what purpose they came, for he had heard report of the Queen's fearful sickness, and thereupon goes up to Burcot, who was then walking in his chamber, and told him how the Queen was very sick and had sent for him. But he grew into a great rage, and sware by his ordinary oath, "By God's pestilence, if she be sick, there let her die! Call me *knave* for my good will!" Which when Roach heard, he told him that if he could save his sovereign's life and would not, he would surely (whatsoever became of him) make him pay for it with the loss of his own, therefore bade him resolve either to go unto her or to die presently. So down Roach goes to those which were sent, and tells them the Doctor would come to them by and by, and then carries up his boots and his cassock and lays them down before him, and drawing out his poniard bids him dispatch, for one way or other he should quickly go. Whereupon in a furious rage Burcot snatches up his cassock and boots and puts them on, runs to his cupboard, catches a bottle of liquor he kept there, puts it in his pocket, flings down over the stairs, mounts on horseback without so much as saluting the parties who were sent for him, posts to the Court, and comes thither a good while before the messengers could come after him.

'He was presently brought to the Queen, and as soon as he saw her, says, "Almost too late, my liege," causes a pallet to be made for her, calls for a remnant of scarlet, laps all her body in it, save one hand which he would have to be out, lays her before the fire, then gives her his bottle to drink of, which when she had tasted, he asked her how she liked it, when she answered, "Well, for we found it comfortable." Then he bade her drink more, all if she would, as she did, and a little after, looking on that hand which was out, seeing divers red spots rising thereon, asked him, "What is this Mr Doctor?" "'Tis the pox," says he. At which, when she complained, because she much loathed that disease, he replied, "By God's pestilence, which is better, to have the pox in the hands, in the face and in the arse, or have them in the heart and kill the whole body?" '

Carew then tells how the grateful queen, on her recovery, gave Burcot a pair of gold spurs that had belonged to Henry VII, and land in Cornwall worth £100. This, it is interesting to note, was part of the forfeited Winslade inheritance, but Cecil, thinking it too much for a mere doctor's fee, managed to cancel the gift, much to the doctor's rage – 'By God's pestilence, me care not for it!' Of course the story must have improved with the telling, but there is no reason to doubt its essential truth. Elizabeth really did very nearly die of smallpox in 1562 when, the succession unsettled, her death would have been a national disaster, so it looks as though this German-Cornish engineer-doctor changed the course of history.

Carnsew was to have further trouble with 'Dutch mineral men'. In the early eighties he was managing a mining company, financed from London, with the aid of a German engineer, Ulrich Frose. They reopened Treworthy copper mine near Perranporth, which Burcot had worked so disastrously twenty years before – it must have been one of the first – but the shaft was deep, water poured in, while funds from London merely trickled, and Frose was sent to Neath to manage their smelting works. Another copper mine at St Just was more promising, the ore being shipped to St Ives and thence to Neath for smelting, 'either to save cost in fuel, or to conceal the profit', Carew commented rather sourly. It was almost certainly to save cost in fuel, very scarce in north Cornwall, for the ships returned with Welsh timber for the mines, and the St Just venture had to close down shortly before Carnsew's death in Armada year.

The trouble was that mining at depths of two or three hundred feet was uneconomical with the primitive equipment of the day, or as Francis Godolphin put it, 'the tin mines also growing more chargeable to be wrought, by the greater depth, the greater quantity of timber required, the greater charge for drawing up water springs, and the scarcity of wood'. Copper mining proved even more expensive – there were no copper streams, and lodes were even deeper – and another century was to pass before it became profitable. The result was that, despite the development of capitalist mining, Elizabeth's reign was a period of depression in the industry, and Godolphin estimated that in 1597 there were '10,000 idle loiterers in this small county'. Of course that was a gross exaggeration, and all the unemployed would not be miners. But many of the tinners must have been in desperate straits. Unlike the medieval gilds, the stannaries afforded no protection to their distressed members, most of whom were in the toils of usurers, and they often added to their plight by preferring 'tribute' to wages, a gamble whereby they received a proportion of the value of the ore that they raised. The government tried to relieve their distress by offering loans at a low rate of interest, and by buying tin at a fixed price. But a fixed price was not very helpful when all other prices were rising rapidly, and the output of tin was less at the end of the reign than it had been at the beginning.

When the war began the two most vulnerable parts of England were Kent and Cornwall, the one opposite the Spanish Netherlands, the other the nearest point to Spain and, as Godolphin put it, though he was referring primarily to his charge of Scilly, 'the fairest inn in the direct way between Spain and Ireland'. But even if invasion were planned from the Netherlands – which was in fact the plan for the first Armada – the fleet would have to sail past Cornwall, which thus became the country's most important outpost, although its defence was left to the local levies. Under Raleigh, with Godolphin and Sir William Mohun as deputy-lieutenants, the tinners and peasants of the militia were given a few days' training, earthworks were thrown up behind the beaches, much as they were in our own time, and beacons manned on hills and headlands, in forts and citadels of the Iron Age. By 1587 Philip's invasion fleet was almost ready, but in April Drake slipped out of Plymouth and into Cadiz, where he burned some ten thousand tons of Spanish shipping – a singe indeed for Philip's beard – and returned with an East Indian carrack, the *San Felipe*, all its silken treasure intact. Though the Armada was not destroyed, there was little chance of its sailing that year.

It came in the high summer of 1588, if such a season of gales may so be called. On July 19th it was sighted off Scilly, driven by the south-westerlies that confined Lord Admiral Howard and Drake in Plymouth Sound. All that day, a Friday, the sombre crescent of nearly one hundred and fifty ships sailed along the Cornish coast, past the Land's End and the Lizard, Pendennis and St Mawes. During the night the hastily provisioned English fleet beat out of Plymouth, forcing its way westward until by Sunday morning it had got to windward of the Spaniards and was pursuing them up-Channel past Rame Head and Mount Edgcumbe, the house that the Spanish commander is said to have reserved for himself when his troops had conquered England. It was from here, at about nine o'clock, that Carew, commanding a company to defend Cawsand Bay, saw the

'Spanish floating Babel' and the first engagement, in which one great galleon was blown almost to pieces and another crippled. And then the two fleets faded into the eastern haze. Of those proud Spanish ships only half returned to Spain.

The English counter-armada of the following year, which might have been decisive, was an anti-climax. Drake, much the most popular man in England, was the foremost exponent of the policy of carrying the war into Spain – 'to propagate religious piety', as Peele the dramatist put it – but Elizabeth and Hawkins favoured the less hazardous course of looting the traffic on the sea routes. Drake was given his chance, but the expedition, lacking wholehearted support, was crippled from the start. There were heroic actions, some Spanish property was destroyed and a number of ships taken; above all, Drake proved that, with proper backing, Spain could be defeated on her own soil. But Spain was not defeated; Drake was discredited and retired to Buckland, the abbey near Plymouth which Grenville had converted into a house and sold to him.

And so Elizabeth had her way. English squadrons were to patrol the Azores and waylay the convoys of Spanish treasure. Grenville was there in the summer of 1591, when he was trapped by a fleet that sailed from Spain. For fifteen hours the *Revenge* engaged its fifty-three opponents, until her upperwork was razed and she lay a helpless hulk. Grenville was a proud and grasping man, but his last heroic action transformed him into the sea-counterpart of Sidney, a legendary figure who, 'finding none other to compare withal in his life, strived through a virtuous envy to exceed it in his death'. He was succeeded at Stowe by his son Bernard.

The character of the war now changed, and the danger to Cornwall became even greater. In 1590 the Spaniards occupied Brittany to support the Catholics in the French civil war, and for almost eight years they had a base from which they could descend on the Cornish coast. The government took alarm, and while Raleigh and Drake pushed forward the fortification of Plymouth, Godolphin was sent to Scilly to supervise the building of a fort on St Mary's.

He was back at Godolphin in July 1595, when in the early morning of the 23rd four Spanish galleys appeared out of the mist off Mousehole and landed two hundred men who fired the village and the church of Paul. Sir Francis saw the smoke as he was riding over the hills towards Penzance and galloped through the town until he met the fugitives, now rallying and eager to march against the enemy who were destroying their homes. Godolphin, thinking that invasion had come, sent a messenger to warn Drake and Hawkins at Plymouth, and then led his band of about a hundred ill-armed men towards Mousehole, two or three miles away. Suddenly, however, the Spaniards re-embarked and landed their whole force of four hundred at Newlyn in an attempt to cut off Godolphin from Penzance. There followed a race for the town, the Cornishmen being swept by fire from the galleys' guns as they ran, and when they reached the market place, where Godolphin tried to make a stand, were so demoralised that barely a dozen remained under his command. He was forced to withdraw towards Marazion, leaving Newlyn and Penzance to be fired by the enemy, who then returned to their ships.

Fresh squads of militiamen arrived in the afternoon and evening, and Godolphin camped that night in the fields west of Marazion and the Mount. Next day the Spaniards made as if to land again, but seeing a more formidable opposition withdrew a little into the bay where they rode at anchor. By the following morning Drake's ships were bearing down from the Lizard on the south-easterly wind that prevented the Spaniards' escape, when suddenly it shifted to north-west, and 'away pack the galleys with all the haste they could'.

It was the nearest thing to invasion that the country was to experience in the whole course of the war. The government had had a fright and tightened up its defence measures, and Raleigh pleaded for the better defence of Falmouth, which was in his opinion 'every way more to be sought for by the enemy than Plymouth'. But little was done to strengthen either Pendennis or St Mawes, and Raleigh sailed on his expedition to Guiana, taking with him John Grenville, Sir Richard's second son. John won golden opinions but, like his father and grandfather before him, died at sea, and 'the ocean became his bed of honour'.

The Penzance raid brought it home to Elizabeth that Spanish sea-power was recovering and that her current policy of lying in wait for treasure ships was no longer good enough. Drake was recalled from Buckland and set off with Hawkins, now well over sixty, to repeat his classic raids on the Spanish Main. In April 1596 their battered ships returned to Falmouth, but without either of their commanders. Hawkins had perished at Porto Rico and Drake had died on board his ship in January. The old generation was passing and the heroic age almost over, yet something of their inspiration remained. At Plymouth Raleigh and Elizabeth's new favourite, the Earl of Essex, were making ready to repeat Drake's singeing of Philip's beard. In June they sailed into Cadiz bay, captured the town and crippled the armada that Philip was preparing. Yet it sailed in October, though only to be scattered and driven back by gales. The patient Philip could afford to wait, and he began to build a bigger and even better armada for 1597.

In March, while Essex and Raleigh were refitting their fleet in Plymouth for another raid, a Spanish ship appeared in Cawsand Bay. Carew, who was responsible for its defence, was at Bodmin for the assizes with the other magistrates. Under cover of night the Spaniards landed a few men who 'hanged up barrels of matter fit to take fire upon certain doors, which by a train should have burned the houses. But one of the inhabitants, espying these unwelcome guests, with the bounce of a caliver chased them aboard and removed the barrels before the trains came to work their effect'. It was a small affair, but it made a deep impression, for rumours of Philip's new armada were arriving, and Treffry reported a number of other Spanish warships in the Channel.

There was no time to be lost, and in July Essex and Raleigh sailed to destroy the Spanish fleet in the harbour of Ferrol. Off the Land's End, however, they were struck by a fearful storm which drove Raleigh back to Plymouth and Essex to Falmouth. The fleet was repaired and sailed again, but on reaching Ferrol an easterly gale held them off the harbour, so, abandoning the attack, they made for the Azores to intercept the Spanish treasure ships. They failed and turned for home, having accomplished precisely nothing. Meanwhile England had been left virtually defenceless. Philip's chance had come at last, and he ordered his armada to leave Ferrol, to seize the castles of Pendennis and St Mawes, and to destroy the English fleet on its return from the Azores, after which their ten thousand men could march on Plymouth and London. In October, two days before Essex and Raleigh left the Azores, the Spanish fleet put out to sea, but it was caught in the Channel approaches by the autumn gales, and all that remained of the third armada struggled back to Ferrol. No wonder the English talk about the weather: it has been a major determinant of their history.

Raleigh was now the most unpopular man in England, and all the blunders and failures of Essex, the people's darling as well as Elizabeth's, were attributed to him. Yet what success there had been at Cadiz and on the Islands Voyage was mainly his doing, and he had been right about Falmouth – that it would be the objective of the next Spanish invasion scheme. At last he had his way, and the defences of Falmouth were brought up to date. St Mawes was left under the able command of Hannibal Vyvyan of Trelowarren, but the day of reckoning had come for Killigrew. Hopelessly in debt, now known to be hand in glove with the Helford pirates, and even his loyalty suspected, he was removed to prison and succeeded at Pendennis by Sir Nicholas Parker, a professional soldier. For the government, realising that Cornwall could no longer bear the brunt of the Spanish attack unaided, sent down three hundred regular soldiers to Plymouth and another two hundred to Pendennis. A more efficient method of training the militia was also devised, and soon Raleigh, as Lieutenant General, could muster a force of six thousand men armed with pikes, muskets and calivers, while the number of deputy lieutenants was raised from two to seven: Sir Francis Godolphin, Sir Nicholas Parker, Sir Reynold Mohun, Peter Edgcumbe, Bernard Grenville, Richard Carew and Christopher Harris of Trecarrel.

No doubt the organisation looked better on paper than it proved in practice, and when Tyrone's rebellion flared up in Ireland the drain on the Cornish forces began again. A hundred men were demanded in 1597 and three hundred in 1598, almost as many as from the richer and more populous Devon. The country was weary of war, and no part of the country had better reason to be weary of the seemingly endless and fruitless struggle than Cornwall, once again threatened on either flank. There was defeatist talk, but the gentry kept the people together. Indefatigable Godolphin made plans for the building of a bigger fort on St Mary's, and his son William was one of those who followed Essex on his ill-fated expedition to Ireland in 1599. There he was knighted by Essex, but fortunately took no part in the subsequent follies of the earl, which two years later brought him to the block in Tower Yard.

While Sir Francis was busy with his tin mines and the defence of Penwith and Scilly, his great friend at the other end of the county, Richard Carew, found time for more solitary enchantments, for fishing in the saltwater pond that he made on the bank of the Lynher, for reading omnivorously – he was to read himself blind – and for writing. From Godolphin he borrowed a Spanish book which he translated as *The Examination of Men's Wits*, enlivening it with marginal snooks cocked at Philip of Spain, and publishing it in 1594 with an affectionate dedication to Sir Francis. In the same year the first five cantos of his translation of Tasso's *Jerusalem Delivered* were surreptitiously printed by a stationer into whose hands they had fallen. This was Christopher Hunt, who may well have been engaged at the time in pirating an even more important quarto, Shakespeare's lost play of *Love's Labour's Won*. Then in 1598 appeared the mock-heroic poem, *A Herring's Tail*, in which a snail climbs the steeple of Uther Pendragon's mausoleum at Tintagel, and after a dreadful battle defeats the weathercock. Though not one of the great poems of the period it is by no means the least entertaining.

But these were what Carew would have called petty commodities, for all this time he was revising and bringing up to date his greatest work, *The Survey of Cornwall*, the principal source of our knowledge of the county in Elizabeth's reign, and incidentally one of the minor classics of English prose. There is a vivid and sympathetic description of the tinners and the new technique of mining. Some of the mines were already so deep that 'from their bottoms you shall at noonday descry the stars. The workers are let down and taken up in a stirrup by two men who wind the rope'. The almost insuperable difficulties were splitting the rock with wedges, for there was as yet no blasting, and draining the water. Pumps were inefficient and the work so strenuous that the men could endure it for only four hours a day, while the adits that they drove into the hillsides to the shaft bottoms often proved too expensive to complete. Then sometimes the timber-framed galleries collapsed, pressing the moldwarp miners to death or burying them alive behind barriers of rock.

The decline in production was not altogether loss, for formerly the Cornish people were so anxious to make quick money out of tin that they neglected agriculture, and even let their pastures to Devon and Somerset graziers. But when the tin works began to fail there was a healthy return to farming, import of corn giving place to self-sufficiency and even to a surplus for export. The process was helped by enclosure, for though much of the high ground in the centre of the shire remained waste, there was still good agricultural land along the coast which had not been divided by hedges, and when this was enclosed and dressed with seaweed and sand it yielded a profitable return. There was now plenty of corn ground, and pasture enough for cattle and sheep, which improved out of all recognition, though some of the sporting gentry still let their beasts run wild, hunting them with crossbows and guns in the manner of deer.

After farming and mining came the third main industry of fishing, and Carew describes the way in which pilchards, 'least in bigness, greatest for gain and most in number', were caught with the seine net. It is a method which must have had a long tradition behind it, and one that is still practised in some places. 'The seine is in fashion like that within harbour, but of a far larger proportion. To each of these there commonly belong three or four boats carrying about six men apiece, with which, when the season of the year and weather serveth, they lie hovering upon the coast and are directed in their work by a balker, or huer, who standeth on the cliff side and from thence best discerneth the quantity and course of the pilchard, according whereunto he cundeth (as they call it) the master of each boat (who hath his eye still fixed upon him) by crying with a loud voice, whistling through his fingers and wheazing certain diversified and significant signs with a bush which he holdeth in his hand. At his appointment they cast out their net, draw it to either hand as the shoal lieth or fareth, beat with their oars to keep in the fish, and at last either close and tuck it up in the sea, or draw the same on land with more certain profit.' The fish were then salted, pressed and packed into hogsheads for export to France, Italy and Spain.

Although some of the displaced miners found employment in a reviving agriculture, unemployment was a serious problem, and Carew detested the vagabonds who swarmed into the towns, mainly from Ireland. But the condition of the workers had improved in the last half-century. In the old days they had lived in earthen hovels without floorboards, chimneys or glass windows – little wonder that there had been three rebellions in fifty years – but now they were able to maintain themselves in comparative decency with money to spare for little luxuries. On the whole it is a contented people that we see at the end of the Elizabethan era, despite the war, the alarms and musters. Work was hard, but they had fun. There were church ales at Whitsuntide, harvest dinners in the autumn, and saints' feasts were still celebrated despite the Reformation and the Puritans. Then there were miracle plays in the rounds, though in a degraded form, shooting, hurling and wrestling, all benevolently patronised by the gentry.

And for the gentry, his own class, Carew has a special word. 'They keep liberal, but not costly builded or furnished houses, give kind entertainment to strangers, make even at the year's end with the profits of their living, are reverenced and beloved of their neighbours, live void of factions amongst themselves (at leastwise such as break out into any dangerous excess), and delight not in bravery of apparel ... They converse familiarly together, and often visit one another. A gentleman and his wife will ride to make merry with his next neighbour, and after a day or twain those two couples go to a third, in which progress they increase like snowballs, till through their burdensome weight they break again.'

It is almost impossible to exaggerate the importance of the gentry in Cornwall at this period. They were the landowners, magistrates, commanders of the land and sea forces, and parliamentary members for the county and many of the twenty-one boroughs as well. It is true that in theory the Stannaries were outside their jurisdiction, but in practice most of the members for the Convocations or Parliaments of tinners were drawn from their ranks. Then again, although forty-five Cornish manors were held by the Duchy, there was no Duke in Elizabeth's reign – there was indeed no peer living in the county – and the offices of the Duchy were filled mainly by the local gentry. And so we must imagine these country gentlemen, most of them related by marriage, for 'all Cornish gentlemen are cousins', presiding over the fortunes of the county: Godolphins of Godolphin, Vyvyans of Trelowarren, Bassets of Tehidy, St Aubyns of Clowance, Killigrews of Arwennack, Trevanions of Carhays, Arundells of Trerice, Arundells of Lanherne, Treffrys of Fowey, Trelawnys of Trelawne, Mohuns of Boconnoc, Eliots of Port Eliot, Carews of Antony, Bullers of Shillingham, Edgcumbes of Cotehele and Mount Edgcumbe, Grenvilles of Stowe, and others whose inheritance and influence were scarcely less. The extreme Catholics had been weeded out – Winslades and Tregians were gone, the Lanherne Arundells reduced – and most of them were staunch Protestants well aware of their divine right to their position in the established political order. But the time was not far off when some of them were to challenge the divine right of the most exalted member of the hierarchy, and factions of a most dangerous excess were to break out among themselves.

Carew finished his *Survey* on April 23rd, 1602, Shakespeare's thirty-eighth birthday, and dedicated it to his kinsman, 'Sir Walter Raleigh, Knight, Lord Warden of the Stannaries, Lieutenant General of Cornwall'. In the following spring Queen Elizabeth died, but it was not the Lieutenant General who proclaimed the new king, James I, in Cornwall, but the Colonel General, Sir Nicholas Parker.

IX

The Stuarts
1603–1714

As James was already King of Scotland before coming to the throne of England, he was the first sovereign who could call himself King of Great Britain. At last the four Celtic countries on her northern and western fringes were attached, with varying degrees of security, to Saxon England, and perhaps it was only appropriate that one of the leading members of the commission that arranged the treaty with Scotland, the latest partner, should have come from Cornwall, the earliest acquisition. This was Richard Carew's younger brother George, who was knighted for his services and after a distinguished tenure of the post of ambassador to the court of France wrote the important *Relation of the State of France*. He died in 1612, leaving a fortune of £10,000 and a widow, Thomasine, daughter of Sir Francis Godolphin.

And at last Cornwall had a Duke again. Even the beloved octogenarian Hugh Atwell, for half a century parson of St Ewe and prescriber of milk for all infirmities, would scarcely remember the last one, Edward VI. The new Duke was James's eldest son, Henry, 'that most vertuous prince of most blessed towardness', as honest John Norden called him. Norden had just completed a *Description of Cornwall* with maps of the county and each hundred, and thirteen views of 'the most remarkable curiosities', a delightful book supplementing Carew's *Survey*, but though he dedicated it to James it was more than a hundred years before it found a publisher. His account of the Duke's authority is an admirable summary. 'His Highnes, by this Honor is privileged with sundrie jurisdictions and Royalties, (as have bene the former Dukes) who hath the returne of writs, Custome, Toll, Treasure founde Wardes, and mariages of wards. The benefite arising by Minerals, as of Golde, Silver, tynn, Copper, and such like; the two laste muche abounding within this Duchie. And withall his Highnes hath powre to give libertie and (as some say) to inhibite the Borrowe towns within the Dukedome, to send Burgesses unto the Parliament of estate: Having within his govemmente a peculiar parliament, for the pryvate governmente of Stannerye causes. Moreover, the Duke by his auctoritie appointeth all officers, as the Shirife, an officer of greateste comaunde, beyng vicegovernour of the shyre ...' There is an ominous note in that parenthetic 'as some say'.

James found the Duchy sadly reduced. In 1601, at her wit's end for money, Elizabeth had sold eighteen of its manors, including Trematon, Tintagel and Restormel, though she had done this without the consent of Parliament, which according to the original charter was illegal. For the first and almost only time, therefore, James invoked the power of Parliament and, quite justifiably, recovered the alienated estates. There was a pretty ceremony in London in 1610 when Henry was created Prince of Wales, the loyal citizens greeting him on the Thames with pageants – Amphion on a dolphin representing Wales, and Corinea on a whale saluting him on behalf of Cornwall. But unfortunately for England the Duke was never to become King. Two years later he was dead, and James, following the precedent of Henry VII, transferred the dukedom to his second son Charles.

'Like an Eclipse of the Sunne, wee shall finde the effects hereafter,' was Raleigh's sombre prophecy when he heard of Prince Henry's death. He had good reason to be sombre, for he wrote from the Tower where he had been imprisoned by James at the beginning of his reign as one who opposed his succession and his policy of peace with Spain. For one of James's first acts was to end the twenty years' war, and the next twenty years were a period of peace. Peace of a sort, for, now that the Dutch were getting the better of Spain, the captured Channel ports, notably Dunkirk, became bases for privateers who preyed on English shipping which a neglected and decaying navy was unable to protect. One Dunkirker took four ships off the Lizard in a single day, two of them coming from Looe and Fowey, ports that suffered severely from their activities. But even worse than the Dunkirk privateers were the Mohammedan pirates from Algiers and Salee in Morocco, whom the Dutch introduced into the Channel, and who naturally concentrated at the western approaches. Hovering off Cornwall and Scilly in their long swift ships these very professional pirates descended on the fishing fleets and merchantmen who ventured into the Channel, and even raided the coast to carry off men and women to slavery. As English sea-power declined their depredations increased, and during a black ten days of 1625 they took twenty-seven ships and two hundred men, eighty of them from Looe. A few weeks earlier sixty men, women and children had been snatched out of a church on Mount's Bay. No wonder the people of Penzance were so 'terribly terrified by the Turks' that they petitioned the Council for a fort to protect them.

The Killigrews of Arwennack were being beaten at their own game. The disreputable John, abettor of pirates and ex-captain of Pendennis, died in 1605 and was succeeded by another John, who had to turn his hand to other methods of restoring the family fortunes. He remembered an old scheme of his father's, and in 1619 obtained a patent for the erection of a lighthouse on the Lizard. This, he protested, he did purely 'out of Christian and charitable considerations', hoping only for voluntary contributions from ships that profited from his philanthropy, though his real object was to establish a fixed charge for all vessels passing the Lizard. By Christmas the tower was built and the light burning at a cost of 10s a night for coal. But it raised the indignation of the good people of the Lizard who complained, wrote Killigrew, 'that I take away God's grace from them. Their English meaning is that they now shall receive no more benefit from shipwreck. They have been so long used to reap purchase by the calamity of the ruin of shipping as they claim it hereditary'. This virtuous protest loses some of its force when we find that earlier in the year, when a Spanish ship carrying silver had been wrecked off the Lizard, Killigrew had led the local inhabitants in trying to salvage the treasure, and threatened death to anyone who interfered. By January 1620, he had spent £500 without receiving a penny for his charitable services, and soon afterwards the light went out. However, in 1622 he did succeed in getting a fixed imposition on shipping. The light reappeared and burned for ten years, but the difficulty of collecting the money and the jealousy of Trinity House proved too much, and in 1631 it flickered and went out for good. Yet the venture was the beginning of lighthouses in England.

Killigrew was scarcely more fortunate in his other enterprises. Though he succeeded in advancing the development of Falmouth and establishing a custom house there, the requisite bribing of government officials was more than he could afford, and of course he roused the fury of the ancient ports of Truro and Penryn. Then, he further impoverished himself in obtaining a divorce from his unfaithful wife, who found refuge and support in the rival borough, to which she presented a cup inscribed, 'To the town of Penryn, where they received me in great misery, Jane Killigrew, 1613'. Sir John died in debt in 1633, but by this time other Killigrews had long been prosperously established within Court circles at Whitehall.

Like Killigrew, to compare great things with small, King James had an unhappy knack of rousing antagonism wherever he meddled. His policy being one of peace at home as well as abroad, the Catholics naturally hoped for some amelioration of their lot. Among them was the new Sir John Arundell of Lanherne, like his father a recusant and an exile in London, his sisters having entered a convent in Brussels. He asked for leave to go and live in his house at Chideock in Dorset, but Gunpowder Plot shattered his hopes; he had to go on paying the ruinous monthly fine of £20 as the price of his recusancy, and Lanherne fell into decay. Catholicism in Cornwall was a waning faith, and by the end of the reign there was only one redoubtable recusant,

John Trevelyan of St Clether, 'a bould active spirit, and the greatest of that faction in the West'.

James also roused the resentment of the left-wing members of the Anglican Church, the Puritans, who assumed that the king's Presbyterian upbringing would make him sympathetic towards their ideals. They were mistaken, for after listening to their demands for a more democratic form of Church government, James angrily threatened to expel any Puritan clergy who refused to conform, and three hundred were deprived of their livings. Puritanism in Cornwall was a growing though never overwhelming force, as in East Anglia, and was checked by the Bishop of Exeter, William Cotton, who in 1606 suspended a number of non-conforming clergy. Then under the tolerant rule of Bishop Hall, who turned a blind eye on the preaching of additional sermons, sufficient puritanical steam was allowed to escape to prevent an explosive fanaticism. Launceston, Bodmin and St Ives were the main centres of the cult, though it was strongest in the east where some of the leading families were that way inclined.

There were the Carews of Antony, or rather the eldest son of the author of the *Survey*, another Richard. Born in 1580, he had married Bridget Chudleigh of Ashton in Devon, by whom he had a son, Alexander, born in 1608. Alexander was only three when his mother died, but he was present at her deathbed and was never to forget her last words: 'Lord, though thou killest me, yet will I put my trust in thee.' Eleven years later, shortly after the death of his father, Richard married another Devonshire girl, Grace Rolle, their eldest son John being born towards the end of 1622. Both Chudleighs and Rolles were to play important parts in the Civil War, as were Alexander and John.

Just across the river from Antony were the Bullers of Shillingham, great friends of Richard's, and it was to Mrs Buller that he gave his little treatise on medicine and his invention of the warming stone, precursor of hot-water bottles. A little higher up the Tamar at Halton, famous for its cherries, lived his father's old friend Sir Anthony Rous, whose son Francis and stepson John Pym had been the playfellows of his boyhood. Then on the delectable lands that had once belonged to Bodmin Priory, at Lanhydrock, the Robartes family had established themselves. They had made a fortune out of tin and moneylending in Truro, and in 1620 Sir Richard bought the Lanhydrock estate and began the building of one of the most beautiful houses in Cornwall, facing down the valley of the Fowey towards Restormel and Lostwithiel. This was the year in which the Pilgrim Fathers sailed from Plymouth, but Robartes was a Puritan of another mould, and in 1624 secured a peerage from James's favourite, the Duke of Buckingham, now virtual ruler of England – at a price of £10,000.

Meanwhile James, having offended both Catholics and Puritans, had alarmed and antagonised his Parliaments. 'Kings', he told them, 'are God's lieutenants upon earth,' and 'it is sedition in subjects to dispute what a King may do in height of his power.' Moreover, the House of Commons, he assured its members, sat not in its own right, but of his grace. The Commons replied that His Majesty had been misinformed, and were dismissed. A second Parliament, the 'Addled', called in 1614, lasted only a few weeks, but is memorable for the first appearance of John Eliot as one of the members for St Germans. John was the grandson of Richard Eliot who had inherited the Priory of St Germans from his uncle, the Devonshire merchant who had bought it from the Champernownes. Born in 1592, he was knighted in 1618, and in the following year appointed Vice Admiral of Devon, in which capacity he succeeded in capturing the notorious pirate John Nutt. Unfortunately, Sir George Calvert, secretary of state, was in the pay of Spain and encouraged Nutt's activities against the Dutch, so that while the pirate was allowed to return to his prey, the Vice Admiral was detained for four months in the Marshalsea. It was important to keep on good terms with Spain when James was angling for a Spanish princess for his son.

James had made a more tragic sacrifice to Spanish friendship than Eliot. Released after fifteen years in the Tower to find gold for James in Guiana on the impossible condition of not offending Spain, Sir Walter Raleigh sailed on his last hopeless expedition, in which his son was killed in a skirmish with the Spaniards. He was executed on his return, as James had promised the Spanish ambassador. So perished the last of the Elizabethans. The irony was that within a few years England was again at war with Spain.

James died in 1625, and the fateful reign of Charles I began – on a modest note of popularity, for the anti-Catholic war was popular, though Buckingham's shameful mismanagement of it and Charles's marriage with the Catholic Henrietta Maria of France soon disillusioned the country. War gave Parliament a chance to assert itself, for the king needed money for its prosecution, and when it met in 1626 after the disastrous Cadiz expedition, Eliot led the Commons in the impeachment of Buckingham, for which he was dismissed from his office of Vice Admiral. Charles dissolved Parliament and, to finance Buckingham's maritime and military catastrophes, resorted to a forced loan. Cornwall, with disabled sailors and soldiers in its ports, was particularly hostile to this unconstitutional way of raising money. The county was to pay £2,000, but the justices reported that 'the gentlemen of most sufficiency were not able to give in that manner', though ready to give satisfaction 'in a Parliamentary way', and Sir Francis Godolphin, one of the collectors, apologetically told Jonathan Rashleigh, from whom he demanded £10, how unpleasing it was to him 'to be employed in this kind'. Eliot and William Coryton, Vice Warden of the Stannaries, were imprisoned for refusing to pay, while Sir Richard Buller, Nicholas Trefusis and Humphrey Nicoll were struck off the roll of magistrates.

All those who suffered were returned to the Parliament of 1628 which brought matters to a head. Under the leadership of Eliot and Pym the Commons forced Charles to accept the Petition of Right, which declared illegal all forms of taxation without the consent of Parliament, and the imprisonment of any subject without cause shown. Eliot, the most eloquent orator in the House, then proceeded to attack Buckingham, who was, however, to the great joy of the nation, assassinated. Parliament, which was predominantly Puritan, then turned its attention to the king's

Anglican friends, but Charles had had enough, and decided to manage without Parliaments. He withdrew from the war on the continent, but before he could dismiss the Commons they passed three resolutions declaring that anyone who introduced innovations in religion or advised or paid taxes without the consent of Parliament was an enemy to the kingdom. Ignoring the Petition of Right, Charles imprisoned nine of the leaders, including the greatest, Sir John Eliot, who died in the Tower three years later. When his son asked permission to remove the body to Port Eliot for burial, Charles pitilessly replied, 'Let Sir John Eliot be buried in the church of that parish where he died.' Yet although his body is not at Port Eliot, his image is there. A few days before his death he had his portrait painted in the Tower, an invalid of forty in a dressing gown, a whimsical protest against the tyranny of kings.

For eleven years of peace, 1629 to 1640, the king dispensed with Parliament, raising money without its consent, and, supported by the Earl of Strafford and Archbishop Laud, tried with fanatical pedantry to impose the Anglican system on the Presbyterian Scots. The Scots rose in rebellion, collected a formidably efficient army with which the toast-and-butter English militia was unable to compete, and forced Charles to ask for a truce. The period of personal government was over, and the king had to call a Parliament to pay for his Scottish war. But the Short Parliament of April 1640 refused to grant supplies until its grievances were redressed. Charles dissolved it, and the Scots occupied northern England, demanding £25,000 a month for their upkeep. By November Charles was compelled to summon another Parliament to buy them off.

The Long Parliament went round to work, and practically without dissension passed a series of Acts that reduced the Crown to financial dependence upon Parliament, and laid the foundation of a limited monarchy. This involved a reform of the prerogative courts outside the Common Law, among them the Stannary Courts. All kinds of people remotely connected with the tin trade had come to claim their privileges, but now a Bill was passed confining their jurisdiction to working tinners. These financial reforms, however, marked the end of unanimity, and a more moderate party, both in politics and religion, began to emerge when Laud was thrown into prison to await his death, Strafford executed by a high-handed Act of Attainder, and a Root and Branch Bill introduced for the abolition of episcopacy. Then when Pym by a narrow majority carried the Grand Remonstrance, declaring no confidence in the king, and a Militia Bill depriving him of the command of the armed forces, a well-defined Royalist party came into being. Encouraged by this support, Charles went to the House of Commons to arrest Pym and four other members, but they escaped and returned to Westminster followed by the City trainbands. A few days later, on January 10th, 1642, the king fled from London; compromise was no longer possible, and in August the royal standard was raised at Nottingham. The Civil War had begun.

In Cornwall the popular party gained ground in the decade of the thirties. The government, with some justice, was blamed for the neglect of its defences: there was scarcely any ammunition for the obsolete guns of Fowey, the Mount, Pendennis and St Mawes; Algerine and Salee pirates could be sighted daily off the coast, and in a single month of 1636 they snapped up fifteen fishing boats from Looe and Helford. Then when peasants and tinners were pressed for the Scottish war, there were not enough men to get in the harvest or to keep water out of the mines. The example of Sir John Eliot was a constant inspiration, and ship money, a tax devised by another Cornishman, Attorney General William Noy of Carnanton, was bitterly resented as unconstitutional, though the county paid up most of the £26,000 demanded. But opposition was almost entirely confined to economic and political abuses, for the conservative Cornish had a deep reverence for the king himself and for the Anglican Church, which only a hundred years before they had revolted against as an innovation, and the great majority followed the lead of Sir Bevil Grenville, the most influential and best-loved man in the county.

Sir Bevil, grandson of Grenville of the *Revenge*, succeeded to Stowe in 1636 on the death of his father, Sir Bernard, whose life had been a model of quiet devotion to county affairs. A man of forty, generous and vigorous, Sir Bevil was adored by his servants, tenantry and wife, 'My deare Love', to whom in 1625 he sent pictures of 'ye Kgs and Sr Jo. E'. It was symbolic, for Sir Bevil was a Royalist born and lost no time in sending down to Stowe from London a portrait of the new king, Charles, while Sir John Eliot was his greatest friend. When, therefore, Charles despotically clapped Eliot in the Tower his allegiances were torn, but Eliot's death made him for a time a leader of the opposition to unconstitutional government. The Scottish war, however, brought out all the simple, primitive loyalties in him, and he itched to be where 'the King of England's standard waves in the field upon so just occasion'. It was therefore as a Royalist that he rode up to London in October 1640 to attend the first session of the Long Parliament as one of the county members for Cornwall.

The other member for the county was puritanical Alexander Carew, who looked for leadership to his father's old friend Francis Rous, one of the members for Truro, the other being his brother-in-law, John Rolle. Of like persuasion were Sir Richard and Francis Buller and one or two more, who could count on the fanatical support of Lord Robartes in the Upper House. But most of the forty-four members belonged neither to one extreme nor the other, and were merely constitutionalists eager to redress political wrongs. Such was Edward Hyde, member for Saltash, one of the few non-Cornishmen, who was soon to become one of the king's most ardent supporters, and Earl of Clarendon, historian of the Rebellion.

The representatives of Cornwall acted together, and in concert with the rest of the Commons, over the first measures that were passed limiting the power of the Crown, but the Root and Branch Bill and attainder of Strafford soon revealed fundamental cleavages of opinion. Francis Rous led the Puritan extremists in the attack on episcopacy, and was supported by Carew and the Bullers, while Hyde and his followers fought the measure clause by clause. Then, when the attack on Strafford was reaching its climax, Grenville turned to Carew with, 'Pray, Sir, let it not be said that any member of our county should have a hand in this ominous business, and therefore pray give your vote against the Bill'; to which Carew replied, 'If I were sure to be the next man that should suffer upon the same scaffold with the same axe, I would give my consent to the passing of it.' Most of the Cornish members still hoped for a compromise, but when the Militia Bill was passed and Charles replied by declaring it illegal, issuing his own Commissions of Array for calling up the militia, the zealots declared for one side or the other and the rival parties formed, soon to be joined by others whose consciences or interests compelled them to make a choice.

Among the leading Royalists in Cornwall were Sir Bevil Grenville, Sir John Arundell of Trerice, Sir Richard Vyvyan, Lord Mohun, Sir Henry Killigrew, Sir Francis Godolphin and his son Sidney, while Sir Francis Basset was Lord of St Michael's Mount and Sir Nicholas Slanning, a young Devonshireman, held the key position of Captain of Pendennis. On the side of Parliament were Lord Robartes, Alexander Carew, Sir Richard Buller, John St Aubyn, Richard Erisey, Anthony Nicoll, Edmund Prideaux and many others. On the whole the Parliamentary party was strongest in the east, where they were supported by those with Puritan sympathies, but the great majority of clergy stood firmly for the Anglican Church and carried their parishioners with them into the Royalist camp. Most of the towns remained prudently neutral while the rival forces gathered, though Plymouth, on the Devonshire side of the Tamar, declared for Parliament. It was the religious issue rather than the political that divided Cornwall, though there were few clear-cut divisions: a man might be Puritan yet Royalist, Anglican yet Parliamentarian; friends and neighbours took opposite sides, and families were riven by greater loyalties; though most of the Arundells and Godolphins were for the king, some of them threw in their lot with Parliament, and the days were over when the Cornish gentry lived 'void of factions amongst themselves'.

Although the Civil War began on August 22nd, 1642, in Cornwall there was a preliminary period of manoeuvring for the allegiance of the towns and control of the militia, and it was another month before Bodmin and Truro had been secured for the King, while Sir Richard Buller, from his Parliamentary headquarters at Saltash, occupied Launceston. The Royalist command of the Mount and Pendennis was invaluable for the King's cause, not only in Cornwall but throughout the country, for Francis Basset and Sir Nicholas Slanning were able to organise the import of arms and munitions from France, paid for by the sale of tin, even though the navy, which had gone over to Parliament, attempted to blockade the ports. On the other hand, Buller had one big advantage: he could look for reinforcements from the east, for Somerset and the greater part of Dorset and Devon had risen for Parliament, leaving the Cornish Royalists isolated at the end of England. Yet this very advantage proved his undoing when the Royalist leaders, Sir Ralph Hopton and Sir John Berkeley, having been driven out of Dorset, managed to reach Cornwall with a small force of cavalry. Hopton, lovable as loyal and an experienced professional soldier who had seen service in Germany, was a rare acquisition, and it was he who advanced from Truro on Launceston in command of some three thousand raw militiamen raised in the west. Buller was outnumbered and withdrew from Launceston and Saltash to Plymouth, and by the beginning of October Cornwall was in Royalist hands.

But the untrained Cornish militia, even if they had been prepared to leave their own county, were no match for the Parliamentary forces gathering on the other side of the Tamar, and Hopton with the aid of Grenville and the other Royalist gentry set about organising an army of volunteers. It was an expensive business to equip and maintain them, but their leaders were prepared to sacrifice everything in the cause, while the men, mainly their own servants and tenants, were bound by a simple, semi-feudal devotion. It was a small force, only fifteen hundred foot with a few guns, but it was loyal, and the nucleus of the formidable Cornish army – Parliament called them the Cornish Malignants – that was to make such a name for itself.

By November Hopton felt strong enough to take the offensive and advanced on Exeter, hoping to rally the Devonshiremen to the King's cause. But the expedition was a failure: Exeter, like

Plymouth, remained firm for Parliament, provisions ran short, his men were insufficiently disciplined, and he had to retreat to Bodmin, Saltash having been retaken in his absence. It was the prelude to a Parliamentary invasion, and in January 1643 the Scottish Colonel Ruthven crossed the Tamar with the advance guard. Hopton had no choice: he must attempt to destroy Ruthven before he was joined by his main body under the Earl of Stamford. Ruthven played into his hands by not waiting for Stamford, and, advancing from Liskeard, drew up his army on the downs in front of the little church of Bradock. Hopton, reinforced by militiamen prepared to fight on Cornish soil, was at Boconnoc, only two miles away, and on January 19th on that lovely ridge between Bradock and Boconnoc the first battle in Cornwall was fought. It did not last long. After prayers had been said the Royalists advanced, the foot in the centre, cavalry on the flanks, and Grenville, emulating his ancestors, led the foot in so fierce a charge that at the first shock the enemy broke and fled, while the cavalry, helped by the men of Liskeard, turned defeat into a rout. 'But when resistance was over,' wrote Clarendon, 'the Cornish soldiers were very sparing of shedding blood, having a noble and Christian sense of the lives of their brethren.' Hopton was a Puritan, Grenville himself had leanings that way, and in the early days the Cornish army had a religious discipline that gave them an enviable reputation for mercy. Unhappily, it was not always to be like that.

The Royalist losses were light as the enemy's heavy – two hundred killed, twelve hundred captured and five guns – and having reorganised in Liskeard, Hopton set off in pursuit, making for Saltash where Ruthven was throwing up defences. In the afternoon of January 22nd Hopton attacked, carried the barricades, and drove the garrison down the steep slope into the river. Those who were not killed or drowned escaped in boats to Plymouth, leaving twenty guns and another hundred prisoners behind them. It was an astonishing little campaign, those four days from Bradock Down to Saltash. The first Parliamentary invasion had been flung back with heavy loss, and at the beginning of 1643 Cornwall was again in Royalist hands.

In the far west the war had become almost a private affair between Royalist Cornwall and Parliamentary Devon, the two forces facing each other across the frontier of the Tamar. For the moment Devonshire was on the defensive, but once again the Cornish militia refused to leave its native soil, and it was only with his small army of volunteers that Hopton could take the initiative and attempt to reduce Plymouth from bases at Tavistock, Plympton and Modbury. But now it was the turn of the Devonshire peasants to rise and defend their county from the invading Cornishmen, and in February the Royalists were driven back on Tavistock with severe losses in men and equipment. It was on a raid during this operation that Sidney Godolphin was killed at Chagford by a stray shot fired in the dark, 'from an undiscerned and undiscerning hand'. One of the minor Cavalier poets, 'a young gentleman of incomparable parts', as Clarendon called him, he was loved by all and a sad loss to the fellowship of Cornish Royalists.

Neither side was strong enough to take the offensive. The Cornish withdrew behind the Tamar, and there followed two months of truce while Stamford and Hopton increased and reorganised their forces. Barriers were thrown up about Bodmin, and by the time the truce ended, at midnight on April 22nd, Grenville, Basset and other Royalist leaders had brought their regiments into Launceston for the general muster that Hopton had ordered for the 23rd. At the same time the Parliamentarians concentrated at Lifton just across the river. As Stamford was ill, they were under the command of Major General James Chudleigh, Alexander Carew's cousin, a brilliant young soldier of twenty-five, who decided to attack Launceston before all the Royalist forces had arrived. Early on the morning of the 23rd he crossed Polston Bridge and began the difficult ascent of the steep hill on which Hopton was entrenched. But the defence was stubborn, he failed to carry the hill by assault, and in the course of the day the remaining Royalist columns arrived under Mohun, Berkeley, Slanning and John Trevanion. Chudleigh's problem was now to extricate himself and prevent being cut off at Polston Bridge, but he was saved by the arrival of a regiment from

Plymouth, and succeeded in withdrawing to Okehampton with little loss.

Hopton, with a force of four thousand newly equipped men, was now in a position to advance; it was indeed his duty to do so, for he had just received a letter from the King ordering him to join the Royalist army in Somerset. On the 25th, therefore, he set off gaily in pursuit of Chudleigh who was still at Okehampton, though with only a hundred horse and a thousand foot. When Chudleigh heard of his approach it was too late to save his infantry by anything but a stratagem, so dividing his cavalry into a number of small squadrons he posted them in hollows on Sourton Down, a few miles south of the town, with orders to charge and make as much noise as they could when the Royalists rode into the ambush. It was dark when the overconfident Cornishmen began their careless passage of the down, and suddenly squadrons of shouting horsemen appeared on all sides and charged their leading troops. All was confusion: the van was driven back on the main body and only the steadiness of the commanders saved the situation. They took up a position behind an old earthwork and awaited the attack, but all they saw was the blazing furze that Chudleigh set on fire. Their discomfiture was not yet over, for suddenly a thunderstorm broke over the moor. It was too much for the shaken and superstitious Cornishmen, who broke and fled to Bridestowe, where in the morning Hopton collected them and returned disconsolately to Launceston.

Many of Chudleigh's men disappeared that night, but he was left with the spoils of the demoralised Royalists scattered over the down, among them Hopton's despatch case containing the King's order to march into Somerset. This plan Stamford decided to prevent, and collecting an army of nearly six thousand men he joined Chudleigh and crossed the upper Tamar near Stratton on May 15th, at the same time sending Chudleigh's father, Sir George, with a thousand horse to make a diversion by a raid on Bodmin. At Stratton Stamford took up a strong position on a spur running north and south, its eastern side falling steeply into the valley of the little river, the gentler western slope defended by an earthwork on which he mounted his guns.

Although the Royalist army was barely half the size of Stamford's and not yet fully reorganised and equipped, Hopton marched rapidly north from Launceston, reaching Stratton on the evening of the 15th, soon after the Parliamentarians had taken up their position. Short of food and ammunition and already badly outnumbered, he could not afford to wait and risk Sir George Chudleigh's rejoining Stamford, and decided to attack the next day.

In the early morning of May 16th the assault began, the Cornish foot advancing up the hill from south and west, while the cavalry covered their rear. Time and again they charged, fired, reloaded and charged, led by Hopton and Mohun, Grenville and Berkeley, Slanning and Trevanion, but by three o'clock their powder was almost spent and the hill still held by the enemy. Then Hopton gave the inspired and inspiring order for a general advance without pausing to fire until they reached the top. This final flood tide of the Cornish foot proved irresistible – though Chudleigh led a dangerous counter-attack – and half an hour later they broke over the summit; the enemy fled and the hill was theirs. So were thirteen guns, £5,000 and seventeen hundred prisoners, including Chudleigh, who was so disheartened by Stamford's timid incapacity and full of admiration for the courage and godliness of the Royalists – they sang a *Te Deum* after their victory – that he changed his allegiance. A few weeks later Sir George Chudleigh, whose troops had been savagely handled at Bodmin when news of the battle of Stratton arrived, followed the example of his son.

Cornwall had now been made secure for the King, and could safely be left in charge of its energetic sheriff, Francis Basset, while the army moved eastward into a larger sphere of action. It was a force to be reckoned with, for after the battle of Stratton the Cornish foot acquired an almost legendary reputation, not only because of its fighting qualities but also because of its religious discipline, its chivalry and devotion to its commanders. It was indeed this devotion to men of the calibre of Grenville and Hopton that fused it into such a power, and the record of its exploits in the first heroic year of the war has something of the quality of Arthurian romance. Certainly, if their Celtic ancestors fought under Arthur as they fought under Grenville we can understand why the Saxon invaders were halted for so long.

At the end of May Hopton left Launceston with a force of nearly four thousand men and by June 4th reached Chard in his native Somerset, where he joined the Royalist army under the Marquis of Hertford and Prince Maurice. This was composed mainly of cavalry, Cavaliers whose laxness was a sad contrast to the discipline of the Cornishmen, and whose plundering activities made them feared and hated wherever they passed. Yet it was this cavalry, brilliant and reckless, that gave the Royalists their superiority until Cromwell had trained horsemen who were more than a match for them.

Having occupied Taunton and Bridgwater the Royalists advanced on Bath, held for Parliament by Sir William Waller, Hopton's friend. Hopton wrote to him, in the hope of arranging a meeting, but Waller replied sadly, 'Certainly my affections to you are so unchangeable that hostility itself cannot violate my friendship to your person, but I must be true to the cause wherein I serve', and a few days later, on July 5th, the friends confronted one another with their rival armies on the high escarpment of the Cotswolds north of Bath. Waller's position between Hopton and the town was immensely strong, on the fortified summit of Lansdown ridge, so strong that Hopton began to withdraw. Seeing this, Waller ordered his cavalry to attack, but after a fierce engagement it was repulsed, and the Cornish foot, flushed with success and infuriated by the enemy's fire, asked to be led up the hill to seize the guns. It was Stratton fight over again, though on a bigger and more desperate scale, and when Grenville reached the top he had to hold the edge of the plateau with his stand of pikes against repeated charges of the Parliamentary horse. Slowly Waller was forced back, but when he took up his final position within a walled enclosure it was already dark and the Royalists were too exhausted to continue the attack. It was a barren victory, for though Hopton had gained the ridge, Waller was able to withdraw into Bath under cover of night, and the losses were terrible. Worst of all, Grenville had been mortally wounded in the moment of victory. He died the next day, and his body was taken back to Kilkhampton for burial. It was the death that he wished for, but his loss was irreparable, and for many of the Cornishmen all brightness and meaning had fallen from the war, for it was for Grenville whom they loved and not for a remote and unknown King that they had fought.

While Waller rested and reorganised his troops in Bath, the Royalists, who were in hostile territory, prepared to retire, but as Hopton was riding over the field an ammunition wagon exploded, almost blinding him and burning him so severely that his men despaired of his life, and, Hopton gone as well as Grenville, their plight would be desperate. It was sufficiently desperate in any event, for Waller was now in pursuit, reinforced by part of the Bristol garrison, and on the 9th he caught them at Devizes. As it was too late to attack that night, he took up his position on Roundway Down to the north of the town, so cutting them off from Oxford where the King lay. Fortunately Hopton was recovering and, while Hertford with the cavalry burst through the enemy lines to fetch help from Oxford, he organised the defence of Devizes. There was little ammunition left after the explosion, but the town, which was Royalist, supplied gunpowder, while bullets were made from the lead on the church roofs and fuses out of bed-cords. For three days the Royalists held out – 'the Cornish defend it bravely', wrote Waller, who tried to persuade Hopton to surrender – and then on the 13th the relieving force arrived from Oxford. Waller turned to meet it on Roundway Down, at once ordering his crack corps of cuirassiers to charge. But the 'Lobsters', too heavily armed for the steep and difficult ground, were swept back by the light Royalist horse, while the Cornish foot from Devizes attacked Waller's position from the rear. The Parliamentary army was routed; about a thousand were killed, most of the foot taken prisoner, the rest escaping into Gloucestershire. 'My dismal defeat at Roundway', wrote Waller, 'the most dismal stroke of any that did befal me.' It was the most dismal stroke that had yet befallen Parliament, and the way was open for the seizure of Bristol, after

London itself the greatest city and most important Parliamentary stronghold in the country.

The Royalists turned west, occupied Bath, and on July 23rd were joined before Bristol by Prince Rupert from Oxford. Their army was now nearly fifteen thousand strong, while the Bristol garrison was under two thousand, many of their men having been lost with Waller on Roundway Down. But its defences were immensely strong, particularly on the south side where the Cornish division was posted. There was no great hurry, for the city could have little hope of relief, and the Cornish officers counselled a siege, but the impetuous Rupert, facing the weaker northern defences, favoured an assault, and finally succeeded in imposing his plan.

The Cornish division began the attack at dawn on the 26th, Slanning in the centre, Sir Thomas Basset with Grenville's and Godolphin's regiments on his left. Facing them was a broad ditch, backed by the city walls, and finally the central citadel of the castle. It was madness to attempt to take such a position by storm, yet the ditch was bridged with wagons from the top of which the Cornishmen attempted to scale the walls. But their ladders were too short and, exposed to a murderous fire from the ramparts, they were compelled to withdraw after an assault of three hours and loss of a third of their number. As they were re-forming, Rupert sent word that the northern defences had been breached, and asked for reinforcements of Cornish foot. Five hundred answered the call and helped to force a way through the narrow streets into the city centre. Even then, however, Bristol was by no means theirs, only one fort having fallen and the castle remaining intact; but the Governor, Colonel Nathaniel Fiennes, considering the position hopeless and anxious to prevent unnecessary destruction, surrendered. The next day the Parliamentary garrison marched out, and the great city and port was in the hands of the King.

But the price was high, for the losses had been fearful, particularly among the Cornishmen, who had suffered so severely in the futile assaults on the southern defences that of the three thousand foot whom Hopton had led out of Launceston two months before only about half remained. And most of their leaders had gone. Godolphin and Grenville, and now John Trevanion and Nicholas Slanning, both mortally wounded as they led their men to the assault.

> The four wheels of Charles's Wain,
> Grenville, Godolphin, Trevanion, Slanning, slain.

They had fought together throughout the war, and now they died together, 'hurt almost in the same minute and in the same place, both shot in the thigh with a musket bullet'. 'They were both very young,' wrote Clarendon, 'of entire friendship to one another, and to Sir Bevil Grenville.' It was like the break-up of the fellowship of the Round Table, another echo of Arthurian romance.

And it was the end of the fellowship of the Cornish army as a whole. Their loyalty had been to their leaders, who had fused them together and inspired them with a crusading zeal; now they were dead, while the wounded Hopton was to be left in Bristol as Lieutenant Governor. The heroic year was over; the men were infected with the laxity of the Cavaliers; some deserted and stole home with their booty, and the remainder flatly refused to be led to the siege of Gloucester. There was another dangerous Parliamentary stronghold nearer home, and they marched westward towards Plymouth, the foot under Prince Maurice, the horse under the Earl of Carnarvon.

Although the Cornish army was no longer the fighting force that it had been, its reputation after the fall of Bristol was almost fabulous, and as it marched through the west country many of the Parliamentary towns surrendered with scarcely a blow. Dorchester, hearing that the Cornishmen could run up walls twenty feet high, yielded at the first summons, and Weymouth and Portland followed their example. Bideford and Barnstaple fell on August 28th, and by that time Exeter itself was on the point of capitulation. It would soon be the turn of Plymouth.

There, Sir Alexander Carew, a baronet since the death of his father in March, was in command of the vitally important defences on Drake's Island in the Sound. He had watched events uneasily since the battle of Stratton when his cousin and uncle, the Chudleighs, changed their allegiance, and as one town after another surrendered to the returning Cornish army he lost his nerve. He approached some of his Royalist friends and offered to surrender the fort and island if they would obtain a full pardon from the King. Sir John Berkeley, who was with Prince Maurice besieging Exeter, guaranteed his safety and urged him to carry out his plans at once, but Carew insisted that he must have the King's written word. It was too late: a trusted servant betrayed his design to the mayor, and he was arrested in his fort and shipped off to London for trial. A year later he was executed on Tower Hill. 'Dost thou hear,' he said to the executioner, 'when I say, "Lord though thou killest me, yet will I put my trust in thee," then do thou cut off my head. For it was the last words that ever my mother spoke when she died.' Then, kneeling down with his head on the block, he spoke the words – and the executioner did his office.

He too was young, and many older men than he changed sides. Then, after the death of his mother he had been brought up by his fanatically devout father, who took complete charge of his spiritual and physical welfare, even nursing him alone through an almost mortal illness. It was an unhealthy, emotionally overcharged atmosphere, which might have sapped the strength of any boy's character; but perhaps his convictions suffered a genuine change after his father's death, and it was never definitely proved that he intended to surrender the fort. His portrait still hangs at Antony House, and the story is that when he sided with Parliament his family cut it out of the frame, replacing it when he changed his mind. It is most unlikely. His father was a Puritan and Parliamentarian, and died six months before Alexander's defection. It is much more probable that any slashing was done by his half-brother John when he heard of his attempt to join the King. Whatever happened, the canvas has certainly been cut and stitched together again.

Carew's apparent treachery was followed on September 4th by the capitulation of Exeter, and a month later by the fall of

Dartmouth. All the west country, save only Poole, Lyme Regis and Plymouth, was in Royalist hands, and from his camp at Sudeley Castle in the Cotswolds the King sent a 'Declaration unto all his loving Subjects in the County of Cornwall', thanking them for their extraordinary zeal, patience and courage in his cause, and ordering copies to be published in every church, where they were to be kept, 'That as long as the History of these Times and this Nation shall continue, the Memory of how much that County hath merited from Us and Our Crown may be derived with it to Posterity.' The message can still be seen on the walls of some of the Cornish churches.

Plymouth might have fallen soon after Exeter had not Prince Maurice spent a precious month in the reduction of Dartmouth, allowing time for Parliament to reinforce the garrison and strengthen its defences. But its position was still perilous in the extreme: closely invested by the Royalists, its fate could well be a decisive factor in determining the issue of the war.

At the beginning of 1644 the Royalists were heartened by the arrival of another Grenville, Sir Richard, a fine soldier though a very different man from his elder brother Sir Bevil. Brutal and cynical, he had fought in Germany and Ireland before returning to England in 1643, when he was wooed by Parliament, who gave him £600 and a troop of horse, with which he at once rode off to join the King at Oxford. The impotent Parliamentarians hanged him in effigy and ever afterwards referred to him as Skellum Grenville.

About the next move in the west there were divided counsels in both camps, but in June the Parliamentary commander, the Earl of Essex, encouraged by Lord Robartes of Lanhydrock, insisted on marching into Devonshire to relieve Plymouth. As his army passed through Dorset, Prince Maurice retreated on Exeter from Lyme, which he was besieging, while Weymouth and Taunton were both occupied by the Parliamentarians. Meanwhile the King himself was hard on the heels of Essex, joining Prince Maurice at Exeter on July 26th, the day on which Essex crossed the Tamar into Cornwall. It was a rash move, but his arrival at Tavistock had secured his primary objective by drawing off the besieging Royalists from Plymouth, and Robartes assured him that he had only to appear in Cornwall for the peasants to rise for Parliament. If he believed that he was sadly mistaken, but then Robartes was hardly disinterested so long as Lanhydrock was in Royalist hands.

Sir Richard Grenville disputed Essex's passage of the Tamar at Horsebridge, but was repulsed and retreated on Truro, while Essex advanced through Liskeard to Lanhydrock and Bodmin. He was now in the centre of Cornwall, but instead of the friendly peasants he had been led to expect, he found himself surrounded by a savagely hostile people, all their latent hatred of the foreigner roused by his invasion. He was, indeed, in an extremely critical position: the King and Prince Maurice were now at Launceston, having been joined by Hopton who had raised another army in Somerset, while Grenville threatened him from the west. His one chance was to secure a base from which he could be reinforced or withdraw by sea, and he moved south to Lostwithiel and occupied Fowey.

But reinforcements never arrived, and by the middle of August the Parliamentarians were surrounded by the four Royalist armies, confined to the Gribbin peninsula and the valley of the Fowey between Lostwithiel and the sea. Grenville had taken Bodmin and was at Lanhydrock on the west bank of the river, in contact with the King, whose headquarters were at Boconnoc, the site of Bevil Grenville's victory on Bradock Down. The King had been careful to warn his troops not to alienate the Cornish people, whom he regarded as peculiarly his own, so many of them being tenants of Duchy manors, and Prince Maurice hanged at least one of his men for looting at Lanhydrock. On the other hand, the Parliamentary army of ten thousand men, confined within an area of a few square miles, was compelled to live largely off the country, seizing what the natives would not render freely, though it was also guilty of wanton plunder and destruction, completely sacking Jonathan Rashleigh's houses at Fowey and Menabilly, and at Lostwithiel burning the Exchequer records and attempting to blow up the parish church with Royalist prisoners inside it.

Yet Essex had only himself to blame: he had acted against the advice of Parliament, and did singularly little to retrieve the situation. He allowed the King to seize the east bank of the river, from Beacon Hill overlooking Lostwithiel to Polruan opposite Fowey, thereby losing control of the port, and he left Restormel so inadequately defended that on August 21st it was taken by Grenville. At the same time the King sent Goring with three thousand men to seize the little port of Par, west of Fowey, thus depriving him of the only remaining harbour from which he could reasonably hope to escape.

By the 30th the position was desperate, and Essex, who had resolutely refused the King's appeals to surrender, decided to try to cut his way out that night. While the cavalry under Sir William Balfour broke through the Royalist lines to the east, he would lead the foot down to Fowey and attempt to embark them there for Plymouth. The cold wet weather had added to the misery of his half-starved troops, but the mist and darkness of that night were all that could be wished, and Balfour managed to elude the Royalists and gallop over Bradock Down towards Saltash, where he crossed the river and got safely into Plymouth. The foot were less fortunate. The rain had made the road to Fowey almost impassable, and Skippon, who was in the rear with the artillery, had to abandon four of his guns in the mud. On the morning of the 31st they had got only as far as Castle Dore, and there, within the ramparts of King Mark, Essex made his last stand. All day they fought, the Cornish foot leading the attack, and as darkness fell the Royalists broke through the eastern gateway – it had ever been the weak point in the defences – cutting the line of retreat to Golant and the river. Early the next morning Essex and Robartes slipped away and sailed for Plymouth in a fishing boat.

Skippon, finding himself and the army thus deserted, rose nobly to the occasion and proposed following the example of the horse and cutting his way out, but he was overruled by the other officers and forced to accept the King's terms of surrender. They were honourable: the wounded were to be sent by sea from Fowey to Plymouth, while the remainder of the army, the officers being allowed to retain their arms, was to march out of Cornwall under guard. But their guard was powerless to prevent the plundering of the Royalist forces, and even worse was their treatment at the hands of the Cornish peasants, women as well as men, who assaulted the drenched, starving and ragged troops, robbed them of the little food they had and stripped them of their clothing, sometimes even of their boots. By the time they reached the Tamar half of them had died of ill-treatment, starvation, sickness or exposure, and of the six thousand men who left Lostwithiel on that terrible retreat only a thousand reached the safety of Poole in Dorset. At last the Celts had avenged themselves on the invading Saxons.

While Skippon set out on his ill-fated march the King knighted Francis Basset at Boconnoc. He well deserved the honour, for since the beginning of the war he had raised the money to finance the King's cause in the west, levying taxes, selling tin and collecting plate, and after Slanning's death had taken over the organisation of the privateers who brought many profitable prizes into Cornish ports. Moreover he spent more than £1,500 of his own money in strengthening the defences of St Michael's Mount and paying its garrison of fifty men. No wonder the King said before his departure, 'Now Mr Sheriff, I leave Cornwall to

11. St Michael's Mount at sunset.

you safe and sound.' Charles Trevanion of Carhays and John Arundell of Lanherne were also knighted, while Sir Richard Vyvyan of Trelowarren was made a baronet. Sir Richard Grenville also had his reward. He received the sequestrated estates of Lord Robartes at Lanhydrock and of Sir Francis Drake, another Parliamentarian, at Buckland. Once again there was a Sir Richard Grenville at the Abbey. He celebrated the occasion by taking Saltash and, in the manner of the German wars, hanging those who had helped Balfour and the Parliamentary horse to escape to Plymouth.

The King left Boconnoc on September 4th, and two days later joined Grenville before Plymouth, but, remembering his failure at Gloucester, he had no mind to begin a regular siege, and he hesitated to repeat the storming of Bristol until all his Cornish forces had been brought up. The delay was fatal, for the arrival of Lord Robartes, who had been made governor, put new heart into the citizens and garrison, still eager to be avenged on the 'cursed Cornish'. When, therefore, Charles called upon the town to surrender, he received so defiant a reply that he abandoned the idea both of siege and assault and began his march back to Oxford, leaving Grenville to blockade the town. There was little love lost between the governor of Plymouth and the Cornish commander, and when Robartes executed young Joseph Grenville on a charge of treachery Sir Richard replied by ordering the execution of three hundred prisoners, and only the King's intervention prevented his hanging them. The war in the west was degenerating into one of atrocities and reprisals in the continental manner; the chivalry of Sir Bevil Grenville giving place to the brutality of Sir Richard.

The King reached Oxford safely after fighting the indecisive second battle of Newbury, in which the Cornish contingent was severely handled by the survivors of the retreat from Lostwithiel. It had been a triumphantly successful campaign: Essex's army was virtually destroyed and Cornwall saved for the Royalist cause. Yet so long as Lyme, Taunton and Plymouth were held for Parliament the west country could not be considered secure.

In the spring of 1645 the King appointed his son Charles, Prince of Wales and Duke of Cornwall, commander of the western army, in the hope that his presence would rally the Royalists and lead to the fall of the Parliamentary strongholds, though as the Prince was only fifteen his position was merely titular and he was accompanied by a Council, the chief members of which were Sir Edward Hyde and Lord Hopton. It was not easy for them to control the commanders in the field, either the dissolute and unpredictable Lord Goring, whose pillaging troops were the terror of the countryside, or the savage and rapacious bully Grenville, who, however, did at least enforce discipline among his men, and in spite of his partiality for hanging retained some popularity in Cornwall because of his name. The two men were profoundly jealous of one another, continually quarrelling and quite unable to cooperate, while they both disliked Hyde as much as he distrusted them. The result was that Taunton, which might have fallen to a combined attack, resisted the separate assaults of the two commanders, and Grenville was severely wounded. To make matters worse, the New Model Army under Fairfax and Cromwell, having routed the Royalists at Naseby, was marching into the west.

At the beginning of July Fairfax was in Dorchester, while Grenville, Achilles-like, sulked at Ottery St Mary, and Goring drank and diced near Langport. On the 9th Fairfax occupied Yeovil, and on the following day stormed Goring's position, his cavalry under Cromwell pursuing the routed Royalists as far as the gates of Bridgwater, which capitulated a fortnight later. It was a shattering disaster, for Bridgwater was the Royalist arsenal, and vast quantities of arms and ammunition fell to the Parliamentary forces. The Prince and his Council retired to Launceston, and at Bodmin Hyde and Hopton appealed to the 'noble Cornwallians, both gentry and commonalty', to rally to the King's cause as they had done in the first heroic year of the war. But the Cornish were exhausted, disillusioned and impoverished, and the example of the two squabbling commanders was scarcely encouraging: while Goring boasted that one of his Irish soldiers was worth ten of Grenville's

Cornish cowards, Grenville ordered the people to rise and drive out Goring's troops if they should enter the county.

Hyde was fortunate in having a breathing space in which to order the finances of Cornwall and organise its defence, though the period was a calamitous one for the Royalist cause as a whole. After the fall of Bridgwater, Fairfax wisely secured his rear before crossing the Tamar, and followed up the storming of Sherborne Castle with an assault on Bristol, which capitulated on September 10th. The King lost immense quantities of stores as well as his greatest port, and the way was open for the final invasion of Cornwall.

Fairfax resumed his westward march, and by the middle of October had taken Tiverton, where Goring had dallied before retiring to Exeter and then embarking for France on a holiday, leaving Lord Wentworth in command of his demoralised troops. Meanwhile Grenville was engaged in putting down an insurrection in St Ives, where some of the leading men, notably Major Peter Ceely, were supporters of Parliament. There he ordered a Zennor constable to be hanged, and on the following day two other St Ives men suffered the same fate, one at Helston, the other at Truro, while he committed the mayor, Edward Hammond, to Launceston gaol for refusing to pay a fine of £400. Grenville had lodged with Hammond while in St Ives. He had a grim sense of humour, and it was an even better joke to hang the lawyer who had conducted his wife's case when she divorced him.

When Fairfax swept Wentworth and the remainder of Goring's army out of Devonshire all the Royalist forces withdrew into Cornwall, the long siege of Plymouth was abandoned, and the Prince removed to the safety of Pendennis Castle. It was the beginning of the end of the Cornish tragedy, though fortunately the last act was to be worthy of the first, and played under the lead of the man who had conducted the campaign from Bradock Down to Bristol. On January 15th, 1646, Lord Hopton was given the supreme command, Wentworth and Grenville agreeing to serve as his generals of horse and foot respectively. With a man of Hopton's ability and integrity in charge there was just a chance that the King's cause would yet be saved in Cornwall, but Grenville contrived to wreck the new harmony. Two days later he refused to obey Hopton's orders and was promptly arrested by the Prince's Council and delivered into the custody of Sir Arthur Basset at St Michael's Mount. His arrest was as unfortunate as it was essential, for Hopton and Hyde were 'foreigners' while Grenville was a Cornishman and brother of Sir Bevil. The peasants as well as the troops demanded his release, and when it was refused Hopton found himself in command of a sullen and reluctant army.

While Grenville was disobeying orders, Fairfax was storming Dartmouth, and sending off each Cornish prisoner with two silver shillings jingling in his pocket to pay for his journey home, a very different treatment from that meted out by Goring and Grenville, and one that encouraged thousands of Devonshiremen to join him. He now gathered his forces to attack Exeter, and Hopton advanced from Stratton with his undisciplined little army in a desperate attempt to relieve the town, but Fairfax met him at Torrington, threw him back over the Tamar, and occupied Launceston.

Before pressing farther west Fairfax sent an emissary to negotiate with the eastern Cornish gentry. This was his chaplain, Hugh Peters, son of Thomas Dickwood, *alias* Peters, and Martha Treffry of Fowey, a fanatical preacher whose eloquence was used to inspire the Parliamentary troops before battle, and he had little difficulty in extracting promises from Colonel Edgcumbe and his friends to keep the eastern peasants quiet while Fairfax advanced. When, therefore, Fairfax entered Bodmin on March 2nd he could be reasonably certain that his rear was secure. That night, while Hopton camped on Castle-an-Dinas, Hyde left Pendennis with the Prince of Wales and sailed for Scilly.

The position of Hopton was now hopeless, and he must have thought bitterly of the early days of the war when he had led the devoted and irresistible Cornish foot with Bevil Grenville and his peers from Bradock Down to Bristol. Now he commanded the demoralised fragments of an army eager only to surrender in a war-weary county that welcomed the disciplined Parliamentary forces and their magnanimous general. But it was only when pushed back to Truro that he consented to treat with Fairfax, and even then he refused to surrender the Mount and Pendennis, reinforcing the one with two hundred men and sending a further nine hundred under John Arundell of Trerice to defend the other. On March 12th he signed the treaty of surrender before joining the Prince in Scilly, and the remains of his army in the field laid down their arms. A few days later St Mawes Castle and Dennis Fort at the mouth of the Helford river capitulated. Pendennis was thus robbed of protection on either flank, and Fairfax called on John Arundell to surrender, giving him two hours in which to reply. But Arundell, for all his seventy years, was made of the same stuff as Bevil Grenville, and replied:

> Sir, The Castle was committed to my government by His Majesty, who by our laws hath the command of the Castles and Forts of this Kingdom, and my age of seventy summons me hence shortly. Yet I shall desire no other testimony to follow my departure than my conscience to God and loyalty to His Majesty, whereto I am bound by all the obligations of nature, duty and oath. I wonder you demand the Castle without authority from His Majesty, which if I should render, I brand myself and my posterity with the indelible character of Treason. And having taken less than two minutes resolution, I resolve that I will here bury myself before I deliver up this Castle to such as fight against His Majesty, and that nothing you can threaten is formidable to me in respect of the loss of loyalty and conscience. Your servant, John Arundell of Trerice, 18th March, 1645.

It was clear that the capture of Pendennis was going to be a lengthy business, and Fairfax, leaving the siege to Colonel Hammond, marched back through Bodmin, Launceston and Plymouth to Exeter, which capitulated on April 19th, and so to Oxford, which fell two months later.

The Royalist strongholds were tumbling. On April 16th Sir Arthur Basset, who had succeeded his brother Sir Francis, surrendered the Mount, and on the same day the Prince with his Council and three hundred Royalist refugees left Scilly for Jersey. By the end of June the Prince was an exile in France and the King a prisoner in the hands of the Scots, but still the loyal old Arundell held out, resisting the honourable terms offered by Colonel Hammond and Admiral Batten, who blockaded him by sea. Some of the garrison deserted, but the remainder stood firm although plague had broken out and they were reduced to 'eating horses for beef'. On June 27th Arundell wrote to the Prince telling him that 'it is now come to the last with us', yet it was another two months before starvation drove him to surrender: he could not allow the women, children and the sick, 'fedd upon bread and water', to die of hunger. On the afternoon of August 17th 'Jack for the King' and his garrison marched out with their horses and arms, 'colours flying, trumpets sounding, drums beating, matches lighted at both ends, and bullets in their mouths'. It was a fitting close to the Civil War in Cornwall.

Some of the Royalist leaders chose exile rather than submission to Parliament. Sir Francis Godolphin, Governor of Scilly, and young John Grenville, Sir Bevil's son, had already joined the Prince of Wales – they were both of an age – and now there was Sir Henry Killigrew. Although he had never accepted high command, he had fought throughout the war from Bradock Down to Pendennis, and was one of the rare fellowship of Bevil Grenville and his circle; but he did not long survive defeat, dying of wounds in France a month after the surrender. Those who remained were forced to compound for their confiscated estates by paying huge fines varying from a sixth to half their value. Jonathan Rashleigh was almost ruined, and Sir Richard Vyvyan of Trelowarren would have suffered even more severely than he did had it not been for the intervention of Fairfax, who also saw to it that Peter Edgcumbe, William Coryton and the other eastern gentry who had surrendered when he entered Cornwall were more lightly treated. The Bassets were so impoverished that in 1657 they sold St Michael's Mount to John St Aubyn of Clowance, the Parliamentary leader.

The Anglican clergy received equally harsh treatment. The Prayer Book service was forbidden, and those who would not conform to the law were deprived of their livings. Altogether some two thousand were expelled, about a hundred of them being in Cornwall. Richard Tucker, rector of Ludgvan, a widower with eight young children, was driven out of his house without food or belongings, and Thomas Harrison of Lanivet was thrown into prison and received such treatment that he went blind. No doubt these were extreme cases, but few of the ejected clergy received the small pension to which they were entitled. The churches suffered too. Much of their medieval beauty had been destroyed by the zealots of the Reformation, and now the Puritans had their way. 'Payd the Joyners for takinge downe the Organs and Railings of the church £1 15s 7d', reads one item in the accounts of the Mayor of St Ives for 1647–8. The 'railings' were the fifteenth-century rood screen, and men were similarly paid to smash any stained glass that had escaped the attention of previous reformers. Although the vicar of St Neot was one of the evicted clergy, somehow the windows of his church survived to bear witness to what has been lost.

Not only the Royalists and Anglican clergy, but the Cornish people as a whole were in a pitiful condition. Apart from the loss of many of their best men, they had suffered the depredations of invading armies, the marauding of Goring's Cavaliers and the exactions of Skellum Grenville; harvests had been lost, tin mines flooded and bridges broken; and now they had to support an army of bureaucrats busily collecting taxes and fines. To make matters worse the end of the war was followed by bad harvests, and plague spread from Pendennis to the western towns. St Ives was isolated and, though food from neighbouring parishes was placed on the boundary of the stricken area, more than five hundred people, about a third of the population, died of famine and pestilence. By 1648 Cornwall was ripe for another revolt.

In the spring of that year the Second Civil War, fomented by the King, who played off the Scots, Parliament and Army against one another, broke out in Wales and was quickly followed by insurrections in other parts of the country. Cornwall was of course suspect, and Sir Hardress Waller was sent down to preserve order. Having learned who were the most dangerous Royalists, he arrested Sir John Trelawny and Robert Harris, but this did not prevent a rising of lesser men from the Mount's Bay region in May. The rebels were caught in Penzance, but no sooner had the town been seized than the men of the Helford area were up. From Mullion and St Keverne they converged on Mawgan, threatening Helston from their position in the ancient earthwork of Gear between Trelowarren and the Helford river, but the troops from Penzance arrived just in time to scatter them, and they fled over Goonhilly Downs, some, it is said, jumping into the sea in despair. John Arundell of Trerice, the suspected instigator of the revolt, was heavily fined, as was Sir John Trelawny, while his son Jonathan suffered the first of his many imprisonments. It was a forlorn little affair, for Cornwall was too exhausted to do much, but failure on the mainland was redeemed by a successful revolt in Scilly, which under Sir John Grenville became for a time a Royalist base for privateers.

The Second Civil War left the Army in control of England. Cromwell had defeated the Scots, and now Colonel Pryde forcibly excluded the Presbyterian members from Parliament. All that remained of the Long Parliament of 1640 was a Rump of sixty, Independents dependent on the Army, among them ten Cornish representatives, including Francis Rous, now Provost of Eton, and John Carew, half-brother of the unfortunate Sir Alexander. The Rump had its orders, and in January 1649 dutifully appointed a Commission to try the King for treason. John Carew was one of his judges and, although not of the Commission, another Cornishman was active in the proceedings, Hugh Peters, who, in sermon after sermon, incited them to find the King guilty: 'Turn to your Bibles,' he preached to Cromwell and Bradshaw, 'and ye shall find it there: Whosoever sheds man's blood, by man shall his blood be shed.' Peters was not a vicious man, merely a fanatic finding justification for his actions in the Old Testament. The King was found guilty, and John Carew and the other two Cornish representatives on the Commission, Gregory Clement and William Say, signed his death warrant. He was executed at

Whitehall on January 30th, when 'there was such a grone by the Thousands there present', wrote one of the spectators, 'as I never heard before and desire I may never hear again'. The elements themselves seemed to play a part in the tragedy. On the same day a great storm broke over west Cornwall; a ship carrying the King's belongings to France was wrecked on Godrevy Island with the loss of all on board, and rocks were overthrown at the Land's End.

England was now a republic governed by Cromwell and the Army through the agency of the Rump, and as there was no longer a King, Prince of Wales or Duke of Cornwall, the Duchy was abolished and an Act passed for the sale of 'the Honors, Manors, Lands heretofore belonging to the late King, Queen and Prince'. There were very few small buyers, as most of the tenants, fearing or hoping for a restoration of the monarchy, which would invalidate their contracts, preferred to remain as tenants. But some of the Parliamentary officers acquired large estates, Colonel Robert Bennett for example, who bought the honour of Launceston Castle and the manor of Tintagel, now 'totally out of repair, ye material not being worth taking down'. Despite the change of ownership, life on the Duchy manors went on much as usual.

Although England was a republic, the Scots recognised the Prince of Wales as their new King – after all the Stuarts were Scottish – and the Royalist exiles in Jersey and Scilly proclaimed him as Charles II. Their cause now had a martyr, and the danger of a western rising was correspondingly increased. 'The news of that most horrid murder and treason,' wrote Sir John Grenville, 'has so transported me with grief as that I am not able to expresse it to you, this barbarous and most inhumane action being without president the greatest that ever has byn committed,' and Hopton from his base in Scilly preyed on the Parliamentary shipping, and exhorted the gentlemen and people of Cornwall to support the new King Charles.

The government was on the alert, strengthened the army of occupation, and made a number of precautionary arrests: Francis Godolphin, Sir Charles Trevanion, John Arundel of Trerice, Sir

Nicholas Prideaux and others were seized, and when Sir John Berkeley and Colonel Walter Slingsby were discovered at Carhays they were imprisoned in Pendennis Castle. Those who were left at large, however, wisely refused to act rashly, demanding the landing of Sir Richard Grenville with forces from Scilly before they rose, while Sir John Arundell of Lanherne asked Charles for an assurance that he would grant toleration to Catholics if he were restored. Charles, ready to promise anything, assured him that he would, but when the Scottish Royalists were defeated he came to terms with the Presbyterians, promising to impose their religion on England and to enforce the penal laws against Catholics. Such perfidy cost him the support of some of the most honourable men in his cause, the respect of those who still followed him, and prejudiced the chances of a rising on his behalf.

Meanwhile the government tightened its grip on the county, exacting crippling fines from those, like Sir John Arundell of Lanherne, whose loyalty – quite rightly – it suspected, and getting smaller men out of the way by pressing them for the navy. Then in the spring of 1651 the Royalists suffered a serious reverse. In March a Dutch fleet appeared off Scilly to demand reparations for the damage inflicted by privateers on their shipping. The government protested, ordered Admiral Blake to seize the islands from Grenville and to fight the Dutch if they intervened. Blake, with five times as many men as Grenville, took Tresco by night assault, but it was another six weeks before St Mary's surrendered. The terms were honourable: the garrison, many of them Irish, were allowed to go home, and Grenville himself joined the Court of Charles II in France.

There things were in a bad way, largely owing to the dissension and suspicion sown by Grenville's uncle, Sir Richard. On the slenderest evidence he accused Hyde of treating with Cromwell, but when Charles discovered how baseless the charge was he banished him from Court for his malicious calumny. Grenville wrote a lachrymose defence: 'As for Sir Richard Grenville, let him go with the reward of an old soldier of the King's. There is no present use for him.' There was not, and he died poor and unlamented in Ghent shortly before the Restoration.

After the loss of Scilly the prospect of a successful Royalist rising faded, and when in 1653 Cromwell established a dictatorship it was virtually extinguished. In April he dissolved the Rump, and in December the little assembly of the 'Saints' nominated by the Independent congregations. The Speaker of this, the so-called Barebones Parliament, was Francis Rous, and it was he who submissively offered its resignation without putting the motion to the vote. Four days later, on December 16th, Cromwell assumed the office of Lord Protector. John Carew protested, and shortly afterwards he and other leading republicans and Fifth Monarchy men – those who expected the coming of the Empire of Christ – were imprisoned. So too was George Fox, founder of the Quakers. Arrested by Major Ceely at St Ives in January 1656, he was removed to Launceston where he was imprisoned until released in September by order of Colonel Bennett, the owner of the castle.

If religious sects were thus persecuted by Cromwell and his agents, his political opponents could scarcely expect more generous treatment. After there had been another short experiment with a Parliament, in which the Cornish representatives were reduced from forty-four to twelve, the Royalists at last rose in desperation, but the insurrection was ill-concerted and hopeless from the start. In March 1655 Sir Joseph Wagstaffe proclaimed Charles II in Salisbury, marched into Dorset with some two hundred men, but failing to raise further supporters made for Cornwall in the hope of being joined by the Royalists there. But his little force was caught at South Molton, twenty miles short of the Cornish border, and scattered. Wagstaffe escaped, but a number of his followers were executed, others imprisoned and many more transported to Barbados. This savage repression was followed by the setting up of a naked military dictatorship under ten Major Generals, each responsible for ordering a part of the country with an army paid for by taxes levied on the Royalists. Starting as an opponent of despotism, Cromwell had been driven to reduce England to a police state.

As the Cornish Royalists had not risen in 1655 they escaped the persecution of the other western counties. But it was well known that Sir John Grenville, now back at Stowe, Jonathan Trelawny, the Arundells of Lanherne and Trerice, and many others were intriguing on behalf of the King, and in the spring of 1657 many of them were arrested as a precautionary measure. The Royalist cause seemed lost, when on September 3rd, 1658, all was transformed by the death of Cromwell.

There followed a period of confusion in which Cromwell's son Richard, the new Protector, was swept aside, and England fell into the power of the generals. One of these was George Monk in command of the army in Scotland, a Devonshireman and a cousin of Grenville's. Moreover Monk's brother Nicholas was vicar of Kilkhampton, the Grenville living near Stowe. In July 1659, therefore, Grenville sent Nicholas to Scotland to persuade his brother to declare for a free Parliament and the restoration of the monarchy. Monk made no promises, but in November Grenville wrote to the King, 'We shall still endeavour to promote and if possible to invite him to the loyalty and Dutie to your Majesty.' In January the enigmatic Monk crossed the Tweed and marched south, brushing aside the rival generals who opposed him, and in March met Grenville in London. There, in a secret interview, he embraced his cousin, thanked him for his fidelity and prudence, and gave him a message for the King. Charles accepted Monk's terms and sent Grenville back with letters, one of which was read in the House of Commons on May 1st, 'which,' wrote Pepys, 'will be remembered for the happiest May Day that hath been many a year in England. Thanks were given by the House to Sir John Grenville, one of the bedchamber to the King, who brought the letter'. On May 25th King Charles II, a tall swarthy man of thirty, more French than English, landed at Dover.

Although Hyde persuaded the Convention Parliament which had restored Charles to the throne to pass an Act of Indemnity and Oblivion, it had no intention of allowing its extreme opponents to escape its vengeance. Cromwell's body was dug up, dragged to Tyburn, hanged in sight of the people and buried at the gallows' foot. Another scaffold was set up at Charing Cross, and there the surviving regicides, those who had signed the death warrant of Charles I, were butchered. One of these was John Carew, who, refusing to make any attempt to escape, obeyed the proclamation ordering all regicides to surrender. At his trial at the Old Bailey in October, he pleaded 'Not guilty, saving to our Lord Jesus Christ his right to the government of these kingdoms.' He was found guilty of high treason and sentenced to death, which he faced with such high courage and unshaken faith that he comforted and inspired all those who saw him. On October 15th he was drawn on a hurdle from Newgate to Charing Cross, where he was hanged, cut down and hacked in pieces, his reeking heart plucked out and displayed to the people. His dismembered body should have been exposed above the City gates, but the King granted his family's earnest petition and in the same night it was obscurely buried. Hyde could scarcely have accused John Carew, as he accused Sir Alexander, of having 'no other motives than of popularity and interests, neither courage enough to obey his convictions'. If the honour of the Carews of Antony had been tarnished by the treachery of one brother, it had been scoured clean with the blood of the other.

Hugh Peters suffered on the following day. Although not a regicide, he was accused and found guilty of inciting 'the soldiery to take off the King'. He too died courageously, although subjected to even greater brutality. After he had been made to watch the disembowelling of his friend John Coke, the hangman, rubbing his bloody hands together, asked him how he liked that work. He told him that he was not at all terrified, and that he might do his worst, and when on the ladder he turned to the sheriff: 'Sir, you have slain one of the servants of God before mine eyes, and have made me to behold it to terrify and discourage me, but God hath made it an ordinance to me for my strengthening and encouragement.'

In the following May the King's first Parliament met. For the most part it consisted of young, triumphant and insolent Cavaliers, eager to avenge themselves on the Puritans, two thousand of whom were expelled from their livings. In Cornwall at least forty refused to accept the Prayer Book, and the Anglican clergy returned. The old way of life beyond the Tamar was resumed much as it had been twenty years before; once again forty-four members were sent up to Parliament, the Duchy was re-established, those who had bought its estates being either ejected or allowed to remain as tenants, and the Royalists were restored and richly rewarded.

Old John Arundell did not live to see the Restoration, but his son Richard was created Lord Arundell of Trerice in recognition of his father's services and of his own eminent exploits during the war. A hundred years later the title and family became extinct, but the house remains, one of the loveliest relics of the Elizabethan age. General Monk became Duke of Albemarle and his cousin Sir John Grenville was honoured above all Cornishmen. For his devotion and that of his father Sir Bevil, the King made him Earl of Bath, Viscount Lansdowne and Baron Grenville of Kilkhampton, while offices and other rewards were showered upon him: Steward of the Duchy of Cornwall, Lord Lieutenant of the county, Captain and Governor of Plymouth, Lord Warden of the Stannaries with a pension of £3,000 a year paid out of the tin revenue, and the reversion of the Dukedom of Albemarle. The old house of his forefathers at Stowe was no longer good enough for the greatest man in the west country; he pulled it down and built in its stead a splendid red brick mansion in the latest classical style. Under James II his fortunes faltered, for he was too staunch a Protestant for the Catholic king's liking, and after some hesitation declared for William of Orange, seizing Plymouth and admitting the Dutch fleet into the harbour. Yet William III mistrusted him for his long loyalty to the Stuarts, and when the second Duke of Albemarle died without an heir he granted the title to his young Dutch favourite Keppel. Disappointed and his estate impoverished, Bath died in 1701, and a fortnight later his son Charles, the second earl, died too, some say by his own hand. They were buried together at Kilkhampton on the same day. Another ten years and the last Earl of Bath was dead, and his aunt the Countess Grenville pulled down the great new house at Stowe. Bricks, timber and all were sold, and once again, on the cliffs looking down to Tintagel, grass grew over the site of the home of the Grenvilles.

The great house of the Godolphins at the far end of the county was not forgotten by Charles, for after all it was they who had offered him refuge in Scilly after his flight from Pendennis, and supplied him with money in exile. Francis, brother of Sidney, the poet killed at the beginning of the war, and now head of the family, was rewarded with a knighthood and the old manor house of Rialton, once the retreat of Prior Vyvyan of Bodmin, while his young son Sidney was taken into the royal household as a page. If, as is said, a Godolphin never wanted wit, very rarely did he want a flair for business; the fortunes of the house had been founded on tin, indeed the house itself was founded on tin, on the fabulous columns of ore beneath it, and Sidney Godolphin, the silent and cloudy member for Helston, soon won a reputation in Parliament as a financial genius. We see him, easily but unambitiously, ascending the ladder of power: Privy Councillor, Commissioner of the Treasury, Baron Godolphin, Lord High Treasurer, Knight of the Garter, Viscount Rialton and Earl of Godolphin. And we see him too with 'the affairs of a nation in his head, and a pair of cards or a box of dice in his hand', or at Newmarket watching the Arab racehorses which, to the great profit of England, he bred in his stables. For, sober and prudent public servant though he was, his private passion was gambling.

The one romance of his life was his marriage with John Evelyn's devout and melancholy young friend, Margaret Blagge. But it was a romance of only three years, for in 1678 she died of puerperal fever after giving birth to their only child, Francis. In case of mortal accident she had written a letter to her husband, concluding, 'Now, my dear, I have done. I know nothing more I have to desire of you, but that you will sometymes think of me with kindness, butt never with too much griefe. For my Funerall, I desire there may be noe cost bestowed upon it att all; butt if I might, I would begg that my body might lye wher I have had such a mind to goe myselfe, att Godolphyn, among your freinds. I believe, if I were carried by Sea, the expence would not be very great.' And so she was brought down to the county she had never known, but loved for her husband's sake, and buried in Breage church between Godolphin and the sea.

Sidney Godolphin did not marry again, but in 1698 Francis married Henrietta, eldest daughter of his friend and political ally, the Duke of Marlborough. And it was Godolphin who, as Queen Anne's Lord Treasurer and First Minister, financed Marlborough's triumphant campaigns from Blenheim to Malplaquet. But in 1710 the great partnership came to an end; Anne quarrelled with the Marlboroughs, Godolphin was dismissed, and two years later he died. The great days of the Godolphins in Cornwall were over, and the house among the accumulating rubble from the mines gradually fell into decay.

A different sort of reward was reserved for another loyal Cornishman, Thomas Killigrew, great-grandson of John Killigrew the first, builder of Arwennack. His grandfather and father had both been courtiers, so that young Thomas became a page to Charles I, followed Charles II into exile, and returned with him at the Restoration. Pepys met him on board ship the day before the royal party landed at Dover: 'walking upon the decks, where persons of honour all the afternoon, among others, Thomas Killigrew, (a merry droll, but a gentleman of great esteem with the King) who told us many merry stories.' No doubt they were as bawdy as the comedies that he had written, for Tom's passion was the stage, and as a boy he had contrived to play at the old Red Bull. Since the beginning of the Civil War the theatres had been closed and most of them destroyed, so that it was most fitting that Charles should reward his faithful Tom and another courtier-dramatist, Sir William Davenant, with the monopoly of the London theatres. Killigrew formed the King's Company, built the first Drury Lane playhouse and, to his honour, lost no time in reviving the half-forgotten plays of Shakespeare; Pepys saw his production of *Othello*, 'which was well done', as early as October 1660. Rake, wit, almost indeed the King's jester, his licence, in both senses of the word, allowed him to speak more roundly and give more salutary advice to his royal master than many a better man. He died in 1683 as Master of the Revels, and was buried – final jest – in Poet's Corner in Westminster Abbey. Yet perhaps it was more appropriate than being carried back to the home of his ancestors which he had never seen. Arwennack had been half ruined at the time of the siege of Pendennis, and the Cornish Killigrews were failing. The second Sir Peter, after the death of his sons, the younger one killed in a tavern brawl in Penryn – a characteristic Killigrew ending – retired to Ludlow, where he died in 1704, last of the main line of Killigrews. His body was brought back to Arwennack and buried in the church of King Charles the Martyr which had been built by his father. Yet the chief ambition of the Killigrews had been fulfilled: in 1661 Falmouth, the child they had fostered for a century, received its charter.

No Cornish family had shown greater devotion to the Stuart cause than the Trelawnys, yet the religious policy of James II was to strain their loyalty to breaking point. Jonathan, second son of the Sir Jonathan whose Royalist activities had been a constant source of anxiety to the Commonwealth government, was ordained in 1673, but succeeded to the baronetcy on the death of his elder brother a few years later. He did not desert the Church, but compromised by assuming a dual role: 'When I swear,' he explained, 'I do not swear as a priest, but as a baronet and a country gentleman.' In 1685, when the Duke of Monmouth led the western rebellion against James II, he took an active part with his younger brother, Major General Charles Trelawny, in putting it down, an exploit that earned him the titles of Spiritual Dragoon and Christian Turk, and the bishopric of Bristol – although he asked for Exeter. When, however, James issued the Declaration of Indulgence granting toleration to Catholics, Trelawny was one of the bishops who protested and, according to the King, 'My Lord of Bristol was the most saucy of the Seven.' Imprisoned in the Tower and brought up for trial, he was triumphantly acquitted, and all England rejoiced; the bells were rung in his native parish of Pelynt, and the old popular refrain was adapted to fit the new hero:

> And shall Trelawny die?
> And shall Trelawny die?
> Here's twenty thousand Cornishmen
> Will know the reason why.

It was mere rhetoric, for Cornishmen had had enough of wars of religion, but it served – in Hawker's elaborated version – to immortalise his name. He had his revenge. A few weeks later William of Orange landed in England, and James offered him the bishopric of Exeter as the price of his loyalty. But it was too late. Trelawny supported William, and in the following year got Exeter. He died as Bishop of Winchester, but his body was brought back to Cornwall and buried in the church at Pelynt, close to the old grey house of Trelawne.

That was in 1721, sixty years after the Restoration. By that time the Hanoverians were firmly established on the throne, and Walpole, at the head of a mercenary phalanx of Whigs, many of them representing, or misrepresenting, the twenty-one Cornish boroughs, was Prime Minister. A new age had begun, the age of reason, of prose and of material progress.

A History Of Cornwall

X

The Eighteenth Century

The independent political history of Cornwall may be said to have ended at the Restoration. Impoverished and weakened by the Civil War, the Cornish people took little interest in the events that followed the death of Charles II – the Monmouth rebellion, the Revolution of 1688, the Jacobite rising of 1715 – and passively accepted the decisions of the English. But if adventures beyond the Tamar were over, Cornwall was by no means absorbed by England: remote and still barely accessible save to the hardy adventurer, its people pursued their own peculiar way of life, preserving their Celtic legends, festivals and folklore, and in the far west even their own language. It was still a foreign country with a culture of its own, and even if its independent political history was finished, its distinctive economic history was not; indeed, it might be argued that it was only just beginning. Geologically the county was unique: no other region in Britain had a comparable wealth of metal below its surface, and as yet it had scarcely been worked. The next two centuries of the history of Cornwall, therefore, are essentially the history of its mining industry.

Although most of the Royalists got back their estates after the Civil War, one result of the turmoils of the middle of the century was a considerable redistribution of property; lawyers, merchants and other businessmen were not slow to appreciate the advantage of investing in land that might prove rich in metal, and their professional approach had its effect on the established gentry.

Land was no longer to be developed primarily as a source of food, but to be exploited for the minerals beneath its surface. As nearly all the then-known lodes of ore were in the western part of the county, between St Austell and St Just-in-Penwith, landowners in this magical area were particularly fortunate: Godolphins, Bassets of Tehidy, Pendarveses of Pendarves and Roscrow, St Aubyns of Clowance and the Mount, Boscawens of Tregothnan, Tonkins of Trevaunance, and Borlases of Pendeen.

There is no better introduction to eighteenth-century Cornwall than the account of the aristocratic, puritanical and adventurous young lady, Celia Fiennes, daughter of the unfortunate defender of Bristol, who made her 'Great Journey' from Tamar to the Land's End in the autumn of 1698. Of course she travelled on horseback, for there was no question of drawing a coach up and down those steep, miry roads, pocked with holes full of water, into which her horse sometimes stumbled and almost drowned or broke its neck. It is true that Charles I travelled by coach on his Lostwithiel campaign of 1644, but then he had an army to pull him out of the mud, and even as late as the middle of the eighteenth century a coach in Cornwall was a rarity.

Miss Fiennes crossed the Tamar by the Cremyll ferry, a wet and hazardous passage that took an hour and cost her a cold, and then rode up the hill past Mount Edgcumbe, a house and situation that she thought the finest she had ever seen, though the road to Looe was so bad in places that she deserted it for the seashore. From Looe she followed the 'main' road through Fowey and Par, and 'over the heath and commons by the tinn mines' to St Austell, where she was much pleased with her supper, with her west-country tart and Cornish cream, though not with the custom of the country, 'which is a univerall smoaking; both men, women and children have all their pipes of tobacco in their mouths, and soe sit round the fire smoaking'.

Her description of tin mining is an admirable piece of reporting. 'Halfe a mile from hence they blow their tin, which I went to see. They take the ore and pound it in a stamping mill, and when it is fine as the finest sand they fling it into a furnace, and with it coale to make the fire; so it burns together and makes a violent heate and fierce flame, the mettle, by the fire being seperated from the coale and its own drosse, being heavy falls down to a trench made to receive it at the furnace hole below. This liquid mettle I saw them shovel up with an iron shovel, and soe pour it into molds in which it cooles, and soe they take it thence in sort of wedges or piggs. I went a mile farther on the hills, and soe came where they were digging in the Tinn mines. There was at least 20 mines all in sight, which employs a great many people at work, almost night and day, but constantly all and every day, including the Lords day, which they are forced to, to prevent their mines being overflowed with water. More than 1000 men are taken up about them. Few mines but had then almost 20 men and boys attending it, either down in the mines digging and carrying the oare to the little bucket which conveys it up, or else others are draineing the water and looking to the engines that are draineing it, and those above are attending the drawing up the oare in a sort of windless as is to a well: two men keeps turning, bringing up one and letting down another. They have a great labour and great expence to draine the mines of the water with mills that horses turn, and now they have the mills or water engines that are turned by the water which is convey'd on frames of timber and truncks to hold the water, which falls down on the wheels, as on an overshott mill. Those mines do require a great deale of timber to support them and to make all these engines and mills, which makes fewell very scarce here. They burn mostly turfs, which is an unpleasant smell; it makes one smell as if smoaked like bacon.'

She passed scores of mine shafts after leaving St Austell, some 'that were lost by the waters overwhelming them', crossed the Fal by the long stone bridge at Tregony, and so reached Tregothnan, the home of her cousin Hugh Boscawen, so perfectly placed at the confluence of the Fal and Truro rivers. It was a pleasant house, and evidently the refinements of civilisation had reached even these outlandish parts: two parlours, one wainscotted in cedar, a drawing room opening on to the garden, and of course a smoking room, bedrooms newly decorated in the latest manner, the beds made up well, one red damask, another green, another wrought. A balcony looked very pleasantly over the park, and from the cupola on the roof she could see 'the Great Ocean which runs into Falmouth', and to the west the 'hills full of Copper mines'. They were indeed, and of tin mines too. There was Poldice, for example, on the hill west of St Day, of which William Hals had just written: 'Not far from St Day is that unparalleled and inexhaustible tin work called Poldys, which for about forty years space hath employed yearly from eight hundred to a thousand men and boys labouring for and searching after tin in that place, where they have produced and raised up from that time yearly at least £20,000 worth of that commodity, to the great enrichment of adventurers in these lands.'

A seventeenth-century Cornish autumn was very much like its twentieth-century successor, and the melancholy rain almost persuaded her to turn east again, but a sparkling day changed her mind, and from St Columb Major she 'went for the Lands End by Redruth, 18 mile mostly over heath and downs which was very bleake and full of mines', a landscape we can so well imagine, when the earth was being flayed and turned inside out by those early miners. Copper was mined, she noted, in the same way as tin, though it was not smelted in Cornwall owing to lack of fuel, but shipped off to Bristol and South Wales. And she wondered at the way in which everything was carried on the backs of the little Cornish horses: tin and copper ore, fish and even the corn which they were then cutting.

It is good to know that the enterprising explorer reached the Land's End, scrambled romantically over the rocks as far west as she could, saw 'the Island of Sily', fell in love with Truro, 'formerly a great tradeing town' but now 'a ruinated disregarded place' (thanks to the Killigrews of Falmouth), was awed by the 'great mountaine' of Brown Willy, impressed by the Delabole quarries, and, before reaching Launceston and crossing the Tamar, admired the Earl of Bath's fine house and gardens at Stowe, whence she caught a glimpse of Lundy Island which her grandfather, William Fiennes, Lord Saye and Sele, 'Old Subtlety' as he was called, had captured from the Grenvilles during the Civil War.

Celia Fiennes describes graphically enough the main hazard of mining in the early days – the flooding of shafts as they were sunk deeper, and of levels driven out from them in pursuit of the lodes of ore. When the deepest workings could be drained by adits, almost horizontal galleries that carried away the water to openings lower down the flank of a hill, the problem was relatively simple, but when they were too deep thus to be drained by gravity, the water had to be raised to adit level by some means or other: by a simple windlass and bucket, by a 'horse-whim', a large vertical drum round which the rope was drawn by horses, or by rag-and-chain pumps, which, however, might need six or seven times as many men to work them as there were miners below. Or, where surface water was available, there were wooden pumps worked by waterwheels, as seen by Celia Fiennes at St Austell. A few years later, about 1710, that 'noble machine the fire engine' was first harnessed to a Cornish mine by Thomas Newcomen, probably to the Godolphin mine of Wheal Vor. The age of steam had arrived, but the engine devoured coal at such a rate that the cost of running it was almost prohibitive, and even as late as 1740 there were only three of these steam pumps at work.

The primary difficulty of mining, the sheer sinking of shafts and driving of levels through granite, had been overcome, or partly overcome, by the end of the seventeenth century. The old method had been simply to hew a passage with picks and gads, sometimes at a rate of no more than an inch or two a day, and anyone who looks down the black mouth of one of these old mines and listens for the plunge of a stone in its depths, would be insensitive indeed if he did not marvel, with a feeling of pity, at the lifelong labours of those long-since-vanished workmen. In 1689, however, their labours were lightened, for in that year the parish register at Breage records the burial of 'Thomas Epsly of Chilchumpton parish, Sumersitsheere. He was the man that brought that rare invention of shooting the rocks which came heare in June, 1689, and he died at the bal [i.e. mine] and was buried at breag the 16 day of December 1689.' It looks as though Epsly was the first victim of the blasting that he introduced, the first of many, for during the eighteenth century, before William Bickford invented a safety fuse, gunpowder was the cause of untold disasters.

Another invention of the period had important consequences: the smelting of tin with coal in a reverberatory furnace. This of course meant importing fuel, and the smelting industry fell into the hands of the merchants and ship owners who supplied it, though not entirely, for some of the old charcoal-using blowing houses were retained for smelting stream tin, which was of a finer quality than that from the mines. The use of coal probably saved Cornwall from being completely denuded of timber, the demand for which for shoring up the workings was enormous, and one of the last services that Godolphin did his native county was to cheapen the price of coal by securing a drawback of the duty on that used for smelting. A few years before, in 1703, he had been responsible for the favourable terms of pre-emption granted to the Cornish tinners.

Pre-emption, the right of the Crown to buy before others at a fixed price, had been resorted to in the last years of Elizabeth to relieve the distress of the tinners, most of whom were in the clutches of usurers. The intention had been good, but the result was unfortunate, for while other prices and the expenses of deep mining rose rapidly, the price of tin remained the same, and production in 1650 was only about five hundred tons, less than it had been in 1600. In 1650, however, the Stannary regulations were abolished by the Commonwealth, coinage duty as well as pre-emption, and there followed a decade of unprecedented prosperity when the price of tin doubled, mines flooded and abandoned during the war were reopened, and production reached a record level of a thousand tons. Despite the reimposition of the Stannary apparatus this high rate of production was maintained and even increased after the Restoration, though the earnings of the working tinners were deplorably low, which was why Godolphin raised the price of tin by a third in 1703. When, however, Walpole succeeded Godolphin at the Treasury, the Norfolk farmer the Cornish mine owner, pre-emption was abolished for good.

It was left to Sir John St Aubyn, 'the little baronet', of whom Walpole said, surveying his opponents in Parliament, 'All these men have their price but him', to look after the interests of the Cornish tinners. He built a new pier at the Mount for the export trade, and when in 1727 the miners, made desperate by a shortage of corn, rose and plundered the granaries, he advanced a considerable sum of money to relieve them. A very different type was Sir William Pendarves, who, when he entertained his friends, mixed his punch in a coffin made of copper.

For by this time copper was beginning to compete in importance with tin. A little copper had been raised in Elizabethan times, but it was only as the shafts sank deeper at the end of the seventeenth century that rich lodes were discovered below the tin, particularly in the Redruth-Chacewater region. An attempt was made to extend the stannary laws to copper so that its smelting should be confined to Cornwall, for if the refined metal had to be taken to the coinage towns to be assayed and assessed for Duchy duty, as white tin was, the ore would not be shipped to South Wales for smelting. But Walpole and the Whigs were not interested in state intervention, the scheme came to nothing, and though one successful smelting business was established for a time at Copperhouse near Hayle, nearly all the ore was carried off by 'foreigners' who gained a controlling interest in the industry. Cornish landowners, notably Hugh Boscawen, first Viscount Falmouth, leased mineral rights to them, while others formed companies to work the deposits themselves.

In the eighteenth century, therefore, both tin and copper mines were developed on capitalist lines. The shareholders, or 'adventurers' as they were called, left the general management of the mine to a purser, usually himself an adventurer, who was responsible for the financial side and the all-important payment of dividends according to the cost-book system. This was really the system of the old tin streamers, who had divided their product every so often in proportion to the share that each had in the working. Once every few months, therefore, or even once a month, the eager adventurers or their agents met the purser, who presented his accounts. If there was no profit each adventurer might be called on to subscribe more capital according to his share, or if there was a profit the whole, after payment of the mineral lord's 'dish', was distributed as dividend. It was a complex system, for it entailed frequent stocktaking and keeping of elaborate accounts, and it left no capital in reserve; on the other hand, the division of the capital into shares, and fractions of shares, allowed the adventurers to spread their risks and encouraged them to invest in a number of mines. The adventurers in Wheal Virgin in Gwennap must have rubbed their hands when the purser told them that the first fortnight's working in 1757 had produced copper ore worth £5,700, equal to more than £60,000 today. On the other hand, Wheal Bounty, so ironically named, made regular monthly calls and was eventually abandoned without ever having paid a dividend.

The detailed mining operations were directed by 'bal captains', experienced foremen who had risen from the ranks, responsible for the underground workings, keeping them in repair, supplying the men with material and setting the pitches where they were to dig for ore. The miners themselves were divided into two main classes, both of which had paid assistants, often boys. First the tutworkers, who were generally employed in the more mechanical processes of burrowing down and outwards towards the lodes. They worked in small gangs or 'pares', offering to move so many cubic fathoms of earth and rock for a certain price. All was intensely competitive, there was nothing resembling a trade union organisation, one pare competing against another for the work and the purser accepting the lowest tender. Obviously, if the ground proved more difficult than anticipated, the tutworkers might be a foul way out. So too might the tributers. These were the men who dug the ore, contracting to work a certain 'pitch' of mineralised ground in return for a proportion of the value of the ore they extracted. Once every month or so, on 'setting' day, these pitches were put up for auction by the chief captain, standing on the steps of the count house, the men bidding against one another and forcing down their reward, until the bid that offered the greatest proportion to the adventurers was accepted. Thus a pare might obtain the right to work a moderate pitch for half the value of the ore they raised, while a rich one might be worked for only one shilling out of every pound's worth sent to surface. The advantage of the tribute system to the adventurers is clear enough: they bought labour in the cheapest possible market and paid only for results, which the workers had every incentive to make as good as possible. Yet the system appealed to the tributers too: they were virtually free miners, supplying their own tools and materials, profit-sharers rather than wage earners, and there was always the chance that they might strike richer than they had ever dared to hope. It appealed both to the innate Cornish individualism and the primitive hunting instinct in man. They, and not the shareholders, were the true adventurers, and the tributer was drawn to the mine by a passion as strong as that which draws the gambler to the gaming table.

From the pitch the ore was trundled in wheelbarrows, or even dragged on trays, along the narrow levels – some of the old workings were little more than two feet wide – to the shaft, where it was loaded into kibbles and hoisted by horses to the surface. There, under the direction of 'grass captains', it was broken into small pieces by women, 'bal maidens' with long-handled hammers, ground into powder by stamping mills worked by water power, and washed by children until all the waste had been removed. The black tin was then ready for smelting and coining, the copper for the ceremony of 'ticketing'. On sampling day the agents of the smelting companies visited the mines to take samples of the copper ore piled up in 'doles', sometimes as much as a hundred tons of it, for their inspection. Then, having tested them at their leisure, they met the representatives of the mines at an inn at Redruth or Truro, where they handed in sealed tenders or tickets, stating the price they were ready to pay for the various doles. The chairman opened the tickets, read them aloud, and the doles fell to the lot of the highest bidder. The sales, thus expeditiously concluded, were celebrated by a splendid dinner at the expense of the mine owners, and a few days later the ore was collected and shipped for south Wales or Bristol to be smelted.

In this free-for-all early-eighteenth-century capitalist society, great fortunes were quickly made by men more fortunate, astute, enterprising, ruthless or unscrupulous than their fellows. There was William Lemon, son of a poor man of Germoe, who was lucky enough to find employment with John Coster, inventor of the horse-whim and manager of copper mines in the Chacewater district. Lemon himself became manager of the Chyandour tin-smelting house at Penzance, which served at least twenty mines in West Penwith, from Ding Dong to St Just and St Ives. In 1724 he married and invested the money his wife brought him in developing the so appropriately named Wheal Fortune in Ludgvan, a venture that is said to have brought him some £10,000. After this he moved to Truro, where he began to work the Gwennap mines on an unprecedented scale, at the same time making up for his neglected education by studying under the master of the local grammar school. He rendered Cornwall a signal service by securing from Walpole the abolition of all duties on coal imported for working the new 'fire engines', bought Carclew, the great estate on Restronguet Creek, and died a baronet in 1760.

The manager of Lemon's immensely rich Poldice mine in St Day was John Williams of Scorrier, who drove the Great Adit from Bissoe Bridge near Carclew to drain Poldice some four miles away. It took him almost twenty years to do so, and when all the branch adits had been driven the complete system was thirty miles long and drained some fifty mines. The Williams family was one of the toughest of that bustling age, and a few generations later moved from Scorrier into Carhays Castle, where the last of the Trevanions had amused himself after dinner by shooting the eyes out of his family portraits with a pistol.

One result of this driving of adits in the mid-eighteenth century, before there were steam engines capable of pumping water out of the deepest workings, was the discovery of tin and copper lodes in places thought to be outside the mineral zones. One of these was at Pool, between Camborne and Redruth, which proved to be so rich in copper that it brought the Basset family, who owned all the shares, an income of over £10,000 a year. The Bassets also controlled Cook's Kitchen and Dolcoath, two of the richest of all the mines, while their great rival, Lord Falmouth, drew an immense income from the mines of Chacewater and Gwennap, where he was the principal landowner.

Great wealth had come to Cornwall, but although certain favoured families and individuals, owners of land within the magic aureoles encircling the granite bosses, shrewd businessmen and fortunate adventurers, many of them 'foreigners', made their fortunes out of the rapid development of mining in the first half of the eighteenth century, the great majority of Cornish people profited little. It was nobody's fault. The industrial revolution, with its attendant rapacious capitalism, had struck west Cornwall early, upsetting a simple economy based primarily on agriculture and fishing, when there was neither a philosophy nor a political machinery to prevent the grotesque maldistribution of wealth, and the exploitation of the labour that helped to produce it. The population of Cornwall seems to have grown from about 100,000 to 150,000 in the century after the Restoration, but as this growth was entirely in the western half, partly owing to migration from the agricultural east, the number of people in the mining areas probably doubled. There was, therefore, an abundant supply of labour, quite unorganised, fiercely competitive and scrambling for the privilege of employment. As a result, wages were pitifully low.

According to *The Tinners Greivances* of 1697, some of the men had to work day and night to earn 15s a month, or about £10 a year. Of course the value of money was much more than it is today, some fifteen times more, but even then 4s a week was perilously near starvation level, and in times of unemployment, sickness or injury there might be nothing but a trickle of relief from the parish. Wives and children, therefore, had to supplement the men's wages, the women working as bal maidens, 'spalling' the ore, small boys and girls helping to wash it, and at the age of twelve or so the boys went underground to learn the art of mining. By 1730 a good miner was making about 24s a month, but even fifty years later that seems to have been the average reward of a St Just miner. However, wages varied with the district and prosperity of the mine, and a tributer working at a good pitch might make as much as £10 a month for a short time, though the average in the middle of the century was probably little more than 30s. 'Grass men' employed in dressing the ore at surface, generally those too old or unfit for mining, received 18s a month, while bal maidens were paid 5d a day and children 4d. These were gross wages, for fines were often deducted for various misdemeanours, such as cluttering up the levels with debris, arriving late or taking an unauthorised holiday.

The hours were desperately long, sometimes 'cores' of twelve hours a day, though even in the eighteenth century it was discovered that such long spells underground were uneconomical, and day and night shifts of eight hours each became normal. Conditions were appalling. At the beginning of his core a miner would descend the dripping shaft by slimy ladders, often with broken rungs, while on the other side kibbles raced and rumbled up and down, spilling lumps of ore and sometimes dislodging a rock. A few fathoms down the only light was that from the smoky hempen candle stuck on his hat with a piece of clay, and by this glimmer he sank a hundred fathoms or more to the deepest workings. (No wonder the mines were thought to be haunted by 'knackers', mischievous elves who were said to be spirits of Jews who crucified the Lord.) There perhaps he scrambled another fifty fathoms along the narrow level to his pitch at the end, far from any ventilation, where the temperature might be 90°F. and the air so stifling that a boy had to fan the candles to keep them alight. There was of course a constant danger of accidents, a fall of rock, a mistimed explosion of gunpowder, while the powder smoke added to the lethal contamination of the air. After eight hours' work with a pick the miner climbed a hundred fathoms to the surface, where, dripping with sweat, he might find a freezing January evening. Then in an open shed, with no facilities for washing, he changed his clothes, cold and wet if he had been caught by rain on his way to the mine, and walked home, sometimes five miles or more away.

There was little material comfort to be found there. The typical miner's cottage was a thatched hovel of cob built by himself on the moors, for like his Celtic forbears he did not take kindly to village life. One room with a damp earthen floor had to serve for all purposes, unless a kind of shelf rigged up under the rafters could be called a bedroom. The usual food of the family was fish, mainly pilchards, potatoes, barley bread and gruel made of a kind of oatmeal. Meat was a very rare luxury. Of course conditions in the home varied with the housewife, but even though a capable woman could prevent a lapse into squalor, she was helpless against poverty, overcrowding, lack of sanitation and disease. We have no statistics of mortality in the eighteenth century, but there is no reason to think that conditions were better in 1750 than in 1850, when the average age of those buried in the mining parish of St Just-in-Penwith, male and female, was twenty-seven. The miners' occupational diseases of tuberculosis and silicosis were taking their toll, smoke and dust were destroying their lungs, but the main killers were the common diseases attendant on poverty and malnutrition.

It is scarcely surprising that men working and living under such conditions sought a temporary oblivion in gin and other spirits obtained from the numerous dram shops or 'kiddleywinks' that invited their patronage, resorted to violence when drunk, hungry or angry, or when an opportunity to plunder occurred, and gained the reputation of being little more than savages. In years of bad harvest there simply was not corn enough in Cornwall to feed the growing population, and when merchants exported it to gain higher prices abroad the miners rose in revolt. The food riots of 1727, so humanely quelled by Sir John St Aubyn, were followed two years later by a more serious rising of the tinners, who 'ravaged up and down the country in a very insolent manner and great numbers'. This time they were more severely dealt with: four of their leaders were hanged, and Thomas Tonkin noted with satisfaction, 'one of them is now hanging in chains on St Austell Downs, for leading a mob to plunder the mowhays, barns and cellars'. There were similar risings at least once every decade, and in times of scarcity the gentry and middle classes lived in fear of a general insurrection.

Sometimes the miners found an outlet for their violent passions in a kind of interparochial warfare, as when the men of Redruth attacked those of Gwennap in the early part of the century. The Redruthers swore to take the life of the first thing they met in Gwennap; this happened to be a dog, in the blood of which they dyed a handkerchief to serve as a flag. In the ensuing

fight, however, they were routed, partly owing to the intervention
of the women of St Day, and at least one of their number was
killed. Then there was the celebrated 'Siege of Skewis' in 1734,
when Henry Rogers seized his old family home from the widow
of his elder brother, and held it for more than a year against the
attacks of the sheriff and his men, five of whom he killed. It was
only when troops brought up guns from Pendennis that he fled,
though he was caught at Salisbury, tried at Launceston assizes
and hanged. Skewis was only a mile from Clowance, Sir John
St Aubyn's estate, and the affair, which gained a widespread
notoriety, confirmed the opinion of the English that Cornishmen
were lawless barbarians whom their masters could not, or would
not, control.

There was some truth in this, for Cornishmen had more
opportunity for lawless practices than the less fortunate Saxons
on the other side of the Tamar, and as they were by no means
unprofitable they took them. Thrust out into the Atlantic athwart
the main trade routes, with a coast as cruel as it was beautiful,
Cornwall was the graveyard of more ships than any other county
in Britain, and its people had long had a reputation for wrecking.
If by this was meant that they lured ships on to their rocks by
waving confusing lights from the cliffs, the accusation was
probably unjust; there was no need to do that, for the ships came
without their intervention. But if it was wrong, or unnecessary, to
lure ships to their doom, it might be equally wrong, as it was
certainly undesirable, to interfere with the will of God and warn
them of danger. 'Thou shalt not kill; but need'st not strive
officiously to keep alive,' so that when Sir John Killigrew built
his lighthouse on the Lizard in 1619 the people naturally
complained that he 'took away God's grace from them', and
almost two centuries later Parson Troutbeck of Scilly is said to
have prayed, 'Dear God, we pray not that wrecks should happen,
but if it be Thy will that they do, we pray Thee let them be to the
benefit of Thy poor people of Scilly.' All too frequently they were,
as when on that October night of 1707 three men-of-war went
down off St Mary's with the loss of nearly two thousand men.
Legend has it that their commander, Sir Cloudesley Shovel, was

cast up alive on Porth Hellick beach, where he was murdered by a woman for the sake of an emerald ring.

All things conspired to make wrecking in Cornwall a callous and brutal business: natural greed, the poverty of the wreckers, remoteness, and the law itself, which defined a 'wreck of the sea' as anything from which no living creature reached the shore. If man or beast escaped, the vessel was not legally a wreck, but if all perished it became the property of the lord of the coastal manor, though in practice of those who got there first. There was, therefore, every incentive to fail to see a drowning man, or, if his shouts and struggles could not be ignored, to shove him back under the waves. Moreover, corpses cast up by the sea were not allowed Christian burial until 1808, when Davies Giddy (later Gilbert), member for Bodmin, secured an Act of Parliament for their burial in a churchyard at the expense of the parish.

The stretch of coast from the Mount to the Lizard was perhaps the most fatal in Cornwall, and the tinners of Breage and Germoe, strategically placed in the middle, had a particularly sinister reputation for wrecking. If we are to believe George Borlase, who wrote in February 1753, it was well deserved. 'The late storms have brought several vessels ashore and some dead wrecks, and in the former case great barbaritys have been committed. My situation in life hath obliged me sometimes to be a spectator of things which shock humanity. The people who make it their business to attend these wrecks are generally tynners, and, as soon as they observe a ship on the coast, they first arm themselves with sharp axes and hatchetts, and leave their tynn works to follow those ships ... They'll cut a large trading vessell to pieces in one tide, and cut down everybody that offers to oppose them. Two or three years ago, a Dutchman was stranded near Helston, every man saved, and the ship whole, burthen 250 tons, laden with claret. In twenty-four hours time the tinners cleared all. A few months before this, they murdered a poor man just by Helston who came in aid of a custom-house officer to seize some brandy ... I have seen many a poor man, half dead, cast ashore and crawling out of the reach of the waves, fallen upon and in a manner stripped naked by those villains, and if afterwards he has saved his chest or any more cloaths they have been taken from him.'

Borlase was not entirely disinterested, for the mines of St Just had enabled his family to move from bleak Pendeen to the comforts of Castle Horneck near Penzance, and something more than his humanity was shocked by the tinners' barbarities: 'Sometimes the ship is not wrecked, but whether 'tis or not the mines suffer greatly, not only by the loss of their labour, which may be about £100 per diem if they are two thousand in quest of the ship, but where the water is quick the mine is entirely drowned, and they seldom go in a less number than two thousand.' Perhaps the prosperous adventurer inadvertently weakens his case, for £100 a day divided among two thousand men is one shilling, and one cannot help feeling some sympathy for those wreckers, who had at least the chance of salvaging more than a shilling's worth of firewood.

George Borlase was full of complaints in 1753. 'The coasts here swarm with smugglers from the Land's End to the Lizard,' he groaned, 'so that I wonder the soldiers (who were late quartered here) should have been ordered off without being replaced by others.' It was true enough, for sheer poverty drove streamers, miners, peasants and fishermen alike to develop this unconventional form of free trade, until by 1750 it had reached a pitch of unprecedented prosperity. Moreover it added excitement and adventure to their humdrum lives, and formed a bond with the gentry and clergy, most of whom appreciated a practice that supplied them with luxuries free of duty. We shall never know how much tin escaped coinage duty, hidden away under hogsheads of pilchards shipped to the Mediterranean, or how much ore served as ballast in boats running over to Brittany, whence they returned with cargoes of brandy, gin, tea, lace and salt, which were hidden in caves before distribution, or by miners in their workings and moorhouses. We do know, however, that by 1770 some 470,000 gallons of brandy and 350,000 pounds of tea were being smuggled into Cornwall every year at a cost of about £150,000 to the Exchequer.

Depriving the government of revenue extorted by making prices artificially high was regarded by most people as a legitimate game: magistrates turned a blind eye, juries refused to convict, short-sighted excisemen had their douceurs of ankers of brandy, and the law against smugglers was far less ferocious than that against thieves. Many of the smugglers had rare reputations for honesty, and John Carter, the 'King of Prussia', who reigned at Prussia Cove near Germoe from 1770 to 1807, set a high standard of conduct. On one occasion, the Penzance excise officers seized a recently run cargo while he was away. His reputation as an honourable merchant was at stake, for he had promised to deliver the goods by a certain day. On the night of his return, therefore, he broke into the custom house and took his own again, and when the officers found what had gone and what remained they remarked that John Carter had been there, for he was a man who would never take anything that did not belong to him. Captain Harry Carter, his brother, was even more of a precisian: he would have no swearing or unseemly talk on board his ship, and when living in enforced retirement at Roscoff in Brittany, conducted Sunday services for the benefit of the English smugglers in the town. 'The men took off their hats,' he noted in his diary, 'all very serious, no laffing, no trifling conversations.'

Yet, although running a contraband cargo by night into a picturesque cove lit by beacons on the cliffs was more than a little romantic, and though the game was played in a comparatively gentlemanly fashion, Cornish smuggling has been over-romanticised. There were fierce and bloody clashes between smugglers and excisemen, murder was by no means uncommon, and one would not willingly have got in the way of a gang of drunken tinners lugging their liquor up into the moors. Smuggling must have been responsible for much of the violence of the times; it was itself often a brutal business, and the traffic in cheap spirits encouraged an even deeper drunkenness and savager brutality.

Never before had the Cornish people been in such need of material and spiritual help, but never before had the clergy had so little to offer. The age of enthusiasm was over and, lapsed in sloth, they comforted themselves rather than their flocks with the doctrine that all is for the best in this transitory life, and that man must endure his lot or suffer the consequences of his rebellion. There were solid reasons for this pastoral *laissez-faire*, particularly in west Cornwall, where most of the livings in the mining districts were held by younger sons and relations of Godolphins, St Aubyns, Bassets and Pendarveses, while William Borlase held Ludgvan and St Just, and his elder brother Walter combined Madron and Kenwyn. 'I have a share in a very flourishing tin mine,' wrote Walter Borlase to his friend, the famous Dr Oliver of Bath, another Ludgvan man. 'I receive it from the hand of providence with a humble and thankful heart. I have none to thank but Him whose service is perfect freedom.' Then there were those who took orders not from conviction but from convenience. John Wolcot, for example, who sailed with Sir William Trelawny when he was appointed Governor of Jamaica, found that the incumbent of a rich living was dying, and returned to England to be ordained. The obliging Bishop of London admitted him deacon one day, ordained him priest the next, and the newly fledged parson returned to Jamaica only to find that the dying man had recovered. He accepted a poorer living, but soon tired of his new calling and returned to Cornwall as a doctor. Of course there were honourable exceptions, men like John Bennet of Laneast and George Thompson of St Gennys, but the Anglican Church as a whole had entered on a century of somnolence, and the connection of the Cornish clergy with the mine-owning gentry was conducive to slumber. Then, in August 1743, into this society of starving and hard-drinking tinners, wreckers, smugglers, smug clergy and stubborn capitalists, John Wesley fearlessly advanced.

It was not that Wesley taught anything new; he was himself, like his brother Charles, an Anglican clergyman, but one in revolt against apathy, an evangelist calling sinners to repentance. It was not so much what he said as his way of saying it that made the difference; full of compassion, and never faltering in conviction, he was the greatest preacher of his age, each hearer feeling that every word was aimed at himself. There was nothing in his doctrine to which the resident clergy could legitimately object, yet the itinerant Wesley and his Methodist followers roused much the same resentment as the medieval friars, wandering busybodies interfering in the work of the parish and implicitly criticising the incumbent. We can understand why most of the parsons refused to let him preach from their pulpits, or to lead his congregation in singing his and Charles's hymns in their churches, and even incited their parishioners to break up the services that he had perforce to hold out-of-doors, on the downs or in the market place. Yet in spite of persecution Wesley conquered: local societies were formed, preachers appointed, chapels built, and Methodism became a living faith. The industrial revolution and Wesley's evangelism are the two central themes of eighteenth-century Cornish history.

Wesley's energy was prodigious. For almost half a century he travelled some five thousand miles every year, mostly on horseback, preaching two or three times a day, from northern Scotland to western Ireland, from eastern England to Wales and Cornwall. That he should have visited Cornwall nearly thirty times may seem surprising, but it must be remembered that the mining areas of the western half were then among the most densely populated parts of England, St Just almost as big as Manchester, St Ives considerably larger than Liverpool, and the rough and godless Celtic miners were the sort of men whom Wesley set out to save.

On Monday, August 29th, 1743, accompanied by the Rev. W Shepherd, John Nelson and John Downes, Wesley rode forward from Exeter, and by eight that night the little party was quite lost in the 'great pathless moor beyond Launceston', until they were guided to Bodmin by the sound of its bells. By seven o'clock on the following evening Wesley was preaching his first sermon at St Ives. Charles had been there in July to prepare the way, though not without opposition in the district. The vicar of Illogan, the Basset country, had hired his churchwarden and a mob to chase the preacher out of his parish, a victory celebrated at the old alehouse at Pool, nine shillings of the parochial funds being expended at 'Anne Gartrell's on driving out the Methodist'.

John made St Ives his headquarters, riding out to preach to the miners of Redruth and Gwennap, and in the opposite direction visiting Zennor, Morvah, St Just, Sennen, the Land's End, and even Scilly, where he presented the Governor, the second Earl of Godolphin, with the latest copy of the *Sherborne Mercury*, the only newspaper circulating in the west. He stayed three weeks in Cornwall, preaching about forty times to somewhat apathetic congregations of two or three hundred. There was little organised rowdyism, apart from one attack on the St Ives preaching house, where he was savagely handled by a roaring mob, but in the course of the winter the local clergy and gentry prepared a warm reception for the next visit of the meddling Methodist. It may have been William Hoblyn and William Symonds, the vicar and curate of St Ives, who incited James Roberts, a tinner, and his confederates to destroy the preaching house, and Lord Falmouth, then engaged in raising a regiment of Cornish volunteers to suppress the threatened Jacobite rebellion, who spread the rumour that Wesley was in league with the Young Pretender, while Walter Borlase, a magistrate as well as Vice Warden of the Stannaries, his old tartar of a father, John, who thought nothing of horse whipping a man in church, and the drunken William Usticke of St Buryan prepared their own surprises.

Wesley returned at the beginning of April 1744. On the 2nd he stayed with Digory Isbel, a granite mason, at Trewint on Bodmin Moor, and two days later reached St Ives, where he stayed with John Nance. He was received with some consternation by those awaiting him – but the story of this second visit should be told in Wesley's own words, as recorded in his Journal.

'*Wed*. 4. About eleven we reached St Ives. I was a little surprised at entering John Nance's house, being received by many, who were waiting for me there, with a loud (though not bitter) cry. But they soon recovered; and we poured out our souls together in praises and thanksgiving. As soon as we went out we were saluted, as usual, with a huzza and a few stones or pieces of dirt. But in the evening none opened his mouth while I proclaimed, "I will love Thee, O Lord, my strength."
'*Thur*. 5. I took a view of the ruins of the house which the mob had pulled down a little before, for joy that Admiral

Matthews had beaten the Spaniards. Such is the Cornish method of thanksgiving. Both this morning and evening the congregation was as large as the house could well contain.

'*Fri.* 6. I spoke with the members of the society severally, and observed with great satisfaction that persecution had driven only three or four away, and exceedingly strengthened the rest. The persecution here was owing, in great measure, to the indefatigable labours of Mr Hoblyn and Mr Symonds, gentlemen worthy to be "had in everlasting remembrance" for their unwearied endeavours to destroy heresy.

'*Sat.* 7. About eleven John Nance and I set out for Morvah. Having both the wind and rain full in our faces, we were thoroughly wet before we came to Rosemergy, where some of our brethren met us. I found there had been a shaking among them, occasioned by the confident assertions of some that they had seen Mr Wesley a week or two ago with the Pretender in France; and others, that he was in prison at London. The wind and rain beat hard upon us again as we walked from Morvah to St Just, which also frighted many from coming. However, some hundreds were there. It is remarkable that those of St Just were the chief of the whole country for hurling, fighting, drinking and all manner of wickedness; but many of the lions are become lambs, are continually praising God, and calling their old companions in sin to come and magnify the Lord together;

'*Sun.* 8. I preached here at five and at twelve, and in the evening at Morvah.

'*Mon.* 9. I preached at noon on Tregavara Downs, about two miles from Penzance. A great congregation was deeply attentive while I described the "sect" which "is everywhere spoken against". At four I preached near Gulval, regulated the society and returned to St Ives.

'*Tues.* 10. I was inquiring how Dr [Walter] Borlase, a person of unquestioned sense and learning, could speak evil of this way after he had seen such a change in the most abandoned of his parishioners; but I was satisfied when Jonathan Reeves informed me that, on the doctor's asking him who had been the better for this preaching, and his replying, "The man before you (John Daniel) for one, who never before knew any work of God upon his soul," the doctor answered, "Get along: you are a parcel of mad, crazy-headed fellows", and, taking him by the shoulder, fairly thrust him to the door. In the afternoon I walked over to Zennor and, after preaching, settled the infant society.

'Wed. 11. Being the Public Fast, the church at St Ives was well filled. After reading those strong words, "If they have called the Master of the house Beelzebub, how much more them of his household?" Mr Hoblyn fulfilled them by vehemently declaiming against *the new sect*, as enemies of the Church, Jacobites, Papists and what not! After church we met and spent an hour in prayer, not forgetting the poor sinner against his own soul. In the evening I preached at Gwennap. I stood on the wall, in the calm still evening, with the sun setting behind me, and almost an innumerable multitude before, behind and on either hand.

'Thur. 12. About eleven I preached at Crowan. In the afternoon we heard of the success of Mr Hoblyn's sermon. James Wheatley was walking through the town in the evening, when the mob gathered, and began to throw stones from all quarters. He stepped into an house, but the master of it followed him like a lion, to drag him out. Yet, after a few words, his mind was changed, and he swore nobody should hurt him. Meantime one went for a Justice of the Peace, who came, and promised to see him safe home. The mob followed, hallooing and shouting amain. Near John Paynter's house the Justice left him: they quickly beset the house. But a messenger came from the mayor, forbidding any to touch Mr Wheatley, at his peril. He then went home. But between seven and eight the mob came and beset John Nance's house. John Nance and John Paynter went out and stood before the door, though they were quickly covered with dirt. The cry was, "Bring out the preacher! Pull down the house!" And they began to pull down the boards which were nailed against the windows.

But the mayor, hearing it, came without delay and read the proclamation against riots: upon which, after many oaths and imprecations, they thought proper to disperse.

'About six I reached Morvah, wet through and through, the rain having continued with scarce any intermission. However, a little company were gathered together, to whom I preached. The next day I had time to dry my clothes at Mr John's, near Penzance. At noon I preached on the Downs; about three at Gulval, and at St Ives in the evening.

'*Sat.* 14. I took my leave of St Ives, preached at two in Camborne, and at Gwennap in the evening.

'*Sun.* 15. I preached here again at five, and at eight in Stithians parish. At five I preached at Gwennap. It rained from the time I began till I concluded. I felt no pain while I spoke, but the instant I had done my teeth and head ached so violently that I had hardly any senses. I lay down as soon as I could, and fell asleep. In the morning I ailed nothing.

'*Mon.* 16. In the afternoon we came again to Trewint. I learned that notice had been given of my preaching that evening in Laneast church, which was crowded exceedingly. Mr Bennet, the minister of Laneast, carried me afterwards to his house, and (though above seventy years old) came with me in the morning to Trewint, where I had promised to preach at five. Before we parted, Digory informed me of an accusation against me current in those parts. It was really one which I did not expect; no more than that other, vehemently asserted at St Ives, of my bringing the Pretender with me thither last autumn, under the name of John Downes. It was that I called myself John Wesley; whereas everybody knew Mr Wesley was dead.'

By the end of June 1745, a few weeks before the Young Pretender landed in Scotland and began his march on London, Wesley was back in Cornwall and, at this perilous crisis in English history, faced all the forces of a panicky persecution deployed against him. Walter Borlase swore that there should be no more preaching in his neighbourhood and, on warrants from him and

Usticke, lay preachers and prominent helpers and converts were pressed for the army or hurried aboard men-of-war, while at Gwennap an attempt was made to seize Wesley himself 'for his Majesty's service'. On Sunday evenings at St Ives there was always the danger of an attack 'from some of the devil's drunken champions, who swarm here on a holy-day, so called', but Falmouth was the scene of the worst riot of all. Wesley was trapped in the house of an invalid lady by a mob roaring 'Bring out the Canorum! Where is the Canorum?' – the Cornish cant term for Methodist – and, helped by the crews of some privateers shouting 'Avast, lads, avast!', broke open the doors. The indomitable little man faced his persecutors, talked some of them into being his protectors, and eventually escaped to Penryn, where the last of the rabble pursued him with curses.

But with Culloden and the fading of the Jacobite scare the worst was over. Nerves no longer on edge and worn out by Wesley's persistence, clergy and gentry became less actively hostile, while the Cornish people, admiring his courage and recognising him as their champion against the indifference of their rulers, flocked to hear him in greater and greater numbers. 'How strangely has one year changed the scene in Cornwall', Wesley mused in 1747. All was quiet in St Ives; James Roberts, the drunken tinner and puller down of preaching houses, a reformed character; John Rogers, the Camborne persecutor, was nowhere to be seen, and even some of the gentry came to hear him at Penryn. It is true that he still had to overcome opposition from the fisherfolk and inhabitants of the new towns that he now began to take within his circuit: St Agnes, Port Isaac, Camelford, Grampound ('a mean, inconsiderable, dirty village; however, it is a borough town!'), Newlyn, Mevagissey ('See, the Methodees are come!'), Polperro. Ten years later, however, 'both persecution and popular tumult seem to be forgotten in Cornwall'. Helston, where once 'a Methodist preacher could hardly go through the streets without a shower of stones', was as quiet as Falmouth and Penryn. None opened his mouth at Breage in 1755, 'for the lions of Breage too are now changed into lambs. That they were so fierce ten years ago is no wonder, since their wretched minister told them from the pulpit that "John Wesley was expelled the College for a base child, and had been quite mazed ever since; that all the Methodists, at their private societies, put out the lights," &c., with abundance more of the same kind. But a year or two since it was observed he grew thoughtful and melancholy, and, about nine months ago, he went into his own necessary house – and hanged himself'. Redruth, once the roughest, had become one of the quietest towns in England, Camelford and Port Isaac two of the liveliest centres of Methodism. Thanks to the Methodists and a zealous clergy in these parts, 'the line is now laid, with no considerable interruption, all along the north sea, from the eastern point of Cornwall to the Land's End. In a while, I trust, there will be no more cause on these coasts to accuse *Britannos hospitibus feros'* – the Britons of being inhuman to strangers, or in other words, the Cornish of wrecking.

This, however, was over-optimistic, for sixteen years later, when Wesley asked if 'that scandal of Cornwall, the plundering of wrecked vessels, still subsisted', the old vicar of Cubert replied, 'As much as ever; only the Methodists will have nothing to do with it. But three months since a vessel was wrecked on the south coast, and the tinners presently seized on all the goods; and even broke in pieces a new coach which was on board, and carried every scrap of it away.' Wesley blamed the gentry for their laxity in enforcing the law, and recommended their making an example of ten of the next plunderers; or, there was a milder way: 'Let them only agree together to discharge any tinner or labourer that is concerned in the plundering of a wreck, and advertise his name, that no Cornish gentleman may employ him any more.'

Then, there was smuggling. When examining the society at St Ives in 1753 he was horrified to find 'an accursed thing among them: wellnigh one and all bought or sold uncustomed goods'. He told them plainly that they must put that abomination away, or they would see his face no more, and on their promising to do so felt that that plague was stayed. Perhaps he was right, for ten years later he congratulated himself that the 'detestable practice of cheating the King is no more found in our societies'. Yet the King of Prussia and his devout brother were just setting up in business, smuggling was entering on its classical and heroic age, and it is difficult to believe that there were no members of Methodist societies to leaven the mystery.

Wesley first preached in Gwennap Pit in 1762, and since then came to love that 'round, green hollow, gently shelving down', with the 'glorious congregations' assembled there, better than any other preaching place in the kingdom. 'I think this is the most magnificent spectacle which is to be seen on this side heaven', he wrote in the fullness of his heart after preaching there to thousands of tinners one fine evening in September 1775, and though the Pit has since been trimmed and tiered, it is in this

12. Wesley preaching at Gwennap Pit.

strange hollow on the hill overlooking St Day and the deserted mines of Gwennap that we can best recapture the atmosphere of eighteenth-century Cornish Methodism.

Wesley was now seventy-two, as grey-headed as his friends at St Ives. His old adversary Walter Borlase was dead, and his antiquarian brother too. He had always been generous in praise of William's books, particularly of his *Antiquities of Cornwall*, antiquities which he himself interpreted in terms of the doctor's odd archaeology, finding Druid altars in the rocks, and conveniently assigning everything older than the Romans to those ancient British priests. Yet William Borlase was a very remarkable man. The friend of the incorruptible Sir John St Aubyn and correspondent of Pope, he was one of the pioneers of archaeology and his *Observations on the Isles of Scilly* was praised by Johnson as 'one of the most pleasing and elegant pieces of local inquiry that our country has produced'. Another opponent of a very different kind died in 1777, Samuel Foote of Truro, the actor, mimic and dramatist, who had satirised the Methodists in his comedy, *The Minor*, a play which the Archbishop of Canterbury would have dearly liked to censor, but dared not, knowing very well that Foote would advertise it 'as altered and amended by his Grace the Archbishop of Canterbury'. In the same year died Dolly Pentreath, the old fisherwoman of Mousehole, reputed to be the last person to speak the Cornish language. Shortly before her death she was visited by Daines Barrington, who sent a report of his adventure to the Society of Antiquaries, and was ridiculed for his pains by John Wolcot in a poem about pilchards. Wolcot was then practising as a doctor in Truro, and had just discovered a boy of fifteen, the son of a carpenter of St Agnes, who got up at three o'clock in the summer to draw. Remembering perhaps his own early-morning attempts to paint as a youth at Fowey, he supplied him with materials, gave him the run of his house, taught him all he knew, and introduced him to patrons who paid half a guinea for a portrait head. Then in 1781, having quarrelled with everybody in Truro, Wolcot carried off his young genius to London, where he himself, as Peter Pindar, became the most popular, and often the funniest, of all English satirists, and John Opie, for that was the boy's name, the most fashionable portrait painter of a decade.

The decade was by no means a fortunate one for Cornwall. Between 1750 and 1770 the average yearly coinage of tin, of metal that is, had risen from about one thousand seven hundred to two thousand eight hundred tons, while the production of copper ore had more than doubled, from some twelve thousand to twenty-eight thousand tons. This was largely owing to the deeper mining made possible by more efficient draining; by the enterprise of John Williams in driving the County Adit, of the elder Jonathan Hornblower who erected some forty improved Newcomen engines, and of the elder Richard Trevithick who extended the Dolcoath mine by making a deep adit, introducing a system of artificial ventilation, and transforming a Hornblower engine so that it could work at a higher pressure. They were years of prosperity for the fortunate adventurers, but then in the early seventies the market was suddenly swamped by a great flood of cheap copper from the Parys mine in Anglesey.

Parys was not so much a mine as a mound of copper. The ore rose to the surface; there was no problem of drainage, and all that had to be done was to dig and carry the stuff away. It was more like quarrying than mining. The price of copper ore fell from over £7 to little more than £5 a ton; nearly all the Cornish mines were reduced to working at a loss, many of the smaller ones closed down, and even the great Dolcoath and other giants were eventually brought to a standstill. Thousands of miners were thrown out of work, some of whom found employment in the tin mines, but the increased production and consequent fall in price of the metal, coming at a time when cheap alluvial tin from Malaya was beginning to compete with the Cornish product, and porcelain was replacing pewter on the tables of the middle classes, added to the desperate hardships of the last quarter of the eighteenth century.

Fortunately there were two developments that helped to alleviate the distress. In the middle of the century the china clay deposits of St Austell had been discovered; some of the clay was exported to Worcester and Staffordshire, and attempts were made to establish porcelain works at Calstock and Penryn, but it was only after 1768, when William Cookworthy, who had founded a factory at Plymouth, began to work the deposits that the industry became at all important. 'From Truro we went on through a swiftly improving country to St Austell', wrote Wesley in 1787, and a few of the copper and tin miners – though they despised the work – were absorbed in the new and prosperous industry.

Then, in 1777 James Watt came to Cornwall to superintend the erection of one of his engines at Ting Tang mine in Gwennap. He was not well received by the jealous Cornish mining engineers, nor was Watt impressed by the barbarous country and its inhabitants, who scraped the grease from his machines and ate it. But his engine was a triumphant success. Fitted with a separate condenser, it easily drained the water which two of the biggest old engines had failed to do, and used only a quarter of the fuel in the process. By the end of 1778 there were five engines with the revolutionary separate condenser at work in Cornwall, and this saving of fuel and reduced cost of production enabled the Cornish mines to compete to some extent with the cheap, though inferior, ore that poured out of Anglesey. But Watt and his partner Boulton not unnaturally demanded their reward, and the owners of mines that used their engines had to sign contracts promising to pay premiums equal to one-third of the value of the coal saved.

Such an arrangement was bound to lead to trouble, and it was inevitable that attempts should be made to circumvent Watt's patent and gain the advantages of his invention without paying the premiums. In 1781 the younger Jonathan Hornblower patented an engine with two cylinders instead of one, and a few years later Edward Bull transformed the engine at Wheal Virgin in such a way that he claimed that it did not infringe Watt's monopoly. Boulton and Watt secured an injunction against Bull and prevented his completing the engine that he was erecting at Ding Dong, but they failed to stop Hornblower, who was commissioned to build a number of his compound engines in the Camborne area. Moreover, they failed to stop the far more dangerous younger Trevithick, a young Camborne giant who completed Bull's work at Ding Dong and threatened to throw anybody who tried to stop him down the engine shaft.

Meanwhile Boulton and Watt were quite legitimately demanding payment of their premiums, most of which were sadly in arrears, but the Cornish adventurers, many of whom were genuinely in a bad way, had little difficulty in persuading the hordes of unemployed and starving miners that the real villains responsible for their misery were the Birmingham vultures who demanded their thirty per cent. The result was serious rioting at Poldice mine in 1787. Boulton disclaimed any responsibility for the unhappy lot of the miners – why should his firm waive its royalties and bear the loss when trade was bad? – and recommended migration to the Midland coalfields. He was not altogether unsympathetic, but the dyspeptic Watt hoped that no improper concessions would be made to the miners, and suggested that soldiers should be posted at Redruth and Truro. They were there for the riots of 1789. 'We went on to Truro,' wrote Wesley on August 18th, 'but could not get through the main street to our preaching house. It was quite blocked up with soldiers to the east, and numberless tinners to the west, a huge multitude of whom, being nearly starved, were come to beg or demand an increase of their wages, without which they could not live.' It was an ill wind that blew the Methodists no good, and Wesley preached outside the Coinage Hall to twice as many people, rich and poor, as the preaching house would have held. 'How wise are all the ways of God!' was the pious reflection of the strange old man.

There was further trouble at Poldice in 1795, and in the following year Sir Francis Basset put down food rioting in Redruth by enrolling fifty special constables and arresting the ringleaders in their beds. One of them was transported and another hanged, his body being carried back from Bodmin to Camborne by a thousand mourners. Soon after this prompt and vigorous action, by which Sir Francis claimed to have changed the manners of the people from rudeness and disrespect to proper obedience, and while Pitt was engaged in suppressing the traditional liberties of England, he was created Baron de Dunstanville of Tehidy.

Perhaps the most vivid picture of these unhappy times in Cornwall is William Beckford's description of his visit to the Consolidated Mines of Gwennap in March 1787, whilst he was waiting for the Lisbon packet at Falmouth, a picture very different from the oriental luxuries of *Vathek* and the Gothic glories of Fonthill Abbey. 'They are situated in a bleak desert, rendered still more doleful by the unhealthy appearance of its inhabitants. At every step one stumbles upon ladders that lead into utter darkness, or funnels that exhale warm copperous vapours. All around these

openings the ore is piled up in heaps ready for purchasers. I saw it
drawn reeking out of the mine by the help of a machine called a
whim put in motion by mules, which in their turn are stimulated
by impish children hanging over the poor brutes and flogging
them without respite. This dismal scene of whims, suffering mules
and hillocks of cinders extends for miles. Huge iron engines
creaking and groaning invented by Watt, and tall chimneys
smoking and flaming, that seem to belong to old Nicholas's
abode, diversify the prospect. Two strange-looking beings, dressed
in ghostly white, conducted me about and very kindly proposed a
descent into the bowels of the earth, but I declined the initiation.
These mystagogues occupy a tolerable house with fair sash
windows, where the inspectors [adventurers] of the mine hold
their meetings and regale upon beef, pudding and brandy. While I
was standing at the door of this habitation several woeful figures
in tattered garments with pickaxes on their shoulders crawled out
of a dark fissure and repaired to a hovel, which I learnt was a gin-
shop. There they pass the few hours allotted them aboveground
and drink, it is to be hoped, in oblivion of their subterranean
existence. Piety, as well as gin, helps to fill up their leisure
moments, and I was told that Wesley, who came apostolising into
Cornwall a few years ago, preached on this very spot to about
7,000 followers. Since this period Methodism has made a very
rapid progress and has been of no trifling service in diverting the
attention of these sons of darkness from their present condition to
the glories of the life to come.'

Beckford wrote even more wisely than he knew. Six months
later Wesley was back in Gwennap, preaching to a 'very serious
congregation, for such are all congregations in Cornwall'. In 1789
the old evangelist of eighty-six was there for the last time, and
before passing over the Tamar, which he had first crossed nearly
fifty years before, he made the final Cornish entry in his Journal:
'So there is a fair prospect in Cornwall, from Launceston to the
Land's End.'

For Methodism there was, for at St Ives and Redruth he had left
two of the most important societies in England, and in Cornwall
an organisation and apostles who were to spread his simple

doctrine of fearing God and working righteousness throughout the county. He had brought hope to hopeless thousands, and thanks largely to him the Cornwall of 1790 was a far less barbarous place than it had been in 1740. Drunkenness had declined and, though smuggling had never been so prosperous, the inhumanities of wrecking had been checked. When in 1802 the *Suffolk* was driven ashore in St Ives Bay, the people rescued all but two of the crew, salvaged the cargo and even the ship itself. Again, when the *Anson* was wrecked off Gunwalloe in a tremendous gale in 1807, many of the local men risked their lives in saving the women and children on board, an exploit that led Henry Trengrouse of Helston to devote his life and fortune to the invention and official adoption of a rocket apparatus for ships.

But the reformation had been achieved at a cost. By diverting attention from the miseries of this life to the glories of the life to come, Wesley was reinforcing what the share-holding clergy preached and playing into the hands of exploiting capitalists, and the lot of the miner was little better in 1840 than it had been when he began his ministry a century before. Many innocent diversions, hurling and wrestling for example, were frowned on, others discouraged as undesirable fripperies, a puritanical Sabbatarianism was enforced, and much of the old Celtic gaiety disappeared at the same time as the language. Cornish congregations were serious congregations. No wonder. The thundering denunciations of sin and threats of hell fire must have brought untold terror to thousands of simple folk, and it cannot have been easy to be gay, or even prepossessing, after singing some of the Methodist hymns, or if such lines as,

The soul there restless, helpless, hopeless, lies;
The body frying roars and roaring fries,

were taken seriously instead of being the occasion for ridicule and laughter.

Fair though the Methodist prospect was in 1789, the economic prospect had never seemed bleaker. As Wesley was leaving Cornwall for the last time, news arrived that the Paris mob had stormed the Bastille, and by 1793 Britain had been drawn into war with revolutionary France, a desperate struggle that was to last until the field of Waterloo a generation later. The consequent dislocation of trade and loss of markets intensified the depression, while rising prices added to the hardships of employed and unemployed alike, for there was little advance in wages. The fishing industry was also badly hit, not only by the loss of markets but also by the heavy duties that Pitt levied on salt, which was essential for curing pilchards. Fishermen could not earn enough to buy salt to preserve sufficient pilchards for their own families, and sometimes the fish were carried direct from the seine nets to manure the fields. Once at least the St Ives men, with a great haul of pilchards in their nets, left them in shallow water until salt had been smuggled from France to cure them. Small wonder that smuggling became a major industry in Cornwall during the 'starving times' of the French wars.

Unemployment, if not distress, was to some extent reduced by the demand of the navy for men, though if Dr Johnson was right, that an eighteenth-century ship was worse than a gaol, there can have been few volunteers. But press-gangs had a way of snapping up likely looking young fellows, and in addition Parliament sanctioned a measure whereby each county had to supply a certain number of men, one hundred and ninety-four being demanded from Cornwall in 1795, two hundred and fifty-two in 1796, and many of these must have been unemployed miners. A more attractive service was the Sea Fencibles, a volunteer force for repelling invasion, and as its recruits had little fear of impressment and were paid a shilling a day when on duty, we can understand why two thousand men were enrolled. They made a great show of manning the guns supplied by the government, four to Looe, ten to Fowey, twelve to St Ives and so on, even though there was never any real threat of a French landing in Cornwall. It was just as well, for the officer who inspected the Mount's Bay volunteers reported that they were a very indifferent corps, their officers so inefficient that he could only conclude that they had been hired and dressed up for the day.

In one respect at least the Cornish were better off at the end of the century than they had been before the onset of the depression.

They were less isolated. Even as late as 1760 there was scarcely a stretch of road in the county fit for wheeled traffic, and it is said that there was then only one cart in Penzance, but within the next twenty years the old routes from Truro to Launceston and Torpoint, the one by Camelford, the other by Lostwithiel, had been improved out of all recognition. These both skirted the 'pathless moor' on which Wesley had lost his way in 1743, but at last a highway was driven over the moor from Launceston to Bodmin and the 'Indian Queens' inn, where it joined the Camelford–Truro road. Along these new turnpike roads – the smaller ones remained much as they had been after the Flood – rumbled the huge cumbersome stage wagons drawn by eight horses, in which London could be reached in three weeks. Considerably quicker than these 'flying-wagons', as they were called without irony, were the stage coaches, that plying between Truro and Torpoint doing the journey in a day, and quicker still was a post-chaise. When Robert Southey, the poet laureate, left Falmouth by chaise early one morning in 1802, he breakfasted in Truro, changed horses at the 'Indian Queens', dined in Bodmin and reached the 'White Hart' at Launceston about six. 'What a country for travelling is this!' he wrote while waiting for his supper. 'Such rapidity on the roads! Such accommodation at the resting places! We advanced fourteen leagues to-day without fatigue or exertion.' There is a confident ring about that; a good note on which to leave the eighteenth century.

XI

The Nineteenth Century

The first third of the nineteenth century, the period up to the accession of Queen Victoria, was to witness the transformation of Cornwall. It was an age of invention and expansion, a new heroic age of common miners and uncommon men. There was Humphry Davy of Penzance, handsome and vivacious, a passionate angler and minor poet as well as major scientist, who was succeeded as president of the Royal Society by generous Davies Gilbert of St Erth, and it was Gilbert again who encouraged and helped impetuous Richard Trevithick of Camborne and Goldsworthy Gurney of Padstow, inventor of the steam jet and Bude light. And in other spheres of action there were Edward Pellew, Viscount Exmouth, liberator of slaves, Henry Martyn, melancholy missionary and oriental scholar, Richard Lander, explorer of the Niger, and Edward John Trelawny, 'beautiful and terrible as a tempest', friend of Shelley and companion of Byron, who fought for the independence of Greece and married the sister of an Albanian chieftain. Most of these passed under the rod of Cornelius Cardew, who, to his great satisfaction and profit, managed to combine the Mastership of Truro Grammar School with the livings of St Erme and Lelant, his 'western living', where, for £45 a year, he was represented by a curate.

The very dawn of the century brought new hope. In 1800 Watt's patent came to an end, and with it the burden of royalties and freedom to combine his invention with others in an attempt to produce an engine that would drain mines three hundred fathoms deep. They could afford to dig deep now, for the Anglesey deposits were almost exhausted, leaving Cornwall the biggest copper producing region in the world. As always happens, war stimulated invention, and before it was over Trevithick had built a high-pressure engine which was not only much more powerful than the old low-pressure engines, but considerably smaller and cheaper. But Trevithick was too restless and full of ideas to concentrate long on one problem. After making a steam threshing machine for the borough-mongering Sir Christopher Hawkins – Trelawny's uncle – he sailed for Peru in 1816 to reopen the old silver and gold mines there, was ruined by a revolution, made a fortune by salvaging treasure, lost it in a pearl fishing speculation, turned surgeon, was pressed as a soldier, and finally rescued from the jaws of an alligator before returning penniless to Cornwall in 1827.

Meanwhile invention had been further stimulated by Joel Lean's system of duty reporting, a scheme whereby mine managers published monthly reports of the efficiency or 'duty' of their engines, the duty being the number of pounds of water raised one foot by one hundredweight of coal. In 1811 the average duty of twelve engines reporting was seventeen million, by 1820 that of forty-five engines was twenty-nine million, and when Trevithick returned he found Arthur Woolf and Samuel Grose competing for the honour of being the first to reach a hundred million, though the first to do so was William West, who broke all records in 1835 with 125,000,000. The average duty of sixty-one engines was now nearly fifty million, four times as much as it had been at the beginning of the century, and a few years later one pound of coal in a perfected Cornish engine could raise a ton of water four hundred and fifty feet at a cost of about half a farthing.

As a result the shafts plunged deeper, Wheal Virgin down to three hundred fathoms and a temperature of 100°F., and the new engines, which had been virtually confined to mines working deep for copper, were now installed in the shallower tin mines. Greatest of all these, Wheal Vor, which had been drowned in 1715 when a Newcomen engine failed to drain it, was reopened in 1814, and shortly afterwards the richest lode of tin ever discovered in Cornwall was struck at a hundred and fifty fathoms and worked down to three hundred through ground worth £100 a foot. Copper mines that had been closed during the depression were also pumped dry and reworked; Dolcoath was reopened, and so was Levant mine on the cliffs near St Just, the fortunate adventurers in which cleared a profit of £200,000 in the first twenty years of working. Even more important was the opening up of a new area. In 1837 a small company of adventurers, many of them working tinners, found a rich lode of copper at Caradon, a few miles north of Liskeard, and in the

13. Levant Mine.

following year sold a hundred and thirty tons of ore for £1,200. The Caradon region was soon to prove itself one of the richest mineral areas in Cornwall.

It was a revolution indeed. In 1800 there were seventy-five mines, employing some 16,000 people, at work in Cornwall. By 1837 there were more than 200 mines employing 30,000 men, women and children; 170 engines drained the workings, and steam had replaced mules and water in driving many of the whims and stamps. Wheal Vor alone had sixteen engines and more than a thousand workpeople, and was mainly responsible for raising the amount of tin produced from 2,500 tons in 1800 to 4,100 in 1837. The increase in copper was even more spectacular, from 5,000 to 12,000 tons, and during this period Cornwall produced two-thirds of the world's supply. No wonder the 'bleak desert' round the Consolidated Mines of Gwennap, visited by Beckford just fifty years before, was reputed to be the richest square mile of ground in the Old World. The population of the county increased almost in proportion, from 200,000 to 350,000 – more than it is today – and many of the mining parishes more than doubled, Gwennap, for example, rising from 4,500 to 10,000.

One result of the increased tin production was the promotion of Hayle and St Austell to the rank of coinage towns. By this time, however, the medieval ceremony of coinage was merely an embarrassing anachronism: the privileges formerly enjoyed by the tinners had long since lapsed, the delay incurred by having to wait for coinage days was infuriating to businessmen like Michael Williams, while the innumerable fees demanded by petty officials when added to the standard duty of 4s a hundredweight represented a tax of almost ten per cent on Cornish tin, most of which was swallowed up by the cost of collection. In 1838, therefore, the whole system was swept away in favour of a small excise duty levied at the smelting house, the Duke of Cornwall – though there was no Duke until the birth of the future Edward VII in 1841 – being compensated out of government funds. It was just five hundred years since Edward III had made over the coinage revenue to the Black Prince.

310

The enormous increase in demand for engines and machinery led inevitably to the establishment of iron foundries near the mining centres. In 1800 most of the engine castings were supplied by Boulton and Watt of Birmingham, who sent them by canal and sea to Hayle, Portreath and the Fal estuary; but one or two firms at such a distance could not cope with the growing demand from Cornwall, and Trevithick's father-in-law, John Harvey, transformed his blacksmith's shop into a foundry which, by the middle of the century, was one of the biggest engineering firms in the country. The works are now only a shell, but the massive ruins and great early Victorian houses with cast-iron Corinthian pilasters are a melancholy reminder of the town's former prosperity, when the port was full of ships and orders poured in from all over the world. A rival foundry was set up nearby at Copperhouse on the site of the abandoned smelting works, and the Gwennap area was served by another great foundry at Perran on Restronguet Creek, while in 1839 Holman's mining machinery works were established in Camborne.

Transport had become a pressing problem. Iron castings and great quantities of coal and ore could scarcely be carried between port and mine on the backs of mules, and in 1809 the Williams family built a tramway from Portreath to Scorrier and Poldice mine, along the iron rails of which horses and mules, with stationary engines at the top of steep inclines hauled goods with comparative ease. The venture was so successful that in 1824 the Gwennap mines laid a similar line from Redruth to Restronguet Creek, and by 1830 a short line from St Austell to Pentewan was carrying passengers as well as china clay.

Long before this Trevithick had been experimenting with locomotives. As early as 1797 he had made a model 'road carriage' which was driven at his house in Camborne by Lady de Dunstanville and stoked by Davies Gilbert. Then on December 28th, 1801, his full-scale Puffing Devil was given its trials on the road between Camborne and Tehidy. There were minor disasters, upsets and explosions, but Christmas was perhaps too festive a season to give the machine a fair trial, and in 1803 another engine was successfully driven through London and put through its paces on Lord's cricket ground. The next step was to place the locomotive on rails, and in 1808 one of his engines ran round and round a circular track at Euston to the vast entertainment of the passengers, until one of the rails broke and the machine overturned. Having got so far, Trevithick characteristically abandoned railway locomotives for ship propellers and threshing machines, leaving George Stephenson to finish his work.

The short, steep stretches of rail in the mining districts were not suitable for locomotives, and the first railway engine in Cornwall ran along the almost level course of the Camel from Bodmin to Wadebridge when the line was opened in 1834. In that year, however, an Act of Parliament incorporated the Hayle Railway Company, with power to construct a line from the port up to Tresavean mine in Gwennap. Starting from Hayle foundry, it crossed Copperhouse Creek by a drawbridge and ran along the northern shore through Phillack before climbing up to the mine clusters of Camborne and so on to Redruth and Tresavean. As there were no viaducts, a stationary engine and wire rope were necessary on the steep Angarrack incline, but east of that locomotives, assisted by ropes in two places, could be used. The line was finished in 1837, and a year later the first locomotive built in Cornwall, the *Cornishman*, from the Copperhouse foundry of Sandys, Carne and Vivian, completed its trials on this line. Trevithick was dead, but Davies Gilbert lived just long enough to see the dawn of the Victorian era and the beginning of the railway age in Cornwall.

While tramways were being laid in the mining districts of the west, the transport problem was partially solved in the broader lands of the agricultural east by building canals. The first and biggest of these, begun in 1819, was to link Bodmin with the Tamar and Launceston. It was never quite finished, however, though one of its main purposes was achieved when barges brought sand to the inland farmers who, in the traditional Cornish fashion, spread it on their fields as a fertiliser. Another canal of the same period carried coal up to Liskeard and granite down to Looe, a traffic that was supplemented by copper ore when the Caradon mines were opened and linked by railway to Liskeard.

The growing prosperity of Cornwall, or at least of its landowners and adventurers, was given tangible expression in its building. Some of the great country houses had already been altered or rebuilt in the eighteenth century: the old home of the Carews at Antony had been demolished and replaced by a new mansion, probably by Gibbs; Sir Richard Vyvyan had added a delicate little Gothic chapel to Trelowarren, and additions were made to Lanherne, though the great Arundells were gone, and since 1794 the house had been a convent – as it still is – occupied by nuns who fled from Antwerp at the beginning of the revolutionary wars. The first decades of the nineteenth century were a transitional period when architects, according to the whims of their clients, wavered uneasily between the old classicism and new romanticism inspired by the quickened interest in the Middle Ages and Middle East, a period that produced Beckford's precarious Fonthill Abbey and the Sino-Gothic fantasy of Brighton Pavilion. There is nothing quite so fanciful in Cornwall, though Carclew – now a ruin – has its picturesque Neo-Gothic chapel, Penzance its Egyptian House, and P F Robinson, who favoured the Egyptian, rebuilt Trelissick in an uncompromisingly Neo-Greek manner, while the new Clowance of the St Aubyns, with its porch of Tuscan columns, was equally severe. In the skilful hands of Sir John Soane medieval Port Eliot assumed a classical air, an elegant compromise of battlements and sash windows, as was the house erected within the ruins of Trematon Castle, but John Nash ruthlessly converted Carhays into a vaulted and turreted stronghold. William Wilkins out-Tudored the Tudors in the ingenuity of his chimneys when rebuilding Tregothnan on a massive scale for Lord Falmouth, and it was Wilkins who built picturesque Pentillie Castle overlooking the last great loop of the Tamar, close to the tower in which the embalmed body of Sir James Tillie had been placed in a chair when he died a hundred years before.

The towns too were being transformed – a Doric Methodist chapel at Truro, a new church at Penzance, and another at St Day, now doomed like the mines that surround it, where the single word 'Williams' carved on a granite headstone was epitaph enough for the members of that powerful dynasty. Then there were new public buildings: a Market House at Penzance, a Custom House at Falmouth, and everywhere new houses and streets were going up, from Launceston and Bodmin to St Ives, but finest of all, Lemon Street in Truro. In those late Georgian days, when roads were good enough for coaches, and railways had not yet brought London within a few hours of the Land's End, the little Cornish towns were centres of fashion as they had never been before and will never be again. Formerly, the county families entertained exclusively in their country houses, but now many of them had a town house as well, and all flocked to the new assembly rooms to dance and enjoy themselves with the families of the wealthier townsmen, and again, although Bodmin was the county town, Truro took the lead. There, in the Assembly Rooms faced with Bath stone, and indeed worthy of Bath which they emulated, de Dunstanville and Vyvyan paired with Williams and Trevanion, Falmouth and Lemon stepped off with Hawkins and St Aubyn. It was a brief flowering, this Jane Austen world of routs and revels; another twenty years and it was over; the great houses of Boscawen Street were long ago converted into offices and shops, the Assembly Rooms are now a garage, incongruously displaying medallions of Shakespeare and Handel.

Less frivolous and less ephemeral were the societies founded at this time. Shut off from all great centres of learning and the arts, townsmen combined to form their own associations, literary, scientific, philosophical and musical. There was the Royal Geographical Society of Cornwall with Davies Gilbert as its first president, Penzance had its Natural History and Antiquarian Society and its Library, Falmouth its Royal Cornwall Polytechnic Society, the first of its kind in England, Truro its Philharmonic Society, and at Truro the Royal Institution of Cornwall was founded in 1818. Even the small fishing towns had their little societies, concerts and balls, for with the end of the Napoleonic wars prosperity returned.

In 1827 there were more than ten thousand people engaged in the fishing industry: two thousand seven hundred seinemen, sixteen hundred driftmen and six thousand women and children, who cured and packed the pilchards in fish cellars, and in the next ten years the number of hogsheads exported was doubled. St Ives had become the chief centre of pilchard fishing, and between 1829 and 1838 supplied the Mediterranean market with nearly nine thousand hogsheads, some thirty million fish, every year, in 1834 ten thousand hogsheads being encircled by its seines within an hour. Such catches, of course, were exceptional, and there were years when the pilchard shoals were very thin. Moreover, seine fishing was merely a seasonal occupation lasting at best only three or four months, at worst only three or four days, and few of these shore fishermen were sailors, but farmhands, labourers and miners, tributers and tutworkers who took time off when the fish appeared in the autumn.

Agricultural labourers could well do with something to supplement their wages, for the post-war period was a wicked time for farming. During the Napoleonic blockade, when corn was at famine prices, cultivation had been pushed up the hills and into the moors, while the better land had been driven until it was exhausted, so that with peace and falling prices the whole farming economy was thrown out of gear. Wages were appallingly low: in the Morwenstow region, where Hawker was appointed vicar in 1834, they were still 7s a week in the middle of the century, and for one harvest at least Ludgvan farmers were able to hire pauper labour for 3d a day. It is hardly surprising that a steady stream of emigrants passed through Padstow on their way to the New World.

The era of reform was at hand, however, of Poor Law Act and Factory Act, though the one was universally unpopular and the other scarcely affected Cornwall; but the measure that made these reforms possible affected Cornwall more than any other county in the kingdom. For more than two centuries Cornwall had returned forty-four members to the House of Commons, until in 1821 a defeated candidate at Grampound revealed that Sir Manasseh Lopes had bought the forty voters for £50 apiece, less £300 that had stuck to the fingers of the mayor. No government could ignore this exposure of corruption, and the borough was

disfranchised. Lopes was by no means the only large-scale
borough-monger; there was Sir Christopher Hawkins with St Ives
in his pocket, and Boscawens wrestled with Bassets for Michell,
Tregony and Truro. Cornish seats were transferred like shares in
a joint stock company; only half a dozen of the members were
natives of the county, and electors were kept down to a
minimum; St Ives had most with a hundred and eighty, but
seven had less than thirty, the two Looes had ten, Michell five,
and for some years a single voter returned two members for the
little village of Bossiney. Then at last, in 1830, the Whigs were
returned to power, and Lord John Russell introduced his Reform
Bill. Only six of the forty-two members for Cornwall supported
the Bill, but in 1832 it was carried through the Commons and
forced through the Lords.

Pocket and rotten boroughs were abolished, thirteen of them
in Cornwall; Launceston, Liskeard, Helston and St Ives were
reduced to one member, and only Bodmin, Truro, Penryn-
Falmouth and the county itself were left with two. Cornwall thus
contributed thirty of the hundred and sixty seats made available
for distribution among the big new towns of the Midlands and
north. Cornish reformers rejoiced, and Trevithick proposed –
it was his final project – the erection in London of a
commemorative, perforated, gilt, cast-iron column a thousand
feet high, up which sightseers would be shot to the summit in
a tubular air elevator.

The Reforming Thirties were followed by the Hungry Forties,
a decade of agitation and distress during which the population of
the agricultural hundred of Stratton declined by more than ten
per cent, and seven thousand miners and their families left for the
lead regions of Wisconsin. Despite the repeal of the Corn Laws,
bad harvests doubled the price of grain, and after the hard winter
of 1846–7 bands of hungry miners and labourers invaded the
towns – Wadebridge, Callington, Launceston, Redruth, St Austell,
Penzance – to prevent merchants sending corn out of the county
and to enforce the sale of food at what they considered
reasonable prices. They were remarkably well behaved and there

was nothing worse than a little mild rioting; then food prices fell, and with the fifties farming entered on a period of relative prosperity. But if the workers had combined under a leader to demand higher wages there might have been another story to tell.

However, nobody thought of raising wages, although the fortune of adventurers with shares in the right mines continued to flourish. Even though the duty on foreign tin ore was abolished in 1843, demand was so great that production rose from five thousand to six thousand tons between 1840 and 1860, while copper reached its maximum in 1856 with 13,247 tons – more than twice the amount and twice the value of the tin – largely owing to the rich new deposits of Caradon, and the opening of Devon Great Consols on the other bank of the Tamar, the shares in which rose from £1 to £300 in 1844. The western copper of Gwennap and Camborne was not yet exhausted, but the balance had shifted; great wealth had come to east Cornwall.

Wealth for a few and work for many. 'The Caradon Copper Mines,' wrote the genial author of Black's *Guide*, 'have been excavated out of solid granite at the base of Caradon Hill (1,208 feet), and are connected with the seashore, *via* Liskeard and Looe, by a small railway worked by horses. The scene is a fantastic one; a clear swift stream runs into a deep valley between the twin hills, West and South Caradon. On the slopes of these hills, and in the hollows of the valley, are the banks of the copper mines, and the ground is dotted with groups of workpeople – women and girls, in bright-coloured attire, hammering at lumps of ore, or sifting and washing them in the numerous watercourses which ripple around.' Most of these women and girls, and their husbands and brothers down the shafts in which 'a succession of ladders wearies the legs and tests the patience of the curious explorer' would come from St Cleer, once one of the loveliest villages of Cornwall, surrounded by memorials of the past from neolithic to medieval times, Trethevy Quoit, the Hurlers, the Doniert Stone, a Holy Well, but now swollen into a mining town of four thousand souls, almost as big as modern Launceston. In 1830, before the mines were opened, the average age of those buried in the parish was forty-five, in 1860 it was under twenty-two; the proportion of those dying before the age of five had doubled, and only fifty, twenty-six men and twenty-four women, lived to be seventy in the decade of the fifties. Death, as well as wealth and work, had come to east Cornwall.

It is true that there had been some improvement in conditions underground. Bickford's safety fuse saved the eyes and hands of many a miner, though it did not reduce the fumes that made him cough and spit black. Tram roads had been laid in some mines at the same time as those on the surface, but even in 1864 when the Mines Commission made its report they were by no means general, and boys wheeled heavy barrows along the levels with hands so sore that they had to take the weight with slings about their necks. Perhaps the greatest improvement was Michael Loam's man engine installed in Tresavean mine in 1841, a device whereby men travelled up and down the shaft by stepping from one moving platform to another, yet in 1864 most of the mines reported that they had been unable to afford such a luxury.

Without any standards of safety or government inspection, disasters were frequent, and in 1847 it was estimated that one out of every five Gwennap miners died as a result of accident. According to Dr Richard Couch, however, the mortality was much higher than it need have been owing to lack of hospitals and skilled nursing, while the men lived in such isolated and inaccessible places that it was almost impossible for a doctor to attend them speedily – even if he had wished to. Mine surgeons were appointed by the adventurers, and, in return for a small monthly deduction from his pay, the miner was entitled to free medical attention, but only too often the doctor drew his salary and left the work to unqualified assistants who lived nearer the miners' cottages.

Couch was himself a mine surgeon, a devoted and dedicated one working in the St Just region, where in 1857 he found that the average age of the miners was only twenty-eight and a man of forty already an old man. He attributed more than half the deaths to chest complaints brought on largely by the damp and smoke-sodden air, the Great Beam mine near St Austell being particularly notorious. 'To see the men from such mines arriving at surface after eight hours' work is a most sickening sight,' he wrote. 'Thin, haggard, with arms apparently very much lengthened and hanging almost uselessly by their sides, they seem like men worn out rather than tired.' Another hazard was the great change in temperature from three hundred fathoms, where men cooled themselves in steaming water, to surface conditions fifty degrees lower. Then there was the strain of climbing two thousand feet of ladders after an eight hours' shift; it took the men three-quarters of an hour to go down that depth and twice as long to return, so that eight hours became ten, followed by a normal hour's walk home.

Boys were subjected to the same conditions, though of course they could not do the heavy work of men. At Ding Dong, high on the Penwith downs, Couch found that nearly a third of the two hundred miners were boys under fifteen, two of them being children of eight. They were better off than boys in the coal mines, where children of four sat in the dark opening and closing trap doors, but sometimes when the tributers were cutting a rich lode they worked seventy or eighty hours a week.

In 1850 wages were almost twice as high as they had been a century before, but as prices had just about doubled there was little difference in real wages, in what the money would buy. By working hard a skilled bal maiden could make a shilling a day, 24s a month, though the average was probably no more than 20s. Miners' earnings varied: a tributer might make £6 one month and nothing the next, but the average monthly wage of tributers, tutworkers and surface workers was rather less than £3 – twice that of many farm labourers. As at the end of a month a tributer on a poor pitch might actually be in debt to the adventurers after all deductions had been made for fines, powder, candles and so on, there was a system of 'subsist' by which the firm advanced money to be deducted from the next month's pay. The adventurers did not hesitate to take advantage of their debtors' weakened position, and placed them still further in their power by setting up truck shops where the miners could buy – were expected to buy – their goods on credit. There was, for example,

14. Building a Cornish haystack at Tregaminion, Lizard, c.1864–6.

the highly successful mining adventurer Collan Harvey of St Day, brother-in-law of John Williams of Scorrier, who owned the biggest store in Gwennap parish. One of his clerks attended every pay day at the mines of the Williams group to collect the amounts due from the men, and if any had failed to visit the shop a deduction was made to bring them there to explain their negligence. Such exploitation was no worse than that of serfs under the feudal system, the exploiters themselves no worse than feudal barons, but after all it was the middle of the nineteenth century. Harvey died in 1846 at Pengreep, the great Georgian house which even the fastidious Beckford had admired.

'Everything was very dear, and the working people were half starved,' wrote the miner, Thomas Oliver, of this period. 'My father had the standard wages for surface hands, which was £2 5s a month, and I was earning 10s a month, so that £2 15s a month had to provide for five of us. For our breakfast we had barley gruel, which consisted of about three quarts of water and a halfpenny-worth of skimmed milk thickened with barley flour, a concoction which went by the name of sky-blue and sinker. We lived about half a mile from the mine, and I had to go home to dinner. I can assure the reader that I was sometimes so feeble that

I could scarcely crawl along. For dinner we had sometimes a barley pasty with a bit or two of fat pork on the potatoes, and for supper a barley cake or stewed potatoes or turnips with a barley cover. Everything was very dear; groceries such as raisins and currants were 10d per pound, tea 4s a pound and the common brown sugar 5d a pound. I never saw at that time such a thing as jam.' Dr Couch described the hovels in which such families lived, refuse heaps and slimy puddles surrounding the two rooms in which sometimes eight or nine people of all ages were crammed. No wonder the mortality was high, the average age of burial at St Cleer twenty-two, for these were the real killers – poverty, malnutrition, overcrowding and filth.

Of course there were philanthropists, devoted doctors such as Richard Couch and Tobias Mitchell, and enlightened adventurers like those at Redruth who tried to set up a hospital, a scheme that was defeated by the conservative and suspicious miners themselves; they preferred to die at home. But when, after the report of the Mines Commission of 1864, Lord Kinnaird proposed introducing legislation for government inspection, the adventurers and 'gentlemen interested in mining property' raised such an outcry that the matter was dropped. Cornwall produced no Lord Shaftesbury to champion the miners' cause, nor any leader to combine the workers into trade unions for the redress of their grievances. Tributers, and to a lesser degree tutworkers as well, were in a sense free men, not wage earners, and Celtic independence, an almost fanatical individualism, made nonsense of the Cornish motto 'One and All'. Combination, save in small groups for working a pitch or owning a fishing boat, was unnatural, interest in politics elementary and demagogues rare. Cornishmen looked elsewhere for their comfort and oratory, to simple but intensely moving miner preachers like Billy Bray who continued the work begun by Wesley.

As a result there were no labour troubles comparable to those that convulsed nineteenth-century trans-Tamar England, and in the improving literature of the period Cornish miners – many of them teetotallers by now – were very favourably contrasted with their turbulent Saxon cousins who never seemed to be satisfied and were always going on strike. It was not until 1857 that Cornishmen spoiled their record, when the surface workers at Balleswidden, a tin mine near St Just, refused to work when the adventurers proposed to cut their pay.

By this time, the decade of the Great Exhibition, Crimean War and Indian Mutiny, there was alternative work to be found in Cornwall. Strung along the threads of the great network of railroads that was lacing Britain were two hundred thousand navvies – inland navigators who used to dig canals – shovelling, tunnelling and blasting, easy work for miners and better paid. Already, in 1849, the South Devon Railway had reached Plymouth, and a four-horse omnibus leaving Camborne early in the morning whisked its passengers across the county to catch the

15. Royal Albert Bridge from Saltash Station, c.1862–3.

evening train up to London. That, however, was not good enough. Cornwall was a great industrial centre, Falmouth the most westerly landfall, a position of unique importance in the days of sailing ships, and plans had long been made to link the port with London, though it was not until 1846 that the Cornwall Railway

Company was formed. A single broad-gauge line was to run from Plymouth to Truro and Falmouth, and I K Brunel, the engineer, proposed bridging the Tamar at Saltash. In 1847 work was begun on the stretch from Truro to St Austell, but owing to difficulties of finance as well as of construction it was 1858 before the line from Truro to Saltash and, on the other side of the Tamar, to Plymouth, had been completed. Meanwhile the base of the central pier of the bridge had been fixed in the middle of the river, and slowly the two huge iron trusses were hoisted as the stone piers were built under them, until they were a hundred feet above the water. By the end of February 1859 the work was finished; on April 11th the first train ran from Plymouth to Truro, and on May 2nd the Prince Consort came down to open the great Saltash Bridge.

It was a memorable occasion. Cornwall was no longer all but an island, remote and inaccessible. A few years before, a journey from Truro to London was the event of a lifetime experienced by very few Cornishmen, and very few Englishmen penetrated far beyond the Tamar; but now space was folded like a fan, the far west within a few hours of the great cities of the east and north, Exeter, Bristol, Oxford, Birmingham, London, and Celt and Saxon were brought together in daily intercourse to the great advantage of both. Although something would inevitably and irretrievably be lost by the dilution of an ancient Celtic culture, far more was to be gained, and it is scarcely too much to say that the coming of the railway at this critical juncture was to prove the salvation of Cornwall.

It was a remarkable achievement as well. Although the line from Truro to Plymouth was only fifty-three miles long, it was one of the most difficult – and most beautiful – stretches in the country; there was barely a mile of level ground, and the steep valleys cutting across its course had to be bridged by thirty-four viaducts, lacelike structures of stone and timber, for which the Cornwall Railway was famous. Altogether there were four miles of viaduct apart from the great bridge at Saltash, which with its approaches was almost half a mile long, the river itself, more than three hundred yards wide, being crossed by two great spans under which the tallest ship could pass. Brunel died six months after its completion, and the directors commemorated him by the simple inscription over the shore archways: 'I K Brunel. Engineer. 1859.' Eight more viaducts were added to the Cornwall Railway when the line from Truro to Falmouth was completed in 1863.

Meanwhile there had been developments west of Truro. On the day of incorporation of the Cornwall Railway Company, August 3rd, 1846, another projected line received the royal assent. This was the West Cornwall, which was to take over the little narrow-gauge Hayle Railway between Hayle and Redruth, and extend it westward to Penzance and eastward to Truro, where it would link up with the Cornwall. The ropes on the inclines between Hayle and Camborne were scrapped, the line relaid, steep gradients avoided by building viaducts, and by the autumn of 1852 trains were running between Penzance and Truro. It must have been an enchanting little line; guards signalled with green and white flags to restrain or encourage their drivers, though the directors spoiled some of the fun by forbidding their workmen to wear 'apparel of a Red or Pink color'. Perhaps they were touchy after the year of revolutions, 1848, or more probably they wished to avoid a man being mistaken for a signal.

When, seven years later, the line from Plymouth reached Truro, Penzance was in direct communication with London. Not quite direct, however. The position was somewhat absurd. From Paddington to Truro the line was broad-gauge, from Truro to Penzance narrow, so that all had to change, passengers and goods alike, and there was no through traffic until the West Cornwall had been converted to broad gauge by the addition of an outer rail in 1867. This gave further scope for eccentricity: mixed-gauge goods trains composed of narrow-gauge engines hauling a medley of broad- and narrow-gauge trucks, a tricky business when it came to negotiating points.

By this time the South Devon Railway from Exeter and Tavistock had reached Launceston, but there it stopped just over the threshold of Cornwall, and it was at Launceston that the young architect, Thomas Hardy, arrived by train one afternoon in March 1870, having left Dorchester early that morning. He had come to make sketches and a plan of St Juliot church, which was to be restored, and drove the sixteen miles to the rectory near Boscastle over the road taken by Leland more than three centuries before, and still very much the same: 'Scarcely a solitary house or man had been visible along the whole dreary distance of open country. The only lights apparent on earth were some spots of dull red, glowing here and there upon the distant hills, smouldering fires for the consumption of peat and gorse-roots.' He was received by the rector's sister-in-law, the girl who was to become his wife and inspire the writing of his first great novel, *A Pair of Blue Eyes*, and the lyric, 'When I set out for Lyonnesse'. St Juliot was a very poor agricultural parish, but Hardy was not to know that industrial Cornwall was even more desperately impoverished.

Copper production reached its peak in 1856 when 209,000 tons of ore were raised, yielding 13,300 tons of metal worth almost £2,000,000, and £300,000 were distributed to adventurers

16. Botallack Mine, c.1864.

in dividends. Yet the prosperity was deceptive: most of the profit came from the new eastern mines of Caradon and the Tamar, even Botallack was running at a loss, and in 1857 only three

Gwennap mines paid dividends. Moreover the quality of ore was deteriorating; the hills full of copper which Hugh Boscawen had pointed out to Celia Fiennes from Tregothnan nearly two centuries before were now almost empty; costs of production were rising while prices were falling, and prices were falling because of foreign competition.

In the decade of the thirties Cornwall had produced 116,000 tons of fine copper as against the rest of the world's 102,000, but the figures for the fifties were 122,000 and 384,000. Cornish production was slightly higher, but that of the rest of the world was nearly four times as great, and in the sixties the proportion was 90,000 to 810,000. The chief competitor was Chile, but more ominous was the rapidly rising output of Australia and above all of the United States which, in spite of the Civil War, was producing more than Cornwall.

Some of the younger and more enterprising miners, realising that there was little future for them in Cornwall, joined the gold rush for California as early as 1850, and during the fifties hundreds of men left Hayle and other ports in small ships that took them to Bristol and Liverpool, where they embarked for New York or San Francisco by way of Cape Horn. Some went to the newly discovered Australian goldfields, others to the copper mines of Michigan, and even the allied industry of engineering began to leave the county when the Vivians transferred their works from Camborne to Pittsburgh. But as yet emigration was not on a grand scale, and in 1861 the population of Cornwall reached its maximum with 369,390, though the decennial rate of increase in the forties and fifties was only four per cent, whereas that of the country as a whole was fourteen.

The threat of slump and unemployment at last drove the miners to try to protect themselves by combination. At the beginning of 1866 the eastern men formed the Miners' Mutual Benefit Association, a friendly society which, however, claimed the right to decide whether the rate offered to tributers and tutworkers was sufficient. The adventurers refused to recognise the claim or to employ any member of the trade union, for such it really was, and the men replied by refusing to work. There was some disorder, troops were brought up, but the strike was broken by the importation of unemployed men from the west, where wages were even lower. When so much blackleg labour was available there was little chance of organising a successful trade union, and even less chance of raising wages when profits were falling.

For the western mines were closing down: Wheal Abraham, Basset United, Wentworth Consols and others were already 'knackt bals' when the financial crisis of 1866 struck Cornwall and turned depression into disaster, precipitating the inevitable end, more merciful in the long run than a protracted consumption. Already tottering copper mines could not withstand the pressure that brought down firmly established businesses all over England, and the melancholy roll of casualties continued: Treloweth, Wendron Consols, Wheal Talgus ... it is said that five thousand miners left Cornwall that year. And 1867 was even worse: Wheal Reath, Hallamanin, St Day United ... thousands of men were thrown out of work and hundreds of families were on the verge of starvation. Production of copper ore fell from 160,000 tons in 1865 to 120,000 in 1867, and by 1870 it was only 80,000; ten years later it was 40,000 and by the end of the century less than 500.

It was particularly hard for the conservative Cornishman, so proud of his heritage, so deeply attached to his native country, so ignorant of the world outside, to tear up his roots and leave his home, but for many there was no alternative, and after the collapse of 1866 there was a continuous stream of emigrants to the newly discovered mining areas of other continents – the United States, South America, South Africa, Australia – and soon it became almost literally true that 'where a hole is sunk in the ground, no matter in what corner of the globe, you will be sure to find a Cornishman at the bottom of it, searching for metal'. While the population of England and Wales grew steadily at the rate of thirteen per cent every ten years, that of Cornwall fell two per cent in the sixties, and a further nine per cent in the seventies, when a third of the mining population left the county. In that decade St Just fell from 9,000 to 6,400 and even St Cleer from 4,000 to 3,000, while Gwennap parish, which had 11,000 inhabitants in 1841, was reduced to 6,000 by 1881. Houses were empty in the little towns, on the moors cottages were crumbling, their hard-won fields and gardens reverting to waste, couch grass and bracken were obliterating the old mule tracks and ivy crept up the pointing fingers of the silent engine houses.

Fortunately a number of factors helped to reduce the scale of the disaster to Cornwall. In the seventeenth century copper had been found below the tin, but when the copper had been almost exhausted there were signs that the lodes were changing again to tin at an average depth of about a thousand feet. There followed a brief period of what might be called mixed mining, but the weaker concerns without capital reserves could not afford to dig deep in the hope of exploiting this new wealth, and they were the ones, the great majority, that had to close. A few, however, managed to raise more capital and to change over from deep copper to even deeper tin mining. One of these was the great Levant mine at Pendeen, another the venerable Dolcoath at Camborne. After paying prodigious dividends at the beginning of

17. East Pool Mine in 1893, 180 fathom level.

the century, Dolcoath began to falter as the vast copper lodes gave place to a not very valuable mixture of copper and tin, but thanks to the efforts of the manager, Charles Thomas, the adventurers agreed to subscribe more capital, shafts were driven deeper and in 1853 the first dividend was paid on tin. After that riches once again poured out of the mine: by 1868 the adventurers had received £148,000, and during the next twenty-five years a further £650,000 were distributed. The great run came to an end in 1894 when the bottom of the mine collapsed, more than four hundred fathoms down, burying eight miners and the richest tin ground. A few more mines succeeded in making the transition to tin – Botallack, South Crofty, East Pool, Wheal Kitty – and there were some, like Wheal Vor, that had always been tin producers. The output of tin rose while that of copper fell catastrophically, and tin mines enjoyed another thirty years of prosperity, largely owing to the introduction of rock drills and machines for dressing the ore, though they could absorb only a fraction of the copper miners thrown out of work.

More found employment in the china clay industry. The region between Roche and St Austell was rapidly being transformed into a lunar landscape of spectral craters and foolscap hills whose rivers ran milk; it had a remote and dreamlike beauty, but more immediately important this seemingly aimless geological

18. St Austell viaduct, mid 1880s.

upheaval was profitable. In addition to its primary function in the manufacture of porcelain, a hundred and one new uses had been found for china clay, from paper making to paint, and in the decade following the copper crisis production was more than doubled. Here at least was an urgent demand for labour and, though miners professed contempt for the clay men and their work, two or three thousand of them found employment in the industry. It was the salvation of the St Austell district.

Then there was the railway. It had arrived just in time. In 1861 the directors 'observed with pleasure' that 1,063 tons of fish, 1,787 of potatoes and 867 of broccoli and other vegetables had been carried over the Cornwall line during the season. It is the first mention of the carriage of perishable goods to the almost insatiable market of London. This rapid transport and the warm equable climate made it possible for the farmers of West Cornwall to turn their fields into market gardens supplying vegetables to the eastern cities, and by the end of the century nearly twenty thousand tons of broccoli were being sent by train every year. Flowers soon followed, though mainly from Scilly. In 1871 a Mr Trevellick of St Mary's sent a box of narcissi to Covent Garden, where it sold for £1. Fifteen years later sixty-five tons of flowers were exported, and ten times that amount after another fifteen years. The barren island of St Mary's became a chequerboard of tiny fields surrounded by towering hedges of veronica, escallonia and privet to protect the flowers from the gales, for the harvest began in winter, long before eastern England saw daffodil, narcissus and anemone.

The coming of the railway was equally a blessing to the fisheries. Although seine fishing still flourished, particularly at St Ives where a record catch of seventeen million pilchards in one seine was made in 1868, drift fishing had become even more important. Drifting was practised by night and some ten miles from land, the nets forming a mile-long underwater fence in the meshes of which the fish entangled themselves. Pilchards were caught in this way as well as in seines, but by the middle of the century scores of boats and hundreds of men were drifting for mackerel, which swarmed in Mount's Bay. The difficulty was to find a market for fresh fish. Pilchards were cured and packed off to Italy, but owing to lack of rapid transport mackerel had to be disposed of locally, by the scarlet-cloaked fishwives of Newlyn and Mousehole. The opening of the through line to Penzance in 1859, therefore, was revolutionary. In the following year fish to the value of £80,000 were sent to London, and most of the 1,063 tons on which the directors of the Cornwall Railway congratulated themselves would be spring mackerel caught by the drifters of Mount's Bay. Never before had there been such a building of boats, and by 1875 there were about four hundred of them landing some fifty tons a day throughout the season.

19. Landing fish at St Ives, c.1887.

And with the railway came the tourists. Not at a great pace, however. Even when the Great Western company took over the whole line from Paddington to Penzance in 1876, the 11.45 express took six and a quarter hours to reach Plymouth, and then sauntered through Cornwall for another four. It stopped at every station, but by changing at St Austell the tourist could go to

Newquay by the branch line opened in that year, and in 1877 he could change at St Ives Road, rechristened St Erth, and travel the four enchanting miles to St Ives along the last stretch of broad-gauge railway ever made. In 1878 he could even stay at a Great Western hotel, the Tregenna Castle.

However, Black's *Guide* for 1876 was not very encouraging for the would-be holidaymaker. 'A dirtier, squalider, less interesting town than Hayle is not to be found in all Cornwall. Its population is composed of fishermen and miners, of labourers in its two iron foundries, or tin smelting works, and railway employees.' So much for the town that had a history long before London was heard of, and the tourist is recommended to hurry on to St Ives which can be seen over the water. Yet even the Capri of Cornwall is better seen at a distance, for 'it is to be regretted that the favourable impression which at first the tourist necessarily forms, should be dissipated on his entrance into the town by its accumulation of nastiness. The streets are narrow and crooked; the houses old and shattered; the shops mean and squalid; and everywhere pervades an intolerable fishy smell.' Penzance is better: even though it possesses no buildings of architectural importance, it 'commands a full view of the beautiful shores of Mount's Bay, and communicates with hills bold and romantic, with valleys as fair as they are fertile'. And there are five hotels, two of which announce their amenities in the advertisement section of the guidebook, the only hotels in Cornwall to do so. There is the Queen's on the Esplanade, 'the only Hotel that commands a full and uninterrupted view of Mount's Bay'; and then there is Mount's Bay House, also on the Esplanade, 'commanding an *uninterrupted and unsurpassed* view of St Michael's Mount, and the whole of the magnificent Bay'. Another attraction of Penzance is that an excursion to the Land's End (respectable inn here) can easily, and positively must, be made, and for ten shillings the intrepid tourist can even make a trip down Botallack mine (1,050 feet) – Wilkie Collins climbed halfway down in 1850 – though the 7 a.m. descent would seem to be over-early for the Penzance visitor.

There is no mention of bathing beaches, of Bude, Perranporth or Prah Sands, even though as early as 1820 Looe had optimistically provided a bathing machine, which, however, for lack of patronage had long since disintegrated. The only suggestion of such frivolities is at 'New Quay, a small but thriving watering-place', and the tourist of 1876 is assumed to be either an invalid in search of a mild climate, or an archaeologist with a sensitive appreciation of the picturesque and a passion for rambling. Of Cornish towns Truro seems likely to have pleased him best: 'its public buildings are of more than ordinary pretensions, its churches large, handsome and decorously preserved', particularly the church of St Mary. But the writer was sadly behind the times: in 1876 St Mary's Church had become Truro Cathedral. After eight and a half centuries the old diocese of Cornwall, merged in that of Exeter since Saxon times, had been restored, and Truro rather than Bodmin or St Germans selected as the cathedral city.

20. St Mary's Church, Truro, probably around 1870.

It was high time that a bishop should come back to Cornwall. Many of the clergy were still very lax, their churches falling to pieces. When Hardy arrived at St Juliot he found the tower so cracked and unsafe that the bells lay mute on the floor of the transept, the bench ends were rotten, ivy and bats hung from the roof timbers where sparrows nested, and nobody seemed to care. The diocese of Exeter was too big, and few of the western churches were ever visited by the bishop; had he done so he would have found some odd goings-on. There was one parson who, just for a change, would order white wine for communion, and another who positively refused to enter his church, though, clad in flowered dressing gown and smoking a hookah, he chatted amiably enough to his parishioners when they came out. Then there was Buryan, which lay outside the bishop's jurisdiction, a Royal Peculiar whose dean was appointed by the Duke of Cornwall. The last dean was the Hon. Fitzroy Stanhope, a Waterloo veteran who not unreasonably expected a pension in return for the loss of a leg. In 1817 the Prince Regent appointed him to Buryan, a post that he held until his death in 1864. He never went there, though he conscientiously drew his stipend of £1,000 a year and paid three curates £100 apiece to do the work of looking after his parishes of Buryan, Sennen and St Levan. A Church that allowed its places of worship to crumble and tolerated such Trollopian comedy could scarcely hope to compete with nonconformists who, inspired by preachers like Billy Bray and Soli Stone, built trim little chapels with their own hands.

But reformers were already busy, and Truro was fortunate in its first bishop, Edward Benson. He came full of zeal from the Mastership of Wellington College and threw himself wholeheartedly into the work of organising his diocese, visiting the remotest parishes and driving their patrons to repair the derelict churches. He loved the Cornish, vowing that of all mankind they were the most God-fearing and best-hearted, though unfortunately they had gone astray in their religion, and he waged open war against the Methodists who, while respecting him, did their best to defeat the intruder. A citadel was essential; he insisted that Cornwall should have its own cathedral, the first to be built in England since the Reformation, and work was begun in 1880. The old parish church of St Mary's was pulled down, all but the south aisle, which was incorporated in the new building, but when Benson died in 1896 as Archbishop of Canterbury there was only half a cathedral, a chancel without a nave, a stump instead of a spire. There was not the money to finish it.

After the collapse of copper mining the Cornish economy had had to withstand still other blows. The great agricultural depression suddenly descended in 1874 when the Middle West of America was opened up by railway and steamer, and cheap wheat from its virgin prairies flooded into Britain unprotected by any tariff barrier. Cornwall, it is true, was less shrewdly hit than eastern England. Although corn growing was then an important branch of her husbandry, the county was better suited to dairy farming, and in spite of inevitable dislocation and distress the transition was made, and cattle browsed in the fields where formerly corn had grown.

Then, the railway that had brought prosperity to the mackerel fisheries of Mount's Bay, St Ives and Mevagissey was to prove by no means an unmixed blessing. For many years trawlers from Plymouth and Brixham had been visiting western waters, dragging their trawls over the bottom of the fishing grounds by day, and carrying their catches back by night in order to reach the

21. Truro Cathedral under construction.

nearest big market at Plymouth. As the Cornish drifters fished by night this did not greatly matter, but with the opening of the Cornwall Railway foreign trawlers could fish day and night and send off their catches from Penzance like the local men. Then, this easy access to eastern markets attracted boats from farther afield, from Yarmouth and Lowestoft, their trawls fouling and cutting the Cornishmen's drift nets. Moreover, the foreigners fished on Sundays as well, a practice so abhorrent and apparently unfair to the Mount's Bay Methodists that at last they could bear it no longer, and one Monday morning in 1896 they attacked their rivals when they put in to Penzance to land their catch. It was a final gesture of despair. Steam trawlers arrived and steam drifters as well with nets three miles long, and the days of the Cornish mackerel fleets were numbered.

By 1896 tin mining was in a far worse plight than fishing. After twenty years of prosperity, of deep mining and reckless exploitation, the more easily accessible deposits were becoming exhausted just when large quantities of cheap alluvial tin from Malaya and other sources were coming on to the market. In 1891 the price fell from £100 to £86 a ton; by 1894 it was £64, and round about this price it remained until a recovery in 1898. But by that time the damage had been done. The weaker concerns were soon driven out of business, then one after another well-established mines were forced to close down – Great Work in Breage, Trumpet Consols in Wendron, Providence Mines in Lelant, St Ives Consols, Ding Dong – and mines once flooded were rarely reopened. Production fell from eight thousand to four thousand tons, tin miners followed into exile the copper miners of a generation before, population shrank still further, the model village of Halsetown where Henry Irving had spent his childhood was desolate, and mining parishes like Breage and Germoe were left with only a few hundred inhabitants.

The old Cornish toast of 'Fish, Tin and Copper' had become tragically ironical; a more relevant one would have been 'China Clay and Tourists', and in 1898 Arthur Quiller-Couch, editor of the newly established *Cornish Magazine*, asked his readers for their opinions on how to develop Cornwall as a holiday resort. Some did not want development, some offered helpful suggestions and others awful warnings: Bude had already been spoiled by promiscuous building, and even Tintagel was threatened by the erection of a great modern hotel on the cliff overlooking King Arthur's Castle. The correspondence was judicially and sadly summed up by Q himself. The author of *Troy Town* did not wish to see his Delectable Duchy turned into a holiday resort, 'but these are private feelings. On the other hand I see Cornwall impoverished by the evil days on which mining and (to a less degree) agriculture have fallen. I see her population diminishing and her able-bodied sons forced to emigrate by the thousand. The ruined engine-house, the roofless cottage, the cold hearthstone are not cheerful sights to one who would fain see a race so passionately attached to home as ours is still drawing its vigour from its own soil. In the presence of destitution and actual famine (for in the mining district it came even to this, a little while ago) one is bound, if he care for his countrymen, to consider any cure thoughtfully suggested … Were it within human capacity to decide between a revival of our ancient industries, fishery and mining, and the development of this new business, our decision would be prompt enough. But it is not. Well then, since we must cater for the stranger, let us do it well and honestly. Let us respect him and our native land as well'.

A History Of Cornwall

XII

The Twentieth Century

Although Cornwall's development was to follow roughly the pattern sketched by Q, the condition of the county was not quite as desperate as he saw it at the end of the nineteenth century. There was still plenty of tin in Cornwall, indeed the immense riches underground had scarcely been worked owing to the scramble for copper, and one salutary result of the depression was to awaken owners of surviving mines to the need of bringing their methods up to date. At the surface machines replaced the singing bal maidens; ladders and man engines were scrapped for 'gigs' in which the men rode swiftly up and down the shafts to the lowest levels, where they bored and tunnelled like beetles with long mechanical drills. Costs were reduced, though a new hazard was added to the miner's life. In 1904 a government Commission reported that there was an alarming increase in lung diseases among Cornish miners, whose death rate from these complaints was eight to ten times greater than that of coal miners. The cause was the fatal dust that filled the air when boring into dry rock, the cure to keep drilling-holes damp and to draw the dust out of the workings with fans.

Cost of production fell as the price of tin rose, and mining revived. Although on nothing like the scale of fifty years before, when nearly four hundred copper and tin mines were working, yet in 1914 a dozen large mines employing some seven thousand workers produced almost seven thousand tons of black tin. The urgent wartime demand not only for tin but for wolfram and arsenic as well, subsidiary products of some of the mines, fanned prosperity into boom. But the stimulus was over-intense and unhealthy, for workers were concentrated on extracting as much ore as possible in the shortest possible time, and little thought could be given to opening up ground for future production. The inevitable result was another collapse. By the spring of 1920 the price of tin had soared to £400; a year later it had dropped to £140. There was a recovery in 1923, but again it was too late. The all too familiar story of distress was repeated; Camborne was so impoverished that there was not money enough to light the streets, and miners were reduced to forming choirs to tramp the country singing for their bread. Although a relief fund was opened, another generation of miners was driven overseas, and by 1929 only three thousand were employed in and about the mines.

A brief recovery was followed by another slump in the early thirties, and most of the poor remainder of the mines closed down: Levant, Wheal Kitty, East Pool, Polberro ..., until by 1939 there were only five mines working, employing fewer than a thousand men. With the second world war the pressing demand for tin and wolfram was renewed, and the Korean war drove the price of tin up to the fantastic height of £1,600 a ton. Yet there were only four mines left: Geevor in St Just, South Crofty in Camborne, New Consols in Callington and Castle-an-Dinas in St Columb, the last producing wolfram. Altogether they employed eight hundred and forty workers. A hundred years before there had been fifty thousand.

Cornish fisheries suffered an almost comparable decline. Already at the beginning of the century east coast trawlers were driving local drifters out of business, and the great days of seining were almost over. The fisherman's toast was still 'Long life to the Pope and death to the thousands', but for some reason or other the thousands, or rather millions, of pilchards that used to darken the waters no longer came to be killed, and the last catch on an epic scale was made in St Ives Bay in 1907. Moreover, though Popes and Catholic feasts still flourished, the Italian peasant was no longer buying Cornish pilchards as he used to do. His standard of living had risen, and he was offered more savoury fare that came in tins from California. To tempt him back to his old love, the Mevagissey men invented another way of curing pilchards in brine vats instead of by the traditional method of bulking. But it was no use: the adoption of brine-vat curing merely threw out of work the army of women and children who formerly salted the fish for export, a serious loss of income to the fisherfolk.

As most Cornish fishermen were naval reservists, they were called up on the outbreak of war in 1914, many of them never to return, so that in 1918 there was a shortage of fit and active young men to work the boats. However, the grounds had been rested, prices were good, and for some years the industry flourished. Then in 1924 a steady fall in prices set in, and the great fleet of St Ives seine boats was broken up for firewood. There remained three other forms of inshore fishing: drifting for mackerel, pilchards and herring; long-lining for skate, turbot and ray; and crabbing for lobsters, crayfish and crabs. But by this time French and Belgian trawlers were working the offshore grounds with meshes so small that nothing escaped their nets, and the fish moved farther out to sea each year. The Cornishmen in their small boats could not follow so far afield, sailing a hundred and more miles out instead of a former thirty or forty, and even those with diesel engines who managed to hang on found that they had to double the amount of their gear to catch the same quantity of fish. In 1924 there had been 953 boats and 3,110 men; in 1936 the numbers were 704 and 1,849.

Again there was a recovery during and after the 1939–45 war, for trawlers were requisitioned and most of the Cornish fishermen were too old to be called up. But by 1950 evil days had returned. The enormous rise in price of every kind of equipment was too heavy for the weakened industry to bear, the cost of building was prohibitive, and ageing boats were left with ageing crews, with eight men over sixty for every five under thirty. But then there were not many either of one or the other. In 1950 there were four hundred and twenty boats and eight hundred and twenty men, almost exactly the same as the number of miners.

'Fish, Tin and Copper'! In 1870 there had been three times as many engaged in drifting alone.

It was fortunate for Cornwall that she had a prosperous agriculture as the basis of her economy – a county of small farms specialising in stock rearing, dairying and horticulture – and a number of subsidiary industries to support it: granite quarries and the venerable slate quarry at Delabole, worked perhaps in Roman times and now a mile in circumference and nearly four hundred feet deep, china clay works at St Austell, ship repairing at Falmouth and mining engineering at Camborne. Yet all these together provided work for only a quarter of the people who had been employed in mining a century before, and without the great new tourist industry the plight of Cornwall would have been desperate indeed.

The railway opened up the country for the visitor. In 1892 the main line was converted to narrow gauge, and by 1904 it had been made into a double track with branches to Newquay, Looe, Bude, Padstow and Perranporth, as well as to St Ives. Then came the motor car, and in the twenties Cornwall, or rather Cornish

22. The beach at Newquay.

beaches, were discovered by English holidaymakers, and so rapid was the rush, so ruthless the exploitation of her coast, that a Survey was hurriedly compiled by the Cornwall branch of the Council for the Preservation of Rural England in an attempt to protect the county both from the excesses of ignorant foreigners and the rapacity of thoughtless natives. 'Since we must cater for the stranger,' Q had written thirty years before, 'let us do it well and honestly. Let us respect him and our native land alike.' And now he wrote a preface to the Survey. 'I merely ask it to be noted how rapidly the strain has come upon us, an ancient people, with its inrush of motors and descent of the ready-made-bungalow builder, the hotel-investor, the holidaymaker who thinks no cove complete without a minstrel (negro) and a gramophone, the *paterfamilias* who brings his youngster to Tintagel with spade and bucket. Cornwall is not an improvised playground; it is not a "Riviera", and the use of that word, whoever first applied it to Cornwall, was and has been a commercial "inexactitude". To any right Cornishman, Cornwall is a mother with a character, a most egregious one, definite and dear. Having that character, she has a character to lose.' And he concluded, 'At least let me implore the reader beyond Tamar to help us in protecting our noble coast from defacement by the Philistine. It used to be ours, the priceless if barren inheritance of a little clan. Let those whom we welcome to share our love of it help us to preserve the primitive beauty of this delectable Duchy as a national possession.' The Council recognised that 'the increasing importance of Cornwall as a centre for holidays and for retirement now constitutes a definite commercial asset', and after surveying both coast and countryside proposed the creation of a Planning Authority to carry out its recommendations.

The Survey included a chapter on the Antiquities of Cornwall by Charles Henderson, the brilliant young historian who had collected a fabulous amount of material for a projected Parochial History. But he did not live to write it. He died in Rome in 1933 and was buried there in the Protestant Cemetery, where Keats and Shelley already lay, and Shelley's friend, another Cornishman, Edward John Trelawny. One of Henderson's mentors had been the great Celtic scholar Henry Jenner, author of a *Handbook of the Cornish Language*, and Grand Bard of Cornwall. This second English invasion, although only an annual one confined to the main roads and beaches, seems to have revived the stubborn Cornish nationalism, and moved those of the western hundreds in particular to a protest, mainly unconscious, comparable to that of a thousand years before when hundreds of Celtic crosses were set up in the newly conquered county from the Land's End to Bodmin Moor. Under the inspiration of Jenner and R. Morton Nance a Celtic Gorsedd was formed after the Welsh model, and in 1928 the first picturesque ceremony of robed Bards was held in the Bronze Age stone circle of Boscawen-Un. A Federation of Old Cornwall Societies was formed to revive the ancient language and customs; Morton Nance, Jenner's successor as Grand Bard, published *Cornish for All* and Hamilton Jenkin wrote *The Cornish Miner*; once again midsummer bonfires blazed from the Land's End to Tamar, and the last corn was cut to the ceremony of Crying the Neck.

With the tourists came the artists, attracted by the grandeur of the coast, picturesque fishing villages, and romance of the foreign scene, particularly in the far west. Whistler and Sickert were in St Ives in 1883, Anders Zorn soon afterwards, and by the turn of the century there was a flourishing colony of painters there: Adrian Stokes, Arnesby Brown, Moffat Lindner, Julius Olsson, Elmer Schofield, to mention only a few. Stanhope Forbes founded another colony at Newlyn, and Lamorna Birch settled in his cottage at Lamorna. All these were painters of what may roughly be called the impressionist school, but in the late thirties there came a change when Ben Nicholson and Barbara Hepworth moved from London to St Ives. It was not picturesqueness, romance, or any literary quality that attracted them, but the all-pervading light that gave the landscape a definition and clarity of form, an intensity of colour that is not to be found elsewhere in Britain, a primitive structural quality which they abstracted from all that was accidental and ephemeral and interpreted in terms of their non-figurative paintings and sculptures. It was a new art, but the theme was as old as Cornwall. Inspired by their work other artists came, and as a result St Ives has become an art centre with an international reputation.

It was Ben Nicholson who discovered and recognised the genius of the old Cornish fisherman and rag-and-bone merchant Alfred Walls, who painted ships and the coast on any material he could find, from the walls of his cottage to pieces of wood and old cardboard. He died in 1942 and was buried in the old St Ives cemetery by the sea, where he is commemorated by tiles designed by Bernard Leach. After studying and practising pottery in Japan for ten years, in 1920 Bernard Leach founded the Leach Pottery in St Ives, and has long been recognised, in the East as well as in the West, as one of the world's master potters. Another Cornish painter of distinction was Peter Lanyon, who died after a gliding accident in 1964, aged only forty-six. He was a founder member of the Penwith Society of Arts in Cornwall, a group who, led by Ben Nicholson and Barbara Hepworth and encouraged by the marine painter Borlase Smart, in 1948 broke away from the old St Ives Society of Artists, and in 1975 an additional gallery will be opened to house a permanent collection of the visual arts. Among the exhibits will be work by the Cornish painters John Wells and Bryan Pearce.

In the non-visual arts, the most distinguished living Cornish writer is A L Rowse, whose *Tudor Cornwall* is the product of his unrivalled knowledge of Elizabethan history, a knowledge that has enabled him recently to throw light on some of the major obscurities in the life and work of Shakespeare. He is also a poet, as is his near neighbour Jack Clemo, and in the far east of the county, at Launceston, lives one of the best-known poets of our time, Charles Causley.

Although the Cornish, like the Welsh, are a musical people, their towns are too small to support professional orchestras, but few counties, relatively to their population, can have as many amateur musical societies and festivals as Cornwall, from Penzance, Falmouth and Truro to the Tamar, and one of our leading contemporary composers, Michael Tippett, is a Cornishman.

In 1969 an event of some significance took place when for the first time for nearly four hundred years the Cornish cycle of miracle plays, the *Ordinalia*, albeit in a modern translation, was performed in Piran Round. Then, in the following year Cornwall County Council and the University of Exeter jointly founded an Institute of Cornish Studies, appointing as its first Director the Cornish archaeologist Charles Thomas, who was also given a new Chair of Cornish Studies at the University.

Systematic excavation of sites had begun in the 1930s with the formation of the West Cornwall Field Club, which, however, was only a small body of enthusiasts, and in 1961 it was enlarged and its activities greatly extended by its transformation into the *Cornwall Archaeological* Society, the first of whose annual publications, Cornish Archaeology, appeared in 1962. Among the most interesting sites excavated in the last decade are those of the Iron Age village of Carn Euny in West Penwith, the Iron Age cliff castle at Rumps Point near Padstow, and the Roman fort at Tregear near Bodmin.

The last two sites used to lie within the Hundred of Trigg – which according to Carew 'signifieth an inhabitant' – but since the recent reorganisation of local government throughout the country names and boundaries of some of the old Hundreds have been changed, and Trigg has now become part of the area administered by the North District Council. Even the sea between Cornwall and Ireland has become – less prosaically – the Celtic Sea, from beneath which the new adventurers hope to extract oil. Perhaps oil drilling will one day become as important to Cornwall as were the old industries of tin mining and fishing.

The Celtic revival of the 1920s was a defensive action to prevent the culture of Cornwall being swamped by the foreigner rather than an attempt to check the English invasion, for prosperity, survival almost, depended on its visitors. Yet when Q wrote, the influx was only a trickle in comparison with the torrent of the seventies, by which time the tourist trades employ far more people than agriculture, and the industry as a whole is much the most important in the county. The traffic, however, is only a seasonal one, a sort of human late-summer monsoon between solstice and autumnal equinox – a season that rarely compares with the earlier one of daffodil, bluebell and gorse – and when the last tents have gone down on the beaches the primeval magic and mystery return to the desolate downs and deserted coast. For in spite of all mechanical progress, of railway, motor car and aeroplane, Cornwall remains an all-but-island, un-English, seaward- and southward-looking 'toward Namancos and Bayona's hold', and beyond Spain to the Mediterranean, ultimate source of her first primitive culture. And in spite of English invasion the succeeding Celtic culture has not altogether been lost in the kingdom of lost causes and almost lost, though slowly reviving, industries, for although their numbers have shrunk, while those of foreign residents increase, there are still many times twenty thousand Cornishmen, independent, clannish, parochial even, proud of their separate history symbolised by quoit, saint, huer's hut and sky-fingering mine chimney.

When, therefore, the visitor from the east crosses Saltash Bridge he enters a country scarcely penetrated by the English until a few centuries ago, peopled by men whose origins are different from his, who not long since spoke a strange language. And as he travels westward, back in geological time, he also travels back in the history of man, passing as it were through the varied strata of Cornwall's story, rich in memorials, until he reaches its beginning at the end of the land. Trematon Castle, Norman stronghold of the Valletorts, and on the southern bank of tidal Lynher the salt-water pond made by Richard Carew, and the Elizabethan angle of Antony House and Mount Edgcumbe, so coveted by the commander of the Armada; St Germans, Saxon cathedral of Cornwall and nurse of Sir John Eliot; Liskeard and Richard of Cornwall's castle; neighbouring St Neot with its medieval glass; and St Cleer, the Doniert Stone, memorial maybe of a Cornish king, the petrified Hurlers, Trethevy Quoit, and the abandoned mines of Caradon; Bodmin of the many churches and shrine of St Petroc; the Civil War country, that precious square of down and woodland set between the rivers Looe and Fowey, where names are music as well as history: Bradock,

Boconnoc, Lanhydrock, Lostwithiel, former capital of the Duchy; and above Lostwithiel, Restormel, once gay with the coloured chivalry of the Black Prince, first Duke of Cornwall; the country of King Mark, his palace at Castle Dore and the trophy erected to Tristan, and Malpas at Truro, where Iseult crossed the river to Blanche Lande; Chacewater, St Day, Redruth and Camborne, once the richest region in the Old World, dominated by granite Carn Brea where neolithic man settled more than four thousand years ago; the country of the Saints, of Gwithian, Gwinear and his sister Piala, massacred on Connor Downs by Teudar, King of Cornwall; Hayle at the head of the prehistoric trade route to Marazion and the Mount, where the granite front of West Penwith, so nearly another island beyond Cornwall, brings the railway to a stop.

A hundred years ago its hills were loud with miners, but grass and bracken have covered their trackways and workings, and along the coast from Pendeen to Botallack stretch ruined mine buildings, massive as a deserted Roman city, some of them plunging sheer into the sea. Yet these are but recent memorials to the passing of man's achievement, and centuries before the miners came, centuries before the Saints and Romans, the land was peopled, perhaps more thickly peopled than any other part of Britain, by the builders of hilltop citadels and promontory forts, of megalithic monuments, stone circles, menhirs and the chambered tombs of the Land's End. And westward still beyond the Land's End, beyond the legendary Lyonesse of King Arthur, the Fortunate Isles, along whose sunken shores it may be that relics of even earlier men have perished.

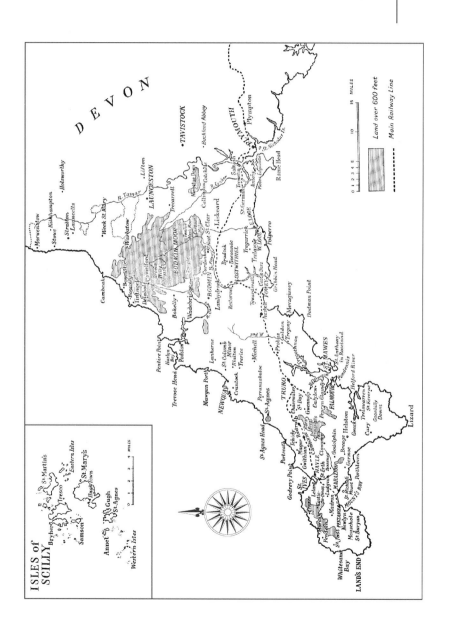

23. Map of Cornwall.

Epilogue

These few pages are not intended to be a full update of my father's book. They aim to provide no more than an outline sketch of major developments in Cornwall in the latter part of the twentieth century.

This period has seen the continuation of most of the trends described in the last chapter. In particular, traditional industries have continued to decline while improved communications have opened the door to increasing levels of tourism, inward migration and contact with England, Europe and the world at large. Against this background of continuity there have been some new developments, unguessed at forty years ago, which offer new promises for Cornwall in the third millennium.

In the years following the Second World War Cornish mining went through a period of stagnation. There was a lack of enthusiasm among the local workforce and miners had to be recruited from abroad. Investment in plant, equipment and technology was inadequate and Cornish mines lagged behind their competitors in mining methods. This all changed in the 1960s; a rise in the price of tin attracted new investment and, with more vigorous management, the mines became profitable again; once again Cornishmen were keen to work in their traditional industry. Plans were made for a number of mines to reopen and some went into production, including Wheal Jane, Mount Wellington, Wheal Concord and Wheal Pendarves. However, following an all too familiar pattern, the tin price collapsed in 1985 and put paid to most of the new ventures, leaving only Geevor, South Crofty and Wheal Jane. Geevor closed in 1986, reopened briefly in 1988 but ceased working again soon after. After Wheal Jane closed in 1991, only South Crofty remained to represent an industry which had been the source of most of the world's tin for much of the last three thousand years. The mine had been in continuous production since the 17th century but in 1998 it was also forced to close and, despite an attempt to reopen it in 1999, it seems unlikely that it will go into production again.

The end of the millennium thus saw the final demise of Cornwall's most ancient and famous industry.

Fishing, that other traditional Cornish pursuit, has fared somewhat better than mining, but is a shadow of its former self. The numerous Cornish harbours, which once were crowded with fishing boats, now depend almost entirely on tourism; trips along the coast and berths for leisure craft provide some income. Padstow, Mevagissey and Looe have retained small fishing fleets and individual fishermen engaged in coastal fishing from many small coves and harbours. Newlyn alone has managed to maintain its place as a major fishing port with one of the largest deep-sea fishing fleets in the country. In the 1980s the annual value of the catch exceeded £20 million; a new pier was opened by the Queen in 1980, and a new fish market in 1988. However, like the rest of the UK fishing industry, the Newlyn fleet is threatened with decline as a result of reducing fish stocks and the efforts to preserve them. The future of Cornish fishing increasingly depends on factors beyond local control. Government and, in particular, EU regulations impose restrictions on days-at-sea and strict quotas on catches; complex rules regulate when and where fishing can take place and the types of net that may be used. Traditional Cornish fishing grounds have been opened to foreign fishing fleets and there has been particular animosity against the Spanish. Dissatisfaction was strikingly expressed in 1995 when Cornish fishing boats flew the Canadian flag as a signal of discontent with the British government's perceived failure to stand up for the Cornish fishing industry. (The Canadian government of the time had taken robust action against Spanish interlopers.) Equipping boats has also become more and more expensive and there has been a lack of investment in modern vessels, with consequential reductions in safety and efficiency. Finally, decommissioning has brought down the numbers of working boats. Unless there is a market improvement in these circumstances Cornish fishermen cannot look to the future with much confidence.

Historically, Cornish agriculture has been relatively prosperous and Cornish farmers have been quick to seize such opportunities as the market for spring flowers and early vegetables which was opened up by the coming of the railway. In more recent times the market for vegetables has become truly global – supermarkets sell produce from every continent and seasons for particular vegetables are almost a thing of the past. This has inevitably affected the trade in early vegetables. Farmers have responded not only by increasing the use of plastic sheeting and tunnels to protect and advance their crops, but also by turning to organic and specialist cultivation. There is a widely supported move to make Cornwall a GMO-free zone, while farmers' markets are on the increase. The last ten years of the century have been exceptionally difficult for UK farming as a whole, and not least for Cornwall. The BSE crisis, sharply falling milk prices, the impact of the 'green revolution' and rising costs have had a disastrous effect on farm incomes, which have fallen by well over a half. Many farmers are staring ruin in the face; their uncertain future has had a knock-on effect on sales of farm machinery and agricultural supplies, as well as on the network of industries and services supporting agriculture. Farmers have been encouraged to diversify and many have converted barns and outbuildings to provide holiday accommodation or developed farm holiday schemes or a variety of small-scale tourist attractions. Despite these efforts farming remains in a state of severe depression.

There are, of course, other industries in the county: quarrying at Delabole, china clay around St Austell, shipbuilding and repair at Falmouth, and a variety of light industries. Nevertheless, with the decline of mining, fishing and agriculture, Cornwall's dependence on tourism can only increase. Here too things have changed. Today Cornwall has to compete not merely with other British resorts but with destinations throughout Europe and, more recently, the world. A package trip to the Mediterranean may now cost less than a holiday in Newquay. Forty years ago the weekend trains from the midlands and the north would be packed with holiday-making families who would spend the greater part of their time on the beach in their chosen resort. Since then many of the Cornish branch lines have been closed and the A30 has largely been converted to dual carriageway. Over 90% of today's tourists arrive by car and, although the beach retains its attraction, they also expect to travel and visit other sights during their stay. The tourist industry in Cornwall has responded by providing a range of new attractions, ranging from theme parks to nature reserves. Heritage has become a major theme, with ever increasing numbers of houses and gardens opening to the public and providing good quality cafes, craft centres and special attractions such as children's trails or musical evenings. There has also been a major revival of interest in the industrial past, in particular tin mining; in 1999 the Great Flat Lode, the mining area to the south of Redruth, was nominated by the government as part of a potential 'World Heritage Site'. Surfing is another major tourist attraction with its own sub-culture; it brings in large numbers of enthusiasts to the north Cornish beaches and has spawned a variety of secondary economic activities. A range of fine restaurants have sprung up throughout the county, taking advantage of the excellent local fish, meat and vegetables; visitors can now eat as well in Cornwall as in any part of the country. The most exciting development of all is emerging in the lunar landscape of a disused clay pit near St Austell; the Eden project will present the world's flora and its uses in a fabulous series of linked geodesic domes – the largest greenhouse in the world. The aim is to create a world-class attraction, as familiar internationally as the Eiffel Tower or the Sidney Opera house.

Another significant new development is the Tate Gallery, St Ives. Built on the site of an old gas works and overlooking Porthmeor beach, this striking modern building, designed by Cornish architects, houses a fine collection of works by St Ives artists such as Alfred Wallis, Ben Nicholson, Barbara Hepworth and Bernard Leach. The gallery has already attracted over a million visitors and has had an enormous positive effect on the economy of the town. The visual arts are a major factor in the Cornish economy and tourism; many distinguished artists live and work in St Ives and Newlyn and few areas of the country can provide as rich a range of galleries selling first-class modern painting and sculpture. Craft pottery also flourishes, building on the Leach legacy. Other significant cultural developments of recent times include the Hall for Cornwall in Truro, which now serves as a focus for the spring

Cornish Music Festival. This is but one of numerous festivals around the county including the Daphne du Maurier Festival in Fowey and the International Music Seminar based at Prussia Cove. Together with such traditional events at Helston's Furry Day, the 'Obby 'Oss in Padstow and the recently revived Golowan Feast in Penzance there is much to interest the tourist at almost any time of the year. It is interesting that these events, and others such as Trevithick Day in Camborne, are seen by many local people as a genuine expression of Cornish culture. They therefore contribute to the growing sense of Cornish regional distinctiveness and identity.

Despite these encouraging developments in tourism and the arts, Cornwall is a seriously depressed region. In 1995 average incomes were 26% below the national average and it was recently reported that 46% of homes in Kerrier District had a net weekly income of £125 or less. Levels of unemployment are far above the national average and many jobs are part-time and seasonal. Those who acquire professional skills usually have to leave the county to find employment. In areas such as Camborne/Redruth youth unemployment is as bad as anywhere in the country. In recognition of this Cornwall was awarded Objective One status by the EU in 1999; this provides financial aid to help the poorest parts of the union catch up with the rest. Over £300 million will be available, though matching funds will have to be found from other sources. The primary aim is to increase absolute prosperity, but important subsidiary objectives are to support local communities and to enhance regional distinctiveness. Ideally this programme will revive the Cornish economy and transform it into a 'Celtic Tiger' on the Irish model, but these are early days and many uncertainties remain.

A major social and economic factor in the second half of the 20th century has been the level of migration into Cornwall from other parts of the UK. Between 1961 and 1981 the population of the county increased by no less than 25%, largely as a result of inward migration; in subsequent years the figure has sometimes been as much as 8,000 a year. Some of these newcomers are retired people but a substantial majority have been people of working age aiming to 'escape the rat race' and attracted by the quality of life the county offered. Many came in search of a lifestyle rather than a job and it is arguable that this inward migration has merely imported unemployment. Nevertheless they also brought valuable skills and enthusiasms with them. For example, much of the excellent craftwork now being produced in Cornwall is attributable to inward migrants.

It might have been expected that better communications with the rest of the world, combined with this influx of outsiders, would have served to dilute the Cornish sense of identity. Paradoxically the reverse has happened. Those who live in Cornwall, whether Cornish by ancestry or not, appear to value Cornish distinctiveness more than was the case fifty years ago. The Cornish revival in the first part of the century was deliberately non-political. It focused on the past, the preservation of traditions, such as the 'crying of the neck', and the recovery of the Cornish language. In recent years these interests continue; evening classes in the Cornish Language are over-subscribed, the Gosedd is well attended and the Cornish genealogy pages on the Internet hum with world-wide activity. But these concerns are accompanied by more direct assertions of Cornishness.

One example is 'Trelawney's army', the enormous crowds of black and gold clad supporters of the Cornish rugby team. In 1991 and 1992 almost ten per cent of the population of the county visited Twickenham, and *The Guardian* was moved to remark that 'the lusty spirit of national independence is alive and flourishing in the undeclared Republic of Cornwall'. Then there is the remarkable popularity of the black and white flag of St Piran; virtually unknown twenty years ago, it is to be seen throughout the county on flagpoles and car stickers and it flies next to the union flag outside County Hall in Truro. Cornish names for towns and villages increasingly appear on entry signs beside the road, while the name Kernow is to be seen everywhere; even those who speak not a word of Cornish are aware of the significance of the language. Mebyon Kernow (Sons of Cornwall), which was founded as a pressure group in 1951, more recently converted into a political party committed to Cornish self-government within the

European Community. Despite some notable successes at local levels it has yet to make an impact at parliamentary elections. However, Mebyon Kernow has had a real effect on Cornish politics by pushing the issue of local autonomy up the agenda. This has expressed itself in the resistance to any partitioning of the county in the Local Government Review of 1994, in the claim for a separate Cornish seat in European elections and in the demand for a separate Cornish Development Agency. The idea of a 'Europe of the Regions' fits well with this sense of regional identity; Cornish bodies have established links with various European regions, particularly with Brittany, with which the county shares so much culturally and historically. The establishment of devolved governments in Scotland, Wales and Northern Ireland, together with talk of regional assemblies in England, raises the issue of regional government in Cornwall; this would recognise its special territorial integrity and identity and provide a direct link to national government. A steering group has very recently been set up, with all party support, to make proposals for a Senedh Kernow (Cornish Assembly).

Another less political but even more essential requirement is for a university in Cornwall. There are around nine thousand Cornish students receiving grants for higher education but only a small number are studying for degrees in the county, mostly at the Falmouth College of Art or the Camborne School of Mines. Cornwall suffers from a 'brain drain' with many of its young people leaving to go to university and failing to return. A Cornish university would provide the technical underpinnings for economic development following Objective One funding, it would enhance the county's cultural life and it would undoubtedly attract students from the rest of the UK and abroad. So far attempts to set up such a university have been unsuccessful, however efforts continue and it must be hoped that they will soon succeed.

The last century has not treated Cornwall kindly. The old world of 'fish, tin and copper' is gone for ever and, as yet, little has emerged to take its place. Yet the county appears to face the new millennium with a striking degree of confidence. This is based in part on the emerging sense of regional identity, shared alike by the native Cornish and inward migrants; in part on the opportunities presented by Objective One and the recognition that, in the new technologically driven economy, distance is no barrier to success; in part on pride in such achievements as the Eden Project, the Hall for Cornwall and the St Ives Tate; and in part on the sense that, for once, the tide of history is flowing to Cornwall's advantage. This sense of optimism is splendidly expressed in a book entitled Kernow bys Vyken! (Cornwall for Ever) which has been given to every school-age child in the county. This lively and informative book ends with the following hope:

A vision of Cornwall tomorrow is of a land of sustained and sustainable prosperity, of an enviable environment in which to live, work and play, of a proud people who know that their identity is their greatest strength and who are never afraid to shout:

Kernow bys vyken!

Sebastian Halliday
St Ives, Cornwall.
July 2000.

Chronological Appendix

BC

c. 7000	Mesolithic period.
c. 2500	Neolithic period.
c. 1800	Beaker Folk invasions.
c. 1600	Early Bronze Age.
c. 1400	Middle Bronze Age.
c. 900	Late Bronze Age. First Celtic immigrants.
c. 400	Early Iron Age.
c. 250	La Tène invasions.
55–54	Julius Caesar's raids on south-east Britain.

AD

	Courtyard house culture.
43	Roman occupation of Britain.
c. 250	Romans begin to exploit Cornish tin.
c. 312	Constantine makes Christianity the Imperial religion.
410	End of Roman occupation.
c. 500	Ambrosius Aurelianus defeats Saxons at Badon Hill. Period of King Arthur and King Mark, of Irish raids and the coming of the Saints.
597	St Augustine lands in Kent.
710	Saxons take Exeter.
814	Egbert conquers Cornwall.
838	Battle of Hingston Down.
931	Athelstan creates diocese of Cornwall, with see at St Germans.
c. 1050	Diocese of Cornwall combined with Devon, with see at Exeter.

1066	Norman Conquest.
	Robert of Mortain, first Earl of Cornwall.
1201	King John grants a charter to the Stannaries.
c. 1280	Edmund, Earl of Cornwall, makes Lostwithiel the county capital.
1337	Creation of the Duchy of Cornwall, with the Black Prince as first Duke.
1348–49	The Black Death.
1473	Lancastrian attempt to seize St Michael's Mount.
1497	Cornish rebellion led by Joseph and Flamank, followed by rebellion led by Perkin Warbeck.
1536–39	Dissolution of the monasteries.
c. 1538	Leland's tour of Cornwall.
1545	Loss of the *Mary Rose* and Roger Grenville.
1549	Prayer Book Rebellion.
1558	Accession of Queen Elizabeth.
1577	Cuthbert Mayne executed and Francis Tregian imprisoned.
1588	Spanish Armada.
1591	Death of Sir Richard Grenvillle of the *Revenge*.
1595	Spanish raid on Penzance.
1602	Richard Carew publishes his *Survey of Cornwall*.
1603	Death of Queen Elizabeth.
1619	John Killigrew's lighthouse at the Lizard.
1629	Sir John Eliot imprisoned.
1642	Civil War begins.
1643	Battles of Bradock Down, Stratton, Lansdown (Sir Bevil Grenville killed) and Roundway Down. Royalists take Bristol.
1644	Royalists defeat Essex at Lostwithiel.

1646	Parliamentary army under Fairfax invades Cornwall. John Arundell surrenders Pendennis Castle. End of Civil War.
1651	John Grenville and Royalists driven out of Scilly.
1660	Restoration of Charles II.
1668	Imprisonment and acquittal of Bishop Trelawny.
1702–10	Earl of Godolphin's ministry.
1707	Sir Cloudesley Shovel wrecked on the Scilly Isles.
c. 1710	First steam pump in Cornwall, and capitalist development of tin and copper mining.
1743	John Wesley's first visit to Cornwall.
1754	William Borlase publishes his *Antiquities of Cornwall*.
1777	James Watt erects his first steam engine in Cornwall.
1787	Riots at Poldice mine owing to copper depression.
1789	Wesley's last visit to Cornwall.
1800–40	Rapid development of mining after Richard Trevithick's high-pressure engine.
1818	Royal Institution of Cornwall founded.
1832	Reform Act: Cornish MPs reduced from 42 to 12.
1834	Bodmin–Wadebridge Railway.
1837	Discovery of copper at Caradon.
1838	Abolition of tin coinage.
1842	Man engine installed at Tresavean mine.
1847	Plymouth–Falmouth railway begun.
1852	West Cornwall Railway (Penzance–Truro) completed.
1856	Maximum copper production of 209,000 tons of ore.
1859	Royal Albert Bridge at Saltash completed.
1864	Mines Commission.
1866	Financial crisis, collapse of copper mining, and emigration of miners.

1876   Diocese of Cornwall revived with see at Truro.

_c._ 1890   Decline of tin mining and fisheries, and expansion of china clay and tourist industries.

1928   First Cornish Gorsedd.

1970   Foundation of The Institute of Cornish Studies and of a Chair of Cornish Studies at the University of Exeter

Bibliography

There are probably more books about Cornwall than about any other English county, and the following short list is merely an introduction to that store:

Balchin, W G V *The Making of the English Landscape. Cornwall.* 1954.

Baring-Gould, S *The Vicar of Morwenstow.* 1899.
— *Cornish Characters.* 1908.

Barton, D B *The Cornish Beam Engine.* 1965.
— *A History of Tin Mining and Smelting in Cornwall.* 1967.

Barton, R M *A History of the Cornish China-Clay Industry.* 1966.
— Ed. *Life in Cornwall in the Early Nineteenth Century.* 1970.

Berry, Claude *Cornwall.* 1949.

Betjeman, John *Cornwall* (A Shell Guide). 1964. With A L Rowse, *Victorian and Edwardian Cornwall, from Old Photographs.* 1974.

Black's *Guide to Cornwall.* 1876.

Boase, G C and Courtney, W P *Bibliotheca Cornubiensis.* 1874–82.

Borlase, W *The Antiquities of Cornwall.* 1754. Reprinted 1973.
— *The Natural History of Cornwall.* 1758.

Cardew A *Cornelius Cardew.* 1926.

Carew, Richard *The Survey of Cornwall.* Ed. F E Halliday. 1953, 1969.

Carter, Harry *The Autobiography of a Cornish Smuggler.* 1894.
— *Catalogue of Exhibition of Documents relating to the History of Cornwall.* Truro. 1957.

Chambers, E K *Arthur of Britain.* 1927.

Clarendon, Edward Hyde, Earl of *The History of the Rebellion and Civil Wars in England.* Ed. W D Macray. 1888.

Clark, Evelyn *Cornish Fogous.* 1961.

Coate, Mary *Cornwall in the Great Civil War.* 1933.

Collins, Wilkie *Rambles beyond Railways*. 1850.

Cornish Archaeology The annual publication of the Cornwall Archaeological Society. 1962–.

The Cornish Magazine Ed. A T Quiller-Couch. 1898–99.

The Cornish Review Ed. D Val Baker. 1949–.

Cornwall, A Survey Ed. W H Thompson. 1930.

Cornwall Parish Registers.

County of Cornwall (Cornwall County Council). 1952.

Courtney, W P *History of Parliamentary Representation in Cornwall*. 1889.

Daniel, Glyn E *The Prehistoric Chamber Tombs of England and Wales*. 1950. *The Megalith Builders of Western Europe*. 1958.

Defoe, Daniel *Journey from London to the Land's End*. 1724.

Dickinson H W and Titley A *Richard Trevithick*. 1934.

Dines, H G *The Metalliferous Mining Region of South-West England*. 2 vols. 1956.

Doble, G H *Cornish Saints*. 1923–44.

Elliott-Binns, L E *Medieval Cornwall*. 1955.

Ellis, R B *The Cornish Language and its Literature*. 1974.

Evelyn, John *The Life of Mrs Godolphin*. 1847.

Fiennes, Celia *The Journeys of Celia Fiennes*. Ed. C Morris. 1947.

Gilbert, Davies *The Parochial History of Cornwall*. 1838.

Grylls, R Glynn *Trelawny*. 1950.

Halliday, F E *A Cornish Chronicle: The Carews of Antony*. 1967.

Hardy, Thomas *A Pair of Blue Eyes*. 1873.

Harris, M *The Cornish Ordinalia*. 1969.

Hawker, R S (Author of 'And shall Trelawny die?'). *Footprints of Former Men*. 1870.

Hawkes, C and J *Prehistoric Britain*. 1937.

Hencken, H O'Neill *The Archaeology of Cornwall and Scilly*. 1932.

Henderson, Charles *Essays in Cornish History. 1935*
— *A History of the Parish of Constantine*. 1937.

Hudson, W H *The Land's End*. 1908.

Jenkin, A K Hamilton *The Cornish Miner*. 1927.
— *The Story of Cornwall*. 1934.
— *Cornwall and its People*. 1945.

Jenner, H *A Handbook of the Cornish Language*. 1904.

Journal of the Royal Institution of Cornwall. 1864–.

Langdon, A G *Old Cornish Crosses*. 1896.

Leland, J *Itinerary*. Ed. L T Smith. 1906.

Lewis, G R *The Stannaries*. 1908.

Lysons, D and S *Magna Britannia*. Vol. 3 (*Cornwall*). 1814.

MacDermott, E T *History of the Great Western Railway*. 1927.

MacLean, J *History of the Deanery of Trigg Minor*. 1876.

Matthews, J H *History of the Parishes of St Ives, Lelant, Towednack and Zennor*. 1892.

Nance, R Morton *Cornish for All*. 1929.
— *A Guide to Cornish Place-Names*. Revised ed. 1949.
— *A New Cornish-English Dictionary*. 1938.

Noall, Cyril *A History of Cornish Mail and Stage Coaches*. 1963.

Norden, John *Description of Cornwall*. Written *c*. 1584: first published 1728, with maps: reprinted 1966.

Norris, Edwin *The Ancient Cornish Drama (a translation of the Ordinalia)*. 1859.

Old Cornwall. The Journal of the Federation of Old Cornwall Societies.

Pearce, J (ed.) *The Wesleys in Cornwall*. 1964.

Pevsner, N *The Buildings of England: Cornwall*. 1951.

Piggott, Stuart *Neolithic Cultures of the British Isles*. 1954.

Polwhele, R *The History of Cornwall*. 1803.

Pool, P A S *Cornish for Beginners*. 1961.

Powell, T G E *The Celts*. 1958.

Proceedings of the West Cornwall Field Club. (The 1957–58 issue is a valuable summary of post-Hencken Cornish archaeology.)

Pryce, W *Mineralogia Cornubiensis*. 1778.

Quiller-Couch, A T *Troy Town*. 1888.
— *The Delectable Duchy*. 1898.

Radford, C A R *Tintagel Castle* (Official Guide by the excavator). 1935.

Redding, C *Illustrated Itinerary of the County of Cornwall*. 1842.

Rowe, J *Cornwall in the Age of the Industrial Revolution*. 1953.

Rowse, A L *Sir Richard Grenville*. 1937.
— *Tudor Cornwall*. 1941.
— *The Cornish in America*. 1969.

Smith, A S D *The Story of the Cornish Language*. 1947.

Thomas, Charles *The Principal Antiquities of the Land's End District*. 1957. *Christian Antiquities of Camborne*. 1967.

Todd, A C *The Cornish Miner in America*. 1967.

Tregellas, W H *Cornish Worthies*. 1884.

Victoria County History of Cornwall. Vol. 1. 1906. *The Domesday Survey*. 1924. *Romano-British Cornwall*. 1925.

Vyvyan, C C *The Isles of Scilly*. 1953.

Wesley, John *Journals* (ed. N Curnock). 1909–16.

Since this bibliography was produced many more books have been written about Cornwall and Cornish history. No attempt has been made to update this list in the light of these new publications. Interested readers should consult:

Payton, P *Cornwall*. 1996.

Soulsby, I *History of Cornwall*. 1986.

Index

A

B

C

F

N

Philip II, King of Spain: Catholicism, 211; Elizabeth I and, 207–8; and Mary Tudor, 206; slave trade, 208; war with England, 220, 223–4

Phillack, 94, 156, 312

pilgrims, 141, 161

Pindar, Peter, 299

piracy: Bodrugan, 166; continuing, 196; off Cornish coast, 237; in Elizabeth's reign, 199–200, 208–9; French accuse Cornish, 161; John Nutt, 234; Killigrews, 207; Mohammedan pirates, 231

Piran, St, 95, 98, 120

Pitt, William, 305

plague: Black Death, 156, 157; follows Civil War, 260; returns of, 167, 196

Plymouth: Captain and Governor of, 267; Civil War, 239, 244–5, 242, 250, 252–3, 254, 256, 258; defences, 214; Drake, 211, 215; fish market, 335–6; railway, 322, 323; Spanish war, 220, 221, 224

Polperro, 142, 296

Polruan, 165, 252

Pomeray, Henry de, 125

population: Black Death, 156; early Middle Ages, 116; falls, 327, 336; and labour in eighteenth century, 283; of mining areas, 291; mortality rate, 318, 321; nineteenth-century rate of increase, 326; rise, 148, 151, 167; of towns, 169

Port Isaac, 296, 297

Porthleven, 80, 142

Porthmeor, 71, 76, 79

Portreath, 311

pottery: bar-lip cooking pots, 110; Bronze Age, 27–8, 36; decoration, 36; goblets, 58; grass-marked ware, 99; Gwithian people, 99; Iron Age, 56, 58; mesolithic, 20; neolithic, 21, 22; Samian, 75

Prest, Agnes, 205–6

Prideaux, Edmund, 239

Prideaux, Nicholas, 189

Prideaux, Sir Nicholas, 263

privateering: attacks on English shipping, 231; Civil War, 253; continuing, 196; Dutch demand damages, 263; gentry, 208; increases, 209; Royalist base in Scilly, 261

Probus, 190

Pryde, Thomas, 261

S

T

trade: amber, 40, 50; china clay, 300; Cornish-Irish, 45, 171; Cornish-Breton, 171; under Cunelobin, 68–69; export trade suffers, 170–71; fishing, 227; gold and bronze, 40; pilchard, 315; and smuggling, 288–9; tin, 40, 50, 54, 69, 170, 171, 240; wine, 50, 54
trade routes: Bronze Age, 34–5, 36, 40, 46; Cornish prosperity dependant on, 41; between western Britain and Mediterranean, 69
transport: canals, 312; four-horse omnibus, 322; motor car, 342; railway, 312, 322–4, 342; stage coach and post-chaise, 306; tramway, 311
Trecarrel, Sir Henry, 190
Treffry, John, 209
Treffry, Sir John, 166, 181
Treffry, Martha, 257
Treffry, Thomas i, 164
Treffry, Thomas ii, 186, 195, 204
Treffry, William, 181
Trefusis, Nicholas, 235
Tregian, Francis i, 212, 213
Tregian, Francis ii, 213
Tregian, Thomas, 211
Tregonwell, John, 187, 188
Tregony: bridge, 137, 275; castle, 122; electoral corruption, 315–16; foreign burgesses, 135; martyr's limb exhibited, 213; Parliament, 141
Trelawny family, 201, 270
Trelawny, Charles, 270
Trelawny, Edward John, 307, 343
Trelawny, Sir John i, 163
Trelawny, Sir John ii, 261
Trelawny, Jonathan, 265
Trelawny, Sir Jonathan, 3rd bart., 270
Trelowarren, 72
Trematon: Castle, 117, 122, 129, 159, 196, 313, 347; Grenville finds refuge, 198; market, 139
Tremayne, Edmund, 207
Tremayne, Nicholas, 207
Trengrouse, Henry, 304
Tresilian, Robert, 160–61
Trevanion, Sir Charles, 254, 262
Trevanion, Sir Hugh, 204

TITLES BY F E HALLIDAY AVAILABLE DIRECT
FROM HOUSE OF STRATUS

Quantity		£	$(US)	$(CAN)	€
☐	CHAUCER AND HIS WORLD	8.99	13.95	20.95	15.00
☐	DR JOHNSON AND HIS WORLD	8.99	13.95	20.95	15.00
☐	THE LIFE OF SHAKESPEARE	10.99	16.95	25.95	18.00
☐	THE POETRY OF SHAKESPEARE'S PLAYS	8.99	13.95	20.95	15.00
☐	ROBERT BROWNING: HIS LIFE AND WORK	9.99	14.95	22.95	16.50
☐	SHAKESPEARE AND HIS CRITICS	8.99	13.95	20.95	15.00
☐	A SHAKESPEARE COMPANION	14.99	22.95	34.95	25.00
☐	SHAKESPEARE IN HIS AGE	10.99	16.95	25.95	18.00
☐	THOMAS HARDY: HIS LIFE AND WORK	10.99	16.95	25.95	18.00
☐	UNFAMILIAR SHAKESPEARE	10.99	16.95	25.95	18.00
☐	WORDSWORTH AND HIS WORLD	8.99	13.95	20.95	15.00

A HISTORY OF CORNWALL also available in hardback version, £16.99

ALL HOUSE OF STRATUS BOOKS ARE AVAILABLE FROM GOOD BOOKSHOPS
OR DIRECT FROM THE PUBLISHER:

Internet: www.houseofstratus.com including synopses and features.

Email: sales@houseofstratus.com
info@houseofstratus.com
(please quote author, title and credit card details.)

Tel: Order Line
0800 169 1780 (UK)
1 800 724 1100 (USA)
International
+44 (0) 1845 527700 (UK)
+01   845 463 1100 (USA)

Fax: +44 (0) 1845 527711 (UK)
+01   845 463 0018 (USA)
(please quote author, title and credit card details.)

Send to: House of Stratus Sales Department   House of Stratus Inc.
Thirsk Industrial Park   2 Neptune Road
York Road, Thirsk   Poughkeepsie
North Yorkshire, YO7 3BX   NY 12601
UK   USA

PAYMENT

Please tick currency you wish to use:

☐ £ (Sterling)   ☐ $ (US)   ☐ $ (CAN)   ☐ € (Euros)

Allow for shipping costs charged per order plus an amount per book as set out in the tables below:

CURRENCY/DESTINATION

	£(Sterling)	$(US)	$(CAN)	€(Euros)
Cost per order				
UK	1.50	2.25	3.50	2.50
Europe	3.00	4.50	6.75	5.00
North America	3.00	3.50	5.25	5.00
Rest of World	3.00	4.50	6.75	5.00
Additional cost per book				
UK	0.50	0.75	1.15	0.85
Europe	1.00	1.50	2.25	1.70
North America	1.00	1.00	1.50	1.70
Rest of World	1.50	2.25	3.50	3.00

PLEASE SEND CHEQUE OR INTERNATIONAL MONEY ORDER
payable to: HOUSE OF STRATUS LTD or HOUSE OF STRATUS INC. or card payment as indicated

STERLING EXAMPLE

Cost of book(s):. . . . . Example: 3 x books at £6.99 each: £20.97

Cost of order:. . . . . Example: £1.50 (Delivery to UK address)

Additional cost per book:. . . . . Example: 3 x £0.50: £1.50

Order total including shipping:. . . . . Example: £23.97

VISA, MASTERCARD, SWITCH, AMEX:

☐ ☐ ☐ ☐ ☐ ☐ ☐ ☐ ☐ ☐ ☐ ☐ ☐ ☐ ☐ ☐ ☐ ☐ ☐ ☐

Issue number (Switch only):

☐ ☐ ☐

Start Date: Expiry Date:

☐ ☐ / ☐ ☐   ☐ ☐ / ☐ ☐

Signature: _____

NAME: _____

ADDRESS: _____

COUNTRY: _____

ZIP/POSTCODE: _____

Please allow 28 days for delivery. Despatch normally within 48 hours.

Prices subject to change without notice.
Please tick box if you do not wish to receive any additional information. ☐

House of Stratus publishes many other titles in this genre; please check our website
(**www.houseofstratus.com**) for more details.